CW01659975

Queen of the Silver Screen

Margaret Lockwood

Queen of the Silver Screen

A biography by Lyndsy Spence

fantom
publishing

First published in hardback in 2016 by Fantom Publishing,
an imprint of Fantom Films
This paperback edition published by Fantom in 2023
fantompublishing.co.uk

Copyright © Lyndsy Spence 2016

Lyndsy Spence has asserted her moral right to be identified as the author of this work in accordance with the Copyright, Designs and Patents Act 1988.

All rights reserved.

A catalogue record for this book is available from the British Library.

Hardback edition ISBN: 978-1-78196-264-0
Paperback edition ISBN: 978-1-78196-387-6

Typeset by Phil Reynolds Media Services, Leamington Spa
Printed and bound in the UK by ImprintDigital.com

Cover design by Will Brooks

For Martha

'We've chosen a life for you that can be a splendid one if you choose to make it so, Margaret. But it can also be a very cheap and sordid one if you let it. You must never let it. Once you let this career cheapen you, you yourself are finished.'

– Margaret Evelyn Lockwood

Contents

List of Illustrations

Acknowledgements

When I first set out to write a biography of Margaret Lockwood I quickly discovered a wealth of conflicting information which has contributed to an inaccurate portrayal of her life. As such it would have been fraudulent of me to repeat those stories which have attached themselves to her legacy. Without the help of the individuals who have shared not only their time but their personal memories of Margaret I could not have written this book.

First and foremost I am grateful to Margaret's daughter, Mrs Julia Lockwood-Clark, who patiently answered my questions regarding her mother. Her insights have given me a better understanding of those who have been portrayed in an unfavourable light. I hope I have remained objective in my handling of her family's story.

A special thanks to Betty Elzea, Joy Cheshire, Suzette Singer, Derek Herincx and Graham Clews for their personal memories and information on their Waugh and Lockwood relatives; and to Robert Ward whose research and knowledge of the Lockwood family helped to shape the first chapter of this book.

I am also grateful to Miriam and Tim Harrison who remembered their former neighbour with such affection.

I should like to thank those who have shared memorabilia with me: Tania Todd; Angela Larin; Suzanne Haylerbrown; Hugh O'Neill; and also Audrey Haylerbrown and Belinda

Blanchard (on behalf of her mother Wendy Blanchard) who entrusted me with their private correspondence from Margaret. Thank you to Theo Morgan for providing me with much-needed archived interviews in the early stages of my research.

Thank you to those who offered their time and their feedback: Kendra Bean; Terence Towles Canote; Debbie Catling; Richard Williams; Virginie Pronovost; Robyn Drury; Hannah Betts; Meems Ellenberg; Margaret Lockwood Society; and most especially Andrew Budgell and Tania Todd who offered not only their thoughts during various stages of the manuscript but their generous support, too.

Last but not least I should like to express my deep gratitude to Martha Clark who has been invaluable in assisting me with this biography. It is not an understatement to say Martha brought all the pieces of the puzzle together, and it is to whom I dedicate this book.

I
An Unfamiliar Place

In the cold spring of 1920, the great greyness of London met the Lockwood family as they stepped off the train which had brought them from the Liverpool docks to Gipsy Hill railway station in the city's south-east borough of Lambeth. The two children, Margaret, aged three and a half, and her brother, Lyn, aged seven, had the frail appearance of colonial children who had been raised indoors, their pale skin shielded from the blistering heat of the Karachi sun. Their mother, Margaret Evelyn, guided the children towards a waiting hansom cab, where a coachman lifted Margaret and placed her high on the horsehair chair with its prickly bristles that scratched her bare legs. Hesitantly, Lyn climbed in after his sister, but he did not fidget from the uncomfortable chair nor did he make a sound, for he was a quiet, solemn boy who kept his thoughts to himself. After helping Margaret Evelyn into the cab, the coachman began loading their trunks into the already cramped compartment.

As the horse plodded up Gipsy Hill to Upper Norwood, Margaret knelt up to peer out of the back window at the view below steeped in smog from the thick chimney smoke that piped from the tall, grey houses lining their route. London's concrete skyline paled in comparison to the vibrant terracotta landscape of her birthplace in Karachi, Pakistan, or British

India as it was then known. It had been two years since Armistice Day, yet the austerity Britons still faced was a reminder of the Great War; a striking contrast to the semi-privileged lifestyle that Margaret and Lyn had enjoyed as children of the Raj. Before coming to London, they had resided in a large, airy bungalow perched high in the hills of the great Sind desert, where they lived as a family with their father, Henry Francis Lockwood, their older half-siblings, Frank and Fay, and an ayah who cared for the children.

The family unit was dissolved when Henry made the decision to send his family to London, where the children would benefit from an English education. Margaret Evelyn, whose own formal education had been poor, agreed to her husband's plan. Traditionally, British children were sent overseas to boarding school, as it was feared – particularly among the middle and upper classes – that their children were at risk of developing 'chichi' accents from the servants. However, Henry's children were to attend a day school in London. Lyn was enrolled in the fee-paying Dulwich College, and plans were made for Margaret to attend Belvedere preparatory school when she was old enough. An overseas school was also deemed the safest place for a child, as certain underlying fears, inspired by the Victorian 'curry and rice days', were common. Among the most prominent was the worry that an ayah would give a child some opium on the tip of her finger to quicken sleep. Death and disease dominated parents' thoughts, and the beginning symptoms of any sickness were the cause of much worry as hospitals were hundreds of miles away. There was the knowledge that dogs carried rabies, so children were warned not to pet or entice a dog; likewise the bite of a poisonous snake could kill, and there were haunting sights of armless and legless beggars and lepers lying in the streets. During great epidemics, such as 'flu, the roadside ditches would be filled with unburied corpses whose bacteria would fester in the heat and continue to spread. Typhoid and dysentery were equally feared and a constant threat. As such, the children would bring their own bottle of milk when invited to tea parties because nobody trusted another mother or servant to boil the milk correctly. So, to remedy such rational fears, it was agreed that children should be sent 'home' – though, in many cases, 'home' was an unknown place.

However, unlike traditional families, Henry requested that his wife not return as soon as the children were placed in school, but live with them in London while he remained in Karachi. He made arrangements for his family to sail on the steamship TSS *City of Exeter* departing Bombay for Liverpool, which carried other English families back to their homeland. For the most part, the two-week crossing was uneventful, save for one incident when Margaret almost slipped through the railings of the second-class deck. A fellow passenger screamed, and with lightning speed another grabbed the child by the legs and pulled her to safety before she fell to her death. Shaken by the incident, Margaret quelled her curiosity for the rest of the voyage and retreated into herself. It was to be the only disruption they would suffer, for the separation between Margaret Evelyn and Henry did not cause either spouse much concern. Aside from a visit to England every seven years when a spell of leave presented itself, Henry would remain a distant figure in their lives.

An elusive air surrounded Henry, born in 1879, seven months after the marriage of his parents, Francis Day Lockwood and Sarah Miller. He was named after his paternal grandfather Henry Francis Lockwood, a wealthy architect from Yorkshire who was renowned for his public buildings in Hull; amongst his most notable designs were the Trinity House chapel, the extensions to the Royal Infirmary, the New Wesleyan Chapel, and the Hull Zoological Gardens. Following Henry Francis's death, Francis inherited his father's successful practice, Lockwood, Heathcote and Smith, which had offices in London and Manchester. But, having experienced a conflict of interest with his new partners, the business was dissolved by mutual consent. Thereafter, Francis's share of the family fortune dwindled and his descendants would be forced to make their own way in the world.

Henry's childhood, by his own admission, was unhappy due to his alcoholic mother and neglectful father, who had left his wife and child in London while he ventured to New Zealand to mine for gold. Inventing the story that he had been orphaned at a young age, Henry claimed he was raised by his uncle, Sir Frank Lockwood QC, a Liberal politician and lead counsel for the infamous prosecution of Oscar Wilde who, after losing a libel case against the Marquess of Queensbury, had been accused of sodomy and charged with gross indecency. Although an exaggeration, there was an element of truth to Henry's claim. In 1893, when he was thirteen, his mother, a chronic alcoholic, succumbed to cirrhosis of the liver at the age of thirty-four; and, Henry, now motherless, deeply related with the orphaned status he had once bestowed upon himself. Francis, the boy's father, was still alive and documents show him to have been in the colonial service. Further evidence reveals that Francis Day Lockwood had remarried; his new wife was an Australian, a Miss Mary Stephens, and he was working in Perth, Australia, as chief inspector of the Central Board of Health.[1] The fragments of truth in Henry's account of his early years were given veracity when, in his early teens, Sir Frank Lockwood became his legal guardian. Sir Frank, however, was the boy's father's cousin, and not his uncle. The tragedy Henry had predicted for himself had come full circle when, at the age of eighteen, he found himself entirely alone after Sir Frank's untimely death from influenza.

In September 1900, when Henry came of age, he married Jessie Ramsey, the daughter of a manufacturing chemist. The formality of this marriage was short-lived and the disappearance of Jessie has contributed to stories ranging from an early death to an annulment. Before their marriage, Jessie had had a son, John Alexander Ramsey, who told his descendants that he was 'born on the wrong side of the blanket'.[2] Aside from Edwardian society taking a dim view of illegitimacy, it has been suggested that the marriage was more of a convenience for Jessie, as nobody knew for certain if Henry was the child's biological father.[3]

Theories of Jessie's early death can now be eradicated given the new information that has since come to light. In 1922, Jessie was still very much alive and her presence was recorded at the wedding of her son John Alexander Lockwood (after his parents' marriage he took Henry's name) to Muriel Edith Harriet Fitch in Surrey, with Henry Francis Lockwood listed as the groom's father. What is unknown is the reason for

Jessie's abrupt departure from Henry's life; but, after they had gone their separate ways, she kept their son, who, until now, has also remained a mystery.

Leaving their son behind, Henry and Jessie journeyed to India, but she soon returned to England as she could not tolerate the heat and conditions. Remaining in India without his wife, Henry turned his mind to his career and by 1905 he was sufficiently established to be registered in the official directories of the Raj. After securing work on the state railways, his first job was with the Southern Mahratta Railway as acting district traffic superintendent at Bellary, South West India. He swiftly turned his expertise into a career in administration and would work at various posts across India before he eventually settled in Karachi.

In April 1907, the news of his father's death reached Henry. Still living in Perth and working in his post as Chief of the Central Board of Health, Francis Day Lockwood had committed suicide 'under mental aberration'.[4] Prior to Francis's suicide, he had made continuous threats to take his own life, upon which his wife, Mary, summoned a doctor to tend to her husband, who had complained of insomnia. The doctor diagnosed Francis as suffering from acute mania – 'the probable concomitant of worry' – confirmed when Francis confessed to embezzling £1,000, for which he would have to appear before a jury. Claiming that his 'honour had been impugned', he had no 'alternative but to end his existence'. In the early hours of Thursday 4th April, Mary discovered Francis had ended his life by means of drinking poison. Newspaper notices reveal that Henry attended his father's funeral in Perth. However, with the burial taking place only one day after

Francis's death, Henry (for reasons unknown) was in Australia and not India, and also listed was a Mrs Henry Francis Lockwood. It is uncertain if it was Jessie; the probability of this is slim, given that records for Jessie sporadically listed her in and around England during this time, and also show that their son was in the care of his maternal grandparents.

A year later, in 1908, Henry married for a second time to Marie Anne Whitmarsh, and this was probably the 'wife' to whom the newspapers made reference. Shrouded in mystery, too, were the legal technicalities of his marriage to Jessie. Their marriage had not been dissolved by divorce or annulment[5] and, given that bigamy carried a severe punishment, Jessie decided to exploit the matter for her own gain. According to Jessie's great-grandson, upon Henry's arrival in England he was alarmed to discover that Jessie was waiting for him. An imposing woman, standing six feet tall with a solid build and a no-nonsense attitude, she proposed an arrangement; and Henry, anxious to avoid prosecution, agreed to it. She stipulated that Henry pay her an ongoing allowance which afforded her a house in Golder's Green, a maid, and a generous income.[6]

As with his first marriage, the second union was beset by unfortunate circumstances. It is widely (and wrongly) accepted that Marie Anne died shortly after the birth of her first child, Frank Day Lockwood, in 1908. It has also been reported that she was an unconventional eleven years older than Henry, and was a Roman Catholic. This, too, can be disputed given that no record of Marie Anne's birth, or indeed a record of her marriage to Henry, can be found. Her identity remains something of a mystery, and her descendants believe that she was part Indian, while the logistics of Henry's time in Australia during his father's death and the presence of Marie Anne suggest that she might have been Australian. In 1910, she gave birth to a second child, a daughter named Anne Felicity Whitmarsh Lockwood, known as Fay. However, months after the birth of Fay, Marie Anne died of heart failure.

At the age of thirty-one, Henry was a widower with a two-year-old son and a four-month-old daughter to care for. In his precarious position, Henry was forced to explore his options. There were some factors which he had to consider: he could hire an ayah to act as a surrogate mother to Frank and Fay, but for British children from a good background, his options were limited. Under ordinary circumstances, the children would have been sent home to England into the custody of relatives, but since Henry had no close female relations whom he could approach, his only choice was to remarry.

His third wife, Margaret Evelyn Waugh, seemed an unlikely match for Henry, whose height of six-foot-three, charming personality and sonorous voice drew second glances from the opposite sex. His new bride was not alone when she considered him 'the handsomest man in the East'.[7] At the age of twenty-nine, Margaret Evelyn was, by the standards of the day, close to becoming an old maid, and she had a personality that was unkindly described as 'dour'.

The third of seven surviving children,[8] Margaret Evelyn was born in 1882 to a Scots-born serving soldier, James Nicol Waugh, and Eliza Evelyn (née Shepherd). Although born in Peebles, Scotland, during a visit by her parents to their homeland, Margaret Evelyn's siblings were born in India. A month after the birth of her last child, Arthur, Eliza died at the age of thirty-six from fatty degeneration of the heart. As the eldest daughter, Margaret Evelyn would, in years to come, assume the role of mother figure to her four younger siblings. Shortly after their mother's death, Margaret Evelyn and her two sisters, Kitty and Mary, were sent to live with relatives in North Island, New Zealand. It was a traumatic experience for the young children, though one that remained unspoken about. It is unknown how long they spent in New Zealand, but when the girls returned to India they joined their father in the ancient city of Ferozepur on the banks of the Sutlej River, where he served as a Conductor of Ordnance in the Bengal Regiment.

When Margaret Evelyn met Henry she had known nothing but the colonial way of life. Since her father's death in 1898, she had been a woman of independent means: she first worked as a military nurse in Queen Alexandra's Royal Army Nursing Corps in Calcutta, and then assumed the role of nanny[9] to Frank and Fay. After his second wife's death, and sensing how useful they could be to one another, Henry and Margaret Evelyn were married on 8th April 1911, at St Andrew's Church of Scotland in Calcutta. It should be noted that Henry was still legally married to Jessie.

In the years since his first two marriages, Henry had grown accustomed to moving from post to post, and travelling hundreds of miles for work. His third marriage did not change him, and he and Margaret Evelyn moved a thousand miles from Calcutta to Ferozepur to accommodate his new post as traffic officer on the North West State Railway. But Margaret Evelyn had more pressing matters to concern herself with: not only was she adapting to her new surroundings and caring for her two stepchildren, she was also awaiting the birth of her first child. On 12th October 1912, Henry Evelyn Francis Lockwood was born, though all of his life he would be known as Lyn.

The First World War was imminent, and for young men like Henry there were decisions to be made. Many returned home to their native England and enlisted; but, as the war progressed, India's railways became a vital part in the system for transportation of supplies and men to the Middle East. One of India's two most important terminals for that system would be Henry's next post, when, in 1916, he was appointed district traffic superintendent at Karachi. The family had barely set up their new home when Margaret Evelyn's second child arrived on 15th September 1916: a girl, Margaret Mary, whom she named after herself.

*

The hansom cab reached the top of Gipsy Hill, coming to a halt at 2 Lunham Road. The family's new home, a four-storeyed house at the end of a terrace, was a world away from the life they had left behind in the East. As they stood shivering at the top of the steps leading down to the front door, Margaret was momentarily cheered by the sight of a steep, tree-lined garden which lay behind their new house. To her, it was a welcome alternative to the hot sand which had surrounded their old home four thousand miles away.

Inside the house, Margaret Evelyn bustled the children in front of her as they trudged up the flight of stairs to a maisonette on the third floor. Although their living standards had been reduced, the hexagon-shaped rooms were spacious enough for the family of three to live comfortably, even if Margaret no longer had her own bedroom and had to sleep on a sofa at the foot of her mother's bed. The children gathered at the sash windows where they looked out at the distant rooftops of the city below. Lyn broke his customary silence and announced, 'That's London.' London, Margaret predicted, 'was a city as unknown to the Lockwoods from India as the Lockwoods were to London'.[10]

2
A Solitary Child

Many women in a similar position would have been forgiven if they felt lonely or resentful under such circumstances. But not Margaret Evelyn. She possessed an admirable self-reliance, cultivated from the heavy responsibility she had known as a child and the unexpected turmoil she had experienced as a young woman. Accustomed to solitary periods, she had been parted from her siblings following her marriage to Henry, when the vast distance between Karachi and Calcutta had separated them. The First World War, too, had taken her brothers away from the family who remained in India. And Arthur Waugh, the youngest sibling, whom Margaret Evelyn had cared for since the death of their mother just a month after his birth, was killed by a torpedo on board a hospital ship. Such hardship had strengthened her resilience.

With no close relatives and adapting to their new life in London, the three Lockwoods created a self-contained world for themselves. Margaret Evelyn was not a sociable woman, and Margaret and Lyn barely knew their neighbours, but those who caught passing glimpses of their family life observed Lyn to be 'the quietest little boy'[1] they had seen. Lyn's introverted nature did little to discourage Margaret's companionship; a one-sided friendship, for she had to do all the talking for him, as well as for herself. The children immersed themselves in play acting, and their games were largely inspired by the old Crystal Palace which loomed over the neighbourhood. This imposing structure of glass and steel, built to house the Great Exhibition of 1851, would capture Margaret's imagination for years to come.

Behind closed doors Margaret Evelyn did not exert warmth to her children – especially Margaret – and, having grown up without a maternal influence, displays of affection did not come easily to her. For a sensitive child like Margaret, she viewed her mother's reserved nature as a form of neglect. She never felt her endeavours were good enough, and throughout her life she held the opinion that Margaret Evelyn was not proud of her.[2] Such feelings were exacerbated by Margaret Evelyn's relationship with Lyn, towards whom she was inclined to behave more attentively. Perhaps, having assumed the role of mother to her younger siblings, and then as their sole guardian following the death of her father when she was sixteen, Margaret Evelyn felt compelled to nurture those who needed her most. Margaret, although younger, was more independent than Lyn; and, as such, Margaret Evelyn diverted her full attention to her son, whom she might have viewed as the weaker child. In years to come, this would cast a dark shadow over Margaret's relationship with her mother.

To the outside world, Margaret appeared as a shy child who struggled to make friends. This was common for many children of the Raj who were forced to adapt to a new lifestyle that was a world away from the exotic atmosphere of India. English children had never heard of the brainfever bird or the sound of jackals, and they had never tasted a banana or ridden on an elephant. They simply had nothing in common with her. This loneliness, coupled with the strangeness of their new environment, encouraged Margaret to develop a degree of self-sufficiency, which in many ways mirrored her mother's.

One bright spark appeared in Margaret's lonely world when Mrs Leigh Bennett, an elderly woman who lived in the flat downstairs, befriended the girl. The two struck up an endearing friendship; and, in the privacy of Mrs Leigh Bennett's flat, Margaret could express herself. During bursts of high spirits she would relate her daily routine, chat animatedly about her school lessons, and recite the poems she had learned in class. She also re-enacted the Bible stories that she had heard at the local Christ Church Sunday school.

Sunday school was beginning to consume Margaret's life, and it became the outing that she looked forward to most. Caring little for activities outside of the home, Margaret Evelyn did not attend church but she encouraged the children to go along to Christ Church, a short distance away on the Highland Road, where they sang in the choir. Listening with more than a keen interest to the Bible stories, Margaret's contemplative nature was taken in by Christianity and its teachings. Not one to humour her children, Margaret Evelyn tired of her over-imaginative daughter's fascination with God and the Bible, and she would encourage Margaret to visit 'the lady downstairs', whom Margaret had come to regard as 'the nicest possible person'.[3]

Having made up her mind to become a missionary and live in the Mission House at the top of Highland Road, Margaret confided her decision to Mrs Leigh Bennett. On one particular day she watched with great interest as the elderly woman opened her china cabinet and produced a statue of Jesus on the cross. After studying it for several moments, Margaret announced: 'It's not very much like Him, is it?'[4]

Amused by the child's observation, she concluded the visit by going to her sideboard – a ritual during Margaret's visits – where she kept a supply of small, individually wrapped chocolates. Much to her little friend's dismay, she was only permitted to indulge in one chocolate. Years later, when Margaret questioned Mrs Leigh Bennett about her uncharacteristic meanness, she confided: 'Oh Margaret, you could have had as many as you liked, but I was always afraid you'd be ill and that your mother wouldn't let you come down to see me any more.'[5]

Margaret's love of Sunday school was replaced by a new phenomenon in her life. Although Margaret Evelyn rarely left the maisonette, she did visit the cinema in the Crystal Palace; and, since she could not leave her children at home unattended, she brought them with her. It was surprising that a woman with such a serious nature could find enjoyment in a form of entertainment that was regarded as frivolous in other echelons.[6]

In the darkness of the cinema, as the piano played in time to the silent images on the screen, Margaret felt close to her mother. In a fit of excitement or great terror at the flickering scene unfolding before them, she clutched Margaret Evelyn's hand, and her mother reciprocated the gesture by holding her hand tightly until the fretful moment lapsed. As she watched the popular stars of the day – John Gilbert, Greta Garbo (whom she wrote to but never received a reply), Mary Pickford and Rudolph Valentino – Margaret 'disgraced' herself, and her mother, only once. In an effort to stifle her boredom during a lengthy screen kiss, the impatient child demanded in a loud voice: 'Oh, aren't they ever going to stop!'[7] Eschewing the romantic genre, Margaret decided early on that she preferred dramatic material, in particular *Beau Geste*, and popular serials such as *Fighting Blood* and *Dr Fu Manchu.*

After a visit to the cinema, Margaret Evelyn and the children would return home, where, in their small maisonette, Margaret re-enacted the entire film for her mother. Margaret Evelyn roared with laughter, praising the 'droll little girl' as she shuffled around the room, imitating Charlie Chaplin's famous on-screen walk from *The Tramp*.

Sensing Margaret 'had a flair for this sort of thing', Margaret Evelyn enrolled her in singing and elocution lessons with a local music teacher, Miss Margaret Overbury. Every night, she walked to Miss Overbury's studio above a music shop, two streets away, on Upper Norwood's main street, Westow Hill. Margaret loathed the piano lessons and, although she excelled at elocution, she was not a promising pupil. Much of the music practice was spent sitting on a swivel stool, spinning round and round, biting her nails and gazing longingly at the children playing outside. The music lessons, as tedious as they were, helped Margaret to escape her peers; and as she watched the children on the street below, she knew theirs was a world where she was not welcome.

*

In 1927, Henry crossed the ocean for his first spell of leave since his family had left Karachi seven years before. The joyous occasion quickly soured when he announced that Margaret was old enough to attend a new, more advanced school. Prior to this, Margaret had settled into a comfortable routine at Belvedere College, where the numbers were small and the lessons were undemanding, giving her the freedom to retreat into her make-believe world.

Ignoring the patriarchal view that 'learning in a woman is not only unnecessary but undesirable',[8] Henry decided on Sydenham High School, a school for girls founded in 1887 by four pioneering women: Maria Grey, Lady Stanley, Lady Mary Gurney, and Princess Louise, 'who had the vision and determination to claim as good an education for girls as for their brothers'.[9] But this encouragement of education could have been misconstrued as forward-thinking. With his expenditures (ranging from Jessie's allowance to Margaret Evelyn and the children's living expenses), it might have been his way of making Margaret, as well as Fay, less financially dependent on him as they grew older.

The thought of changing schools filled Margaret with dread, but casting her nervousness aside she delighted in the idea of wearing a uniform to her new school. This feeling swiftly vanished when Margaret Evelyn took her to buy it and, casting an eye over the navy blazers and poplin dresses, she declared she could make it better herself. Furthermore, Margaret would look 'neater and nicer than the other little girls'.

But Margaret did not want to look different, and she reluctantly went off to school in her mother's uniform where she stood out from the others. 'The uniforms were the bane of my young life,' Margaret said as she reflected on her school-days. 'I felt horribly conspicuous on my first day at the big school, and very shy.' And, by her own admission, she was so 'unhappy that I wanted to leave'.[10]

Her shyness made it difficult for Margaret to interact with the other girls, and it took the entire first term before she came out of her shell and began to mingle with her fellow pupils. She preferred to move around under an air of anonymity, and it was her standard practice to find a desk at the back of the classroom where she could daydream without being noticed.

Aware of Margaret's lack of interest in school, her teacher, Miss Hobson, took a dislike to her and found fault with her academic ability. She accused Margaret of tearing a page out of her jotter, a forbidden act worthy of punishment. A self-confessed stickler for rules and regulations, Margaret pleaded that she had not committed the petty crime, but Miss Hobson was adamant that she had, and chastised her furthermore.[11] It pained Margaret enough to confide in her mother, who accompanied her to school the next day. With an air of superiority, Margaret Evelyn pointed out that, in fact, the jotters were badly manufactured, giving the impression of missing pages. This interference only encouraged Miss Hobson's intense dislike of Margaret.[12]

It was also Margaret Evelyn's influence that served to make Margaret unpopular with her peers. 'I had a woebegone time making friends,' she recalled. 'Nobody seemed to want to play with me. I was so dreadfully shy. Somehow I didn't "belong".'[13] It did not help matters when Margaret, who had not been brought up to believe in Santa Claus, told the other children there was no such thing. When she told her mother what she had done, she was punished for daring to repeat what she had heard in the privacy of their home.

Considered a misfit, the other children were not allowed to play with Margaret;[14] and their parents, too, found the

Lockwoods to be bohemian.[15] Their fondness for the cinema, and for Indian cuisine, confirmed this judgement. It was an era when xenophobia was flaunted openly, and 'abroad' was steeped in scandal. When her classmates teased her about her birthplace and accused her of 'being an Indian', Margaret retaliated with, 'Just because you are born in a stable it doesn't follow that you are a horse!'[16]

Reacting to the teasing and the snubs, Margaret realised that other children and their parents did not consider them to be a 'proper' English family, regardless of their origins.[17] When it occurred to her that she did not receive invitations to other children's homes, she asked Margaret Evelyn if she could invite some people over as a last attempt to form a circle of friends. Her mother refused to write the customary note to the other girls' parents and, without adhering to this formality, they were not permitted to visit.

'How difficult this can be when you're a small girl,' Margaret later said. 'And the only thing that matters to you is that you should be just exactly like every other small girl you know. And I was very different.'[18]

3
Miss Margie Day

Like many children, Margaret went through phases where other people's occupations appealed to her. Alongside her dream of becoming a missionary, she aspired to be in charge of the bacon slicer at the local International Stores. But such ambitions were replaced by the siren call of the spotlight and, seeking refuge in the old Crystal Palace cinema, she dreamt of becoming a famous actress. 'My mother always encouraged me, believing that I should in any case eventually do what I had set my heart on,' Margaret later said. It was irrelevant to Margaret Evelyn what her daughter's chosen career should be, actress or bacon slicer; she thought it 'better that I should do it with her help and guidance'.[1]

When she told her mother that she wanted to take dancing lessons, Margaret Evelyn enrolled her in a local dance class where many of her classmates from Sydenham attended. But it was not the type of dancing Margaret had in mind. She complained to Margaret Evelyn that the lessons were dull and that she wanted to learn the 'sort of dancing they do in pantomimes'.[2] Agreeing that Margaret was more advanced than the others, she discovered by chance that the Italia Conti theatrical school in Holborn, formed in 1911, was 'the best in all of London'.

Twice a week, Margaret Evelyn took Margaret to Holborn for her dancing lessons, where the school's founder, Miss

Conti, a former actress, supervised the children. Impressed by Margaret's talent, she put her name forward to play a fairy in two charity performances of *A Midsummer Night's Dream* at the Holborn Empire, a famous London music hall. 'I could think of nothing else,' Margaret recalled. 'A fairy, a fairy – a real fairy in a beautiful frock.'[3]

With her youthful enthusiasm masking a determination to succeed, Margaret attended the dress rehearsal with a dozen other talented children who were ordered to put on a set of wings and run across the stage. Miss Conti praised Margaret but scolded a larger boy, in his late teens, who could not remember his lines. His name was Carol Reed, the future film director. 'I used to want to prompt him,' Margaret said, 'because I knew everybody's lines off by heart... but I never dared to prompt Carol. I was only nine and he seemed very grown up to me.'[4]

After making her debut in *A Midsummer Night's Dream*, Margaret was forced to leave the Italia Conti due to the acute travel sickness she suffered when travelling on buses and trains. A tough decision was reached: she would join the local Haddon School of Dancing at Norwood run by its founder, Miss Haddon. It was a backward step for Margaret and, having experienced the excitement of performing on a live stage and the intoxicating feeling of an audience's applause, she was determined more than ever to succeed.

Although Margaret viewed it as a setback, her career was off to a promising start. Through the Haddon School she had been invited by the Cone School to audition for a part in the chorus of *Babes in the Wood*, which was to open at the Scala Theatre. Miss Haddon sent Margaret home to ask her mother for permission to go to the West End to audition. 'I don't know what these children in pantomimes are like,' Margaret Evelyn said. 'It's a long journey from here every day. Besides, you'll probably catch an awful cold. Still, I'd like to see what you could do…' After a moment of contemplative silence, Margaret stared at her mother's doubtful face and was taken by surprise when she answered, 'All right. Tell Miss Haddon you can go.'[5]

Miss Haddon accompanied ten of her best pupils to the Cone Dancing School, located in a rambling house on Upper Grosvenor Street where its founder, Miss Grace Cone, oversaw the audition. 'Go along, Margaret dear,' Miss Haddon prompted the nervous ingénue. Taking her place on stage, Margaret performed her dance routine, biting her lower lip until it bled. Out of the ten children, Miss Cone chose her.

Then Miss Cone asked if any of the children could sing. The girl originally cast as Babe had contracted measles, and she was desperate to find a replacement in time for opening night. Putting her hand up, Margaret said she could sing. And, after listening to her, Miss Cone handed Margaret Evelyn a script with the news that Margaret had twenty-four hours to learn the part of Babe.

All the way home on the train, Margaret Evelyn continually reminded Margaret: 'This is your big chance.' But Margaret did not need reminding, for the responsibility of carrying the play weighed heavily on her mind. She barely slept that night as she was too busy learning her lines, and Margaret Evelyn stayed awake to help her rehearse. 'None of us thought of anything but the moment when I would really be on the stage in my first pantomime,'[6] Margaret said. The next morning, with little sleep and running on adrenaline ('I was in the seventh heaven of delight'), she was word-perfect.

As was the protocol for child performers, Margaret had to obtain a London County Council licence before she could appear in the theatre. She went along to London County Hall with her mother, who became livid over the small detail of a medical examination which, to her fury, included being checked for head-lice. 'I can understand all this business of making sure the child will be properly escorted and chaperoned, and made to learn her lessons, but when you dare to start looking at my child's head I've had enough. Can't you use any discrimination, can't you see she's a clean, well-brought-up little girl?'[7] She marched Margaret out of the room before the medical examination was complete but, surprisingly, she was given the licence.

With the formalities taken care of, the Cone School suggested that Margaret ought to use a stage name, something plucky and short that would attract attention on a marquee. With the intention of making Margaret a musical star, they decided on Margie Day, with Day[8] being an old family name. There were photographs taken of Margaret striking a wistful pose in Babe's costume of a leotard and tutu; and, with her waist-length hair and petite frame, she looked younger than her thirteen years. The photographs were hung outside the Scala Theatre, with the name Margie Day written below.

At last, Margaret had fulfilled her dream of becoming a leading lady. But it was not to last. Fate dealt her a cruel hand when, three hours before the curtain was due to come up, the original girl returned to the theatre having made a full recovery. Thinking the world 'a very cruel place', Margaret was demoted to her original role of a fairy, but one 'with an entirely broken heart', for which she was paid thirty shillings a week.

Impressed by Margaret's talent, and her dedication in mastering the role of Babe in just twenty-four hours, Miss Cone invited Margaret to join her prestigious dance school. Years later, when Margaret was at the height of her fame, she spoke of her star pupil:

> ...Her face was pretty and petite, with very large, expressive eyes, and framed by long, dark hair. As a child she had a nice little figure, well proportioned and with long arms and legs. Although delicate in build, she had a sturdy look of health about her. When she came to us she had already had some training. She was extremely promising from the start, and I recalled telling her mother that I believed she would go to the top.[9]

When the production of *Babes in the Wood* finished, Margaret auditioned for the role of Alice in the West End production of *Alice in Wonderland*. Again, disappointment was not far off, and shortly after winning the leading role, Margaret was given the supporting part of the White Rabbit. Margaret Evelyn broke the news to Margaret, telling her that, although the casting director thought her 'an exceptionally pretty child', she did not have the experience to carry a show and they had cast somebody else.

Not one to accept defeat, Margaret Evelyn appealed to the casting director and told him it would have to be Alice or nothing. So, it was nothing. At the age of thirteen Margaret was faced with the harsh reality that she was an out-of-work actress.

*

In 1929, Margaret Evelyn's two sisters, Mary Waugh and Kitty Blake, moved from India to London. The sisters had formerly worked as army nurses in Baghdad, Mesopotamia (as Iraq was then known) where Kitty had married her husband, Dr Leo Marley Blake, a doctor in the Irish Army. After Kitty's husband left her, the sisters, along with Kitty's daughter, Betty, joined Margaret Evelyn in London. The family relocated to a spacious Victorian house at 30 Highland Road, paid for by Henry, who was 'banished' [10] from the place. Presumably this was due to his involvement with his first and only legal wife, Jessie,[11] and, when in London, he stayed in boarding houses.

The frequent excursions to auditions during school hours were making Margaret unpopular at Sydenham, and her teachers held a dim view of her competence as a pupil, confirmed when she scored eight out of one hundred in a Latin examination. The headmistress called a meeting with Margaret Evelyn to discuss Margaret's sporadic attendance, and they mutually agreed that she should be removed from school, a place she did not wish to be.

When Margaret Evelyn returned home, she sat Margaret down and delivered the news. 'The head says you're spending too much time going off with the dancing displays,' she told her. Expecting her mother to agree with the headmistress, Margaret's heart sank. 'You're not much good at school because you're not interested. But Miss Overbury says you work very well indeed with her, and Miss Cone is pleased with your dancing.' Margaret tried to stifle her tears of disappointment as her mother continued in a solemn voice. 'If you take up this sort of life it will mean a lot of hard work, for me as well as for you. You can't go to all these auditions and shows by yourself. I've been thinking about it for some time. You've got it in you, I think; but are you sure this is what you want to do, Margaret?'[12] Without hesitating, Margaret told her mother that she was 'quite sure, quite sure'. At the age of fourteen, she left school for good.

Unlike the majority of girls who left school at a similar age with the purpose of finding employment, Margaret Evelyn did not pressure Margaret to find a conventional job. However, Henry was against her dreams of going on the stage and was adamant that his daughter should receive a good education and forget about 'all this play acting'. It was an ironic statement given that Henry himself had once dreamt of going on the stage, but his guardian Sir Frank Lockwood swiftly extinguished any dreams of an acting career. It should be noted that another relative, who earned a living from creativity, was Rudyard Kipling, whose grandmother was cousins with Margaret's great-grandfather. During this period, Henry's eldest children were making their own way in the world. John had sought employment as a railway clerk; Fay had left school at sixteen and was working as a typist for the Post Office, and in 1930 she married a chartered accountant; Frank was staying with the family at the Highland Road house and would soon emigrate to Shanghai; and Lyn continued with his studies at Dulwich College.

During Henry's next visit to London, in 1931, Margaret Evelyn convinced him to watch one of Margaret's performances. He sat through the show, and afterwards he said: 'If she's happy and makes a success of it, I suppose it will be worth it.'[13] Henry, having reached the peak of his career as a divisional superintendent, was nearing retirement. He was also drinking heavily,[14] as he had been when the family left for London in

1920. And, having planned to remain in Karachi, he would soon abandon his distant approach to exerting any parental influence over Margaret.

The Cone School continued to send Margaret on auditions in and around London. She auditioned for and secured a string of engagements at cabaret clubs, smoking concerts and Masonic ladies' evenings. She also danced for Queen Mary and the Prince of Wales at Westminster Hall. As always, Margaret Evelyn accompanied Margaret to her various engagements in places like Croydon and Surbiton, and she rarely complained about the lengthy jaunts across town.

It is interesting that, throughout her life, Margaret never felt her mother was proud of her due to her lack of praise. Perhaps by accompanying Margaret and supporting her ambition – unusual in an era when children were to be seen and not heard – Margaret Evelyn could, in a way, show Margaret that she was proud of her, and this lack of praise was compensated with the belief that she could, and would, achieve her goals.

In those days Margaret would not have denied her mother the occasional negative remark, for she rarely had the luxury of spending an evening at home. However, she did voice her opinion when the Cone School accepted an offer for Margaret to sing at a social event in a large public house. Adamant her daughter would not fulfil the engagement, she told Miss Cone in person, 'I am not taking a child of mine into any public house.'[15] Her decision was final.

It came as a surprise to Margaret when her mother's refusal did not hinder her career: instead it served to enhance her stock with the Cone School. Satisfied that Margaret could hold an audience, Miss Cone sent her on an audition for two of the best engagements in town. One was to sing at the teatime cabarets at the Café de Paris in Piccadilly, and the other was at the restaurant of the smart Regent Street store, Dickins and Jones. She was offered both.

The local newspapers wrote about her recent success, but the small piece of publicity brought repercussions. A neighbour posted an anonymous letter to Margaret Evelyn, which read: 'It would have been much better if your daughter Margaret had followed her wish to look after her black brothers and sisters.'[16] Having experienced the thrill of performing and earning a living from it, Margaret's childhood ambition of becoming a missionary was nothing more than a distant dream.

*

In the summer of 1931 theatre-land was abuzz with the news that Noël Coward, 'the boy wonder' of the 1920s, was planning to stage his latest production, *Cavalcade.* The play, spanning three decades in the lives of the Marryot family and their servants, was set against a backdrop of major historical events at the turn of the century, including the Relief of Mafeking, the death of Queen Victoria, the sinking of the Titanic, and The Great War. Popular songs from the period were incorporated into the score to give an air of historical accuracy, including 'Soldiers of the Queen', 'If You Were the Only Girl in the World', and two of Coward's own songs, 'Twentieth Century Blues' and 'Lover of My Dreams'. There was a proposed cast of two hundred and fifty (forty-three of which were speaking parts), twenty-three scenes, and complex sets complete with hydraulics. With over one hundred walk-on parts, there would be plenty of work to go around. And, responding to a casting call that a large chorus of children were needed for 'a very fancy play', Miss Cone sent Margaret along to the Theatre Royal on Drury Lane.

When Margaret arrived at the theatre, she found Noël Coward sitting in the upper dress circle, barking orders at the electricians who were installing the set. Using his trademark colourful language, he berated the crew: 'What the bloody hell do those electricians think they're doing?'[17] And, finally turning to acknowledge the crowd of children standing on stage, he pointed to Margaret and said, 'I'll take that one.' His decision was prompted by Margaret's long hair, which, in his opinion, 'looked the period', and she was immediately cast as an Edwardian child.

Now that she was fifteen, Margaret Evelyn decided that Margaret was old enough to travel alone on the forty-minute journey, with various stops, by train to and from the theatre. When she granted Margaret this freedom, she was not aware that her daughter would be exposed to a world quite unlike anything she encountered at home. As the rehearsals for *Cavalcade* progressed, Margaret, along with the rest of the cast, grew accustomed to Coward's artistic idiosyncrasies. There were too many supporting cast members to remember their names, so Coward devised a system of dividing the cast into groups of twenty, headed by a leader, and each group was assigned a name and a colour. He, of course, had no trouble remembering the names of the leading actor and actress: they were Edward Sinclair and Mary Clare.

On opening night, the children watched the show from the wings before they were called on stage for the final curtain call, but it never did seem to come down. The applause was never-ending, the audience cheered and demanded an encore.

Peering through the sea of arms and legs of the people standing in front her, Margaret caught glimpses of the standing ovation. 'How wonderful, how wonderful!' she thought.

Racing backstage to meet Margaret Evelyn, who had travelled from Gipsy Hill to Drury Lane for the opening night, Margaret euphorically called, 'Wasn't it wonderful?' Unmoved by the spectacle, her mother said, 'It was terrible.' The response diminished the bright moment in her life and career, and it would leave a lasting impression. 'Mother embarrassed me terribly that night, as she was always doing,' she recalled.[18]

Then a 'tragedy' happened. The children were sitting in the dressing room during an interval when a young boy named Hughie Green[19] used an unusual word in front of Margaret. He had heard it during the first act on the opening night when a mechanical fault caused a brief delay between set changes, causing Coward to react with a tirade of explicit language. Naive to this word, Margaret whispered to the girl next to her, asking what it meant. The girl repeated the word to her, but she remained oblivious and appeared to forget about it.

That evening, Margaret hopped off the train at Gipsy Hill, where Margaret Evelyn was waiting for her on the platform. Bursting with anticipation she bounded up to her mother, shouting, 'Mummy, mummy, what does "fuck" mean?'[20] Margaret Evelyn was livid, her face turned red and she tightly pursed her lips. After a moment of silence, and adopting an authoritative tone, she warned: 'You forget it.'[21]

As they entered the house, Margaret Evelyn, without a word to Margaret, sat down at the kitchen table and wrote a letter of complaint to the management of the Theatre Royal. Under no circumstances, she warned, would she permit her daughter to work in such an establishment where language of that sort was used; and, had she not been an army nurse,[22] she would never have known the meaning of *the word* herself. She sealed the envelope and immediately went outside to post it. When she returned, Margaret Evelyn finally broke her silence when she sat Margaret down and announced: 'I have told them you are never coming back. You have left for good.'

Waiting an entire day before she addressed the incident that had taken place the night before at the theatre, Margaret Evelyn forewarned her daughter of the seedier elements of show business. With a sensible amount of foresight, she began: 'We've chosen a life for you that can be a splendid one if you choose to make it so, Margaret. But it can also be a very cheap and sordid one if you let it. You must never let it. And whenever anything unpleasant like this happens, there is only one answer: walk out. Once you let this career cheapen you, you yourself are finished.'[23]

4
'A Life That Can Be Splendid'

For a year and a half Margaret did not appear on the stage, nor did she audition for any roles. As far as her acting career was concerned, she was convinced that Margaret Evelyn had ruined her chances of being taken seriously. It pained her when she read the newspaper reviews for *Cavalcade*; the production ran for four hundred and five performances, and was later adapted into a film that won an Academy Award for Best Picture. Although she tried to quell any hope of returning to the stage, she often felt her mind straying to the Theatre Royal on Drury Lane and the missed opportunity of performing in a hit show.

Margaret felt her life slipping into a mundane routine although, in spite of her setbacks, a glimmer of ambition still burned within her. On an ordinary afternoon, as Margaret and her mother were going out to tea, Margaret Evelyn paused as they were crossing Tottenham Court Road, and without warning she asked: 'Well Margaret, what do you want to do now?' Without a moment's hesitation, Margaret answered, 'Go to RADA.'

For months, Margaret fed her enthusiasm for the theatre by reading theatrical magazines and books on the subject. She realised that one thing was certain: if she was to advance in her dream of becoming a serious actress, she would have to attend the Royal Academy of Dramatic Art (RADA). Considered the finest acting school in London, RADA was established in 1904 by the former actor and theatre manager, Sir Herbert Beerbohm Tree. Amongst its original council were Sir James Barrie, and George Bernard Shaw, who had donated his royalties from *Pygmalion* to the school.

But getting into RADA was no easy feat as there were three times more applicants than places available for students who wished to study at the academy. The auditioning process was tough and, once that hurdle had been achieved, the potential student faced a difficult entrance examination. Margaret Evelyn believed she could do it,[1] though, as was her wont, she expressed very little by way of praise and set about helping Margaret with her application.

Choosing to read a monologue from the part of Rosalind in *As You Like It*, Margaret gave the reading her own interpretation and portrayed the character as a tomboy. It was a gamble, and she realised if her nerves succeeded in getting the better of her the entire piece would fail. It did not assure her when total silence followed her reading. Intimidated by the judges' lack of reaction, Margaret was certain they were unimpressed. Finally, the principal, Sir Kenneth Barnes, spoke: 'Thank you, Miss Lockwood. Next, please.' As she exited the stage, another judge informed her that she would hear of their decision in due course.

Leaving the building on Gower Street, Margaret dwelled on the judges' parting words. On the way home on the train, she tried to imagine how she looked and sounded. She continuously replayed the scene over and over in her mind, wondering if she had spoken well, if her voice should have gone up instead of down, trying to console herself that it was done and she could only wait for the outcome.

After a week-long ritual of waiting at the front gate for the postman, the fateful letter arrived. Wrought with nerves, Margaret asked her mother to open it. Margaret Evelyn's blank expression gave little away, but Margaret need not have worried. Her future was certain: she had won a place at RADA.

*

In the spring of 1933, Margaret entered RADA as pupil no. 4577: Lockwood, Mary, Margaret. On her first day the teachers extinguished any dreams of fame and fortune with their blunt message. Margaret and her fellow pupils were informed of the realities of the theatre and how little chance they stood of ever seeing their name in lights. Perhaps only one of them would ever make a name for themselves, or ever win a place in the hearts of the public. Great disappointments, they warned, were on the horizon.

For Margaret the disappointments were not in her foreseeable future, and the beginnings of good fortune presented itself during her first term. She won a scholarship – a coveted prize at RADA – but refused the offer because the girl who had tied with her for first place was an Australian whose parents could not afford to keep her at the academy without a grant. Margaret's parents could afford the fees, and she decided it was best to decline the scholarship. It was a gesture that warranted her praise and admiration from her classmates and tutors. RADA's principal later praised Margaret for being 'self-contained, ambitious,' and added: '…she really understood what training and studentship means and was aware of the considerable demands on the personality which are necessary if the actress is to achieve correct expression. Very intelligent, she had a keen sense of technique and was a pleasure to teach.'[2]

However, Margaret's classmates were quick to criticise her appearance, and they pointed to her long plaits and asked, 'Is this a nursery school now?'[3] Longing to fit in with the other girls, who wore their hair in a short, shingled bob, Margaret persuaded her mother to let her cut her hair. A woman of action, Margaret Evelyn listened to Margaret's plea and advised her to sit down on the living-room sofa, where she then fetched a razor blade and sliced off the plaits. There was no tapering, no shaping or expert cutting with scissors, and Margaret's wavy hair sprang out 'like a luxuriant furze brush'.

Although Margaret was not the most fashionable pupil at RADA – she did not wear make-up or care much for clothes – her talent was beginning to attract the attention of her teachers. Violet Vanbrugh, the theatrical *grande dame*, who taught voice lessons, awarded her with the prize for diction. On her way home she decided to visit her first teacher, Miss Overbury, to share the good news. 'It isn't me you have to thank, my dear, it's yourself: you've worked so hard,'[4] she told Margaret. And perhaps to prove that acting was not a waste of time, she cabled the news to her father in Karachi. His response was less than encouraging – he simply ignored her.

*

The first term at RADA had passed and Margaret remained focused on her goal. She had won two double removes which meant she was able to study a two-year course in fourteen months. With her mind fixed on achieving this, it left little time for a social life and no one was more surprised than Margaret when she met her 'first and only sweetheart'. It had happened, by chance, on a Saturday afternoon, when Margaret ran into Betty Leon, a girl she knew from Sydenham High School. After a brief exchange, Betty invited her to a dance at the Leon family home, and she accepted.

When Margaret arrived at the dance she was introduced to Betty's parents, Emile and Daisy. French-born, Emile Armand Leon headed the family's iron and steel business, where he had worked his way up from commercial clerk to managing director of a city commodities firm at the British Iron and Steel Corporation, and had offices in London and in several foreign capitals. Along with his English wife, Daisy Alice (née Kebby), they welcomed Margaret into their home, and in turn she found them 'kindly people'. She already knew Betty's sister, Rhoda, from Sydenham; but she was not acquainted with the girls' nineteen-year-old brother, Rupert, who stood off to the side looking rather self-conscious.

Rupert had returned from a year-long apprenticeship in Saarbrucken, Germany – at his father's request – in the steelworks of ARBED. The political tension simmering below the Baroque city and the rise of Adolf Hitler had an impact on the young man; and when his boss, an ex-soldier of the Kaiser, invited him to a nearby Nazi rally, he accepted. This first sight of Hitler disturbed him and, appalled by his speeches fuelled by racial hatred, he claimed he was 'probably the only one present that could not be reached with those arguments'.[5] Still etched in his mind was the image of the young Germans marching to the Nazi songs. 'I did not like what I had seen in Germany. In one's youth ideals are strong, so I felt I should make a personal gesture of defiance.' Following through with his views he signed up to the Territorial Army and, being a Londoner, he joined the London Rifle Brigade (LRB) – a regiment with an honourable record and an impressive roll of battle honours. Dedicated and disciplined, Rupert spent his two-week holiday from the office at a training camp, learning to shoot straight, and in due course he earned the coveted regimental honour badge, which he wore on his sleeve.[6]

Margaret privately decided that she did not like Rupert very much, and she scrutinised his appearance: he was over six feet tall, lanky and scraggly looking with big feet, hands and teeth, and a mass of straight fair hair. When the dance was over she agreed to let him escort her home, and was further repelled when he tried to kiss her. This, she felt, confirmed her initial instincts. Refusing his advances, she shut the front door in his face and quickly forgot him.

However, Margaret was destined to meet Rupert again when, on a rainy Sunday afternoon, with everyone asleep in the house, she called on Betty and Rhoda. She stayed to tea, and while the girls were engrossed in conversation, Rupert walked in. As he had done before, he insisted on walking Margaret home, and again she accepted. He barely spoke to her as they walked to Highland Road; and, as he guided her across the busy road, she noticed his acute shyness, and empathised with him, for she understood how he felt. 'I've got a car,' he said in halting tones. 'It's not much of one. I only paid five pounds for it, but it goes. Will you come out in it?'[7] Very primly, Margaret said she would. From that Sunday afternoon she never had another boyfriend: it was always Rupert.

Rupert spent Monday to Friday working at his father's office, and every Saturday without fail he collected Margaret to take her dancing at Covent Garden, stopping off at a Lyons Corner House for a cup of tea before motoring home. With his weekly pay of thirty shillings, and his car, they managed to have 'wonderful times'. She thought him kind and considerate, but, in her opinion, slightly possessive. Such behaviour seemed normal to her, as she was used to Margaret Evelyn's domineering personality and, combined with her inexperience, she 'regarded it quite natural to do as he said'.[8]

One evening, as they sat in a Lyons Corner House, she told him about a pupil at RADA who was married to the actress Viola Keats. Through this pupil, she had been given an introduction to an agent, Herbert de Leon, whose office she had visited on Shaftesbury Avenue. Rupert became duly alarmed, and he warned her: 'You should be careful, you know, Margaret. You're so awfully pretty. Who is this man?'[9]

Margaret Evelyn, too, had similar reservations and she accused Herbert de Leon, the son of a Sephardi merchant who was born in Colón, Peru (some sources say it was Panama), of working in the white slave trade. Without telling Margaret, she called at his office unannounced to see for herself if he was genuine or not. It was a bold move and one that might have jeopardised Margaret's future.

An established agent, that same year Herbert had signed Greer Garson, then an up-and-coming theatrical actress. Well connected, his brother was the theatrical impresario, Jack de Leon, who alongside his wife, Beatrice, ran the Q Theatre. Far from offended by Margaret Evelyn's meddling, he appealed to the cynic in her and during their brief meeting he managed to convince her that he was genuine. Before she left, he promised to attend RADA's end-of-term show.

Held at the Theatre Royal Haymarket, the show attracted agents and producers who were eager to sign new talent. But for Margaret, who already knew Herbert was coming to see her, the pressure began when RADA announced its programme. Among the plays chosen was Gerhart Hauptmann's *Hannele*, the tragic story of a German waif who, on the verge of death, hears angels and experiences prophetic visions. It was to be produced by the Austrian-Hungarian director and actress, Leontine Sagan.

Out of all the students who had auditioned for parts, the choice of the lead was narrowed down to two older girls and Margaret. Determined to impress Leontine Sagan, she slept with the script under her pillow; she lived, read and thought *Hannele*. To prepare for the part, she explored the psychology behind the fictional character: how would Hannele look, what would she wear, and how would she speak? Putting this into practice, she sat around her house looking wistful and woebegone, and, she hoped, soulful. For her final audition, she brushed her hair around her face, and chose her simplest and oldest dress. One by one the girls spoke their lines, and after a pause, Leontine Sagan pointed to Margaret and said, 'I'll have that little one.'

But Margaret Evelyn did not share Leontine Sagan's enthusiasm, and she proclaimed the performance 'terrible'. Without mentioning Margaret's sensitive portrayal, she added, 'I couldn't see you half the time!'[10] Although she was disheartened by her mother's response, Margaret had impressed Herbert de Leon, and years later he remarked: 'I knew a star was being born and I was determined to do all that I could to help this young lady.'[11] But her mother's words came back to haunt her when the judges announced the winner of the Gold Medal, and it was not her.

The following morning Margaret, accompanied by her mother, made her way to Herbert's office on Shaftesbury Avenue. She contemplated her uncertain future as she climbed the dark, narrow staircase, at the top of which she was met by Herbert, a short man with dark, wavy hair and a plump, kind face. As she sat opposite him, he noticed that she had a vague, surprised air about her which seemed to ask: 'What am I doing here?' It was this humble approach he warmed to. She thought it best to be honest with him before he took her on as a client, and so confessed that she had not won the Gold Medal for *Hannele*.

Undeterred, Herbert reassured Margaret of her talent, when he said: 'My dear girl, you didn't win it, you didn't win it? I can't understand it; you were by far the best, by far the best. The Gold Medal, you should have won the Gold Medal, you gave a wonderful performance.'[12] Her spirits were raised when he told her, 'You were magnificent; I mean it. One of these days, when you are at the top, you'll believe me. You wait and see.'

He then explained the agent/artist system, as Margaret and her mother were oblivious to how it worked. It was his job to find her work, he told them, and if she secured the job he would take a percentage of her fee. However, no contract was signed. Herbert never signed a contract with his artists: he worked exclusively on a trust system, and if an artist did not trust his judgement or work ethic, they were free to leave.

Although neither of them were aware of it during that first meeting, Herbert was to become the mainstay in Margaret's life. She would count on him more than she did any other man, and in return he was not only her agent, but her mentor, business manager and, despite him being only ten years her senior, her father figure. She would depend on him for the next forty-five years.

5
A Work in Progress

After her meeting with Herbert de Leon, Margaret returned home to sit and wait. She missed the daily routine of RADA and, as she passed the hours at home, she remembered her principal's warning that 'very few of you here, perhaps only one of you, will ever win a place in the public eye'. Before she had time to dwell on the advice, twenty-four hours later, Herbert de Leon sent for her. He wanted Margaret to see Alexander Korda, the Hungarian-born film producer and director, founder of London Films based at Denham Film Studios and owner of British Lion, a film distributing company.

Korda instantly dismissed her; he flippantly advised her 'to go back to her typing or shorthand, whatever it was she did for a living' as she would never make it as a screen actress. Years later, at the peak of her career, Margaret reminded him of his poor judgement, and smiling ruefully he told her of his chance meeting with a German actress whom he advised to return to her role of housewife and mother. Her name was Marlene Dietrich.

The British film industry during this period, in 1934, was dominated by American films and its stars, and home-grown talent such as Gracie Fields, George Formby and Jessie Matthews were the top box office draws. With Britain in the grip of an economic depression, such stars, who were of working-class origins and did not disguise it, appealed to Britons from a similar background who formed a large percentage of the cinema-going public. Not only did those stars have attributes which the audience could identify with, their films were escapism from the drudgery of their everyday life. The latter ingredient would be formulated to mass appeal during WWII, but in the interim it was stars with the 'common touch' who were in demand. And it was, perhaps, with this outlook that Alexander Korda turned Margaret down.

Undismayed by Korda's opinion, Herbert approached his brother, Jack de Leon, the theatre manager and impresario, who was experimenting with a new play, *House on Fire* by Kathleen Leigh, at his little Q Theatre. There was a part yet to be cast: that of a young girl who, having been brought up by nuns in a convent, returns home to find that life is anything but sheltered. Margaret, Herbert told him, was perfect for the role, and trusting his brother's judgement he offered her the part.

Founded in 1924, the Q Theatre's venue was originally a shed that had once been a beer garden, a skating rink, a swimming pool, a dance hall, a cinema and a film studio. By the time Margaret arrived at the present Q Theatre by Kew Bridge it had risen in prestige but retained its shabby air; there was no permanent company of actors and plays lasted only six days. It was an eccentric establishment, with Beatrice de Leon, known as Beattie, running a tight ship. 'Never more than £5 a week,' she would say when hiring talent, regardless of their celebrity, and she refrained from giving the cast preferential treatment. Once, a well-known actress was waiting in the wings when Beattie approached her and said, 'You're not on during the last ten minutes of the first act and you don't come back until half way through the second so you won't mind helping us out in the coffee bar during the interval?'[1]

Eager to learn the ropes, Margaret was the first to arrive at the Q Theatre every day; she was a co-operative actress and could take criticism well. Such traits endeared her to the cast and crew, and Herbert knew his gamble had paid off. The Q Theatre was a stepping stone for many actors who would go on to find fame and have lasting careers on the stage. As Margaret could attest, it was a training ground for young talent and, as Jack intended, a showcase for new playwrights hoping to attract the attention of West End managers. Sydney Carroll, the West End producer, who a year later would launch Vivien Leigh's career with *The Mask of Virtue*, noticed Margaret in *House on Fire* and offered her a small part in *Family Affairs*, a play he was producing at the Ambassadors Theatre. Her confidence was further elevated when Herbert delivered the news that he had secured her a screen test at Elstree Studios.

To celebrate the news, Rupert took Margaret for a drive in his ramshackle car, which had no headlights: instead it had a torch on one side and a bicycle lamp on the other. The consequence of this was that he drove into some railings on the way home, and the impact caused Margaret's head to hit against the windscreen. The result was a black eye. She was devastated; and, with cold water and every other remedy she could think of, she bathed her eye until the swelling went down and she looked somewhat presentable.

The following day, as Herbert drove Margaret down to Elstree, she was stifled by nerves and in awe of the large film studio, founded in 1914 by the Neptune Film Company and sold to Ludwig Blattner in 1928. Margaret was entrusted to two men from the make-up department who would prepare her for the camera. Before that day she had never given much thought to her appearance: Rupert disliked make-up of any variety, including nail polish and other feminine artefacts; like many men of his generation and class, he had been raised with Edwardian sensibilities which promoted beauty in its natural form. 'You're much prettier without all that stuff,' he would tell her. And, since Margaret liked him to think her pretty, she never used it.

However, the film studios shared a different perception of beauty; and along with adopting a German system of recording sound and lighting, imitating Josef von Sternberg's pioneering technique, they favoured Marlene Dietrich's striking look, made popular in *The Blue Angel.* It was an era when leading ladies were transformed by the studios to resemble the opposite of their natural looks. Hollywood did this too, but in possession of larger budgets it could afford to promote glamour in a way its overseas rivals could only dream of.

With Margaret the make-up men at Elstree saw potential in her dark looks, and their transformation would be simple in comparison with that wrought on the various young hopefuls who were plucking their hairline and extracting their back teeth to reach the aesthetic of film-star glamour: that of a prominent forehead and sunken cheeks. They would shave off her eyebrows, by request of the lighting technician who announced: 'I can't photograph that girl: those eyebrows… they've got to come off.'

Bewildered at the thought of losing her eyebrows, Margaret turned to Herbert and pleaded with him to dissuade the make-up men. Taking her to one side, Herbert explained: 'Well, you know it's very important – it's your first test; they've got to come off.'[2]

Although hesitant, she agreed to it, and in place of her prominent eyebrows were two thin pencil-lines. Her thoughts turned to Margaret Evelyn and Rupert's reaction; and before she could settle her nerves, the director called 'lights' and a bright spotlight was shone on her face. As the cameras whirred, she heard herself speaking her lines in a monotone voice as though she were far away. She heard 'cut' and was abruptly brought back to the real world.

Before she left the studio, Margaret telephoned Margaret Evelyn, whom she knew would be waiting for her at Victoria Station, and to avoid a scene she thought it best to warn her mother of her new look. 'Mummy…' she howled into the telephone. 'Something's happened to me. I've lost all my eyebrows. They have shaved them all off.' Margaret Evelyn responded with a horrified wail.[3]

The response to Margaret's screen test at Elstree Studios was, as she suspected, underwhelming, and she happily began work in *Family Affairs* at the Ambassadors Theatre. Although she was intrigued by screen acting – 'where the big money was' – she could hardly scoff at her earnings as an unknown actress. At the end of the first week she had earned £12,[4] a substantial sum in 1934. With her earnings she invested in a wristwatch, and had a telephone installed at home so Herbert could reach her at a moment's notice.

At last she felt like a professional actress. And a professional actress she was; the critics praised Margaret's performance in *Family Affairs*, and Noël Coward noted: 'This girl is worth watching.' Margaret Evelyn, silently proud of her daughter, began a scrapbook and devoted her time to cutting out praise-worthy press releases and pasting them into the book. But, as Margaret began to imagine a long and fulfilling career in the theatre, something came along and threw everything off course.

Associated Talking Pictures, the production company owned by producer and director Basil Dean, who had acquired Ealing Studios in 1929, had viewed Margaret's dubious screen test and, as a result, they offered her the one and only remaining part of a girl named Mary in a screen adaptation of R. D. Blackmore's novel, *Lorna Doone.* Having been adapted twice before, this latest effort – its first foray with sound – was a vehicle for Dean's new wife, the actress Victoria Hopper, who was to be the film's heroine.

It was an unhappy production besieged by setbacks, from an escalating budget to the subsequent nervous breakdown of the second female lead, Dorothy Hyson, who claimed Dean – 'a frightening man' – was the culprit behind her illness. But Dean had little sympathy for Hyson and he ordered the casting director and associate producer, Aubrey Blackburn, to find a replacement to fulfil her part of Annie Ridd. Blackburn thought of Margaret, and he approached her as she rehearsed a country dance for her small scene. 'Dotty Hyson is ill,' he told her. 'I've told Basil Dean you can play her part. I'm sure you can now. Come along, come along.'[5]

Renowned for his domineering personality and harsh treatment of young actresses, it would seem that Margaret, with her shyness and inexperience, would be an easy target for Dean's ill-treatment. However, Dean – who had begun his career as an actor on the West End stage – was quietly impressed by her professionalism on the set and he approved her for Hyson's part.

When the opportunity presented itself, Margaret flew to the nearest telephone kiosk and rang Herbert. 'Herbert,' she yelled down the phone, 'I've got the second lead in *Lorna Doone*.'

'My God,' came Herbert's startled voice. 'You've done it. I knew you would. I'll see if I can get you some more money.'[6]

*

Among the talent scouts at RADA's end-of-term show who saw promise in Margaret was the wife of Herbert Smith, whose brother S. W. Smith controlled British Lion Films, and she returned home to her husband full of praise for 'one particular little girl'. Although nothing came of Mrs Smith's recommendation, Margaret and the Smiths' paths were to cross when Herbert de Leon telephoned Herbert Smith, asking him to see a new client of his. As a favour to his old friend, he agreed to meet Margaret and was pleasantly surprised when she walked in wearing a blue sweater with her hair 'all over the place', looking like 'a young unworldly girl with no perception of how a film actress should look'.[7] He liked her immediately and, two days later, he offered her a contract with British Lion Films. The contract guaranteed £500[8] for fifty days' work in the first year, which then increased to £750[9] for fifty days' work in the second year, and if she worked more than fifty days she earned £10[10] a day and then £15[11] a day in the following year.

At the age of eighteen, Margaret was rich. Appointing herself in charge of her daughter's finances, Margaret Evelyn took fifty per cent of what she earned as it was customary for girls who remained at home to give up half of their earnings to the household. But Margaret was free to spend her money as she wished and, with Margaret Evelyn agreeing that she could afford it, she bought a new wardrobe from Bond Street.

With her mother in mind, she remembered Margaret Evelyn's dream of owning a refrigerator, though she was adamant they could never afford one. 'Oh, if only we had a fridge,' she would say. Inventing an excuse to withdraw some money, Margaret bought a fridge for her mother's birthday and arranged for it to be delivered when she was out. Later, that evening, Margaret casually said, 'I'm making a pot of tea in the kitchen.' Knowing that Margaret Evelyn would offer to help her, she anticipated the reaction when her mother noticed the new fridge. Far from pleased, Margaret Evelyn stared in astonishment at the intrusive item in her kitchen. She called it a 'waste of money', and told Margaret that she 'had managed for years without a fridge and could continue to do so now'. Perhaps the extravagance went against Margaret Evelyn's sensible nature and she rejected the frivolity the fridge represented.[12]

It was an important lesson for Margaret, and at the height of her fame and earning power she maintained the modesty she had been brought up with.

*

Margaret continued with her work on *Lorna Doone* and appearing in *Family Affairs* at the Ambassadors Theatre every night. It was a gruelling schedule with early morning starts beginning at five o'clock and a long journey from Upper Norwood to either Beaconsfield, Ealing or Teddington, depending on where the filming was taking place on the day. In the evenings she would leave the studios and go to the theatre, after which she caught the last train home at night. Recalling her routine from those early days, Margaret wrote:

> I would creep upstairs to my room where, next to my little iron-framed bedstead, I had a hideous alarm-clock which clanked its way through the night till 5 a.m., when it went off with noise enough to wake the dead. Still half asleep, I automatically tumbled out of bed. My bedroom was furnished with a little kidney-shaped, marble-topped dressing table, and there was a rug by my bed so that I would not have to step directly on to the cold lino flooring. There was a big cupboard with a mirror in the middle of it, where I kept my clothes, and the bed had an Indian silk bedspread, one of those which my father had brought home from India. I would dash up to the bathroom, have a quick wash in cold water to wake myself up, and creep down to the kitchen, where Mother was usually waiting with a hot cup of tea for me. Then I waited for Rupert.[13]

Rupert expressed his concerns about Margaret travelling alone during the cold, dark mornings, and he offered to drive her to the studios. He would get up at five o'clock in the morning and call at her house, and after driving her to work he would return to London in time to report to the office. One morning, while they drove to the studios, he confessed his love for her. 'You know I do, don't you, Margaret?' he said.

'So do I,' she replied.

Remembering the 'beautiful morning',[14] passing the milk trucks and early-morning workmen, they envisioned a resplendent life for themselves. She was going to become a famous actress and he was going to be a millionaire. It was as simple as that.

6
Power Struggle

Although Margaret Evelyn had not met Rupert, she was vocal in her dislike of him. She did not approve of their modern courtship, and when Rupert parked his car up the road and sounded his horn (a request by Margaret to prevent the two from meeting), she would watch from the window as Margaret went to meet him. In her opinion, he was an unremarkable young man and not good enough for her daughter, and she knew that a beautiful girl in Margaret's position was bound to attract a lot of interest from the opposite sex.

She had previously acted in a similar manner, although justified as she felt the age gap entirely indecent, when her twenty-four-year-old nephew, Nicol Waugh, known as Pat, visited from Sandhurst Royal Military College to stay with his aunts. Having discovered Pat's infatuation with Margaret, who was sixteen at the time, Margaret Evelyn ordered him from the house and he was told not to set foot in it ever again. As a consequence of this, Pat fled to France where he joined the Foreign Legion; though, pursued by Mary, he was found, and extricated from the Legion.[1]

But Margaret had no interest in other men, and she used what she called 'my drop dead look… my hard stare with which to defend myself'[2] against the lecherous types at the studio who took her out to dinner and 'tried to ply me with different kinds of wine and drink and things'.[3] Others who had observed the young couple had nicknamed them 'beauty and the beast',[4] but Margaret cared little for their unkind comments; she only had eyes for Rupert. 'He was the only person I ever thought about. I was very much in love.'[5]

Rupert's family had grown fond of Margaret and accepted them as a couple, even if Margaret Evelyn refused to acknowledge his presence. But she was unable to avoid Rupert entirely and, at the Leons' request, she went to tea at their home one Sunday afternoon. Accustomed to her mother's brusque nature and habit of speaking her mind, Margaret struggled to relax as they made polite small-talk.

However, the mood changed when the cigarettes were passed around after tea. Margaret rarely smoked and, wanting to make a good impression, she accepted one 'more to be sociable than because I really wanted it'. Without warning, Rupert turned deathly pale, he erupted with anger and accused Margaret of purposely accepting a cigarette to annoy him. He caused 'quite a scene' in front of Margaret Evelyn, saying that it was an 'unwomanly habit' to smoke and that he was 'surprised' Margaret would do such a thing when she 'must have thought he would not like it' and he hoped she 'would never do it again'.[6]

Furious at Rupert's outburst, which confirmed her negative impression of him, Margaret Evelyn departed with a visibly shaken Margaret. When they returned home she ordered her to break up with him. 'If he's like that now, what on earth do you think he will be like later on?' she said. 'I shan't encourage you to see any more of him, and don't you bring him to this house, because I don't want him here.'[7] Margaret, however, continued to see Rupert; and, knowing that her mother 'never changed her mind', his name was never mentioned in their home. 'I think my mother hoped I would grow out of my liking for him, and, probably reasonably, supposed I would meet a lot more young men before I was much older,' Margaret said.[8]

However, Margaret's 'one and only excursion' with another man was disastrous and she 'hated it'. The studio had encouraged her to go out with a rich, middle-aged man, and in her 1948 autobiography, *My Life and Films*, she was understandably coy about the identity of the gentleman in question. She revealed that he was American and the head of a studio 'where I was working a year or two later'. As the 'excursion' occurred around the filming of *Lorna Doone*, the identity of the man appears to have been Sir Stephen Courtauld MC, the financial director of Ealing Studios.

Sir Stephen was fifty-one years old and married, and, as Margaret attested, he was indeed rich – he was a scion of the Courtauld textile family whose money allowed him to pursue cultural and philanthropic interests. During the filming of *Lorna Doone*, Sir Stephen developed a 'powerful interest' in Margaret and would call on her at the dressing room to ask her out. 'I didn't like him, and I didn't want to go out with him,' she recalled. 'But he was so persistent that in the end I agreed to go out with him one Sunday.'[9] A Rolls Royce driven by a liveried chauffeur arrived outside her house, and Margaret Evelyn looked out the window and said: 'I will answer the door.' Taking one look at Margaret's much older suitor, she ordered him to 'take very good care of my little girl'.[10]

They drove to Bray where they had 'a very sedate meal', the mood of which was inspired after Margaret noticed the waiter removing a reservation card which read 'Mr and Mrs…'. And, with Margaret proving to be an unwilling dinner companion, her suitor took the hint and drove her home, much earlier and much more swiftly than he had intended. He had wasted a Sunday on her, and Margaret was upset because she had given up her precious time which she could have spent with Rupert.

Reflecting on the incident, Margaret said: 'There were several times early on in my career when people tried to corrupt me sexually, but I had a basic incorruptibility and it washed over me.' This strength of character she attributed to Margaret Evelyn. 'My mother had very strong moral values which I inherited.'[11]

*

The production of *Lorna Doone* was slowly turning into a disaster and, with one incident after another plaguing the set, Basil Dean took charge and exerted his authority over every minute detail. He became fixated with a particular scene in which Margaret was to open a cage of doves to release them; and, thinking the doves as well as the cast should obey him, he ordered her to repeat it several times. The doves would not co-operate: they simply hopped out of the cage and stood on the ground. After every effort to make them fly up towards the sky, as Dean envisaged, he said through gritted teeth: 'Pick the little dears up, Margaret, put them back in the cage, and do it again.'[12]

Far from disheartened by Dean's meticulous direction, Margaret was flattered that he had devoted so much attention to perfecting her scenes. It was the only engagement she was to have with the director,[13] for as soon as the assistant yelled 'cut', their exchange was over and he went to view the rushes.

Curious to know how she appeared on screen, she approached Dean's protégé, the assistant director Carol Reed, for his opinion. 'Margaret,' he confided, 'it stinks.' He was referring to the production itself and not her performance.

Having viewed the rushes and thinking Margaret was one of the few positive things in *Lorna Doone*, British Lion sent her into her next film, *The Case of Gabriel Perry*, at Beaconsfield Studios. She continued to appear on stage in *Family Affairs* at the Ambassadors Theatre and, amidst her busy work life, it was announced that the premiere of *Lorna Doone* was to be held at the Adelphi Theatre. As she was not yet a star, Basil Dean did not invite Margaret to the premiere despite her appearing as the second female lead in the film.

On the day of the premiere, filming ran late at Beaconsfield and she missed her arrival call time at the Ambassadors Theatre. After berating Margaret for her lateness, the stage manager delivered the damning news: 'Your understudy has gone on. I'll deal with you tomorrow.' Under a cloud of gloom she left the theatre and headed to the Adelphi. Everything else had gone wrong, she thought; what harm could it do to try and get into the premiere of *Lorna Doone*?

When Margaret entered the foyer of the Adelphi, she spied Basil Dean in a tense mood as he paced up and down. She had no way of knowing that, having watched a private screening, the critics had condemned *Lorna Doone* as the worst film ever made in the history of British cinema. Similarly, when it was released to American audiences, the *New York Times* wrote: 'Cynics say that the choice of subject and scenario is not all the battle, and that until British producers realise that in the making of pictures the chief essential is not to be dull, Elstree will trail a long, long way behind Hollywood in the best selling markets of the world.' However, unlike Dean who gambled with his reputation and had lost a fortune, Margaret remained unscathed and the critics agreed that 'in her screen debut, [she] is a ravishing beauty. The story still holds water, even if the acting and the techniques of 1934 may leak a bit.'

Asking Dean if she could go inside, he dismissively said: 'Yes, of course. Here, go in this door, you'll find a seat somewhere.' As Margaret made her way through the darkened theatre, she heard a familiar voice filling the room. She looked up in astonishment to see herself on screen, sitting on a tombstone with John Loder. It was a strange phenomenon and she was unsure if she liked her onscreen presence or not. 'I was rapt for the rest of the picture. I don't know if I liked it or not, I was too fascinated to think about liking it,' she recalled.[14] When the screening was over, she left the cinema to catch the last train home.

Working seventeen hours a day was beginning to take its toll on Margaret. She would often fall asleep on the train and get carried far beyond Gipsy Hill Station. Rupert was concerned, and decided she should have her own car to go to and from work. On the weekends, he taught her how to drive; and, when she passed her test at Croydon, she bought a Standard Eight. The fact that she could afford to buy her own car and earn her own living came naturally to Margaret. 'It was very much a job, to be taken seriously, worked at with pride and diligence of craftsmanship,'[15] she said of her profession.

Margaret had begun to work in 'quota quickies', a practice which had emerged as a consequence of the Cinematograph Films Act of 1927. In an attempt to revive the declining British film industry, the Act called for British cinemas to show a quota of British films for ten years. The idea was introduced to create a market for British films and to provide economic activity in its home industry which had been crowded by American films. Margaret made several quota quickies in 1935, the first of which was the role of the good girl in *Honours Easy*, a vehicle for the Norwegian actress Greta Nissen, co-starring Patric Knowles and Chili Bouchier. Directed by Herbert Brenon and adapted from a play by Roland Pertwee, the plot centred on a man who tries to take revenge on an old rival by framing his son for theft.

The next quota quickie Margaret appeared in was *Man of the Moment* directed by Monty Banks, starring Douglas Fairbanks Jr. and the American star, Laura La Plante. A dark comedy filmed at Teddington studios (the British subsidiary of Warner Brothers), it followed the attempted suicide of La Plante's character, Mary, who is rescued by Tony (Douglas Fairbanks Jr.), a penniless playboy who is engaged to a spoilt heiress, Vera – played by Margaret. After Vera breaks off their engagement, Tony, who is plagued by mountains of debt, proposes that he and Mary make a suicide pact. They go to Monte Carlo to gamble, whereupon they agree that if they lose they will kill themselves and if they win they shall live. However, Vera decides that she wants to marry Tony after all and follows him to Monte Carlo; but, realising that he loves Mary, she breaks up with him and marries his friend instead.

In her third quota quickie, *Someday*, directed by a young Michael Powell, she was given the leading role opposite Esmond Knight. A romance based on two young people who wish to marry but cannot afford to do so, Margaret played a servant girl who falls in love with a lift operator. Upon its release it failed to make an impression on cinema-goers, and little information exists on the film. It remains one of Powell's least favourably reviewed quota quickies, with *Film Weekly* calling it 'feeble entertainment'.

The next was an adventure film titled *Midshipman Easy*, the first film Carol Reed directed alone. It co-starred Roger Livesey, whom Margaret had appeared with in *Lorna Doone*, and Hughie Green, the young boy who had inadvertently lost her the part in *Cavalcade*. Drawing on her dark colouring, she played the small role of Donna Agnes, a Spanish aristocrat's daughter. But, despite her appearance, it was a vehicle for the fifteen-year-old Hughie Green, whose character runs away to the navy and battles pirates and smugglers during the years when Britain was at war with Napoleon and his Spanish allies.

Her final quota quickie from this period was *The Amateur Gentleman*, directed by the American film director, Thornton Freeland. Co-starring Douglas Fairbanks Jr., the film was a period piece set in Regency London, where a young man disguises himself as a gentleman with the purpose of entering a royal court in a bid to prove that his father did not commit a theft, of which the royal party have accused him. The Italian actress, Elissa Landi, was given the leading female role of Lady Cleone whom Fairbanks Jr. falls for, while Margaret played the supporting part of Georgina Huntstanton. Released in January 1936, *The Amateur Gentleman* was voted the tenth best British film of the year.

The studio did not limit Margaret to this genre, and when Maurice Chevalier arrived in England to film *The Beloved Vagabond*, she was sent, along with every ingenue from the studios, to test for the part of the romantic heroine, Blanquette.

Although she won the part, the prospect of working with Chevalier, an international film star who had appeared in thirty films thus far, terrified Margaret as she had not yet considered herself to be an important actress. 'The word film "star" had not loomed on my personal horizon yet.'[16] Overcome by nerves, she never uttered a word to him off the set, except to say 'Good morning'.

Filming *The Beloved Vagabond* was a unique experience for Margaret, as it would also be shot in French with the petite actress Hélène Robert starring in the foreign version. The set, too, had a continental atmosphere, and Margaret was baffled by the French cast and crew's habit of shaking hands with one another. 'Everyone shook hands, constantly – all except the English. I think the others thought we were rather lacking in good manners.' It was also the first time Margaret had experienced professional rivalry[17] on the set.

With both Margaret and Hélène having to replicate one another's scenes for their respective productions, an incident stood out for Margaret. In one scene she had to appear 'like a drowned rat', and she was instructed to have jugs of water poured over her head. 'I didn't mind, and my hair didn't mind, since it curled all the more.' Hélène, however, did not like it at all. Her hair had been especially curled by the studio hairdresser every morning and when the water was poured over her head she 'really did look like a drowned rat'; responding to this unflattering guise, she shot looks of 'pure hatred' in Margaret's direction.

With the majority of the film being shot at Ealing Studios, it was decided during production that many exterior scenes would have to be shot on location in Nice in the south of

France. It would be Margaret's first trip overseas since she had left Karachi at the age of three and a half; and, before she departed, Margaret Evelyn gave her a 'little lecture', warning her to look after herself. She did not advise Margaret against falling in love with a Frenchman, though she held on to the hope that she might fall in love with someone, if only to make her forget Rupert.

The experience was a miserable one for Margaret, and she wrote to Rupert every day. It rained for the duration of filming, prompting the schedule to be moved forward to three o'clock in the morning; and it took three hours to reach the location, high up in the hills surrounding Nice. When Margaret had finished her scenes for the day, she would have to make another three-hour journey back to her hotel. The weather, combined with the loneliness of being in a foreign place, surrounded by an unknown cast and crew, intensified her feelings for Rupert.

Rupert was waiting for Margaret when she returned home to England. The trip had been their first separation since they had met, and, overcome by feelings of loneliness in one another's absence, they decided to get married.

Despite her optimism for their future, Margaret dreaded a confrontation with her mother. Broaching the subject, she gently asked Margaret Evelyn: 'Why won't you see Rupert, Mummy?' It was one of the few times she had mentioned his name, since when she had referred to him in the past it 'always caused friction' between the two.

But any hope of remedying Margaret Evelyn's ill feelings towards Rupert were lost, and she said: 'Don't mention that young man's name to me. I don't want to hear anything about him at all!'

The response left Margaret in tears, and for the first time in her life she rebelled. 'I'm in love with him, and I'm going to marry him; no matter what you say, I'm going to marry him,' she shouted at Margaret Evelyn.

Although startled by Margaret's rare display of defiance, Margaret Evelyn dismissed her threats. 'You're still a child,' she said. 'I won't listen to any more of this nonsense. You don't know what love is. As for marrying him, indeed. You'll never get my permission to do so, so don't talk rubbish. Put this all out of your head and think about your work. And don't you dare mention his name in this house again – ever.' [18]

Margaret had never seen her mother so angry and she herself had never been so torn with misery. She was still sobbing when she met Rupert that night. 'It's no good,' she told him. 'She'll never, never let us marry. She hates you. I've written to father, begging him to say yes.' [19]

The appeal to her father had dangerous repercussions. Henry forwarded the letter on to Margaret Evelyn without responding to his daughter's crisis. Feeling betrayed by Henry's lack of interest for her well-being and his absence in her life, she never sought his counsel again. The estrangement between father and daughter remained until Henry's death in Dorset in 1950. Several years before, he had returned to England from Karachi to live with his first and only legal wife, Jessie.[20]

Margaret felt as though there was no one to whom she could turn. Lyn might have proven a positive influence in the tension between herself and Margaret Evelyn, but he had recently left home to join a touring theatrical company. And Frank, her half-brother who often lived with them, had sailed for Shanghai where he joined the Shanghai Municipal Police.

With the exception of Herbert, she thought Rupert was one of the few men she could rely on.

'Let's run away,' Rupert implored Margaret. 'Let's run away as soon as you're free from the studios and get married at Gretna Green.'[21]

In the past she had been reluctant to disobey her mother, and she thought it was a bold suggestion. But, having failed to convince Margaret Evelyn otherwise, and thinking their happiness was at stake, she agreed with Rupert's suggestion of Gretna Green, the Scottish village renowned for its 'runaway marriages', where couples under the age of twenty-one could marry without parental consent.

*

Work became a welcome distraction for Margaret, and priding herself on being a professional she forgot whatever conflicted feelings she had for her mother and Rupert as soon as she entered the studio gate. The distraction appeared in the form of Carol Reed's small-budget, fast-paced comedy, *Who's Your Lady Friend*? starring Frances Day, and one of Britain's most popular comedians, Vic Oliver. It also marked the screen debut of Oliver's wife, Sarah Churchill, the daughter of Winston.

When Margaret viewed the rushes with Reed she was horrified by her 'appalling' performance, and he 'heartily agreed'.[22] She thought she could forget about the tension between herself and her mother, but it remained on her mind and slipped through to her performance. Reed sensed something was troubling her, but, as they had not yet established their close working relationship, he refrained from prying.

He had troubles of his own: the chief cameraman, Jon Stallich, collapsed on set with acute appendicitis, and, rushing to his aid, the chief electrician, Jack Ford, tripped and injured himself. Preparing to face up to the fact the film would have to be abandoned, Reed delivered the news to his cast.

Fond of their director, who had since advanced from working under Basil Dean at Associated Talking Pictures to directing his own films, they rallied round and offered to work overtime without pay. Margaret, although she never felt it was her best work on screen, managed to give an acceptable performance. The film and Reed's reputation had been saved, and 'she was never so happy to finish a picture'.

In the evenings, as she drove home from the studio, she contemplated Rupert's proposal to elope. On one particular evening, lost in thought, she heard a great commotion ringing through the streets of Norwood. An inferno caught her attention and, certain her family home was on fire, she ran towards the distant blaze. As she reached the top of Gipsy Hill, she could see the old Crystal Palace up in flames. Various conflicting emotions rushed through her mind as she watched the magnificent building of iron and glass succumb in spite of almost four hundred firemen battling in vain to save it. It had been a prominent feature in her childhood. It was one of the first sights she saw as the hansom cab brought her to her new home in London. And it was where, as a starstruck child, she discovered her love of acting. The burning of the old Crystal Palace was not only a great loss to the landscape of London; for Margaret it was a symbolic end to her childhood and all that seemed familiar.

7
Mrs Leon

NOT EVERYONE IN THE Lockwood household was against Margaret's wish to marry Rupert. She managed to form two allies in her aunt Mary and her seven-year-old cousin, Betty, who had grown fond of him. Although he was still forbidden from visiting Margaret at home, she and Rupert would take Betty along on their Sunday outings and it delighted the couple when the child would say, 'When you and Rupert are married…' And in her aunt Mary she found a confidante, to whom she confessed her plan to elope. Alarmed by the extreme measures the young couple were willing to resort to, Mary asked her to reconsider as 'it would kill your mother if she thought you had eloped like that'.[1]

Before Margaret could reach a decision and give Rupert an answer, the studio had made up her mind for her. In June 1937 Maurice Ostrer, the former vice-chairman of Gaumont-British which had been absorbed by Gainsborough Studios of which he was director, and Edward 'Ted' Black, the assistant production manager, approached Herbert with an offer for Margaret to play the female lead opposite George Arliss in *Dr Syn*. It was an ingenue role in a period drama based on eighteenth-century smugglers; and, although she was pleased that her career was advancing, it was Rupert who dominated her thoughts. She was concerned that he would be disappointed because, once again, her time was consumed by work. And, as their respective careers advanced, they were forced to abandon their plan to elope.

Rupert, however, allayed Margaret's concerns when he told her: 'We can wait for each other. We have done for three years. Three months aren't going to make all the difference and you'll be twenty-one then.'[2] As her twenty-first birthday loomed, and realising that Gretna Green had amounted to nothing more than a pipe dream, she was faced with the prospect of fulfilling her promise to marry Rupert and, in turn, disappointing her mother.

With Margaret's work becoming more demanding and her stock with the studio rising, Margaret Evelyn hoped it would triumph over Rupert and their romance would run its course. This seemed a reality when, three days into filming, George Arliss advised Maurice Ostrer and Ted Black to 'sign this nice little actress'. Acting on Arliss's advice and having viewed the rushes, the Ostrer brothers, Maurice, Isidore and Mark – who controlled Gainsborough and some three hundred and fifty British cinemas – telephoned Herbert and offered to buy out Margaret's contract with British Lion and to sign her to Gainsborough for three years. As she was underage, Herbert had to finalise the contract with Margaret Evelyn, who appeared flabbergasted by the terms and conditions. He had negotiated an impressive salary of four thousand[3] pounds per year, and this he related to Margaret Evelyn who was at a loss for words.

'What's the matter?' Margaret asked her.

'Matter, matter!' Margaret Evelyn said, not knowing whether to laugh or to cry. 'Sixty pounds a week for a slip of a girl like you, and he's talking about getting you eighty – I never heard of such a thing.'

Her mother's astonishment was not unfounded: Margaret's salary eclipsed the average earnings of £165 per annum in the mid-1930s. Given her own turbulent start in life – an orphan by the age of sixteen, and raising two children while her husband was thousands of miles away – Margaret Evelyn's pride in Margaret's financial independence must have been tested by her daughter's willingness to marry Rupert. There was no question of Margaret Evelyn considering Rupert as a suitable son-in-law, nor did she consider that he was forging a career that came with its own prospects. It was the cause of her frustration, and given her behaviour and outlook towards Rupert, she must have viewed him as a threat. Perhaps she resented the idea that he might persuade Margaret to adopt a more traditional life. This was certainly true for married women, and it was the norm for a wife to give up her career for a life of domesticity.

But as much as Margaret wanted to marry Rupert she did not consider abandoning her career to become a housewife. Now under contract to Gainsborough, she was given the opportunity to carry a film and for the first time in her career she received unreserved star billing. The film would be *Bank Holiday*, directed by Carol Reed, which depicted several individual stories in and around a seaside hotel. Beginning production in September, the date was significant for Margaret, for she would turn twenty-one on the fifteenth of that month.

As her birthday drew nearer, there was an unspoken tension between Margaret and her mother; and Margaret Evelyn realised that her power to exert her parental authority over her daughter would soon come to an end. Suspecting that something was brewing beneath Margaret's cool exterior, she began to treat her with an air of hostility each time she mentioned Rupert's name or left the house to meet him. Her behaviour was that of any parent who felt they knew best; but, given her strong personality and her inclination for speaking her mind, Margaret Evelyn succeeded only in pushing Margaret closer to Rupert.

Caught between the two people who loved her most, though expressed differently, Margaret sought counsel from Rupert. 'You must not get so upset,' he told her. 'When you're twenty-one you are free to marry; and when you face your mother and tell her firmly, it will be all right.' But, in her heart, she knew it would not be 'all right'.[4]

Margaret began to run on nervous energy: the responsibility of carrying a film and the long hours at the studio were taking their toll. The scenes were emotionally draining; it was a role that forced her to explore many complex emotions as her character, Catherine, a nurse, must choose between her fiancé, with whom she is spending a weekend at a seaside hotel, and her attraction to a suicidal man whose wife dies in childbirth. One scene, in particular, proved to be physically challenging when she was required to remain on the set until two o'clock in the morning, shivering in a bathing suit while buckets of water were poured over her to give the illusion that she had just emerged from a swimming pool. The stress from her private life was also apparent. Her face was covered in spots and she became tearful if anyone asked her a simple question, or offered constructive criticism.

Hoping to elevate her spirits, Rupert asked Margaret once more if she would consider his idea of eloping to Gretna Green. She burst into tears and tried to explain the reason behind her refusal: she was a rising star and a trip to Gretna Green, if discovered by the press, would make newspaper headlines. Far from being discouraged, Rupert came up with another plan. He would find a quiet register office where they could marry and nobody would know. He promised she would not have to tell Margaret Evelyn until she felt the timing was right; the fact that she was marrying him was enough. As he had waited four years, day and night, just to spend one day with her, Margaret agreed to his plan.[5]

They chose a register office in Epsom and the date was set for Saturday 16th October. The filming of *Bank Holiday* was still under way and, as the leading lady, Margaret had to work five days a week, sometimes six if the filming ran through to Saturday. To ensure everything ran smoothly and to avoid disappointing Rupert, she asked Carol Reed if he specifically needed her that day. Reed said he could not confirm if she would be needed or not, and then he asked her why. She explained that she had been invited to a close friend's wedding. Catching her off guard, he asked, 'You're sure it's not you who's getting married?' Margaret said no, but Reed remained unconvinced.[6]

To avoid a clash in her schedule Margaret asked Rupert to swap the day to Sunday 17th October; but, as soon as the date was set, the studio told her she was not needed for Saturday, her original wedding date. The fates were also against the couple when, on Saturday night, the studio rang and ordered Margaret to report for retakes the following morning.

Sunday began like any other working day for Margaret. Margaret Evelyn got up and made her a cup of tea and watched her leave at five o'clock that morning, unaware that her daughter was setting off to marry Rupert, the man she despised.

Following his usual routine, Rupert was waiting at the top of the road in his car. Margaret told him they would have to get married straight away, and there would be no time for a traditional wedding breakfast. Although she sensed he was disappointed, he did not react to the disheartening news. Instead, he quietly retrieved the platinum wedding ring he had purchased using the measurements they had taken with a piece of string because Margaret was too busy to go with him to the jeweller's. And then he seized the moment to be light-hearted when he told her: 'Darling, I believe when you get married you have to wear a hat!' She did not possess a smart hat and had to wear her old school beret.

As the car pulled up outside the register office in Epsom, Margaret glanced in the mirror and fixed her school beret. Accompanied by two witnesses – Rupert's friend, Kenneth Cluitt, and Margaret's friend and stand-in, Kathleen Marshall – she took Rupert's hand and followed him inside. Ten minutes later, they were officially married. Half an hour later, she was at the studio gates ready to report to the set of *Bank Holiday* as though nothing had happened. Pulling off her wedding ring, she handed it to Rupert and promised to meet him for lunch. Kissing him goodbye, she looked forward to their 'precious hour' together, and then at half past six she departed the studio to meet her new husband.

Greeted by a dense fog which had surrounded London that night, Margaret and Rupert must have felt, for once, that luck was on their side. Prior to the elements being in their favour, they had struggled to invent a reason as to why Margaret would have to spend the night away from home. With traffic at a standstill and their fellow commuters stranded for the evening, she had an entirely believable story.

Stopping at a phone box, she telephoned her mother to say she would be spending the evening with a friend. Then, Rupert found a reasonably priced hotel in Marble Arch, and Margaret stood next to him as he signed the register as Mr and Mrs Leon. Finally, she felt married. It was too late for dinner and, exhausted from their early start, they went to their room. Having made arrangements for a five o'clock wake-up call, no one in the hotel suspected they were newlyweds.

Having agreed to continue their lives as though nothing had happened, they each went to their respective homes after work. And although they met up each Sunday, and occasionally in the evenings, the separation felt worse than before. Margaret hated to deceive Margaret Evelyn, and the secrecy of their marriage weighed heavily on Rupert's mind. He encouraged her to tell the truth, but Margaret lacked the courage to face her mother.

On Margaret Evelyn's behalf, she sensed that something was afoot – perhaps she thought Margaret was plotting to elope; however, she failed to realise exactly what had taken place. Margaret remained under her roof, and for Margaret Evelyn that was good enough.

*

In the meantime, it was the studio whose wrath Margaret had to face. Caring little for make-up and clothes, she was told that, as a young star, she was a 'disgrace'. Summoned to the Gainsborough publicity office, Margaret was informed that

Queen Mary would be attending the November premiere of *Dr Syn*, and, as the leading lady of the film, she would be presented to the queen. Worried about her choice of evening dress, the publicity department telephoned Margaret in advance to ask what she planned to wear. 'I don't know,' she truthfully answered. To the publicity department, her response sounded too casual and they took offence at her nonchalance. Frosty silence followed and, with forced patience, they carefully explained the importance of looking glamorous, and how they must know every detail of her attire in order to give an accurate description to the press.

Faced with the frivolous aspect of a film star's life, Margaret felt uneasy about the studio's preoccupation with how she looked. 'It seemed to me they wanted me to be something quite different from my real self and I didn't know how to do that, even if I had wanted to. Furthermore, my mother looked after my money and kept a strict eye upon my activities. It was all very difficult and I'm afraid that unintentionally I quite upset some people.'[7] However, Margaret Evelyn understood the importance of the occasion and she took Margaret in hand. They went to Norman Hartnell's shop in Mayfair, the favourite couturier of the future Queen Mother, where Margaret bought a white chiffon dress trimmed with tiny rosebuds for the princely sum of £20,[8] an expense that horrified her mother. She invested a further £40[9] in a white fox-fur cape and purchased her first pair of white opera gloves.

The publicity department were delighted with Margaret's appearance, and the newspapers reported on her exchange with Queen Mary. The elderly monarch had approached Margaret, who nervously waited in the reception line to meet her, and asked: 'You're the little girl who's in the picture, aren't you?' Steadying her nerves, she managed to whisper, 'Yes, Ma'am.'[10]

*

Margaret and Rupert had been married for six months, during which they had spent a miserable Christmas apart. Their secret was revealed by a journalist who had telephoned Margaret Evelyn, asking her to confirm whether or not Margaret had married. She denied that her daughter had done any such thing; but the journalist checked the official records at Somerset House which validated the rumour, and he printed the story.

When Margaret returned home she was met by her aunt Mary, who rushed to the hallway to forewarn her: 'You'd better see your mother, Margaret. She knows you're married. Oh, Margaret, why didn't you tell any of us?' Without responding to her aunt, Margaret went to the living room to face her mother.

Instead of a scene, which Margaret had been expecting, Margaret Evelyn wept. 'How could you have done such a thing, how could you?' she repeatedly asked. But Margaret had no response; the sight of her mother's tears – she had never seen her mother cry before – silenced whatever defences she had built up. 'I've been shamed by my own daughter. How could you be so ungrateful, and so deceitful?'[11] The tears turned to anger, and Margaret was warned to either annul her marriage or leave home. She chose the latter.

Margaret was aware their marriage was not traditional in the sense that her income was far greater than her husband's, and that, unlike other married women of her generation, she continue to work. Rupert, too, adopted a modern stance on the subject of their expenditures, explaining that, as she earned much more than him, it was impossible for him to assume the role of breadwinner. He would, therefore, play the role of supporter and they would run their household together.

For the first time in her life, Margaret had to take charge of her earnings. Margaret Evelyn had given her half of the total amount which she had earned up until the age of twenty-one. It was a comfortable amount, about £2,000[12] in total, and a healthy sum to invest into her first home. She immediately made two outstanding orders: one for her mother, paid as a monthly allowance, and one for Rupert, which covered her share of the bills.

Allowing Rupert to assume the role as head of the household, Margaret agreed that he should make the final decision on where they were to live. He chose to rent a spacious two-bedroom flat in Frobisher House at Dolphin Square, Pimlico. It was a modern complex containing some 1,250 apartments, and when constructed it was the largest self-contained block of flats in Europe. And, as Rupert pointed out, it had its own arcade of shops on the premises. 'They stay open late,' he told Margaret, hinting that he expected her to take care of the domestic matters when she returned from the studio. But Dolphin Square was a poor choice to inspire Margaret into becoming a housewife. Having written a book in 1935 on the development of the buildings, its author, A. P. Herbert, advised: 'Wives will not have *enough* to do. A little drudgery is good for wives, perhaps. The Dolphin lady may be spoiled.'[13]

Their first nights spent in the new flat proved troublesome for Margaret, who was frequently disturbed due to Rupert being a restless sleeper. To ensure she was well rested for her early-morning start at the studio, she suggested, and Rupert agreed, to their occupying separate bedrooms. Soon they fell into the routine of two polite individuals sharing a flat. They rarely dined together as Margaret often worked late at the studio, and when they did it was at a restaurant for her cooking skills were limited. And, given her early-morning starts, she preferred to go to bed promptly and was asleep by ten o'clock.

On their weekends off, Rupert would visit his family and Margaret would return to Highland Road for a cup of tea with her mother, whom she attempted to maintain a relationship with in spite of her disapproval for Rupert and their marriage. After the visit was over she would walk around the corner to meet Rupert and drive back to Dolphin Square. Often, they would go to the cinema, but never to see one of Margaret's films, for Rupert disliked seeing his wife on screen and felt embarrassed[14] by her love scenes.

But, as Rupert would discover, he could not avoid his wife's film persona altogether. Margaret's popularity was soaring and the studio was insistent that she should carry out personal appearances. Investing in her star image, Gainsborough gave her a new, glamorous wardrobe and they appointed a secretary to read and answer her fan mail, though Margaret personally answered all of her autograph requests. With little choice in the matter, Rupert was faced with the reality that he now had to share his wife with the public.

8
Leading Lady

THE DAY *BANK HOLIDAY* was released was, as Gainsborough had predicted, the day Margaret became a star. A critical success, the film was a satisfying career move for Margaret, and a personal triumph too. Despite the turmoil from her personal life, the conflict with her mother and the burden of keeping her marriage a secret, no traces of those woes were apparent on screen. 'Margaret Lockwood suddenly stands out as an actress,' praised the *Evening Standard*. 'I regard her as one of the best of our younger film actresses. Beware of Hollywood!' wrote the *Daily Herald*. The critics were unanimous when they agreed that she deserved 'bigger and better pictures'.

With Margaret's fame in ascent her next film, *The Lady Vanishes*, was to be directed by Alfred Hitchcock in what would be his last contractual duty for Gainsborough before going to Hollywood to work under contract to David O. Selznick. Adapted from Ethel Lina White's bestselling mystery novel, *The Wheel Spins*, the plot followed Iris Henderson, a beautiful English socialite who is touring the fictional Balkan country of Bandrika with her friends before leaving for London to marry her aristocratic fiancé. As she boards the train on her homeward journey she is hit on the head by a falling plant-pot but is not injured. On the train, she encounters an elderly Englishwoman, Miss Froy, whom she had met at the hotel the night before. Posing as a governess, Miss Froy hides her identity as a spy; and after she goes missing on the train, Iris and her companion, Gilbert, whom she appears to loathe, look for her. However, their fellow passengers claim to have not seen Miss Froy, and they try to convince Iris that the woman does not exist and is the product of her bump to the head. During their search for Miss Froy, Iris and Gilbert realise the passengers are not what they seem – apparent when Iris notices a nun wearing high-heels; they are forced to fight off a knife-wielding magician; and are almost poisoned by a brain surgeon who is involved in the conspiracy to kidnap Miss Froy. When Iris and Gilbert find Miss Froy, she reveals that she is a spy and must deliver a secret message to Whitehall. The message, in the form of a tune, is relayed to Gilbert, who is a musician. They help Miss Froy to escape from the train, but as it stops at the border there is a shootout with jackbooted soldiers. Finally, when Iris and Gilbert reach London, where she is to meet her fiancé, they acknowledge their feelings for one another and hastily marry.

The Lady Vanishes was presented to Hitchcock as a ready-made shooting script written by Frank Launder and Sidney Gilliat, two of Gainsborough's jobbing scriptwriters. But Hitchcock and Margaret almost missed out on the film entirely. Originally scheduled for production in 1936, *The Lady Vanishes* – then working under the title of *Lost Lady* – was to be directed by Roy William Neil, the Irish-born director whose career dated back to 1917, and who had worked with Margaret in *Dr Syn*. However, production got off to a disastrous beginning when the assistant director took the crew to Yugoslavia for location shooting, whereupon he fell and fractured his ankle. The police investigating the incident discovered the script and, offended by Launder and Gilliat's farcical portrayal of their country, they handed it over to higher authorities and subsequently the crew were deported and production was abandoned.

A year later, in 1937, Hitchcock resumed production on *The Lady Vanishes* with the intention of filming it straight away. He also demanded that the cast were to be promptly assembled and, with an eye for emerging talent as well as recasting his leading ladies, newspapers reported that the part of Iris Henderson would go to Nova Pilbeam or Lilli Palmer. Margaret, a great fan of Ethel Lina White's novels and of the mystery genre, abandoned hope of being considered for the part.

With Margaret's availability working in her favour, Ted Black approached Hitchcock with the purpose of testing her for the part of Iris. Charmed by this 'pretty, petite and sincere-looking actress',[1] Hitchcock agreed to cast her as Iris, the pleasure-loving socialite who was both haughty and spoilt, but in possession of a firm moral compass. Black echoed this assessment when he said Margaret 'had something with which every girl in the suburbs could identify herself'.[2] And Margaret herself agreed that she 'was only a little suburban girl from Norwood'.[3] Critics, too, believed that her appeal was founded in the way she 'neatly sidestepped class stereotypes'; her voice 'betrayed neither traces of the Mayfair drawing room nor any hint of a regional accent. She spoke with clarity but without affectation.'[4]

The part of Gilbert, a raffish but penniless upper-middle-class musician, was yet to be cast. Ted Black also encouraged Hitchcock to test Michael Redgrave, a young theatrical actor who was gaining attention in the Chekhov play *The Three Sisters*. A typical thespian, Redgrave was wary of the film world, but he was persuaded by the generous contract offered by the studio. Still, the financial payoff could not detract from the insecurities a serious theatrical actor might harbour about the condescension of their peers. Film acting, to that set, was considered louche, and those who were serious about their stagecraft were reluctant to 'prostitute their talents'[5] for the medium. Hitchcock himself confirmed the differing opinions between the theatre-going public and those who frequented the cinema, stating that 'no well-bred English person would be seen going into a cinema: it simply wasn't done'.[6]

Prior to production, Margaret had not met her leading man. Adhering to the Gainsborough publicity machine, she met Michael Redgrave at a charity ball hosted at the Royal Albert Hall, where they were forced to dance together for the sake of a photo opportunity. Although contrived, it was important to suggest that they knew one another, for the fans expected a sense of camaraderie amongst film stars; or, as Hitchcock said, 'actors are cattle'[7] and could, therefore, be herded into situations beyond their control. Regardless of Hitchcock's meddling, or perhaps because of it, Margaret and Redgrave were to remain 'suspicious of one another'[8] on and off the set.

The aesthetic elements of their acting, with Margaret's experience in film and Redgrave's theatrical style, inspired a certain amount of contempt, though he admitted that he 'respected her professionalism'.[9] Their surroundings contributed to an uneasy feeling between the two, and with the set measuring a mere ninety feet long, including the train used for the majority of the film, they were forced to stay within close proximity of one another. Sensing the unspoken tension between Margaret and Redgrave, Hitchcock would, in an attempt to capture their characters' first meeting – which was 'at a disadvantage', when Gilbert barges into Iris's hotel room and gives her the impression that he would be staying the night – maintain such feelings when filming began.

Furthermore, Hitchcock nurtured a feeling of confusion and uncertainty on the set when he contradicted his reputation for being a perfectionist and adopted a relaxed directorial style. Accustomed to Carol Reed, who was 'quite meticulous by contrast',[10] it unnerved Margaret when Hitchcock refrained from managing her performance. Thinking him disinterested in his cast, she referred to him as a 'dozing, nodding buddha with an enigmatic smile on his face'.[11] Redgrave, who was used to rehearsals lasting for several weeks before the opening night of a play, found it alarming when Hitchcock permitted a maximum of three minutes to rehearse a scene before the camera started to roll. When he approached the director with his concerns, he was ordered 'to do as he was told and not to worry so much'.[12]

The imminent departure for Hollywood contributed to Hitchcock's congenial mood, and Margaret found the set of *The Lady Vanishes* to be a happy yet odd environment. Intrigued by Hitchcock's idiosyncrasies, she was alarmed when the production would break for afternoon tea and, to signify it was over, he would toss the empty cup over his shoulder, causing it to smash on the floor. 'He certainly never did it out of temper or excitement, or any other feeling,'[13] she said. His behaviour soon became the norm, and she found herself growing fond of the director.

But Hitchcock's practical jokes were not always appreciated, and it was Mary Clare, cast as the European Baroness, who was on the receiving end. At a party given by Ted Black for the cast and crew, Hitchcock offered Clare a concoction that he had prepared himself. Claiming it was fruit juice, he had spiked it with liquor; and Clare, a teetotaller, was soon drunk. The cast agreed that it was 'not a very kind thing to do'.[14]

In spite of his 'not very kind' jokes, further endearing Hitchcock to Margaret was the presence of his nine-year-old daughter, Pat. On one occasion he cleared the set during the lunch hour, and ordered mood lighting and a small group of studio musicians to play from a specially made playlist. He then drew up a menu of his favourite dishes and asked for juice to be served in champagne flutes. When the preparation was complete, Hitchcock and Pat ate a special luncheon, served aboard the set of the mock dining-car.

Five weeks later, in December of 1937, production was completed. Spanning the genres of romance, comedy and suspense, *The Lady Vanishes* was released in October 1938 to positive reviews on both sides of the Atlantic. The *New York Times* called it 'the best picture of the year', and, as had been the theme of her previous onscreen efforts, critics wrote that Margaret 'dazzled' and 'sparkled'. And further cementing the film's success, the New York Film Critics Circle awarded it the first prize for the best picture of 1938.

*

For the first time in four years, Margaret experienced the rare luxury of taking a holiday. Doubling as a belated honeymoon, Margaret and Rupert drove randomly for miles before stopping at a 'charming inn' in Slapton, Devon. With their individual careers consuming so much of their time, and Margaret's busy schedule at the studio, they had never spent a considerable amount of time alone. And, having exhausted the topic of talking shop, they discovered they had little to discuss. The strained atmosphere was exacerbated by the weather, as it had rained non-stop since their arrival.

A few days had passed and, to the relief of Margaret, Rupert suggested they return to London. As they drove home, his mood began to falter and, finally breaking his silence, he told her: 'There's going to be a war. You mark my words.'[15] His four-year contract with the London Rifle Brigade was terminated in 1937 and, when Neville Chamberlain returned from Munich 'waving that worthless piece of paper', Rupert was as 'relieved as the next man'; yet he had his doubts that peace would continue. He harboured a deep anger against Hitler, embedded since that first sight of him in Germany in 1932, and a distrust for the British and French Prime Ministers – 'guilty men' – who, in the early stages, had all of the cards in their hands, 'yet they played the game of politics with criminal stupidity'. Disillusioned and frustrated by modern politics, Rupert had become an avid follower of Winston Churchill, 'whose speeches in Parliament struck a chord in my heart'.[16]

Margaret had no intention of marking his words[17] and was relieved when his mood lightened as they drove through the New Forest. Spying a sign advertising a house for sale, he made a turn for a wooded lane where they found a small, dilapidated bungalow. 'Let's look at it, Margaret,' he implored. 'We can afford it now.'[18] That was true: Gainsborough had increased Margaret's contract to what seemed like astronomical figures.

In 1938 she had earned £6,000,[19] and her new contract promised to treble that salary within five years should her popularity endure. Hoping to please Rupert, and to relieve the unspoken tension between them, Margaret agreed to his suggestion and they purchased the bungalow, which they named 'Delcott'. He spoke of renovating the 'shack'[20] which had asbestos walls and a corrugated tin roof into a two-bedroom weekend house, away from London and the studios that monopolised her time.

As they drove back to London, they spoke of Delcott and of their future together. Rupert suggested they might spend their first Christmas as a married couple there, and Margaret agreed. But his plans would have to wait. When they returned to Dolphin Square, she found a telegram waiting for her. It was from Gainsborough, with the news they were sending her to Hollywood.

*

Following the international success of *The Lady Vanishes*, Gainsborough were eager to capitalise on Margaret's popularity both in Britain and overseas. Ted Black spoke of establishing Margaret and Michael Redgrave as a British version of Myrna Loy and William Powell, who had starred together in the Hollywood film series, *The Thin Man*. This idea was eventually abandoned when the war came and Redgrave joined the Royal Navy as an ordinary seaman. But Hollywood loomed on Margaret's horizon; and, further confirming their faith in her as a star, Gaumont British (Gainsborough's parent company) secured a deal with MGM in which *The Lady Vanishes* would be the studio's first release in an American cinema. The studio had also negotiated a transatlantic agreement with Darryl F.

Zanuck, head of Twentieth Century Fox, and he agreed to loan his American contract players to Gainsborough in exchange for Margaret.

Having grown up watching Hollywood films – 'I saw every movie they ever made'[21] – and realising the credibility that it would bring to her career, the offer from Fox was not one Margaret dared to refuse. Rupert, however, sensed this latest venture would involve long absences from his wife, and an upheaval to their private life, and he did little to conceal his dismay. With her attention focused on Hollywood, he brought her down to earth when he asked, 'What are you going to do in Hollywood?' And then, 'How long are you going to be away?'[22] Responding to Rupert's concerns, she attempted to keep his morale up by saying: 'Not long, darling. I won't let them keep me away for long.'

But as the plans for her Hollywood trip were revealed, she began to wonder if it was indeed a sensible career move. She would not be starring opposite her matinee idol, Tyrone Power, as she had hoped, or any leading man for that matter. The film would be *Susannah of the Mounties*, its leading role to be fulfilled by Fox's number one star, the eleven-year-old Shirley Temple. Cast as the second female lead – 'an insipid supporting role' – Margaret felt bitterly disappointed and resentful that Gainsborough had misled her, knowing 'too well [Shirley] would always out-star any adult playing with her'.[23] She wondered why Darryl Zanuck would go to the effort of bringing her to Hollywood for such an unimportant part with so little screen time.

Although Rupert had not been enthusiastic about her going to Hollywood, he sympathised with her change of heart and, not wanting her to travel alone, he suggested she invite Margaret Evelyn as he could not take a leave of absence from the office. Margaret Evelyn declined the offer, claiming she was too old (she was fifty-five) to make such a trip. Finally, Rupert's nineteen-year-old sister, Betty, jumped at the chance to go to Hollywood, and it eased Rupert's mind to know that Margaret would have the company of a 'good and sensible' girl.

Margaret's worries about leaving Rupert behind were temporarily forgotten[24] when Gainsborough's publicity department swooped in and demanded her attention. Advised by Ted Black that she ought to have a wardrobe befitting a Hollywood star, Margaret shopped for a trousseau of dresses, evening gowns, and an array of furs which included a sable jacket costing two hundred guineas, a £150 full-length mink, and an £80 ocelot coat. She spent her days obliging the press who demanded interviews and photographs, and her evenings were filled with leaving parties given in her honour.

There was a brief respite over the Christmas period, and having spent Christmas Day with Rupert in their flat – a poor substitute for the one he had planned to spend at Delcott – Margaret was ordered to resume publicity for the American trip. The studio sent a photographer from the *Daily Sketch* to document her daily life, which consisted of her shopping and packing. Reluctantly, Rupert joined in and was photographed eating a 'last lunch' with his wife, though, quite tellingly, he kept his back to the camera.

To compensate for the disruption (and perhaps the dismal trip to Devon was not far from her mind), Margaret suggested they take a second honeymoon, and this appeared to lift his spirits. But for Margaret, whose fate was in the hands of

Gainsborough and Fox, the six weeks in which the studios said she 'should be away' was an unrealistic prediction. While she fretted about her trip, Rupert concerned himself with the rumours of an impending war. And, although both factors threatened to widen the unspoken distance between them, they clung to the hope that, in six weeks, they could resume their married lives together.

9
Hollywood

The Hollywood trip began with an unpromising start. The acute travel sickness that blighted Margaret's days as a child performer had come back to haunt her, and she spent the five-day voyage locked in her stateroom on the *Ile de France*, bed-bound with debilitating seasickness. Adding to this ominous beginning, three days into the voyage the news had reached her that Vivien Leigh, then a little-known English actress, had landed the coveted role of Scarlett O'Hara in *Gone With the Wind*. Margaret must have wondered, with her similarity in looks to Leigh,[1] if there was room for another British actress; for, prior to Leigh's good fortune, she had been described by David O. Selznick as 'pretty in a Margaret Lockwood way'.[2]

Margaret's concerns were not unfounded. In the midst of 'Vivien Leigh mania', her contemporaries from England, Greer Garson (who had starred with Robert Donat in MGM's *Goodbye Mr Chips*) and Merle Oberon (who played the leading role opposite Laurence Olivier in *Wuthering Heights*), would make an impression on the American public. There was a growing British colony in Hollywood which included Ronald Colman, Charles Laughton, Elsa Lanchester, Maureen O'Sullivan and Maureen O'Hara (both Irish, respectively, but had worked in British films), Ray Milland, Cary Grant, Errol Flynn and

Leslie Howard. It prompted a British scenarist to write: 'The English colony is so large that Americans have been provoked into reviving their forgotten war of independence sentiment in a song entitled "The British Are Coming! Bang! Bang!" '[3] It was also a significant year for importing European talent, the most prominent being Ingrid Bergman, a star in Sweden, who was invited by David O. Selznick to appear in *Intermezzo*, and Austrian-born Hedy Lamarr who was promoted by MGM as the 'world's most beautiful woman'.

While those actresses were brought over to be leading ladies, and were relatively unknown to American audiences when they made their debut in Hollywood films, Margaret had the advantage due to *The Lady Vanishes* being the most popular British film to be shown in American cinemas in 1938. On reflection it seemed a waste of Margaret's talent, and an ill-advised move on Gainsborough's behalf to allow their rising star to play second fiddle to a fading child star.

When the ship docked in New York, Margaret was so incapacitated by seasickness that she had to be examined and given an injection by the ship's doctor before she could leave the liner. Weakened from ill health, and in a strange country, the arrival of a chauffeur-driven car was a welcome sight. The studio had made reservations for Margaret and Betty at the Barbizon Hotel For Women,[4] a residential hotel on the Upper East Side whose clientele was made up of career women who strived for independent living but with the friendly atmosphere of a family home. Perhaps it might have been a comfortable place for Margaret to recuperate but, with the exception of being served breakfast upon her arrival, she was immediately taken to Twentieth Century Fox's offices on West 56th Street.

Inside the Fox offices, Margaret was met by the unforgiving American press. Accustomed to the British press and Gainsborough publicity department who were chivalrous in comparison, Margaret had little experience of handling a press call or answering obtrusive questions. She looked like a star and for a moment she commanded their attention; however, as the gaze was lifted from her ocelot coat and directed to her low-heeled, sensible shoes, the press broke their silence. They ordered her to pose in a negligee, but she truthfully answered that she did not possess such an item. They ridiculed her 'clod-hopping shoes', and mocked her accent. 'Do you always wear your hair like Brenda Frazier?' she was asked. She had never heard of Brenda Frazier, a famous New York debutante, and they misconstrued her ignorance as flippancy.[5] Another reporter, sensing that she was out of her depth, inquired if she expected to see any Red Indians. It was the 'most stupid question' she had ever been asked. Then, she was asked: 'What does your husband do?'

'Steel,' she replied.

'What does he steal?'

The joke did not escape Margaret, and 'bewildered, tired and frozen' she did not respond.[6]

When the interview was printed the following morning the reporters wrote that Margaret 'loffed and loffed. How rilly, rilly funny!' They dismissed her as 'snooty, standoffish, high-hat and dull'.

It was not a promising start. Fox were outraged, not by the interview or how she was portrayed, but with Margaret for admitting that she was married. The mention of a husband would thwart their plan to promote her as a glamour girl reminiscent of her onscreen character, Iris Henderson from *The Lady Vanishes*. But it was not the first time Margaret's candid approach infuriated the publicity department, as Leslie Frewin, a publicity director at Gainsborough, recalled:

> The Margaret Lockwood that I knew in the days of '37, '38 and '39 was something of an enigma to people who did not know her well. I think she will agree that she was not an easy person to understand. But when one really got to know her one got the impression that Margaret was that comparative rarity in the film business, a very sincere person. But she would never suffer fools gladly, nor did she approve or even tolerate empty-headed conceit. She wanted to get to the top of the tree, but unlike some she was not prepared to trample on others beneath her feet in order to achieve her ambition. On the set she was always the essence of sincere charm. Some people were a little mystified because Margaret didn't conform to the recognised pattern of a gushing film star. She was quiet, reserved and unmoved by the usual round of studio excitement and talk. She went her own way, yet always co-operated with everybody from the producer to the clapper-boy, finishing her work and going home in her small car to spend a quiet evening with her family and intimate friends.[7]

After her brief and uninspiring stay in New York, Margaret was driven to Grand Central Station where she and Betty boarded the Twentieth Century Limited for a three-day-long journey to Los Angeles, briefly stopping in Chicago before heading to the west coast. Although a comfortable train, then considered the epitome of glamour with an orchid on every table in the dining car, Margaret's enthusiasm dipped when the newspapers came aboard. Her disastrous interview in New

York made the national papers and much was made about her longing to see Red Indians and her accent. It was not the welcome she had been expecting, and the mockery and ill-treatment of the press intensified her homesickness and longing for Rupert.

When the train reached Los Angeles, Margaret's spirits were momentarily lifted by her new surroundings. Gainsborough had made reservations for Margaret and Betty at the Garden of Allah, a residential hotel made up of twenty-five villas, formerly owned by the silent film star Alla Nazimova who returned to live there in 1939 after becoming impoverished and forced to take bit parts in films. Located east of the Sunset Strip in Hollywood, it had a reputation for being a notorious address since opening in 1927, its controversy springing from the (true) story that during prohibition the residents had attempted to fill the swimming pool with empty liquor bottles. Although the place was still considered somewhat exclusive,[8] the cosmopolitan set was beginning to depart, including the author F. Scott Fitzgerald who left as Margaret arrived.

Unaware of the sordid escapades that occurred behind the stucco walls of the villas, where many residents lived by the philosophy that 'every hour is cocktail hour',[9] Margaret and Betty thought it 'a dear little Spanish-style hotel'.[10] There was a dramatic moment, however, when Margaret saved the costume designer, David King, from drowning in the swimming pool. With the exception of that incident, their stay was a sedate one.

Although it was January and the locals were feeling a chill in the air, to Margaret it seemed like an English summer. A photographer from Fox arrived at the Garden of Allah to photograph Margaret, who posed in a bathing suit and cap next to the swimming pool shaped like the Black Sea.[11] And when she was not obliging the publicity department, she drove herself and Betty to Santa Monica beach in a hired Buick, where they swam in the Pacific Ocean and took in the sights of southern California.

A few days later, Margaret reported to the set of *Susannah of the Mounties* where she met her leading lady, Shirley Temple. At the age of eleven, Temple's career as 'America's little girl' was beginning to wane and, as much as Darryl Zanuck tried, he could not capture the commercial success of her early films. The studio hoped that the plot, based on Muriel Denison's book of the same title, would be a welcome change from Temple's melodramas and musicals. A combination of a western and a musical directed by William Seiter and shot in Technicolor, the film was set in 1880s Canada where a Mounted policeman, played by Randolph Scott, must protect the Canadian Pacific railroad from Indian attack. He is assisted by Temple, the survivor of a Blackfeet massacre, who comes to live on the post. Margaret played the daughter of Scott's commanding officer and, instigated by Temple, over the course of the film the two fall in love.

It unnerved Margaret to witness the pressure the studio placed on Temple, and how her chaperones and formidable mother guarded her from the trivialities of everyday life. Temple would arrive on the lot, film her scenes – usually in one take – after which she was escorted to the custom-designed bungalow that had been installed for her on the lot. The set, too, was a strange one and different from anything she encountered in England. Fox had recruited a dozen Blackfeet Indians to appear as extras but the studio failed to make a good impression on them, prompting an article to be released with the headline 'Indians Heap Much Unimpressed'. However, after a Blackfeet member witnessed Temple rehearsing her tribal dance, the group, led by Big Beaver, applauded and bestowed the nickname 'The Flying Woman' upon her.

As she had done in New York, Margaret unwittingly offended the studio's publicity department. In those days she was not accustomed to sending telegrams, preferring to send handwritten letters home to Rupert and Margaret Evelyn. And, eager to receive their reply, every day she inquired if there were any letters from England. A telephone call came through for her on the set: it was the publicity department and, as usual, she asked if there were any letters postmarked 'London'. None were so, and Margaret casually said she would collect the other letters in due course.

Within five minutes, a man from the publicity department appeared on set and berated Margaret for her lack of interest in her American fans. Before she could explain that she had been expecting letters from her family, and unaware that she even had American fans, the damage was done. The studio considered her to be difficult and, perhaps, they sensed there was a fragment of truth when the New York press had written about her in an unfavourable light.

The filming of *Susannah of the Mounties* was to last for six weeks, and at the end of each day Margaret happily ticked off her calendar. As her anticipated return home to England grew nearer she was disheartened to learn that the six weeks, during which she thought she would be engaged at Fox, was an estimated timeframe given for the production of the film. Post-production, however, could take even longer, for it was far more precise than that of British films. She was told she would have to remain in Hollywood for retakes; but with Zanuck's insistence on viewing every strip of film from every production shot at Fox, she could not be certain as to when he would call for the retakes of her film.

Hollywood, she felt, was the 'most dead-alive place on earth', like a seaside resort out of season; and, to ease her boredom while she waited for Zanuck to call for retakes, Gainsborough loaned her to Paramount to film *Rulers of the Sea*, a seafaring period drama charting the beginnings of the first steamship to cross the Atlantic. Its director, Frank Lloyd, had recently viewed *Bank Holiday* (retitled *Three on a Weekend* for American audiences) and, learning that Margaret was filming at Fox, he was eager to engage her for his next production. Although flattered by Lloyd's persistence, Margaret appealed to Gainsborough to cancel their agreement with Paramount.

The reason for her request was the American newspapers, who – unlike the British press – were forthright about Hitler and the threat of war. Sensing that 'war was definitely coming', Margaret got into 'such a state and was absolutely convinced that she was going to be stuck in Hollywood and never get home'.[12] However, predicting that Margaret's career was on the rise in Hollywood, Gainsborough ignored her request and 'blinded by tears' she reported to the studio.

It was a relief to Margaret that Paramount was smaller than Fox, and the set not quite so large and intimidating. Will Fyffe, her co-star from *Owd Bob* – a film she had made between *Dr Syn* and *Bank Holiday* – was being shipped over to star with her. And unlike *Susannah of the Mounties* where she did not mingle easily with the American cast and crew, she felt this production had a homelier feel. She found her former co-star from two quota quickies, Douglas Fairbanks Jr., to be a 'friendly choice' of leading man, unlike Randolph Scott who had barely spoken to her.

However, not everything ran smoothly during production. Renowned for his seafaring films, Lloyd had a preference for shooting on location, and ferried his cast and crew to Catalina Island for the shipboard scenes. Margaret's seasickness returned and she spent the day being sick over the side of the rail. She was sent ashore and her scenes were reshot against back-projection.

Although Margaret was embarrassed and disappointed at having interrupted production, Lloyd put her at her ease, and in turn she found him to be a sympathetic listener to her woes about Hollywood. He himself had immigrated from Glasgow to America in 1913, where he started out as an actor the following year. He soon found his vocation in directing and, in 1933, he had made the screen adaption of Noël Coward's play *Cavalcade* – a pleasing coincidence, Margaret thought, given her brief involvement in the original stage production. He was also instrumental in introducing her to one of the few friends she would make during her visit.

Without her knowing, Lloyd had approached his friend Joan Bennett and explained Margaret's predicament to her. Bennett invited Margaret to a party at the home she shared with her new husband, Walter Wanger. 'She was very kind to me,' Margaret remembered, and Bennett was 'enchanted' by her new friend's constant refusal of alcohol, preferring to drink only lemonade. This idiosyncrasy earned her the nickname, 'The Lemonade Lady of Hollywood'.

Another social outing presented itself to Margaret when, during the filming of *Rulers of the Sea*, a telegram was delivered to her on the set, inviting her to the Academy Awards. Knowing of her publicity-shy attitude, she was under strict instructions from Fox to attend. As arranged by their publicity department, Richard Greene, a contract player from the studio, was her escort for the event. But he found the assignment tiresome and complained throughout the evening, for his mind was occupied by a young starlet; and, as he worryingly predicted, the next day's newspapers were full of photographs of Margaret on his arm as he escorted her to and from the Biltmore Hotel.

Having achieved so few nominations that year, Fox was allocated the fringe tables far away from the stage. Eager to see the presentations and stand shoulder to shoulder, as it were, with the cinema icons who had inspired her own acting career, Margaret boldly lifted her chair and moved it closer to the stage. The others looked on in astonishment, but for once she did not care. She had not enjoyed Hollywood, did not expect to go far, and decided that she might as well gain some pleasure from the uninspiring trip. Bette Davis, who had attended with eight men including her current lover, the director William Wyler, collected the award for Best Actress in *Jezebel*. Margaret was surprised to discover that Davis 'did not look nearly so attractive off the screen as she did on'.[13]

As she continued to hold a dim view of her future in Hollywood, Margaret was surprised when both Fox and Paramount were considering the idea of signing her to a seven-year contract. Assuming Margaret would readily agree, Gainsborough issued numerous press releases, and they predicted she would split her time evenly between her parent studio and whichever American studio signed her. Her next film, the studio reported, would be starring opposite Richard Greene in *The Blue Lagoon*. 'She's excited [about the film], which was a Victorian shocker concerning a boy and a girl shipwrecked on an island and growing up to learn about love without the benefit of tutelage or clergy.'[14] Nothing came of the production and, in 1949, Jean Simmons played the part of Emmeline Foster, the role intended for Margaret a decade earlier.

Gainsborough delivered the news that Darryl Zanuck had made the decision not to put Margaret under contract with Fox. Drawing on her experience with the publicity department, the studio was further exasperated when Margaret, whom they felt looked too similar to Joan Bennett and Hedy Lamarr, refused to dye her hair blonde. In a bid to change her mind, the hairdressing department experimented with a blonde wig but the results were not to her liking and she remained defiant. In the end, after a personal meeting with Margaret, Zanuck let her go. Paramount were yet to reach a decision, although Margaret hoped they, too, would refuse to put her under contract.

In a professional limbo in Hollywood, she received heartening news from London when Rupert telephoned and asked, 'Are you *really* as homesick as you sound?'

'Yes, yes I am,' she shouted down the static line. 'It's awful.'

The line kept fading; then, booming in her ear, she heard him ask: 'Shall I come over to you?'

'Yes, yes please,' she said.[15]

Later that evening, Margaret received a telegram from Rupert. He had quit his job to be with her – 'it was a big step, and perhaps one which he should not have taken'[16] – and was on his way to America. His arrival coincided with her finishing *Rulers of the Sea*, after which she and Betty headed to New York to meet him.

When he arrived, Betty left for England, and the couple looked forward to the second honeymoon Margaret had promised him before she left for Hollywood. They took in the sights of New York and attended Broadway plays. One particular play, *The Philadelphia Story* starring Katharine Hepburn, left a lasting impression on her. She had a brief respite from the studio: a rarity for, in the past, so much of her time when not filming was consumed by the publicity department; and, for once since their marriage, she could spend this free time with Rupert.

With Paramount still eager to negotiate a transatlantic deal with Gainsborough, Margaret realised she might have to remain in Hollywood as opposed to returning to London. Rupert liked America, which was a relief to her, and he spoke of finding a job with one of the steel firm's agencies there. But the newspaper headlines mocked any hope they had of settling down to a new life. War was imminent, and Rupert threw Margaret into despair when he broke the news that he had signed up to the Territorial Army, and that he was ready to be called up should war be declared.

It was more than Margaret cared to deal with; and, as the threat of war between England and Germany became a reality, she was anxious to return home. It was during this period that *Susannah of the Mounties* was previewed at the Roxy in New York to underwhelming reviews, and the response confirmed Margaret's initial reluctance to partake in the film, believing that it would fail to launch a Hollywood career.

Undecided on her future, a letter from Carol Reed brought her a false sense of security. He wrote to tell her of his next film and to unconditionally offer her the female lead. This, she felt, was a sign that she belonged at Gainsborough and not Paramount, or any Hollywood studio. She was going home.

10
Wartime

On the voyage home from America, Margaret read the script for Carol Reed's screen adaptation of A. J. Cronin's novel *The Stars Look Down.* Alongside the script was a letter from Reed informing her that the role of Jenny Sunley was 'too good to be missed'. However, he confided that Ted Black did not agree with him, and that she 'must persuade' the studio to let her play the part.

With every confidence in Reed, who had previously directed her in sympathetic, intelligent roles, Margaret was furious, and offended, when the part she had been offered was nothing more than 'an ungrateful little hussy'.[1] Throwing the script to one side without finishing it, she turned to Rupert and asked: 'What can Carol be thinking of?' Having made up her mind to reject Reed's offer, Margaret was alarmed when she discovered he had announced to the British newspapers that she would be joining Michael Redgrave in the film.

It was not the homecoming she had been expecting; and, after five months in Hollywood, she found London a hostile place. There were trenches and air-raid shelters being dug in residential squares and parks, and sandbags were being filled and piled along the streets. When she entered her flat there was a leaflet waiting for her in the postbox, advising her on air-raid precautions. She realised Rupert had been right all along:

Britain was preparing to go to war with Germany. However, as much as this unsettled her, she was too preoccupied with the arrangement Reed had marshalled her into.

Before production began, Margaret appealed to Ted Black, who shared her concerns. He was reluctant for Margaret to play Jenny – 'an unpleasant little flibbertigibbet' who tricks a clever young man, Davey Fenwick (Michael Redgrave), into marrying her because she assumes he is going places. But with the miners' strike and the economic depression, Davey's university education is of little use to him and he fights against the injustices faced by the coal miners in the fictional town of Tynecastle. There was also the theme of adultery, an unsettling thought for Ted Black, when Jenny has an affair with the local gangster, Joe Gowlan, played by Emlyn Williams. Margaret was further concerned about the issue of Jenny's illegitimate child; however, Carol Reed assured her it had been removed from the script.

Turning to Margaret Evelyn, a self-confessed puritan, Margaret asked her to read Cronin's novel before she gave Reed her final answer. The response was far from encouraging; Margaret Evelyn was appalled by the plot's 'sordid' nature and she advised Margaret to decline the role of 'a common prostitute'.[2]

Attempting to allay Margaret's concerns, Reed took her to one side and advised: 'Don't judge a part by how many pages it has. Judge it by motivation, by the influence the character you play has upon the whole story.'[3] There was a sense of urgency in Reed's talking Margaret into the part. The impending war with Germany had made banks reluctant to loan money; and, having experienced difficulty in raising the money for production,

Isadore Goldsmith, who produced the film, invested every penny he had into it. As far as attracting investors, the selling point had been the promise of Margaret, Michael Redgrave and Emlyn Williams: it had to be that trio or nothing.

Margaret, still unsure how her character would be portrayed on screen, asked Reed if Jenny could, perhaps, appear more sympathetic. Reed declined, explaining that the entire script would have to be altered and, already on a strict schedule, he was unwilling to do that. Ted Black, however, approached him on behalf of Margaret and ordered a rewrite of the script. The part, he explained, perturbed him as much as anyone; and, conscious of her image on and off the screen, he feared cinema-goers would think Margaret as immoral as the part Reed wanted her to play.

As a conveyor of realism in his work, and with *The Stars Look Down* fitting into the genre of a social drama, Reed refused. He had begun to test Phyllis Calvert in the role of Jenny, but, as talented as she was, he wanted Margaret. Not one to admit defeat, he changed his tactics and approached Margaret about filming a few of Jenny's more pleasant scenes. The gamble paid off, and Margaret admitted that she had been wrong to ask him to rewrite the script to suit her objections. 'I was most impressed by her honesty and great strength of character in making this admission,' Reed said. 'There was something really big about it that I admired immensely.'[4] In the end, she was satisfied with her performance, although still apprehensive as to how the public would receive her as Jenny.

Reed, however, disowned the film. 'It's a gloomy little piece,'[5] he told his colleagues, and he predicted it would fail at the box office. His estimation proved to be wrong. Opening to audiences a year later in 1940, *The Stars Look Down* held the wartime record at the Odeon Theatre in Leicester Square when, in one week, over twenty-seven thousand people viewed the film. Critics, too, praised it as 'one of the finest – if not the finest – British pictures yet produced'.[6]

As filming neared completion, the make-believe world of the studios came to a halt. Margaret and Redgrave were in the make-up department being made up for the last scene of *The Stars Look Down*, when the wireless delivered the news that Hitler had invaded Poland. A stunned silence fell over the room and everybody looked at one another. 'What are we doing here?' their private thoughts seemed to ask. Margaret, for one, had decided there and then to quit acting, thinking she would be of greater service driving an ambulance.

That evening, when she returned to Dolphin Square, Margaret found Rupert in a solemn mood. They talked about the war and what it would mean for them as a married couple, as well as individuals. Rupert had been harbouring an unsettling feeling since their return from America, and he partly blamed her for choosing Gainsborough over Paramount. It was because of this, she assumed, they had not been happy. She felt guilty that he had quit his job to join her on what, at the time, seemed a promising future, and he had not resumed work back in England. Within days, Rupert was warned by the Territorial Army to be on standby for call-up, but to his 'initial disgust'[7] he was told he was too old to become an infantryman, for which he had been trained. Only young men aged between eighteen and twenty could qualify. He was given the job of a gunner, and soon the papers arrived and he went off with the Royal Artillery to a training camp in North Wales.

Life for Margaret continued as before, and in November *Rulers of the Sea* opened in New York at the Paramount Theatre – it had had its world premiere on 12th September 1939 without its leading lady in attendance. Critical response was underwhelming, though Frank Lloyd's attention to detail garnered some praise. 'A handsomely produced film which possesses everything but the spark that kindles interest into enthusiasm – not dramatic at all,' wrote Frank S. Nugent in the *New York Times*. But it was of little consequence to Margaret: she had already drawn a line under her Hollywood experience. She continued to think of the war effort and how best she could assist it. However, Gainsborough had other ideas and she was forced to abandon her plan of driving an ambulance in favour of screen acting.

Her next film, *Night Train to Munich*, written by Sidney Gilliat and Frank Launder, was chosen by Gainsborough in the hope that its familiar setting of a hotel room and train would recreate the popularity of *The Lady Vanishes*. Directed by Carol Reed, and co-starring Rex Harrison and Paul Henreid, the film promised 'laughs, excitement and thrills'. Margaret played Anna, the daughter of a Czech scientist who is kidnapped by the Nazis during their invasion of Prague; and Rex Harrison, as Dickie Randall, is a Secret Service officer who disguises himself as a Nazi officer and pretends to romance Anna in a bid to make her believe in the Nazi cause. The Nazi spy, played by Paul Henreid, befriends Anna in a concentration camp before she manages to escape.

The production was pleasant but uneventful, a welcome change from the financial and artistic tensions which had lingered over *The Stars Look Down*. With the cast and crew's minds focused on war, there seemed to be little that got in the way of real-life issues. More than two-thirds of the technical staff had enlisted in the Armed Forces or had gone off to work in factories, and filming had to be finished by dusk to comply with the blackout regulations. Paul Henreid, considered an 'enemy alien' due to his Austria-Hungary origins, was 'doing his bit' as an air-raid warden in Hampstead, where he lived. Between takes he withdrew from the set to study his ARP (air-raid precaution) manual.

With little to do between takes, Margaret retreated to her crossword puzzles. However, one incident stood out for her when she was almost decapitated by a glass transom that came crashing down, narrowly missing her head. Despite being covered in broken glass and plaster, she managed to escape unharmed. Had she not moved seconds beforehand, the impact would have killed her. She wrote to Rupert, telling him that filming was far more dangerous than the army.

Production ended in January 1940; and, when released to wartime audiences, *Night Train to Munich* was successfully received by critics in both Britain and America. 'If a better comedy-thriller has been made, I should like to see it,' wrote the *Star*.

Immediately moving on to their next production, Margaret and Reed collaborated once more for the crime thriller *Girl in the News*. Margaret played Anne Graham, a nurse acquitted of murder after her elderly patient dies in suspicious circumstances. Changing her name, she finds work as a nurse to a wheelchair-bound man who is deliberately poisoned by his wife and her lover. The film was a poor imitation of their past endeavours, and neither Reed nor Margaret considered it to be good.

Reed, however, maintained an 'unshakeable faith' in Margaret as an actress. 'I consider Margaret Lockwood the most efficient and the most versatile actress I have ever worked with. She is able to put up a very good performance as, say, a chorus girl in one film on a Saturday and then be equally good on the Monday morning as a woman accused of murder.'[8]

It would mark their seventh collaboration; and, although neither of them were aware of it at the time, it would be their last film together.

*

With a break in between films, Margaret set forth from London to Rhyl in North Wales, where Rupert was stationed. Spending his forty-eight hours' leave in a small hotel, they learned that the first bomb had been dropped on London. Worried about her mother's safety, she immediately telephoned Margaret Evelyn and was surprised by her flippant attitude. Assuring Margaret there was nothing to worry about, Margaret Evelyn's dismissive tone turned to one of simmering excitement when she announced that Upper Norwood was the ideal spot for air raids as it offered the best view should more bombs drop on London.

The air raids over London increasingly grew worse, and Margaret left her flat at Dolphin Square to stay with her mother at her house on Highland Road. Since the untimely death of Kitty, who had suffered a stroke in 1939, Margaret Evelyn and Mary cared for Betty. But after a false alarm in September 1939, when the sirens sounded and they all hid under the beds, Mary thought it safer to take Betty to the seaside town of Herne Bay, Kent, where she had a small flat.[9]

With Margaret and her mother alone in the house, they spent their evenings in the living room listening to the Luftwaffe circling London. As the bombs dropped, she realised that Margaret Evelyn had not been exaggerating the thrill of the air raids and that their house, on top of a steep hill, did indeed offer a clear view of the attacks on the city below. An avid bomb-watcher, Margaret Evelyn had created a small lookout station made entirely of cushions positioned against the bathroom window. Happy to leave Margaret Evelyn alone to indulge in her morbid pastime, Margaret retired to bed at her usual hour of ten o'clock. However, if there was a particularly big air raid taking place Margaret Evelyn could not resist waking Margaret so that she, too, could watch it.

During one heavy air raid, a shattering crash threw Margaret from her bed, and, certain the house had been hit, she stumbled out of the room. As she was to discover, the bomb had fallen so close that it shook the house and hurled Margaret Evelyn from her lookout station onto the floor. When Margaret found her mother sprawled out on the bathroom floor, Margaret Evelyn was indignant and furious at being found *there*, 'of all places'.[10] It provided comic relief to a fearful situation, but the lighter moments were beginning to fade. The Battle of Britain was not far away, and life became unfunny, and very uncertain.

*

With the country under threat from enemy bombs and darker days on the horizon, Gainsborough decided that Margaret's next film should be a light-hearted comedy to boost public morale. *Quiet Wedding* was directed by Anthony Asquith, and written by Terence Rattigan and Anatole de Grunwald, adapted from Esther McCracken's hit play of the same title. Margaret was to play the part of Janet, a soon-to-be bride who hopes for a simple wedding to her fiancé, Dallas (Derek Farr); but meddling relatives and a series of unfortunate events threaten to thwart her journey to the altar.

The studio at Sound City in Shepperton was located next door to the Vickers Armstrong aircraft factory which, on more than one occasion, compromised the safety of the cast and crew. Having mistaken the studio for the factory, the Luftwaffe bombed two of the four sound stages. And when the Germans weren't dropping bombs intended for the studio's neighbour, the cast and crew were forever running around extinguishing flames from the firebombs. Adding to the chaos, the air-raid sirens screamed over London, drowning out the actors' dialogue as the cameras rolled.

Eventually it was decided that not only was the bombing disruptive towards production, it had threatened everybody's safety; and, to prevent an injury or fatality, the entire cast and crew of twenty-three were billeted in a house close to the studio – a practicality more than anything as it ensured the cast and crew would not be delayed by the bombings as they reported for work in the morning.

With production commencing as the Battle of Britain was at its height in the autumn of 1940, a particular incident stood out for Margaret, when, on the day of her twenty-fourth birthday, she drove with Margaret Evelyn from the studio to see if their house was still standing. As they drove through Shepperton on that Sunday morning, Margaret thought 'it was getting a bit noisy up there'. An air-raid warden stopped the car as they drove over Wandsworth Common and told them: 'I don't think you ladies ought to go there.'

'Why not?' asked Margaret.

'All hell's going on up there!'

Margaret got out of the car and looked up to find 'he was absolutely right… the most extraordinary things were happening'. She replied: 'Well, I don't know about that, but we've got to get to Norwood to see if the house is still standing.' Realising he 'wasn't going to get anywhere', he let them go.[11]

They pushed on and arrived at the house to find it had not been hit. Afterwards they drove to Wimbledon to visit Margaret's friend and stand-in, Kathleen Marshall, where they celebrated her birthday with a pot of tea in the Anderson shelter.

With London under attack from German bombing, Margaret Evelyn, as much as she delighted in watching the air raids, agreed with Margaret that she would be safer at Delcott, in the depths of the Hampshire countryside. Sensing it was only a matter of time before Dolphin Square was hit, Margaret decided to move the contents from her flat into a storage unit. Her timing was perfect; the following day a bomb landed on the building and her top-floor flat was blown to pieces.

As soon as production on *Quiet Wedding* ended, Margaret escaped London to join Rupert in Rhyl, where he was stationed as an officer-cadet due for a commission. While she waited for the studio to call her back to London for her next film, Margaret was content in her role of a wartime wife. He knew she would be free for some months and had rented a bungalow a few hundred yards from his camp. 'I was going to have another home again,' she recalled. 'I was so happy.'[12]

Margaret bought a bicycle, her only mode of transport due to petrol rationing, which she used for her shopping in town. The locals would stop and stare as she did her errands, but they got used to her and soon she became regular Mrs Leon. And she tried to live up to her role as Mrs Leon, the housewife; but, possessing not a single domestic trait, the everyday duties of running a home baffled her and the task of preparing a meal for her husband became an ordeal. But she soon learned how to cook a few simple dishes, and Rupert, who was proud of her effort, would remark: 'Ah, home cooking.'

To Rupert's embarrassment, word of his famous wife had spread through the camp, and before long his commanding officer asked if Margaret could sing a few songs for the men. Although he agreed to the request, it must have reminded him of the studios and how they would swoop in and steal Margaret away, for he warned her: 'Only a few songs, Margaret, for about a quarter of an hour.' But neither of them was prepared for how demanding the audience would be and, after the quarter of an hour was up, they refused to let her go. Flattered by their calls for an encore, she ended up singing until her voice became hoarse.

As she got up to leave, Margaret scanned the room for Rupert – 'I thought he would be so pleased' – but he was nowhere to be found. The commanding officer escorted her home and neither of them mentioned Rupert's abrupt departure. 'He'll be waiting for me in the hall as a surprise,' Margaret said. But he wasn't. He was in bed, fast asleep, and she realised 'there was nothing to do but swallow my disappointment and go to bed, too'.[13]

The heavy mood soon lightened, and they were happy together. On route-march days, Margaret would stand at the window, watching the long procession of soldiers marching past her bungalow, round the bend in the road and up to the camp. Often Rupert managed to slip away and hide behind a tree, until the rest were out of sight and on their way to perform military commands. Knowing it would take an hour – 'an hour of our precious time together wasted'[14] – before the men marched back, he would rush home to surprise Margaret.

Their happiness was elevated by the news that Margaret was expecting a baby. Rupert asked her to keep it a secret for a few weeks so they could enjoy the news without, as he imagined, Margaret Evelyn's interference and the studio's input.

But, to his disappointment, they had to reveal the news sooner than he anticipated. He had since become fully trained in the Royal Artillery and was to be posted to the 145th Field Regiment RA where he served with the 61st Division at a camp based in County Antrim, Northern Ireland. Before he left, he made arrangements for Margaret to join her mother at Delcott in Hampshire, where he knew she would have companionship and care. Before Margaret could move to the countryside, she had to make the dangerous journey back to London on a blacked-out train which crawled along the tracks, stopping every so often until the air raids passed.

She was going to meet with Herbert, who, to her initial delight, had secured her the leading role opposite James Mason in the screen adaptation of A. J. Cronin's novel, *Hatter's Castle*. Production had been delayed, affording her more time in Rhyl with Rupert, and usually she did not mind such things, but with her pregnancy advancing the timing was crucial.

As she stepped off the train at Paddington Station, Herbert took one look at Margaret and said: 'You needn't tell me,

Margaret. I know. You're going to have a baby.'[15] The role was given to Deborah Kerr, then a little-known actress, and Margaret caught the next train to Hampshire to await the arrival of her baby.

Margaret, aged four months,
in the arms of her ayah.
Karachi, 1916

A portrait of Margaret, taken before the
family sailed for England in 1920

Margaret and her brother, Lyn, dressed
in their school uniforms. Circa 1927

Miss Margie Day in costume
for her song and dance routine
at the Cafe de Paris, 1930

The rising star is given the Hollywood treatment

A promotional still of Michael Redgrave, Margaret, and Emlyn Williams for *The Stars Look Down*, 1939

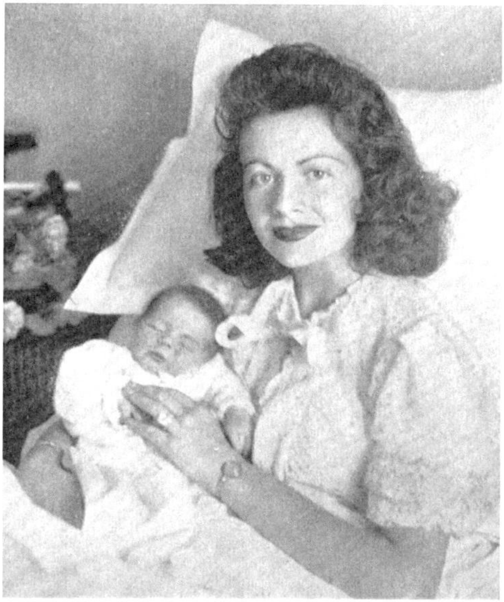

Margaret introduces her newborn baby to the press, August 1941

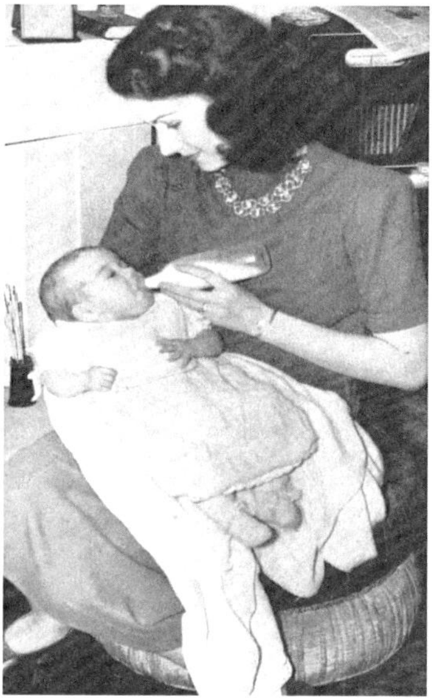

Margaret was 'determined to be a model maternity patient'

Toots keeps her mother company while she convalesces from an operation to remove her tonsils

Margaret teaches Toots a new dance step

The three Margarets: Margaret Mary, Margaret Evelyn and Margaret Julia at Mickey Mouse's

A publicity still of Dennis Price and Margaret for *A Place of One's Own*, 1945

A candid photograph of Margaret with her colleagues at the studio. Keith Dobson lingers in the background, smoking a cigarette

A publicity portrait of Margaret for *The Wicked Lady*, 1945

Margaret with her second *Daily Mail* National Film Award which she won for Best Film Actress of the year, 1947

A festive greeting from Margaret and Toots

A publicity portrait of Margaret and Dane Clark for *Highly Dangerous*, 1950

Margaret on the set of *The Slipper and the Rose*, 1976. After a film career spanning forty years, it would mark her last appearance on screen

II
Toots

It was with open arms that Margaret Evelyn welcomed Margaret to live with her at Delcott. Although purchased by Margaret and Rupert two years before, the uninhabitable building had been transformed by Margaret Evelyn into a comfortable bungalow, and she had every intention of remaining there permanently. But Margaret herself had not glanced too far into the future; with her husband overseas and a baby on the way, she concerned herself with the present. 'Not even Hitler's war could spoil the delight of having one's own baby,' she said.[1] She adopted the slower pace of country life and frequented the nearby historic town of Ringwood where she shopped once a week at the market. The locals would ask for autographs as she stood in line but the novelty soon wore off and, as she had done in Rhyl, she moved around with an air of anonymity.

The past tension between Margaret and her mother appeared to be forgotten and their relationship became friendlier than before. Margaret Evelyn looked forward to becoming a grandmother, and Margaret enjoyed their closeness – something she had not felt growing up. They pooled their ration coupons to buy great quantities of wool and patterns, and Margaret Evelyn taught Margaret how to knit and how to read the hieroglyphics of pattern books, and soon she was turning out clothes for her unborn baby. She was proud of her accomplishment, and she hoped Rupert would be too. But Rupert was the last thing on Margaret Evelyn's mind, and when his spell of leave came round she made it clear that he was not welcome at Delcott.

To avoid any ill feelings that might arise between her mother and husband, Margaret took the train to Oxford to spend two days with Rupert. She brought along her trousseau of baby clothes, but it was not the reaction she had been anticipating. 'Perhaps I expected too much from him,'[2] she later said. She noticed a marked change in Rupert since their time spent apart which, in her opinion, had altered his behaviour towards her. He appeared aloof, which she construed as a lack of enthusiasm for the baby, and it hurt her. Perhaps the circumstances in which their child was being brought into the world troubled Rupert. When he sent Margaret to live in Hampshire with her mother, he had prioritised her safety. But now, with a baby on the way and Margaret Evelyn's warning that he was not welcome at Delcott, he directed his frustration towards Margaret.

Aside from his concerns over his place in his child's life, he was burdened by his war duties in Northern Ireland. His regiment had been sent to act as a deterrent to Hitler, 'for the Germans looked longingly at the southern Irish ports' and, should the enemy set its sights on the north, the British army were ready to defend it against attack. Hauling guns up the mountains and glens where trucks had become bogged down, combined with no sleep – 'a luxury at times' – set his nerves on edge. The looming threat of a German attack provoked a panic amongst those who were stationed there, and everyone made an attempt to get out of Northern Ireland. His command officer pulled strings and joined the commandos, officers disappeared and were replaced, but troops like Rupert had no strings to pull. In the summer of 1941, he was desperate to escape; and on a rare day off that did not include cleaning latrines, guard duty or peeling potatoes, he visited the Giant's Causeway. Walking along the mile-long stretch of hexagonal stones overlooking the North Atlantic, he found a wishing well and, casting his wish, he asked an 'Irish fairy' to help him 'get the hell out of Ireland' – presumably before he got killed.[3]

Although Margaret sympathised with Rupert, their strained reunion consumed her thoughts. When she returned home to Hampshire on the train she replayed his behaviour over in her mind. 'You mustn't be unhappy,' she told herself. 'It will be bad for your baby.'[4] She distracted herself by knitting nightgowns and vests, all in blue, for she was convinced she was carrying a boy. This had been confirmed when a country neighbour tried 'the Japanese method' on her, which meant suspending a needle over her stomach and watching the direction in which it swayed. She was told if it went backwards and forwards, she would have a son; and if the needle circled, it would be a daughter. Margaret copied the method many times and each time her findings leaned towards a boy. So, blue it would have to be, and she chose the name Timothy for her unborn son.

As the baby's birth approached, the doctor advised Margaret that she would have to have a caesarean to ensure the safe delivery of her baby. However, before he could perform the operation, the doctor informed her that she would need her husband's permission. Margaret Evelyn was far from understanding of the patriarchal medical rules of the day, and having brought up her children with her own husband four thousand miles away, she let her feelings be known. 'This,' she announced, 'was quite ridiculous.'[5] Rather than allowing her mother's disapproval to sour the occasion, Margaret optimistically chose a middle name to commemorate the caesarean, and Julius – for Julius Caesar, its namesake derived from his surgical birth – was decided upon.

Rupert was granted compassionate leave for the birth, and he joined Margaret in Bournemouth where she was scheduled to deliver the baby in a nearby nursing home. Margaret Evelyn, not wishing to meet her son-in-law, remained at Delcott. The night before Margaret was due to enter the nursing home, Rupert bought them tickets to see her favourite entertainer, Arthur Askey, perform at the Pavilion. It was a humid evening and as she struggled to get comfortable in her deckchair, Rupert turned to her and snapped: 'Oh do sit up in your chair, Margaret, and don't slump like that; it doesn't look nice.'[6] It evoked memories from their previous meeting in Oxford and she 'felt hurt all over again'. On the eve of their child's birth, Margaret wondered if, perhaps, they had become strangers to one another.

After the show, Margaret and Rupert wandered along the seafront. They spoke of the baby and he said he hoped it would be a boy. She raised his hopes when she told him she was certain it would be. However, when Margaret returned to the nursing home she suddenly felt the urge to knit something in pink. Her instincts proved correct when, on Saturday 23rd August, she gave birth to a baby girl.

Not one to miss out on the birth of her grandchild, Margaret Evelyn travelled down to Bournemouth with the intention of presiding by Margaret's side when she came round from the anaesthetic. But with Rupert also present, Margaret had previously warned the nurse in charge about the family predicament, and the estranged in-laws were allocated separate waiting rooms. Miraculously, given Margaret Evelyn's unbending nature, she and Rupert reached a truce when they met at Margaret's bedside to admire the baby. And Margaret Evelyn was further elated when the nurse remarked how much she thought the baby resembled her grandmother. Still groggy from the anaesthetic, Margaret looked down at the baby's dark hair and swarthy skin, and agreed. Then she asked, 'Is it all right?' before drifting back to sleep.

When Margaret regained consciousness, she settled on a name for her new baby: Margaret – after herself and her mother – and Julia, the feminine version of Julius. The formality of a first name did not last long, and Margaret Evelyn bestowed on Margaret Julia the nickname 'Toots'. And Toots it would always be.

The nurse bathed Toots, and Margaret, still recovering from her operation, sat up in bed watching her. 'She looks like a lion,' Margaret said to the nurse, observing that Toots wore the most ferocious expression on her screwed-up little face. She explained that newly born caesarean babies were always much more alert, but Toots defied her theory when she promptly fell asleep. After Margaret had fed Toots, the press descended into the room to photograph mother and baby together, with the latter sleeping through her first photocall.

Arriving from London, Herbert entered the room wearing a gauze mask, the sight of which caught Margaret by surprise and reduced her to peals of laughter. She asked him to be Toots's godfather, thus confirming the close bond they shared.

He came with the news that Gainsborough had accepted her request to take six months off; however, they warned him that they would be ready and waiting for her once the six months had lapsed.

*

Living arrangements at Delcott were cramped, with Margaret Evelyn in one small bedroom, and Margaret and Toots in the other. The baby slept in a wicker cot and Margaret found a new seventeen-guinea pram, which she considered lucky to get as new: high, springy prams were scarce in the days when the factories were busy turning out munitions for war. Along with cod liver oil and orange juice, she received the standard provisions that went with a green ration book for a wartime baby.

Toots was not a placid baby; she cried day and night, allowing Margaret little time for sleep. And 'determined to be a model maternity patient', she followed the doctor's advice and was reluctantly feeding Toots herself 'because all the best mothers do'. But she instinctively knew that her baby was undernourished. So, after four months of sleepless nights and Toots crying non-stop, Margaret defied the doctor's orders and gave her a bottle. Finally, she experienced a full night's sleep and Toots transformed into a contented baby instead of a 'pathetic, crying little morsel who did not seem to like the world very much'.[7]

Reflecting on her new role of motherhood, Margaret said: 'Like everyone who is a mother I have my periods of looking back over my life and wanting so many things for her which I did not have.'[8] Above all else, Margaret wanted Toots to enjoy a world free from conflict, and she was hinting at a situation closer to home when she expressed those wishes. After their 'armed truce' at Margaret's bedside, Margaret Evelyn had lapsed into her old ways and she was adamant that Rupert was not to visit Delcott. With three generations of Margarets living under one roof, it was the happiest she had felt in years. Although a reunion between Margaret Evelyn and her son-in-law was not on the horizon, Margaret was firm when she told her mother that Rupert would be spending his leave at Delcott. It was, after all, his home too.

Having recently left his artillery training camp in Northern Ireland to train in York for a post in the Intelligence Corps, Rupert's leave posed a threat to his mother-in-law's happy home life. Reluctantly, Margaret Evelyn left for Herne Bay to stay with her sister and niece, only coming back when he returned to his camp in York. Exasperated by her mother's behaviour, Margaret rented a house of her own, close to Delcott, so she, Rupert and Toots could live together as a family whenever his leave came up.

Although their spells of living as a family were few and far between, Margaret was relieved that Rupert's attitude towards fatherhood had changed since the arrival of Toots and he was 'immensely proud' of her. Although she had been hurt at the time, she understood that he had felt 'bewildered about the prospect of becoming a father',[9] given the circumstances of war and what it meant for his own mortality and the separation from his wife and child.

They spent their first Christmas as a family in the rented house, with Margaret buying and decorating her first Christmas tree, adorned with 'all manner of deliciously silly presents' for Toots, whom she acknowledged was too young to understand but it delighted her all the same to spoil the baby. It would be their first and last Christmas together. Rupert was part of a field unit being assembled for sailing to Africa in the New Year of 1942, and it would be five years before he returned home.

In his absence, he imagined that Margaret would finally retire from acting to stay at home with Toots; but it never occurred to her to give up her career, and she was looking forward to resuming her work at Gainsborough. 'That is one of the features of theatrical life. No one ever expects you to give up your career because you have married and had a family,' she said, 'and certainly it never enters your head to do so.'[10]

What Margaret had not considered was the way she would feel when it came to leaving Toots to go to work. 'I was astonished at the agony it cost me,' she later said. With little enjoyment she had read scripts and talked business with Herbert, all the while Toots sat happily on her lap, cooing, gurgling and splashing her with porridge. As much as Herbert sympathised with Margaret, he warned her that the studio was waiting, and they already had a film lined up for her. With this in mind, she began to think seriously about returning to London and how this would affect Toots. She knew Toots could not go to London with her; it was unsafe and she would not put her child at risk, regardless of how much she missed her. The only solution would be to hire a nanny, and she engaged Miss Hetty Hollick in the role.

On the day Margaret was to leave for London, Toots and Miss Hollick accompanied her to the station. She hated to hand over her six-month-old baby, and every instinct told her to stay in Hampshire. As the train pulled out of the station, she waved until they were out of sight. 'I would feel myself in absurd tears,' she later wrote, 'and be on the phone to Nannie as soon as I got to London to make quite sure that everything was all right.'[11]

It was an arrangement that both Margaret and Rupert abhorred. With his war duties separating him from his family, he felt there was little he could do to influence the situation. Margaret, too, felt the pull of her obligations at the studio. She had responsibilities that reached beyond motherhood; and, with the pressure of being the breadwinner, as she was also supporting Margaret Evelyn[12] and the running of her household, she had little choice but to go to work.

12
All Change

When Margaret returned to Gainsborough she discovered that the studio, which had been her home for many years, had changed in the year and a half she had been away. Gaumont-British, Gainsborough's parent company, had been absorbed into the expanding film empire of J. Arthur Rank – of the Rank Organisation, founded in 1937 – who was one of the three owner-operators (eventually becoming the sole owner) of Pinewood Studios, a studio that was formed with the intent to rival the Hollywood studio system. His concept for the British film industry was influenced by his background: he was the heir to a flour-mill fortune and a devout Methodist. The latter was significant in that, as a Sunday-school teacher who showed religious films, he acted on the *Methodist Times* newspaper's complaint that the films shown in Britain were detrimental to family life. With his money and religious values he set about reforming the film industry, which he would come to dominate. Along with Gainsborough, he added Alexander Korda's old Denham Studios and the newly built Elstree Studios to his company. Maurice Ostrer, who had sold the majority of his shares to Rank, remained at Gainsborough where he continued to oversee production alongside Ted Black.

It was decided by Maurice Ostrer that Margaret's first film since returning to the studio was to be *Alibi*, a remake of the

1938 French film, *L'Alibi*, directed by Brian Desmond Hurst. She would be co-starring with James Mason, Ostrer's nephew by marriage; and, as she was to discover, the actor had a reputation for being a taciturn man. On their first meeting, Mason initiated an argument with the studio bosses when he demanded top billing over Margaret. However, as she was the bigger star and her appearance in the picture gave it a commercial draw, Herbert fought for her to receive priority when it came to billing. The 'Mason argument', as Margaret called it, went on for a substantial amount of time, but in the end he was deferred to feature billing.

The plot was of the crime genre, which had worked well for Margaret in *Night Train to Munich*; but *Alibi*, set in Paris in 1937, proved mediocre at the box office. She played Helene, a nightclub hostess whose wages have been docked by her boss and, falling behind on her rent, she finds herself in dire straits. A petty criminal offers her twenty thousand francs if she will provide him with a false alibi. Mason played Andre, an undercover policeman whose assignment is to make Helene fall in love with him, thus hoping to reveal the falseness of her alibi. The final twist in the plot comes when Andre genuinely falls in love with Helene.

Upon its release, the critics were pleasant about *Alibi* – 'an extraordinarily powerful cast of box office names' [1] – although, unlike Margaret's previous efforts, the reviews were inconsistent, ranging from 'a baffling murder mystery' [2] to 'a fast moving melodrama'.[3]

*

Wartime London was a depressing place; the streets lined with sandbags, bombed buildings and air-raid sirens gave everyday life a feeling of uncertainty. The blackouts made the city appear shut in, drab and suffocating in comparison to Margaret's sedate life in the countryside, where she had the luxury of a garden and the company of her baby. Failing to find solace in her work, her feelings of isolation were intensified by the often delayed and cancelled train journeys from London to Hampshire.

When the trains were running, Margaret left her flat at Dolphin Square to spend the weekend with Toots, who was not yet two years old. But on each visit, Margaret could not help but notice her mother was becoming increasingly possessive of the child. She criticised anything Margaret tried to do: the clothes she bought were never good enough, and she overruled Margaret's decisions as to how Toots should be raised. After each brief visit, Margaret returned to London saddened by the separation from her daughter and the realisation that she had become an occasional visitor in Toots's life. The war, combined with her loneliness, had perhaps served to make her feel as though she had been usurped by her mother. Given the circumstances, it presents an interesting paradox to compare Margaret and Margaret Evelyn's relationship, and how forcefully her mother exerted her authority, with Margaret's own personal battle in influencing how her daughter should be raised, though from afar. 'It was useless for me to try to argue that she would have been the first to resent it if anyone had told *her* how to dress, bring up, and look after *me*. She wouldn't, or couldn't, remember that.'[4]

The dispiriting mood continued when Margaret received the news that Rupert's posting abroad had come through. In the five years since they had married, she had come to accept that she and Rupert might never be completely happy. She joined him in York before he sailed to Africa, but she could not ignore 'the intangible rift' between them. As they parted, Margaret felt 'content and at peace' in his leaving, knowing that their last meeting 'had not been spoiled by any jarring note'.[5]

*

With *Alibi* proving to be a commercial failure, Gainsborough were desperate to repeat Margaret's past successes at the box office. This meant veering away from the material they usually presented her with and, having drawn on her experience of playing an unsympathetic character in *The Stars Look Down*, she welcomed this change of direction in her career.

Maurice Ostrer gave her the script of *The Man in Grey*, a period drama set in the Regency era, adapted by Gainsborough's resident screenwriter Leslie Arliss who was also making his directorial debut. Although ordered to read the part of Hesther Shaw, the supporting role, Margaret was initially drawn to Clarissa, the film's heroine who suffers incessantly at the hands of her sadistic husband, Lord Rohan, and her best friend, Hesther, who not only has an affair with Rohan but plays a part in Clarissa's early death.

She was reluctant to play the villain, but after considering the significance of the part and what it would mean for her career, she agreed with Ostrer and accepted.[6]

Again, Margaret was teamed with James Mason – cast as Lord Rohan – who achieved his coveted star billing, and it played to his ego when he was described, in reviews, as 'aptly supported by Margaret Lockwood'. And Phyllis Calvert, not yet a star of the same calibre as Margaret, was given the leading part of Clarissa. However, up until the day before filming, the second male lead was yet to be cast. Numerous young actors had tested for the part of Peter Rokeby – with whom Clarissa is in love – and one by one they were deemed unsuitable. When it seemed there was no one to play the part, it was announced that one more actor had to be tested. Margaret watched the unknown actor, as he moved nervously across the set, and she instinctively knew he would get the part. His name was Stewart Granger.

Stewart Granger, known to his friends as 'Jimmy' because of his birth name James Lablache Stewart, suffered from an inferiority complex which 'came out sometimes in a flow of bad language, and at other times in round abuse of everybody, because he hadn't done his piece as well as he wanted'.[7] Margaret and Phyllis did not appreciate his behaviour, and in due course a letter was sent to his agent, asking the young actor to 'cloak his feelings a little more ably'.[8] Duly noted, and 'with great restraint', Granger censored his language; and in the end he 'got on fine' with Margaret 'who, although having a patrician beauty, also had the raucous laugh of a truck-driver, an endearing combination'.[9] Mason, too, was prone to volatile outbursts; and he expressed himself physically, when, during a disagreement with Arliss on how a scene should be played, he hit the director.

Due to the delay in searching for the second male lead, production on *The Man in Grey* had fallen behind schedule by several weeks. Aside from the financial implications of prolonging filming, the leading lady, Phyllis Calvert, was reaching the confinement stage of her pregnancy, and Arliss had no choice but to quicken the pace.

There was also the matter of Maurice Ostrer and Ted Black's experimentation with the subtle black-and-white colour coding to separate the villains from the heroes. Stewart Granger recalled that he was forced to bleach his hair so that the audience would instinctively trust him. Mason and Margaret, the villains, had dark hair, while Phyllis, the heroine, had blonde hair; and therefore Granger, as the hero, was ordered to be blonde too. It was a unique venture, not only for the studio but for British cinema; and Ostrer and Black refined what would become the formula of the Gainsborough melodrama. 'Spectacle and sex, a dash of sadism, near-the-knuckle lines and an end where virtue is rewarded,' were, according to the London *Evening Standard*, the 'key ingredients'.

Released in August 1943, *The Man in Grey* had two simultaneous openings in West End cinemas, then unheard of for a British film. Although a financial success, critical reception was underwhelming: 'My feelings about *The Man in Grey* are expressed by the Clarissa of the film: "I don't think I can bear this. I can't. I really can't!"' wrote William Whitebait of the *New Statesman*. Rated by the board of censors as 'not suitable for public exhibition', and with critics warning that never before had a British film 'peddled sex and sensation so boldly', the public flocked to the cinema.

Given the box office success of *The Man in Grey*, Maurice Ostrer predicted the public would turn out in droves to see Margaret in any film in which she appeared, regardless of the part she played. But Ted Black, who also weighed a film's worth by the box office takings, disagreed with Ostrer's logic. From the early days of her career at Gainsborough, Black had been careful to choose credible scripts for Margaret and she trusted his judgement as much as Herbert's; thus it came as a professional blow when he was ousted from the studio. By then Ostrer had become greedy, and striking a goldmine with *The Man in Grey* – the first of the 'bodice rippers', or 'Gainsborough Gothics' as they were also known – he began to view Margaret as a commodity in his new 'pulp fiction for the masses' mentality.

Although Ostrer had been right in his estimation that the public would turn out to see Margaret in whichever film she was cast, the studio's efforts after *The Man in Grey* were quickly discarded. The first of these was *Give us the Moon*, a hare-brained comedy set at the end of WWII but ironically filmed during it. It centred on Peter (played by Peter Graves), the son of a hotel proprietor who loathes the thought of working for a living. He discovers a society of 'white elephants' run by Margaret's character, Nina, and her kid sister, Heidi, who are content to be poor so long as they don't have to work. Largely forgotten, the film was best remembered for the onscreen debut of Jean Simmons, who played Heidi. Recalling her fourteen-year-old co-star as 'very pretty with lovely brown eyes and such nice manners', Margaret was later surprised when Simmons married Stewart Granger, the 'young man who had been reproached for his violent language'.[10]

The second in this series of forgettable films was *Dear Octopus*, based on the successful West End play by Dodie Smith and adapted for the screen by Kathleen McCracken, the playwright of *Quiet Wedding*. Co-starring Michael Wilding, the plot examined the relationships between three generations of a large family. McCracken had difficulty with the script, its formula working better on the stage, and neither Margaret nor Herbert considered her part to be sufficiently good. After many negotiations, the studio agreed to enhance her part in the film, but she was not pleased with the outcome. Sensing it had been a backward step in her career, Margaret's concerns were confirmed when it failed to replicate the success of its theatrical run.

To revive her career from its brief and unexpected slump, Maurice Ostrer took inspiration from Ted Black, whose preference for naturalistic cinema had proved successful in the wartime propaganda films *Millions Like Us* and *Two Thousand Women*, made before he had left Gainsborough. Searching for a similar project for Margaret, Ostrer settled on *Love Story*, a melodrama set in the summer of 1939.

This time Margaret was to be the heroine of the film, in the part of Lissa Campbell, a famous concert pianist who retires from the stage to volunteer her services to the army. After a medical examination, Lissa learns that she has a fatal heart disorder; and, upon realising that she is dying, she takes an extended holiday to Cornwall where she meets Kit Firth, a brusque young man who is losing his sight. Stewart Granger, who had been invalided out of the Black Watch, was available for work and he was cast as Kit, much to his annoyance; and Patricia Roc was cast as Judy, an aspiring actress who is in love with Kit and is privy to the secret that he is going blind. Many critics who watched *Love Story* believed Roc had stolen the film from Margaret. Maurice Ostrer sensed this to be true, and he ordered certain scenes to be cut when it seemed as though Roc was 'stealing sympathy' from the main character. Margaret, however, admired Roc's performance and congratulated her on her 'sublime acting'.[11]

With filming taking place on location in Cornwall away from the confines of the studios and the dangers of London,

Margaret invited Toots and her nanny, Miss Hollick, to stay with her. She brought Toots on set to meet her co-stars, and Granger decided that he would be 'nice and very interested in his colleague's dear little girl'. However, Toots took one look at him and screamed until she was blue in the face, and proceeded to do so whenever anyone on the set paid any attention to her. A father of two, Granger took it upon himself to offer parenting advice and he warned Margaret: 'You know, that child is going to turn out a total horror.' And hinting that nanny was to blame, he advised Margaret to dismiss her 'before it's too late'.[12]

The advice was dispensed just as Margaret was mulling over a decision which had been troubling her for some time. On each visit to Delcott, Margaret Evelyn implored Margaret to dismiss Miss Hollick, insisting that she was perfectly capable of raising Toots herself. 'After all,' Margaret Evelyn reminded her, 'she is my grandchild and she is not nearly so much trouble now she can walk.' And pondering the best way to bring up Toots, Margaret wondered if her lack of full-time parenting was contributing to an element of instability in the child's life. More than anything, she wanted Toots to have a sense of normality, whether or not her circumstances were different from those of traditional families.

Giving her mother's proposal much thought, and after careful consideration, Margaret agreed. Toots went to live at Delcott, where she was solely cared for by 'Grannie Lockwood'. Satisfied with the outcome, and feeling useful once again, Margaret Evelyn and Toots formed a close relationship, the type of bond Margaret longed to share with her mother. 'It was a painful position for me... she [wanted] to bring Toots up, and to treat her as though she were me – her own daughter – and she would brook no interference.'[13]

On Monday 9th October 1944, *Love Story* opened to rapturous applause when it premiered at the Gaumont, Haymarket. The film's theme, 'Cornish Rhapsody', a piano concerto written by Hubert Bath and performed by Margaret's character (dubbed by Harriet Cohen), became as popular as the film itself and dominated the music chart of 1944. And, in spite of Stewart Granger claiming the script to be 'the biggest load of crap I'd read',[14] it netted £200,000[15] at the box office – an astronomical figure for its day – making it the second most popular British film during the war years.

Margaret's success at the box office had been restored and her status as Gainsborough's number one star was certain. However, as she reaped the rewards of fame, she began to wonder if her private life could be as fulfilling as her professional one.

13
The Wicked Lady

For two years Margaret and Rupert had been living apart; he remained overseas with the Intelligence Corps, and she carried on with her work at the studios. Living vastly different lives, their letters became few and far between, until it became a chore to write them. There seemed to be little she could tell him: he was not interested in her film work[1] and, now that she was the most popular film star in Britain, there was little else she could talk about by way of normal life.

The world in which she lived served to cut her off from many people. Margaret realised how fast and fickle relationships in the film world were, and when she did forge a friendship she was forever talking shop. With the exception of her child, nothing appeared to exist outside of Gainsborough, and with such a demanding career there was little time for socialising on a personal level that did not involve film parties or publicity events.

Until the age of twenty-six, and forced to do so because of the war and her work in London, Margaret had never lived alone. Now aged twenty-eight, and after two years of being on her own, she had grown tired of the same routine each night. When she returned home from the studios, she dined alone in the residential restaurant at Dolphin Square, and went to bed at ten o'clock. With the exception of film parties and premieres, her schedule left little room for a social life.

When Margaret did have time away from the studio she travelled to Hampshire to visit Margaret Evelyn and Toots. But those precious visits were a rarity due to wartime travel restrictions and, often, the impossibility of leaving London because of an air raid. With all her family living outside of London, more than ever she felt alone. Drawing on those feelings, she concluded that 'loneliness [was] the most damaging single emotion anyone can experience'.[2] And, in her case, it served to make her fall in love.

According to Margaret herself the events which provoked such feelings happened by accident. She entered Dolphin Square's residential restaurant late one evening and was greeted by an apologetic waiter who told her the tables were full and asked if she would mind sharing with another resident. It was her preference to dine alone but, sympathising with the overwrought waiter, she agreed and was led to a small table where an older woman was seated. After a polite introduction, the two women partook in small talk and Margaret learned that her dining companion was named Mrs Dobson, a mother of two sons, both of whom were in the services.[3] The elder son, Keith, was stationed in London, and he spent his leave at his mother's flat. 'London is such a lonely place to be on your own, isn't it?' she asked Margaret. Agreeing with Mrs Dobson's sentiments, Margaret and her dining companion were to meet on several occasions after this first encounter. After a few meetings, Mrs Dobson inquired if Keith could meet Margaret, perhaps over a cup of coffee in her flat. And Margaret, who was shy by nature, found herself agreeing to the impromptu meeting.

Although Margaret wrote about Keith (whom she disguised as 'Bill') in her 1955 autobiography, *Lucky Star*, the information was related in a publicity-friendly way which reflected the period. Information on Keith Dobson is scarce, and Margaret would go to lengths to conceal his true identity and, naturally, she obscured certain facts. Army records show that Keith was not enlisted in the services; therefore he would not have been stationed anywhere in London. Two years younger than Margaret, he was the son of a doctor who was infamously struck off the medical register in 1936 for failing to register purchases of morphine sulphate, cocaine and heroin.[4] He was also married and the father of a young daughter, and evidence suggests that he worked at the studios in the publicity department.[5] So, it would appear that Margaret's account of meeting Keith through his mother was a fabrication.

What was certain was Margaret's feelings of loneliness and how they influenced her feelings for Keith, and, perhaps, her initial blindness to his faults and true intentions. Conveying the story in *Lucky Star*, Margaret wrote: 'It was not one of those "love-at-first-sight" meetings.'[6] But gradually the meetings with Keith became more frequent, and it alarmed her when she found herself looking forward to seeing him, and she felt 'lost and disappointed' if he was not there. Thus, the meeting – regardless of where it had happened, at Dolphin Square, or at the studio – 'changed the whole of my life… and we fell in love with each other'.[7]

In her profession, Margaret had seen many affairs and broken marriages, but those things happened to other people, not to someone who was as careful and as cautious as she was. She was always much too secure in her family life and, despite their faults, Margaret Evelyn and Rupert kept her grounded. Other people, she noticed, went to nightclubs and cocktail parties, but not her. She was always glad to return home after a long day on the set, and she rarely stayed up past ten o'clock. Parties were part of her job, and often she would appease the studio by attending a gala night or premiere, and on her way out Rupert or Margaret Evelyn would off-handedly say, 'Yes, you look all right,' when she sought their opinion.

After one film party, Margaret met Keith, who was struck by how beautiful she looked, and he asked if he could take her out 'looking like that'. Bashfully agreeing to his request, she took him by surprise when she admitted that she had never been to a nightclub; and it inflated his ego to escort her around town, introducing her to London's nightlife. From that evening on, they embarked on a whirlwind of parties and dances, and she could scarcely remember a time when she hurried home so eagerly to change into an evening dress for a night out. Caught up in this new hedonistic lifestyle, she never paused to question whether it was Margaret the person he loved, or Margaret the movie star.

Close associates at Gainsborough began to worry that Margaret was getting carried away with Keith, who had since moved into her flat. Almost every time she was photographed at a premiere, he was by her side. For the first time in her career, a hint of scandal was brewing and people were beginning to talk.

Fans, too, noted his presence. One fan, cannier than the others, found Margaret's address in the directory and also listed there was a Mr Keith Dobson; wondering if he was her husband, she wrote to Margaret to ask her. Quick to dismiss the fan's question, Margaret replied:

> You are quite right, my married name is Mrs Leon and not Mrs Dobson as you thought. I think the reason why you were confused by the directory is that Keith Dobson was the previous owner of this flat, and I think you will find on the new directory that I am listed as the owner. I hope that has straightened it all out for you.[8]

Unsurprisingly, given her puritan values, and rather more surprisingly given her views on Rupert, Margaret Evelyn was the first to condemn their relationship. 'Who is this man?' she demanded. 'You are behaving disgracefully. I have never had much time for Rupert, but I have no time for this man at all! You're making a fool of yourself.'[9] Margaret ignored her mother's scorn; she was determined not to let Margaret Evelyn sabotage this relationship, as she had done with Rupert. But it was Herbert who, with his gentle approach, endeavoured to make her see sense. 'I think Keith can be charming, and you are quite entitled to have a friendship with him,' he said. 'But you are married, Margaret. If this goes on it will mean a great deal of unhappiness for you.'[10]

Herbert was not exaggerating the consequence of Margaret's actions, particularly where her career was concerned. Although J. Arthur Rank presided over a studio that would exploit her villainous characters, he adopted the Hollywood studio system's manner of keeping the unflattering aspects of his stars' careers from the public's gaze. It might have been fun to play 'bad girls' on screen, but in real life he expected Margaret to maintain her exemplary behaviour.

It was, perhaps, a blessing that Margaret's work life was so demanding that it left little time for fan magazines to report on her private life during this period. In her next film, *I'll Be Your Sweetheart*, she played Edie Story, queen of the Edwardian music-halls, in a biopic chronicling the fight composers of popular music-hall songs faced to enforce the new copyright law onto their work. Hoping to replicate the musicals Hollywood was mass-producing, Margaret was given the challenge of partaking in large-scale dance numbers; and, having reminded Maurice Ostrer that her original training was in singing and dancing, she was disappointed when he refused to let her sing on screen, claiming her fans 'wouldn't believe it was her anyway'. In the film Margaret's voice was dubbed by Maudie Edwards, a music-hall artiste.

For the first time Margaret headed a male-dominated cast; she co-starred with Peter Graves (her leading man from *Give us the Moon*), Michael Rennie and Vic Oliver. Directed by Val Guest, it was a happy production for all involved, especially Margaret. This she attributed to her affair with Keith who, unlike Rupert, appeared to revel in her star persona and enjoyed hearing about her working day and the studio gossip. Still, she did not wonder if such flattery concealed an ulterior motive.

Upon its release, *I'll Be Your Sweetheart* was a commercial success; however, the so-called 'quality' critics dismissed its combination of musical and romance. Richard Winnington, of the *News Chronicle*, hastened to plant a dart when he compared the plot with 1940s alcohol rationing. 'Lockwood suggests the robust music-hall belle of that period about as much as the tepid concoction of potato juice and hops we are now allowed occasionally to buy suggests the beer they used to drink in those happy days.'[11]

There was little time to dwell on the critics' response, and, as was the norm, as soon as Margaret finished work on one film, Gainsborough sent her into the next with little respite in between. 'It was just like being a machine,' Margaret recalled. 'You didn't query anything. You just did as you were told and got on with it. You have to remember we were being well paid in those days and you didn't look a gift horse in the mouth.'[12]

However, Margaret's next film, *A Place of One's Own*, offered her a slight change of scenery. She played the role of Annette in the atmospheric ghost story based on the novel by Osbert Sitwell, and was reunited with James Mason, though not as her love interest. Instead, he played Mr Smedhurst, an ageing gentleman who retires to Bellingham House with his wife (Barbara Mullen). Employed as a companion, Annette moves into the house, where she begins to hear strange voices and, having investigated its history, she discovers that a young invalid girl was murdered there forty years ago. When the spirit of the girl possesses Annette, her health declines and, fearing that she's on the brink of death, they send for a doctor. Dr Selbie, played by newcomer Dennis Price, falls in love with Annette and attempts to cure her, but to no avail. In her state of delirium she calls for Dr Marsham, the doctor who had tended to the dead girl all those years ago.

Critical response was divided: some found it 'a ridiculous ghost story without a visible ghost', and *The Gazette* complained that 'the romance has been played up and the eeriness softened'. Much to James Mason's fury, another critic took a jibe at his past role of Lord Rohan in *The Man in Grey* when they quipped: 'Except for the vibrant Mason voice the movie-goer would hardly suspect that this was the masterful character who is in the habit of beating movie heroines.' Margaret did not escape her past either, and they complained that she did not 'lie, cheat or kill' in the film, but they noted that she added 'a little life' to the 'somewhat lustreless part'.

*

The Allied victory over Nazi Germany in May 1945 heralded a new beginning for the British film industry. For six years the studios had adhered to limited shooting budgets, owing to the restrictions on banks loaning money, and a lack of American talent being sent over because of blockades on the Atlantic. As such, there had been little opportunity to exploit Darryl Zanuck's 'star exchange' agreement with Gainsborough. And, with a shortage of column space in newspapers due to reporting on the war, a film's commercial success rested largely on its star as opposed to an extensive promotional campaign in the press. With the war having come to an end, the limitations that were once enforced would be lifted, and the industry would reach new heights of creativity. It was a period of experimentation with Technicolor and special effects – most notably in David Lean's *Blithe Spirit*, and Powell and Pressburger's *A Matter of Life and Death*, both released in 1945.

With Margaret remaining the most popular film star with cinema-goers, Maurice Ostrer viewed this as an indication that the style of her wartime films would be enough to sustain this position. And, inspired by the success of *The Man in Grey*, rather than *Love Story*, Gainsborough purchased the rights to Magdalen King-Hall's historical novel, *The Life and Death of the Wicked Lady Skelton*. Published in 1945 and set during the reign of Charles II, the plot was based on the real-life Lady

Katharine Ferrers, an aristocrat who distracts herself from a dull marriage by disguising herself as a highwayman. The novel and the screenplay drew heavily on the factual story of Lady Katharine; however, in this instance the 'wicked lady' was the fictional Barbara Skelton who steals her cousin Caroline's fiancé, Sir Ralph, whom she marries but meets the handsome Kit Locksby on her wedding day and falls in love with him. To escape Sir Ralph and the boredom of country life, she becomes a highway robber and encounters the infamous highwayman, Jerry Jackson. The two begin an affair with dire consequences, and the wicked lady soon gets her comeuppance.

Written and directed by Leslie Arliss, the screenplay was daring for its day with elements of cross-dressing, infidelity, rape and murder. Hoping to repeat the success of Gainsborough's past wartime productions, Patricia Roc was cast in the saccharine role of Caroline, and, once again to his fury, James Mason was added to the film. Stewart Granger was unavailable for the production, and the role of Kit, intended for Granger, was given to Michael Rennie. The cast was completed with Griffith Jones as Sir Ralph, and character actors Felix Aylmer as the God-fearing servant, Hogarth, and Enid Stamp-Taylor as the snobbish yet witty Lady Henrietta Kingsclere. Jean Kent, who had supporting yet significant parts in films such as *Two Thousand Women*, *Fanny By Gaslight* and *Madonna of the Seven Moons* – incidentally also starring Patricia Roc, Phyllis Calvert and Stewart Granger – stepped into the small role of Jackson's doxy when the original actress who had played her in an earlier scene became ill.

Relishing her villainous role, Margaret experimented with dramatic make-up to emphasise her dark looks. She darkened the mole on her left cheekbone and applied heavier make-up than usual; thus the image she created became her signature look. Turning her attention to the smaller details of Barbara's costumes, she opted to wear her own antique jewellery on screen. And, further getting into the spirit of the character, she learned how to ride saddle; having never ridden a horse before, she was taught at a stable near Elstree Studios where she spent a week learning to be an expert horsewoman.

It was a cheerful set, and Margaret recalled how they all 'giggled' through filming. But Mason found little reason to laugh. Storming off the set as soon as Arliss yelled 'cut', he made no secret of resenting the film; and after delivering his lines he would utter, 'Bloody codswallop'[13] – a jibe at Arliss's ability as a screenwriter.

Mason's behaviour did little to disturb the atmosphere during production. However, the American censorship board, the Breen Office, had viewed the 'indecently provocative' film and objected to it on several grounds. The women's costumes, for one, were deemed too low-cut and, as a result, they ordered those scenes to be reshot with higher necklines. The 'immoral' plot concerned them too, and the Breen Office demanded that certain passages of dialogue be rewritten. Due to Margaret's busy schedule, the studio could not attempt the retakes until a year after the film's British release. The exact detail of every gesture and shot had to be replicated – this time with the ladies in higher necklines – to keep the continuity accurate. It was a tiresome ordeal but, as Gainsborough had predicted when they permitted the retakes for American audiences, the scandal only served to catapult *The Wicked Lady* to resounding popularity.

It was not the first time the Breen Office had been perplexed by a Margaret Lockwood film. *Bank Holiday*, when released in 1938, offended American censors when Margaret's character spends the weekend with her boyfriend at a seaside hotel. Certain lines of dialogue also shocked American audiences, such as: 'We really are a honeymoon couple, aren't we?' as it hinted at the clandestine nature of the trip. The Breen Office had also criticised *A Girl Must Live*, 'an inferior and skimpy romance',[14] directed by Carol Reed and released in 1939. A commercial and critical failure, the predominantly female cast, similar to RKO's *Stage Door*, saw Lilli Palmer and Renee Houston playing gold-digging chorus girls. Reminiscent of their concerns about *The Wicked Lady*, Reed had shot various scenes of the girls in stages of undress; and, furthermore, there was a violent brawl between Palmer and Houston's characters. Although Margaret played the young ingénue and one of the few moral characters in *A Girl Must Live*, American censors still associated her name with the film's so-called depravity.

*

Having completed production on *The Wicked Lady* and with a short break between films, Margaret travelled down to Hampshire to visit her mother and Toots. During the visit, she hoped to find the courage to tell Margaret Evelyn about her love for Keith and how she hoped to marry him. But Margaret's plans were sabotaged when Gainsborough sent her an urgent message, ordering her back to London. They wanted her to do a personal appearance tour but, not wanting to abandon the visit with Toots, Margaret declined. The studio refused to accept her decision, and Maurice Ostrer reminded her that it was not a request, it was a command.

The personal appearance tour was scheduled to coincide with the general release of *I'll Be Your Sweetheart*, and Ostrer expected Margaret to visit many London suburban cinemas, and then venture on to the large provincial town centres. She travelled with her studio dresser and good friend, Gwen Bayliss, who organised her wardrobe for the tour. There were many events which Margaret was scheduled to turn up at, a consistent theme being talent competitions in which she was to judge and hand out the prizes.

Margaret's first appearance set the tone for the rest of the tour. Going on stage in her evening dress, and not quite knowing what to say, she was startled when a cockney voice from the audience called out: 'Oi! Give us a song, Maggie!' Margaret said she couldn't as 'there was no accompanist, no music, no anything'. But the voice continued, 'S'all right. Sing without one.' So, without another thought, she sang the songs from *I'll Be Your Sweetheart*, which consisted of old music-hall numbers like 'The Honeysuckle and the Bee', 'I'll Be Your Sweetheart' and 'I Wouldn't Leave My Little Wooden Hut For You'. To her joy and relief, the audience loved it. The studio found an accompanist and she sang those songs for the remainder of the tour.

As the tour commenced the weather grew increasingly bad with torrential rain, and, with that in mind, Margaret assumed not many fans would turn out to see her. The police, too, shared that thought and did not send as many officers to control the crowds. However, both Margaret and the police had underestimated her popularity. The crowds came out in the rain, flocking to her wherever she went, and it became apparent that there were too many people for the police to manage. As she made her way inside a cinema, she felt a thump on the back of her head followed by the words: 'I touched her nob, I touched her nob.' Margaret turned around to see an excited woman patting her forcefully on the top of her head.

As she left the cinema, the crowds which had gathered outside made it impossible for Margaret to reach the Rolls Royce the studio had provided. They swept her off her feet and carried her far away from the car; but, spying a vacant car, she appealed to the driver to ferry her to safety. 'People! Miss Lockwood,' the driver announced in amazement, 'people!' As the car drove away, a woman who had been standing outside the cinema for hours wailed: 'Me baby, me baby, oh my Gawd I lost me baby!' The baby was found, unharmed, underneath Margaret's car.

Aside from feeling 'strung up' by the overwhelming response of her fans, Margaret was nervous for the people too, 'especially for mothers with young children. I am so terrified they will be hurt.' She wrote of the experience:

> It is always nerve racking to meet so many people, all waiting to see you. It makes you feel very small, and very humble. You are so anxious to please them, always a trifle nervous that they may not like you, and even more nervous when they get out of control, for a crowd when it sweeps along heedlessly, and you are in the middle of it, can be a very frightening thing.[15]

After the success of the personal appearance tour, Margaret's fan mail soared to twenty-five thousand letters a month, and 'touched by this enormous response and kindness' she did not know 'where to start saying thank you'. With her appeal reaching the masses, her name was used to endorse brands and products. She modelled for Pringle of Scotland, endorsed Dreen shampoo and Lux soap; she advertised kirby grips, silk scarves, nylon stockings; and even Toots joined Margaret for an advertising campaign to promote Clarks shoes. In the eyes of the public, she could do no wrong.

14
Sound and Fury

THROUGHOUT HER CAREER, Margaret had been commended by her contemporaries for being 'a star without a star's temperament'. Always happy to oblige the studio, as she had done when she abandoned her holiday to undertake a personal appearance tour, she rightly sensed that Gainsborough were exploiting her star image, and not for the benefit of her career. As Maurice Ostrer had assumed after the box office success of *The Man in Grey*, he could attach Margaret to any production and it would be a commercial draw. However, tired of being treated as a commodity and firmly believing that her fans deserved better, Margaret eventually took a stand against the mediocre scripts that were being presented to her.

The cause of this shift in Margaret's personality was *The Magic Bow*, a biopic of the famous Italian violinist, Niccolò Paganini. In her opinion, the script was badly written and it lacked a substantial plot. Furthermore, Gainsborough had demoted Margaret to the second lead, that of Paganini's childhood sweetheart, the villainous Bianchi, and had given Phyllis Calvert the leading part of his love interest, the aristocratic Jeanne de Vermond. As she had shown with *The Man in Grey*, Margaret was not above taking a smaller part if the role was good; but the final blow was delivered when she realised that, after James Mason had been cast as Paganini, she would be given third billing. Recognising the studio politics at play, she sensed that Maurice Ostrer did not care if she had a star role or not, so long as she was cast as a villain.

Margaret was not alone in voicing her concerns about the script. James Mason shared her sentiments, and after reading the script he refused to appear in the film; no longer under contract to 'Uncle Maurice', he could afford to be choosy. Stewart Granger was brought in to replace Mason as Paganini. Phyllis Calvert also loathed the script – '[I] thought no, this is the end' – but as Margaret pointed out, '[Phyllis], at least, was the heroine. I was... I don't really know what I was meant to be, some kind of mad gypsy who lurked about looking very jealous behind pillars. Absolutely nonsensical.'[1]

Aside from the script, Margaret and Phyllis were concerned about working with Stewart Granger again. 'After three films we did get rather bored with each other,' Phyllis tactfully said. And Granger mirrored her opinion: 'If you're talking about our personal feelings, no,' he said in response to appearing alongside the women again. 'But if you're talking about our public, yes.'[2] Bowing to his loyal fans, Granger went into *The Magic Bow* alongside Phyllis, but Margaret was still fighting against the restraint of the studio.

She appealed to Maurice Ostrer, but her confidence was shaken when he refused to listen and reminded her that she was under contract, and, as such, she should 'do as she was told'. He did, however, take on board her comments about the size of the role and agreed to expand it. Unsatisfied with Ostrer's response, Margaret was prompted by Phyllis to appeal to J. Arthur Rank, who controlled the merged studios despite Ostrer's power over Gainsborough.

Without telling Ostrer of their plans, Phyllis took Margaret 'by the scruff of my neck' to the Rank headquarters in Park Lane. Guided through double doors, they were greeted by J. Arthur Rank, who was sitting at the head of an onyx table. Rising to his towering height, he looked at the women and said, 'I hear you've come to talk about more brass!' The topic of money had not entered Margaret's mind, and she replied, 'No, we've come to try and get out of *The Magic Bow*!' [3]

After listening to Margaret bemoan the lack of good scripts and decent parts, Rank agreed and offered to transfer her Gainsborough contract, due to expire within a few months, to his division, the Rank Organisation. Phyllis was persuaded to stay with *The Magic Bow*, a compromise she agreed to when Rank offered her more money. Jean Kent, rising in popularity, was given the part of Bianchi, the role intended for Margaret.

Although Gainsborough and the Rank Organisation had merged three years before, there was still a code of studio politics which Ostrer felt must be adhered to. He resented Rank for (as he saw it) poaching Margaret, and he did not shirk from directing his resentment at her. He sent her a letter, reminding her that she had only become the number one box office star in Britain because of his careful handling of her career, and telling her she would do well to reciprocate an appreciation towards him for her coveted star status. In his view she had, instead, repaid him with deception by going to Rank behind his back. He made an example out of Margaret by speaking openly about her recent behaviour, and word quickly spread through the studio. Phyllis explained, 'He was angry because Maggie had refused to play in the film. He said that he didn't intend to use her ever again, that he was glad to give up her contract to J. Arthur Rank and that after her next film he guaranteed she would start to go on the down-grade quickly.'[4] Ostrer's vindictiveness might have been common in Hollywood, but in the 'gentlemanly' British film industry, it was unprofessional.

It was a bold step and one Margaret might not have taken had she not been offered a script from an independent producer, John Corfield, who had formed British National Films Company with J. Arthur Rank in 1934. The alternative script was a screen adaption of Vera Caspary's successful novel, *Bedelia.* It was the story of a happy newlywed couple in which the husband, Charlie Carrington (played on screen by Ian Hunter), learns that his wife, Bedelia, has a criminal past. His growing suspicion about the death of her previous husband leads him to discover that she is, in fact, a serial killer who loathes men: 'I hate men!' she screams in the film, 'they're beasts!'

With her bestselling novel *Laura* successfully adapted for the screen and starring Hollywood star Gene Tierney, Caspary was engaged to co-write the screenplay of *Bedelia* with Isadore Goldsmith, who had funded and produced *The Stars Look Down.* The novel's plot, originally set in Connecticut in 1913, was updated to the present day with the Carringtons changed from an American to an English couple, and the setting was moved to Monte Carlo and Yorkshire.

Anticipating the same level of success as *Laura*, Margaret was given the Hollywood treatment. Her face was made up using a new make-up technique, mastered by Ernest Taylor, who specially imported mixtures for shading and highlighting her complexion to 'achieve a new depth of lustre on her screen skin'.

She was loaned £180,000 worth of jewellery, then unheard of in British cinema, and men from Scotland Yard were sent by the insurance company to guard the valuable jewels. And eighteen custom-made gowns were designed by Jacqmar, except for a Raphael housecoat; though, unlike Hollywood, Britain was still in the throes of rationing. Although rumoured to be 'the best dressed British film of the year', the public were reminded that even a star had to adhere to rationing. 'Thanks to coupon-ing, none of the big money Margaret Lockwood is earning as Britain's first lady of the screen can buy Bedelia's lovely dresses, and she casts regretful looks at them as she changes in a little tent off the set and climbs into her old sweater and slacks.'[5]

Filming began three days after *The Magic Bow* went into production; and, although Margaret was relieved to have severed ties with Maurice Ostrer, there was one final obligation she had to fulfil before she was completely free from Gainsborough's influence over her career.

The time had come for *The Wicked Lady* to be released, and with the studio's publicity machine capitalising on the scandal it had attracted for its costumes and dialogue, it was decided that the film was to have a royal premiere in the presence of the Dowager Queen Mary. Opening at the Gaumont, Haymarket on 19th November 1945, it was a gala occasion – 'a night of unreserved glamour' – the first since the war, and tickets were sold with the proceeds going to the British Hospital for Mothers and Babies at Woolwich.

Having viewed a private screening of *The Wicked Lady* on the morning of the premiere, the press retaliated against Gainsborough's publicity campaign. The newspapers printed critical notices, warning the general public of the 'bawdy, disgraceful and salacious' plot. Furthermore, they appealed for monarchists to boycott the picture, seeing it as highly insulting that the eighty-seven-year-old Queen Mary had been invited to view such a 'sordid piece of artistry'.

With hours to go until the premiere at six o'clock, Gainsborough received a telephone call from Marlborough House, asking for an emergency screening ahead of the premiere. Due to the negative response from the critics, an equerry thought it best to view the film and make a hasty decision on whether or not it would be suitable for Queen Mary. For the duration of the screening, the most important men in the British film industry paced the floor outside the viewing room, contemplating the potential humiliation should Queen Mary refuse to attend the premiere. Finally, an equerry emerged and smiled broadly. Approval had been granted.

Margaret arrived at the Gaumont in a heightened state of nervousness, which she tried to conceal by chatting animatedly with J. Arthur Rank as they waited to receive Queen Mary. 'I can't tell you how I felt,' she later recalled. 'You could have cut the atmosphere with a knife.'[6] The tension was provoked by the reunion between herself and Maurice Ostrer, their first meeting since her refusal to appear in *The Magic Bow*, which upon its release was a critical failure. They politely acknowledged one another and posed together for the photographers, aware that both of their professional reputations depended on Queen Mary's response to *The Wicked Lady*.

With her seat in the circle, four or five rows behind the royal party, Margaret could see the journalists and gossip columnists who were in attendance. They did not take their eyes off Queen Mary for a moment, hoping, of course, that she would get up and walk out of the theatre, or at the least give some sign of disapproval.

After a tense one hundred and four minutes, where neither Margaret nor Ostrer watched the film (they watched Queen Mary instead), the credits appeared on screen and the lights came on. Queen Mary rose from her seat and spoke not one word as she left the royal box. She was aware of the panic *The Wicked Lady* had caused her equerries, and she relished keeping the journalists in suspense as she walked towards Margaret.

Wrought with nerves, Margaret dipped into a curtsey and, when she came up, Queen Mary, with a glint in her eye, leaned in and confided: 'That was very good, I enjoyed it very much.' The journalists waited for Queen Mary and her entourage to leave before they besieged Margaret. 'Well, what did she say!' they demanded to know. After all of the fuss they had caused, and very nearly sabotaging the film, she turned to them and replied in an exasperated voice, 'She said she liked it.'[7]

The royal seal of approval kept *The Wicked Lady* on the front pages of newspapers up and down the country. Within a week of its release it had broken all previous attendance records at the Gaumont, Haymarket, and shattered every box office record wherever it was screened.

Although the public flocked to see the film, the critics deplored it and continued to call it 'immoral and crude' and 'an odd mixture of hot passion and cold suet pudding'. The Manchester *Guardian* launched a scathing report on Margaret's performance: 'Miss Lockwood, who might well be the life and soul of a dull sherry party, is quite out of place when she tries to shed glamour over a beer-swilling thieves' kitchen.' Fans might have been taken in by her new screen image, but critics failed to see through the guise of the young romantic heroine who had once enchanted them. 'I just cannot believe in Miss Lockwood as a femme fatale... What I see is no wicked lady, but a nice ordinary girl, with looks and personality as apt to rouse heady admiration and racing pulses in me as a side view of the Albert Hall!'[8]

But nothing could diminish its commercial success. *The Wicked Lady* was the first British film to net one million pounds at the box office (twenty-nine million in today's money). And, in time, it became one of the most successful British films, ranking number seven in the BFI's list of Top 100 British films.

*

To the delight of Maurice Ostrer, *Bedelia* was released on both sides of the Atlantic where it proved a critical disaster. With Margaret's popularity still at its peak in Britain, her loyal fans turned out to see the film and, in turn, this equated to respectable box office receipts. However, failing to capture the same level of success as Vera Caspary's *Laura*, the film was a commercial failure in America. And, objecting to the film's treatment of her novel – in the end Isadore Goldsmith over-ruled Caspary's input – she wrote another screenplay with the intention of having it produced by an American studio. The American film version of *Bedelia* was never made; instead it was aired as a radio play on *Hollywood Star Time* in October 1946, starring Gene Tierney in the title role.

The film's lack of commercial success was attributed to the American censors who, once again, deemed Margaret's latest film of a 'very beautiful, very homicidal' woman as too immoral for its audiences. They were not only shocked by 'the punishment to be meted out to Bedelia' in the ending of the film, but they were equally disturbed by 'the neckline of one of her elegant gowns'.[9]

Having predicted there would be an objection from the Breen Office, Isadore Goldsmith had written two alternative endings. In the British version, Bedelia realises that she will be arrested and commits suicide by drinking poison. But American censors claimed that suicide 'was too good for her'; so to meet with the Breen Office's requirements, and at a cost of $66,000, the second ending showed Bedelia surrendering herself to the police and confessing her murders. However, Goldsmith was not entirely co-operative and, addressing the issue of Margaret's gowns, he was firm that 'it was an unfortunate bit of lighting' and he would not order those scenes to be reshot. The lighting, he claimed, was perfect for its *film noir* theme, and to change it would ruin the subdued mood. He appeased the censors when he said a negative 'may be redeveloped in a darker hue', thus 'toning down the unfortunate lighting'.[10]

Margaret was her own biggest critic when it came to *Bedelia*. She regretted her participation in the film, which she felt on completion was no better than *The Magic Bow*. 'An absolutely dreadful picture,' she later confessed. 'It makes me blush even to think of it.'[11]

The film did not diminish Margaret's popularity overseas. Hoping to exploit the success of *The Wicked Lady* in America, Twentieth Century Fox contacted Rank to offer Margaret the leading role in its film adaptation of *Forever Amber*, to be directed by Otto Preminger. Perhaps recalling her previous experience with Fox, she refused the offer. 'Why should I go? I'd done it in England. Why go six thousand miles away and do it there?'[12] Vivien Leigh had also turned down the role, sensing it was too similar to her portrayal of Scarlett O'Hara in *Gone With the Wind.* But Margaret's refusal was entirely personal; she did not wish to be separated from Keith, nor did she want to go away and leave Toots.

Remaining in England, Margaret's first film under her new contract with the Rank Organisation was to be a screen adaptation of Daphne du Maurier's novel, *Hungry Hill.* She was cast as the spirited Fanny Rosa in the nineteenth-century Irish saga which spanned fifty years as it followed a feud between two Anglo-Irish families, the Brodricks and the Donovans. Although a period drama, Margaret thought it was a move in the right direction to distance herself from Gainsborough's 'pulp fiction for the masses'. However, the production retained an element of Gainsborough, and she was reunited with many of her contemporaries from her former studio. Brian Desmond Hurst, who had directed her in *Alibi*, was engaged to direct *Hungry Hill;* Dennis Price, her co-star in *A Place of One's Own*, returned as her leading man; and Jean Simmons, her sister in *Give Us the Moon*, had a small but substantial role. It also marked the screen debut of Toots, who briefly appeared as Margaret's onscreen daughter, little Fanny Rosa.

Dermot Walsh, the Dublin-born actor, who was given his first film role as Margaret's son, recalled her professionalism. 'Knocked out' by her star status, Walsh said: 'I mean she was *the* star at that time… I learned an enormous amount from watching her. She wouldn't go out of her way to teach you, but she wouldn't try to put you down, either. Her reserve always seemed to be accepted by the people working with her and, as far as I was aware, she was liked. I think the measure of that is that I never heard a joke or a story told at her expense, which is fairly unusual in our business.'[13]

As the film progressed Margaret's character aged fifty years, and this transformation called for her to spend hours in the make-up chair. Greasepaint was applied in the appropriate skin tone and wrinkles were painted on. Next, a special solution was dabbed on with a brush under the eyes which stretched the skin, and contracted it as it dried to give the impression of natural lines. The hollows of the cheeks were shaded and the rest of the make-up was worked into the skin so that the gaunt contours were highlighted without being obvious. The final stage was the liberal application of powder which was brushed off again with a baby's hairbrush. Rather than using a wig, Margaret's brunette hair was treated with a hair whitening formula and set and dressed in the style of the period. It took two bottles of shampoo to remove it from her hair.[14] The effort taken to alter her appearance, and her performance in portraying 'an Irish *femme fatale* who develops into a bitter, drug-dependent matriarch', was hailed as 'startling and ambitious'.[15]

When *Hungry Hill* was released audiences found the plot of the two warring families, the Donovans and the Brodricks, too sprawling for its limited screen time of ninety-two minutes. 'Between the covers of a book such long-drawn narratives may be interesting, but on screen, even with the best intentions and handling, they tend to drag.' Though the critics agreed that Margaret had successfully 'shed her "naughty girl" roles to prove that she can play the part of a self-sacrificing mother'.[16]

Having weathered the currents of her career and, to some extent, reformed her onscreen image, Margaret was quietly confident that her professional life was going in the right direction. But, with the war over and the realisation that Rupert would be coming home, she knew she would have to restore order in her private life, too.

15
THE MERITS OF SUCCESS

AS MARGARET APPROACHED HER thirtieth birthday in September 1946, she decided it was time to take stock of her life. She began with Toots, who, except for the six months following her birth, had not lived under the same roof as her. Now that the war was over it would be safe to bring Toots to London; but, as much as she wanted her child with her, Margaret realised the pain it would cause Margaret Evelyn. Because of this, she delayed breaking the news to her mother.

In the meantime, Margaret focused on her relationship with Keith in the wake of Rupert's homecoming from Germany, which had been delayed. In 1944, a year before the war ended, Rupert had been transferred from his post in Africa to Camp 030 near Hamburg, Germany, seconded to the American Counter Intelligence Corps of the Ninth American Army. He had been the first man on the side of the Allies to learn of Hitler's marriage to Eva Braun and of their joint suicide. He had interrogated Heinz Lorenz, one of three couriers from Hitler's bunker who had tried to smuggle his last will and testament to the West, and various senior SS officers, including the Reich's plenipotentiary in Denmark, SS General Werner Best. He interviewed Baron Von Cramm and another conspirator, both involved in the failed plot to blow up Hitler in 1944. And, remaining in Germany, he was working at uncovering one of the top leaders of the Wehrwolf organisation.[1]

Margaret had written Rupert a 'Dear John' letter,[2] telling him as honestly and as simply as she could that she had fallen in love with Keith. Aside from betraying him, she felt guilty that the war had prevented him from being with Toots and experiencing the traditional family life he had aspired to when they first married. And, given their past meetings and how an unspoken tension appeared to linger between them, she hoped he would understand her wanting to end their marriage.

With Margaret looking to the future, she began to make plans to include Keith in everyday family life. For the past two years they had been living at Dolphin Square, but she found the flat too small and she passed the lease to her brother, Lyn, and his new wife. She then took a lease on a spacious flat on the outskirts of London, in Roehampton, overlooking Richmond Park, where she lived with Keith and Toots – though, in *Lucky Star*, she wrote that Toots came to live with her after her relationship with Keith had ended. The truth was that Margaret had included Toots in this new life with Keith, and the child attended the nearby Froebel School.[3] However, owing to the social mores of the day, she did not disclose that she was not only cohabiting with a man while still married to another, but that her daughter was part of this arrangement, too.

It was a difficult period for Margaret, and for Toots, who had recently left Margaret Evelyn's home after spending five years in her care. When Margaret had told her mother that Toots could no longer live with her, she did not underestimate the damage it would cause to their already brittle relationship. In spite of this, she knew Margaret Evelyn was a kind and loving grandmother to Toots, and over the years she had formed a close bond with her grandchild.

In an attempt to make the separation easier for Margaret Evelyn, Margaret invited her mother to come to the flat, to stay with them for as long as she liked, so she would not be lonely. Rather than accepting the invitation, Margaret Evelyn was deeply offended; Margaret understood, however, that her mother was 'far too independent by nature to share a home with either of her children'.

*

The changes in Margaret's personal life were mirrored in her professional one. In 1946, Maurice Ostrer resigned from Gainsborough, where he had presided for eighteen years. His departure was provoked by a general feeling of isolation and the realisation that he was losing control over the studio he had helped to create. With his wealth and power, J. Arthur Rank continued to dominate a large stake in the British film industry; and, not satisfied with the merging of the film studios, he further invaded Ostrer's territory when he extended his interests towards the cinema industry, too. Beginning in 1938, Rank had bought the Odeon cinemas, and in 1941 he purchased the Gaumont-British and Paramount cinemas. A decade later, he would own six hundred and fifty cinemas across Britain, a calculated move to ensure the distribution of his studio's films.

With his vision for a powerful international future in British film-making, Rank wanted Margaret at the helm; and he offered her a seven-year contract, with a promise of quality scripts and a somewhat free hand in choosing her films. It was an attractive offer, with more freedom than Maurice Ostrer had given her, and she accepted. Sitting next to J. Arthur Rank himself, Margaret signed her new contract under the suitable glare of the press.

The strength of Margaret's popularity was confirmed when it was announced she had won the 1946 *Daily Mail* National Film Award for Most Outstanding British Actress during the war years. 'This,' she said, 'was the greatest evidence I had ever had of the public's liking and affection for me.' It was the first time any such national poll had been conducted, and over six hundred thousand public votes were cast in her favour. In second place was Phyllis Calvert, with only one hundred and ten votes separating the final outcome.

The awards had been created to mark the fifty-year golden jubilee of British films; and the *Daily Mail*, the founder and sponsor of the awards, planned to host a ceremony comparable to that of the Academy Awards in Hollywood. It was to be held at the Royal Albert Hall with the newspaper's proprietor, Lord Harmsworth, and his wife Lady Harmsworth, presenting the awards, followed by a dinner given at the Dorchester hotel. However, to his horror, James Mason had been voted the Most Outstanding British Actor during the war years; and, given his past behaviour when working together, it did not come as a shock to Margaret when he dismissed the ostentatious plans for the awards ceremony. Having developed a degree of animosity for anything to do with his former studio, and feeling that it would hinder his Hollywood career, Mason objected to the ceremony being held at the Royal Albert Hall; and, threatening to pull out of the event should it go ahead, he got his own way and the ceremony and dinner were both held at the Dorchester.

The evening of 21st June 1946 would be a pivotal one for Margaret. Not only was she assured that she had a great career ahead of her, she saw it as a turning point in her relationship with Keith. As her car headed in the direction of the Dorchester, she was surrounded by crowds of fans who spilled onto the roads as a mass of policemen on horseback battled to control the mob. Sitting in the back of the car, as she held onto Keith's hand, she reflected on her past as a child performer and the opportunities which had led her to stardom. 'For a minute I saw myself again as a small girl, in my school uniform, crying because Mother had told me they did not think me good enough for the part of "Alice",' she said. 'Now I was crying because I had reached my wonderland – or nearly. The world seemed at my feet.'[4]

The happiness Margaret felt prompted her to make up her mind about Keith, and their future together. She wanted to marry him, and, in doing so, she 'could expect no further measure of happiness'. In the past, when she had experienced great highs, she often asked herself: 'Am I too happy, can this last?' It was an insightful remark, and perhaps one she subconsciously knew the answer to. When Margaret returned home she wrote a letter to Rupert, asking him for a divorce. All she could do was wait for his reply.

While she waited for Rupert's answer, Margaret and Keith left for the south of France to attend the first Cannes Film Festival, where, ironically, *The Magic Bow* was competing for the Grand Prize of the Festival. Although the film industries from London and Hollywood had descended on the resort, the unspoilt splendour of the Boulevard de la Croisette had exceeded Margaret's expectations. Never before had she seen so many handsome men and beautiful women gathered in one place. One evening in particular stood out for her, 'when everything is suddenly perfect', and in the splendour of the Hotel du Cap-Eden-Roc, Grace Moore serenaded the crowd. 'This was my summer time of happiness,'[5] Margaret recalled. But it was not to last.

*

Remnants from the past were dominating Margaret's life. She returned to Gainsborough to make *Jassy* at Denham Studios, the studio's first and only melodrama shot in Technicolor. Rather than being marshalled into the role, as was the way in which Maurice Ostrer had handled her, Margaret only took part out of loyalty to her former studio. Ostrer's successor at Gainsborough, Sydney Box, had been ordered by J. Arthur Rank to boost production to ten or twelve films a year, each costing no more than £200,000. Taking an inventory of production costs, Box was alarmed when he discovered how Ostrer had allowed the studio to 'slip through his fingers'. Box's wife, Muriel, had taken charge of the script department and she advised him to have a reserve of scripts ready to go into production, waiting to be developed, or under option. *Jassy* was one of the scripts in their 'reserve pile'. Sensing that Margaret's name would give credibility to the film (which was still undeveloped when production began), Box approached her and pleaded for her to help, and reluctantly she agreed.

Like her previous melodramas for Gainsborough, *Jassy* was a costume drama, set in 1830. She played the title role, a half-gypsy girl with the gift of second sight who works for the Hattons until they lose their home by the roll of a dice.

Befriending Dilys Helmer – played by Patricia Roc – Jassy goes to work for her wealthy father, Nick, whom she later marries. But, after a riding accident leaves him invalided, he turns violent towards her. Sympathising with Jassy's domestic plight, Lindy, a mute servant, poisons Nick, and both women find themselves charged with his murder. During the trial, Lindy's power of speech is restored and she confesses to the murder, and thus Jassy is found innocent.

Margaret's initial lack of enthusiasm vanished when she was reunited with her former co-stars. Alongside Patricia Roc, Dermot Walsh and Dennis Price were cast as Barney and Christopher Hatton, both having starred with Margaret in *Hungry Hill.* And, with James Mason no longer under contract to the studio, the menacing role was filled by Basil Sydney – a much-loved character actor, but certainly not a star. Still, Sydney's personality more than made up for his lack of star status, and Margaret recalled he was 'a giggler', a pleasant contrast to Mason's surly disposition. 'It was like being back at school,' she remarked. 'In some of our most dramatic scenes, we'd crease up laughing and couldn't carry on.'

Released in July 1947, *Jassy* consolidated Sydney Box's initial fears regarding the weakness of the script. Critical reception was that of mockery towards what they claimed to be an outdated genre of film; and the critic Paul Dehn accused the studio of showing 'too much sadism in our films', and he directed his critique at Box himself: 'Producers and directors have their recognisable weaknesses. Hitchcock likes appearing in his own pictures, DeMille likes crowds, Lubitsch likes staircases. Sydney Box likes torture, flogging and bloodshed.'[6] However, as was a familiar theme with the Gainsborough 'bodice rippers', the critics were outnumbered by box office receipts, and *Jassy* proved to be a commercial hit.

During the filming of *Jassy*, Rank had ordered Margaret to attend the first Royal Command Film Performance, held at the Empire Cinema on 1st November 1946. Toots had been among the children of popular stars who were chosen to present the bouquets of flowers to Queen Elizabeth, and the Princesses Elizabeth and Margaret. This, Margaret thought, would give Margaret Evelyn the opportunity to see for herself how Toots could be incorporated into her life in London, and at the studios.

They set off in a Rolls Royce to the Empire Cinema, and Margaret noticed that her mother was 'quite excited for once', and that Toots was 'as calm as could be'. Margaret, however, was 'a bundle of nerves' as the car crawled at a snail's pace through the heavy traffic. When they reached the cinema, there were five thousand people blocking the way. London itself was at a standstill (the traffic made headlines the next day) and it was a small relief to Margaret that the Royal car was also delayed. This, to her dread, gave everyone more time in which to grow nervous, and she worried Toots was becoming anxious from the long wait. It did not allay her anxiety when 'foolish people' approached the children to ask them, 'Are you nervous, dear?'

When the Royal party arrived, Margaret gave Toots a discreet nudge whereupon she curtseyed. 'Your little girl is very sweet,' remarked Queen Elizabeth. 'She did that perfectly.' Then, turning to Toots, she asked, 'How old are you, my dear?'

'Five years and two months,' answered Toots.

When the presentation was over, Toots and Margaret Evelyn were driven back to the flat and Margaret followed her contemporaries to a party given in their honour at the Savoy.

As she stepped outside the Empire Cinema, the crowds had turned into an anarchistic mob; and, in their stampede to catch a better glimpse of their idols, they smashed the windscreen of Ray Milland's car. The Empire Cinema, he quipped, was 'among the battlefields I have visited'.[7]

*

It was with mixed feelings that Margaret greeted Rupert when he stood at the door of her new flat: the home he had not seen, nor been a part of. Although his physical appearance had not changed, she felt he was a stranger to her. Almost five years had passed since their last meeting, and Margaret blamed herself for the strained atmosphere between them. 'It's me, I thought, I'm the one who has changed.' Rupert seemed to think so, too. 'I see you wear more make-up now,' he said with an air of disapproval.[8] 'You've gone a long way in four years, Margaret, a very long way. Are you sure about all this?'[9]

They had both 'gone a long way' in the time they had spent apart, and now Rupert had come home. The meeting, although rigid and punctuated by long silences, moved along without emotion.[10] She spoke about his objections to her career, and how the war and their separation had only served to emphasise their underlying differences. 'It was not unreasonable to say that Rupert and I had practically grown up together,' she wrote. 'We had married almost as a matter of course, and doubtless, in the way of young people, had been encouraged to wed by my mother's opposition.'

Rupert agreed with her. 'But, if you are not sure about your feelings for this man, I am willing to try again,' he offered. Margaret confirmed that she was sure. 'Then I must meet him,' he added. 'I want to see what he is like, for your sake as well as for the sake of Toots.'[11]

The meeting between Rupert and Keith was brief and, to her great frustration, it passed without Rupert leaving any indication as to how he felt. Afterwards, when they were alone, he told Margaret: 'I am prepared to accept that our marriage is through. Possibly I was never cut out to be married to a film star, anyway. If we were together now I think I should resent your career. I should want you to stay at home. But that is beside the point. I am not going to divorce you yet.'[12] Although it was not the news Margaret had anticipated, his refusal to divorce her would soon become clear.

Following her meeting with Rupert, Margaret had her answer: there would be no divorce. She felt, at the time, 'bewildered, hurt and torn'. It prompted her to reflect on her feelings for Keith and, according to her autobiography, she asked herself if she had been in love with him all along, or had sheer loneliness made her think this? She was uncertain. It was of little comfort to her that, even if she could get a divorce, Rupert had warned her that it would risk endangering her legal rights to have Toots permanently in her care.[13] She asked herself: 'Was I really so much in love that I would sacrifice the privilege of being her mother? Might not other problems arise? Would my second husband be sufficiently fond of Toots to make her a good stepfather? Would he continue to accept the fact that I was a film star with a career which would make constant demands upon me – a career which would give me a salary far greater than he could ever earn?'[14]

Whether or not Keith could grow to love Toots was irrelevant to the child. Toots, who was aged six at the time, strongly disliked him. Recalling an incident that would ultimately end Margaret's relationship with Keith, Toots remembered sitting down for a meal with her nanny, her mother and Keith and, for some reason (unknown to her), Margaret was angry with him and wanted him to leave. Not one to outwardly show signs of anger, Margaret lifted a bottle of tomato ketchup and hurled it at the wall. Toots and her nanny looked on in bewilderment at the broken ketchup bottle and its contents dripping down the wall. Keith remained seated at the table, unmoved by the outburst.

In a fit of despair, Margaret fled the scene and ran out onto the street where she caught a passing bus. She did not have any money with her, but, to her relief, the bus conductor recognised her and took pity on her. She said she wanted to go to her agent's house and, giving the conductor Herbert's address, he helped her off the bus and pointed her in the right direction. She caught a taxi and Herbert paid the fare on her arrival. Then, he immediately telephoned Rupert and told him of the predicament. Worried about Toots and her nanny left alone in the flat with Keith, Rupert rushed over to remedy the situation.[15]

In *Lucky Star*, Margaret romanticised the ending of her relationship with Keith. She did not disclose the scene of suppressed anger, nor did she relate the sequence of events in a wholly accurate light. She wrote that since meeting Keith she had been 'tremendously happy', and she waxed lyrical about his willingness to escort her to film premieres and gala events. Furthermore, she claimed that he had 'helped her learn how to enjoy being a film star', and for the 'first time she had known somebody with whom she could share her life'.[16]

Further portraying Keith as somebody whom she could rely on, Margaret wrote that she dwelled on the future of their relationship 'night after night until she felt she would go crazy'. With the realisation that obtaining a divorce to marry this man could jeopardise her custody of Toots, 'who meant more to me than anyone else in the world', she made the decision to part from Keith. 'I did not want to do anything so wrong that I might regret it for ever after – not only for myself, but for all the others involved in this emotional maze.' And, somehow, she would 'find the strength to deal with the loneliness'.

Far from understanding, Keith refused to accept Margaret's decision and he pursued her day and night. Overwhelmed by his behaviour, she gathered up Toots and vanished for two weeks. 'It was having my child with me, to love and to think about, and Herbert's friendship and understanding which helped me through those two weeks, two weeks of my life I do not care to remember. I tried to struggle through my personal Gethsemane. But some nights, in panic, I knew I could not face going back to London.' [17]

Herbert delivered the news to Margaret that Keith was going abroad, to South Africa. She returned to London, assured that he could not contact her. Whether or not Keith did indeed go to South Africa is unknown, for his true whereabouts[18] were never revealed by Margaret, and it is assumed that she did not know what became of him.

What is certain is that Rupert's instincts had been correct during that first meeting with Keith when he suspected his devotion to Margaret was driven by ulterior motives. She was a wealthy woman: her new contract with J. Arthur Rank promised a salary of a quarter of a million pounds over the next seven years. And, during the years in which they were together, Margaret had funded his lifestyle[19] and had allowed him to live in her flat; she bought his clothes – expensive suits and monogrammed shirts. It appears he was motivated by money, confirmed when Rupert confronted him at Margaret's flat on the day she had fled to Herbert's house to appeal for his help. He had tried to reason with Keith, but he was defiant in his refusal to leave the flat and Margaret alone. In the end, Rupert paid him off,[20] after which Keith went abroad.

Given his willingness to disappear from Margaret's life, it appears that Rupert had outsmarted Keith, who had previously refused to leave. There would have been no incentive for Keith to do so, given that he was living off her money; and Margaret had, up until then, not succeeded in ending the relationship. However, given the scenario, there is a possibility that Rupert had Keith investigated. Otherwise, would he have got rid of him so easily if he did not have a hold over him, or threatened to expose him?

As Margaret had told Rupert, the separation during the war, her demanding career and his longing for a traditional wife conspired against their happiness. But the guilt of betraying Rupert was not far from her mind, and they both agreed to give their marriage another chance.

They left for a holiday in Brighton, but it was a disastrous attempt. The rise of Nazism and, eventually, the war had set in Rupert 'a deep anger against Hitler which remained with me until the end of the war'. After the cessation of hostilities in 1945, his duties had given him an opportunity to learn much more of Hitler, 'and my anger increased with my knowledge'. He also found it difficult to 'forgive the craven misjudgement of some of our British and French politicians of the pre-war period'.[21] Adjusting to civilian life after six years of service – two years in the Royal Artillery and four in the Intelligence Corps – proved difficult. Aside from his deep-rooted feelings towards the government, and the price he and his fellow comrades paid for their folly, he was still irritated by certain habits of his wife's. He loathed Margaret's smoking, and in spite of his displeasure she continued to do so. The petty differences magnified the underlying tension her affair with Keith had caused, and, unable to resolve their issues, on their return to London they agreed to separate.[22]

Reflecting on the life she had worked hard for, Margaret realised that she had chosen to give everything to her career; and, dwelling on the choices she had made, the mocking little voice inside her head did not hesitate to jeer: 'Or has your career taken everything from you?'

16
Severing Ties

At the age of thirty-one, Margaret held a promising career in her hands, albeit feeling 'sick of playing the type of roles which made Lucrezia Borgia look like Little Miss Muffet'.[1] The public had voted her the best film actress of the year for *Jassy*, and she won the *Daily Mail* National Film Award for the second time. In Canada, too, she had been voted the most popular female star.[2]

Although she had reached the height of her profession, Margaret often wondered if she was becoming cynical, even bitter, over the very successes she had wanted and worked for. Recalling the things that she had sacrificed for her career, she noted that filming had made her work on her wedding day. Filming had taken her away from Rupert, and then from Toots when she was six months old. Filming had kept her in London, away from most of Toots's early childhood. And filming had brought her loneliness.

Silencing the 'mocking little voice' inside her head, she told herself it would be self-destructive to dwell on what might have been different. Without work she would have been 'lost, purposeless and bored'.[3] A great sense of responsibility reminded her that she was Margaret-the-actress, first. But Margaret-the-actress had a restless ambition to be something other than a film star.

In 1948, television was still in its infancy, and many stars in both Britain and Hollywood were reluctant to step away from the cinema screen to appear in a medium that was not yet a mainstream form of entertainment. Although curious about television, Margaret had been discouraged from appearing on it by Herbert until he found a suitable project for her.

The timing could not have been better when the BBC approached him about Margaret playing Eliza Dolittle in their live production of George Bernard Shaw's *Pygmalion*. It would be their most ambitious television programme to date, with a running time of almost three hours: the longest programme yet televised in Britain. Longing for a new challenge and eager for an opportunity outside of Rank, Margaret accepted their offer. It was also a shrewd step towards appearing in the theatre, another ambition she hoped to fulfil.

Although Margaret's experience in film acting had given her a competent knowledge of a sound stage and how it worked, the thought of acting in a similar setting live in front of a television audience filled her with a sense of dread. 'I have been in films for so long, having to remember bits at a time, that I've almost forgotten the art of memorising long speeches,'[4] she remarked during the rehearsals. However, she need not have worried; for, stage fright aside, the final outcome was a success.

Following the first broadcast of *Pygmalion* on 8th February 1948, the play was given a second live performance two nights later, with both receiving high ratings. After the broadcasts, many letters of praise were sent to the BBC, some of which were published in the *Radio Times* on 27th February. One such appreciative letter came from a Mrs Shern in Hertfordshire, who had invited seven friends to watch the teleplay; so impressed were they by its execution, they were 'determined to install television sets at the earliest possible moment'. A pictorial spread of Margaret in various promotional stills followed. A snippet of a letter written by F. C. Poulett from Harrow, who declared the play had 'excelled anything previously broadcast', was placed below a candid photograph of Margaret with her co-stars, Ralph Michael (Higgins), Arthur Wontner (Pickering) and Beatrice Varley (Mrs Pearce).

Pygmalion's success would set the tone for the BBC's latest venture of casting household names in their live broadcasts of Shaw's plays. Four months later, the theatrical actress Margaret Leighton appeared in *Arms and the Man*; and although the television production was a respectable hit, the critics noted that she did not 'have the star appeal of Margaret Lockwood'.[5]

The next step in Margaret's career was ill-judged and a warning for what was yet to come. Exasperated by Rank's enthusiasm to cast her, once again, as the villain, Margaret continued the momentum of her television experience and decided to try something new. Harbouring a desire to hone her skills as a comedienne, she had her heart set on playing Nell Gwynne in the slapstick comedy *Cardboard Cavalier.*

The film was a vehicle for Sid Field, one of Britain's most popular comedians; and its director, Walter Forde, showed little enthusiasm for casting her as Field's leading lady. 'You do realise it's Sid's film: he's got to star in it,' he told her. But Margaret could not be discouraged, and prepared to accept second billing, she said, 'I don't a give a damn about that.'[6] She appealed to the studio bosses, who were reluctant for her to attach herself to *Cardboard Cavalier*, a film set in the England of Oliver Cromwell with Field as a cockney simpleton caught up in espionage for the royalist cause, aided by Margaret's Nell Gwynne. It was casting against type, they warned her. This time, they were right.

The critics deplored the film, and Margaret's performance was singled out as a clumsy attempt at comedy. 'One can only draw an embarrassing veil over the whole enterprise,' wrote the *Sunday Express*. Unwilling to draw constructive criticism from the film's reviews, Margaret defiantly maintained: 'I still think it's a very funny film but the critics absolutely slaughtered it. I can't think why.'[7] Even her most loyal fans were baffled by this change in direction, and they could not fathom her incarnation of a dizzy blonde as the same Margaret who leapt to fame in the Gainsborough melodramas. But the most damning piece of criticism came when she was accused of being 'distinctively wooden'.

It was a bitter blow for Margaret, as her film *Look Before You Love* – released before *Cardboard Cavalier* – had also failed to impress at the box office. It was a sophisticated romantic comedy-drama which, in script form, looked promising. She was cast as a secretary at the British Embassy in Rio de Janeiro who discovers, too late, that her husband plans to sell her to a dying millionaire with the intention of reclaiming her for himself as a wealthy widow. Her co-star, Griffith Jones, recalled: 'We hoped for a comedy of wit and style, but it wasn't to be.' Perplexed by the final shooting script, confusion was apparent both on and off the set, and Margaret would telephone Jones to discuss the next day's scenes. 'Her suggestions were pertinent and constructive and I was impressed by her mental and physical resilience,'[8] he said. The fact that the film was produced by John Corfield, the independent producer who had offered her *Bedelia*, should have been warning enough.

Critical response contained a great deal of foresight. 'If Miss Lockwood makes any more films as bad as this, her outstanding popularity must end with a bang,' wrote the *Manchester Guardian*. The annual *Motion Picture Herald* poll of money-making stars named Anna Neagle in first place, with Margaret listed second, though still ahead of her Hollywood contemporaries, Bette Davis and Ingrid Bergman. The top box office success was Anna Neagle's *The Courtneys of Curzon Street*. Margaret's film *Jassy* came in at seventh place. Although she still had the public behind her, there were quiet whispers in the studio that Margaret's star was fading.

The disastrous outcome of Margaret's latest efforts coincided with the decline of the studio system in Britain. Rank had built up £16,000,000 in debts and reported an annual loss of £3,500,000, and to tackle the financial crisis its managing director, John David, ordered the closure of studio facilities in Islington. He sold Lime Grove Studios to the BBC, Denham Studios were leased, and he closed Independent Producers Ltd. The latter, in particular, alienated some of the top names in British film, including David Lean, the director responsible for some of Rank's most successful films.

Causing further disruption was the industrial action by approximately 1,700 employees who protested over the prospect of redundancies. Meanwhile the stars who were at the height of their popularity during the war years were leaving in their droves. James Mason and Stewart Granger, two of Gainsborough's most popular leading men, had gone to Hollywood. Phyllis Calvert, eager to break out of her saccharine roles on screen, embarked on a stage career where she played less sympathetic characters.

Many critics and film historians felt that British cinema of the 1940s fitted into the traditions of social mobility – that of documentary realism as in Carol Reed's *The Stars Look Down*, and of literary quality matched when, to much acclaim, David Lean had adapted Charles Dickens's *Oliver Twist*. With this advancement in the art of film making, critics and audiences agreed that the film world ought to act on the 'ethic of the middle-class desire for improvement'.[9] To their harshest critics, the Gainsborough and Rank melodramas were a backward step to the days of the music halls which had packed working-class audiences into the penny gaffs to witness the thrilling tales of wicked squires, wronged innocents and virtue triumphant.[10] Film historian Richard Winnington echoed the thoughts of the sophisticated postwar audience when he dismissed *The Wicked Lady* as 'an ugly hodge podge of servant girls' lore'.

With the horrors of war and postwar austerity, the studio's appeal lay in escapism: spectacular costumes, lavish sets, and shocking dialogue fuelled by double-entendres. One such exchange from *The Wicked Lady* had thrilled cinema-goers and horrified the American censors when Margaret (as Barbara) asked James Mason (as Jerry Jackson): 'Do you always take ladies by the throat?' to which Mason gruffly replied: 'No, I just take them.'

But not all of its appeal was founded on lavishness. Gainsborough had done something unique in British cinema: they invented the 'Women's Picture', equal to what Hollywood had done with Bette Davis, Ginger Rogers, Joan Crawford and Olivia de Havilland. This genre was created by need, for during the war years there had been an increase in female cinema-goers; masses of women shift-workers, factory girls, land girls, and the sweethearts of men serving with the armed forces, had created a market that responded to Gainsborough's new product. Such women who had been catapulted into men's jobs identified with Margaret's cry in *The Wicked Lady*: 'I've got brains and looks and personality. I want to use them instead of rotting in this dull hole.'

However, those cinema-goers who had sought escapism during the war had outgrown the genre and were turning to dramatic films which focused on relatable, real-life issues. Margaret had given life to what American writer Gershon Legman labelled 'the bitch-heroine'. Writing in 1948, he explained: 'The bitch-heroine speaks in a loud tone, moves with a firm stride; one hand always on the reins, the other ever-ready with the whip.' To a postwar audience, this characterisation had reached its expiry date; though, keeping within a moral code, as dubious as it seemed, Margaret's immoral characters always got their comeuppance: she was beaten to death in *The Man in Grey*, abandoned on her deathbed by her beloved in *The Wicked Lady*, and was driven to commit suicide in *Bedelia*. This untimely demise was a reminder to those women who felt liberated by their wartime freedom that they must not defy their social roles altogether. It was also an emphasis on the decline of social mores during the war years, when, for example, statistics showed that illegitimate births and divorce rates had risen between 1939 and 1945 – then taboo across the class spectrum. As the decade drew to a close, traditional family values were becoming the focal point of the entertainment industry; thus Margaret's most popular films were no longer topical. It was a symbol that society was returning to normal after the turmoil of the war, and that, perhaps, its virtue had been restored.

With her film career in limbo, Margaret fulfilled the additional clauses of her Rank contract when she agreed to undertake another publicity tour. Amidst the critics sounding the death knell for her popularity, an ominous sign greeted her when, on the first day of her tour, Britain was shrouded in freezing fog and icebound in the coldest winter on record. The weather seemed to mock any prospect of the public turning out to support her. 'You can't expect anyone to endure more of this weather than they have to,' she argued with her studio bosses. 'No one will go to the cinema, let alone go out to see me.'[11]

Having underestimated the public's support, Margaret was astonished and moved to see her loyal fans standing outside for hours in the appalling cold weather just to catch a glimpse of her. Her fans seemed to overlook any unpleasant obstacle which might hinder their chances of seeing their favourite star. But the most important question was not far from Margaret's mind: would they do the same where her films were concerned?

Overseeing the tour was Rank's publicity manager, Theo Cowan. Described as likeable, energetic and easy-going, he had first entered the film industry in 1936 as a publicist with Gaumont-British Pictures and, after his war service, he joined Rank, working in the Special Services division of the publicity office. Theo modestly described himself as the man who looked after the stars; his job was to organise the logistics of personal appearances, attendance at premieres, charity events, garden parties and promotional tours.

Surprisingly, given her popularity, Margaret had never met Theo. But Patricia Roc, a veteran of such tours, assured her there would never be a dull moment while he was around. He kept Margaret in fits of laughter and, as well as organising the tour to perfection, he restored her sense of humour after the turbulent year she had endured with Rupert, Keith and Margaret Evelyn. The friendship between Margaret and Theo was based on laughter. Laughter, Theo recalled, was 'the biggest cementing factor between us… Margaret was a laugh-out-loud lady… that roar of a laugh of hers, you could never miss it or forget it. We laughed at the same things.'[12]

During the tour they spent their free time going to the cinema – 'a privilege for me, for I was expected to be on a screen, not watching one'[13] – with Margaret attempting to blend into the crowd, wearing a scarf tied around her head and no make-up. When a member of the public looked at her in a curious, familiar way, Theo would react on cue. 'You've dropped your glove. Quickly, get down there and go on picking it up', was his code for when someone had recognised her.

Such simple pleasures were rare, and even though Margaret went to great efforts to avoid being recognised, she did not begrudge her fans – 'we just couldn't exist without them' – and the interest they held in her private life. 'I'm told ninety-nine per cent of my public are women and they love knowing about my private life, such as there is of it. They're welcomed as far as I'm concerned, but then I haven't really got what is known – in quotes – as a private life. I have to work pretty hard and when I'm not working I spend all the time I can with my daughter Toots. If I was involved in more complicated domestic circumstances I don't know how I'd feel about it. I will say one thing: we're a darn sight luckier in this respect than the American stars.'[14]

With her popularity defying critics and official box office polls, Margaret was given the *Daily Mail* National Film Award for Best Film Actress of the year. Having won by 166,024 votes, the public had propelled her, once again, to the coveted spot of most popular actress in British films. Standing next to the studio's head, J. Arthur Rank, no one could have predicted the storm clouds forming between them as they smiled for the cameras.

Later in the evening, Margaret was awoken by the incessant ringing of her telephone and, upon answering it, she was met each time by unfamiliar voices. An American newspaper columnist had interviewed her by transatlantic telephone and decided to print her telephone number. And, unbeknownst to Margaret, the British newspapers reprinting the interview had also included the number. The line became jammed with fans, and in desperation she sent someone to contact the Post Office authorities, and was relieved the following morning when they issued her with a new telephone number.

Under any other circumstances it would have seemed a minor, albeit intrusive, incident. But given the frosty relationship between the studio and its star, such obsessive displays of fanaticism were music to Rank's ears. Using the strength of her fan base as a catalyst for his ambitious plans, J. Arthur Rank discussed the possibility of sending Margaret overseas to represent the studio on a six-week personal appearance tour of North America. For once, she was excited about the prospect of returning to America and this time she planned on bringing Toots with her.

However, currency officials rejected the idea. They prohibited Toots from accompanying her mother on a work-related trip since she was not going to earn money for Britain and America. The studio defended their reasoning, and they told Margaret that Toots was bad publicity for 'a glamour girl's personal appearance tour'.[15] Arguments continued between Margaret and Rank, and she maintained that Toots did not need much money, and could live off the studio's allowance of £10 a day. Phyllis Calvert, who was in Hollywood filming *Time Out of Mind*, stepped in and offered to keep the child out of her own earnings which were salaried by Universal Studios. Despite Phyllis's offer to support Toots, it was a dollar crisis in Anglo-American cinema relations that eventually put a stop to the tour.

Although disappointed by the outcome, Margaret was also realistic about the prospects of such a tour. 'Nine times out of ten they don't know how to exploit British artistes,' she explained when questioned about her views on Hollywood. 'I know there have been brilliant exceptions, but on a whole they seem to find us a bewildering problem. Besides, I suppose it's only human nature to prefer being a big fish in a little pond.'[16]

Rank did not dwell on the disappointment of the aborted personal appearance tour, and they kept Margaret busy by sending her the script of her next film, *Roses for Her Pillow*. The storyline was trite and confusing, and the role called for Margaret to play the wife of an army officer who has an affair with her husband's batman, only to wake up and realise it had all been a dream. Having approached the script with an open mind, Margaret hoped Rank would consider her fans, the critics' recent reviews, and her pleas for quality scripts. But as she reached the last pages of the script, she was so furious that she hurled it across the room. She had not been so infuriated since her Gainsborough experience with *The Magic Bow*; and, remembering J. Arthur Rank's sympathy for her predicament, she was disheartened and suspicious of him pulling the same stunt as Maurice Ostrer.

Margaret rushed to the telephone and frantically dialled Herbert's number. When he answered, she greeted him with a rare outburst of bad temper. 'How dare they offer me a part like that! It's no more than that of a stooge. I won't do it!' Herbert tried to reason with her, and said: 'Let's see what can be done to improve it.' She refused to listen; and recalling the incident years later, Margaret explained that she 'did not care if they called me temperamental, self-willed, obstinate. I was going to be all of those things for once. I was thoroughly fed up'.[17]

Prior to this incident, Margaret had always prided herself on her work ethic; she had never missed a day's shooting and had never grumbled when production ran over schedule. Only once in her career had she taken time off, while filming *The White Unicorn* in 1947, due to septic tonsils; having delayed the operation for some time to accommodate the shooting schedule, she finally surrendered to the pain and had them removed. After a two-week convalescence, she returned to the set to resume filming.

Obeying Margaret's orders to refuse the script, Herbert approached J. Arthur Rank; and, despite long conferences and arguments going back and forth, neither the studio head nor the agent managed to reach a compromise. The final word came from Margaret herself. 'Why can't we have more say in the sort of films we have to play in? I've quite made up my mind that in future, unless I feel I can do justice to a part – and the story does justice to me – I shall refuse it.'[18]

Contracted to Rank for seven years, Margaret did not have direct control over the choice of scripts she was offered, and out of those scripts she had to choose one. To refuse all manner of scripts would have been unthinkable, and not something she had had to entertain since *The Magic Bow* incident at Gainsborough. In addition, she could not break the clauses of her contract without suffering the consequences. And, having never challenged Rank in such a direct way before, she was uncertain how the studio would react.

The Rank studio bosses collectively threatened to withhold her fee if she continued to defy their orders. But Margaret remained defiant. She did not care if this refusal jeopardised her chances of earning nearly a quarter of a million pounds for herself in seven years. Neither she, nor the Inland Revenue, who would take more than two-thirds of this, would starve without it. 'Never mind the money, it's my integrity and prestige as an actress I'm thinking about,'[19] she told Herbert. The studio resorted to another tactic, and they threatened to suspend her if she did not comply. 'Let them!' she said.

A man of his word, who believed stars should be kept in their place, J. Arthur Rank personally delivered the news of Margaret's suspension. She lost the £13,000[20] fee she would have earned for the film, but it did not worry her. Some actresses in her position might have viewed it as the end of their career, but to Margaret it meant only one thing: freedom.

Production began on *Roses for Her Pillow* with Googie Withers stepping into the role intended for Margaret. Having starred in the critically acclaimed Ealing dramas *Pink String and Sealing Wax* and *It Always Rains on Sunday*, the role was a step down for Withers, regardless of her outlook that any work was better than none. Retitled *Once Upon a Dream*, the film was a critical and commercial failure, but one that did not hinder Withers's career.

Under suspension for six months, Margaret had made up her mind to enjoy this unexpected holiday. Her fans were in disbelief, for such scandal usually befell Hollywood stars, not British actresses. The newspapers and fan magazines lapped up the gossip; and Margaret, often shy of her public, decided to step into the role of the 'wicked lady' in real life. With her absence from the screen, the public were all the more eager to catch a glimpse of her in person when she appeared at the Royal Film Performance that November. Lining the road, they chanted, 'We want Margaret, we want Margaret,' and they were not disappointed when she stepped out of her car, wearing an elaborate gown of black lace with an ermine trim stole draped across her shoulders. She had become the embodiment of the villainous roles she was famous for, and the public loved it.

J. Arthur Rank could see the suspension did little to harm Margaret's public appeal and, exploiting the situation, he ordered her to go on yet another personal appearance tour. Still in an assertive frame of mind, Margaret told the studio that she and Theo Cowan would choose the locations for the tour. They opted to bypass London and the cities surrounding it in favour of small towns throughout Britain. The exacting schedule was expertly planned down to the last detail, giving her no time for recreation; for, when she was not visiting factories, stores, workshops, cinemas, schools, chemical and heavy engineering works, judging beauty competitions, touring hospitals or attending civic luncheons, she would be travelling.

In preparation for the tour, the studio ordered a small entourage to accompany Margaret, including her dresser, Gwen, and hairdresser, Norah. They commissioned a custom-made wardrobe, and she was fitted for six suits, eight evening dresses, ten afternoon and cocktail dresses, and a dozen hats. The new wardrobe included every colour scheme imaginable except brown, the only shade she did not care for. Her flat had become a revolving door, with dressmakers, photographers, secretaries, and publicity people coming and going, and there were timetables and suitcases everywhere.

Margaret Evelyn, who had temporarily left Delcott to stay with Margaret and Toots, was inconvenienced by the preparations, and she made her feelings known. 'Absurd, rubbish, the whole thing's a lot of nonsense,'[21] she repeated. Feeling that her mother half expected her to cancel the tour because of her disapproval, Margaret tried to explain that it was those 'absurd' practices that afforded them a comfortable lifestyle. The more she tried to explain, the more her mother threatened to go. In the end, she went, 'departing in high dudgeon' a few days after Margaret left for the tour.

After her abrupt departure, Margaret Evelyn rarely visited Margaret, nor did they attempt to resolve their differences. 'Though I constantly regret that we do not see more of her, I think this arrangement is possibly the best solution,'[22] Margaret said at the time. It was, in many ways, the final nail in the coffin on their relationship.

The six-week tour passed quickly, with every hour of the day precisely planned. New Year's Day in Loughborough was typical of Margaret's schedule during the tour:

12.15 p.m. Arrive King's Head Hotel. Reception by Mayor and Mayoress, Town Clerk and wife
1 p.m. Press luncheon
2.45 p.m. Leave King's Head
3 p.m. Visit Loughborough General Hospital
3.30 p.m. Visit Brush Works, Nottingham Road
4.30 p.m. Tea, King's Head
6.30 p.m. Arrive Loughborough Theatre
6.45 p.m. Personal appearance on stage
7.15 p.m. Return to King's Head Hotel
9 p.m. Attend staff dance and party at Loughborough General Hospital
1 a.m. Bed.

Having met hundreds of people on a daily basis, Margaret began to 'appreciate what the life of royalty must be like. Constant crowds awaiting you; the last-minute touch-ups you must always give to your appearance before you alight from a train or car; the smile that must always show people how pleased you are to see them; and always the nervousness of facing them'.[23] One woman, whom Margaret and Theo thought to be an enthusiastic fan, ran alongside their car for such a long time that he urged Margaret to lower the window and speak to her. Having done so, the woman bellowed: 'I'm an Anna Neagle fan!'

A close contender to Margaret as the war years drew to a close, Anna Neagle had usurped her in official polls, then of little consequence as previous public polls had kept her at the top. However, as the public votes were cast to name their favourite star of the screen, it was not Margaret whom they chose, but Neagle. Margaret, for the first time, was ranked at second place.

With the suspension over, Margaret returned to the studio with a year's work ahead of her. Rank had promised Margaret the coveted role of Mary Magdalene in an eponymous biblical biopic. She was full of optimism for the part – 'a magnificent opportunity' – and was deflated when the film became postponed due to script rewrites and was eventually abandoned. Instead, she was given another part, that of Lydia in a film based on the 1941 novel by Flora Sandstrom, *Madness of the Heart.*

The story was adapted for the screen by Charles Bennett, who was also making his directorial debut. Best known as a screenwriter for his collaborations with Alfred Hitchcock during the 1930s, including *The Man Who Knew Too Much*, *The 39 Steps* and *Young and Innocent*, the studio anticipated a similar atmospheric style with *Madness of the Heart.* And, further hoping to capture the success of their past melodramas, the film was produced under Two Cities (also part of Independent Producers Ltd), which had been absorbed by Rank.

On paper, the plot had the makings of a wartime Gainsborough melodrama. Margaret's character of Lydia is gradually losing her sight and she enters a convent so as not to burden Paul, the man she loves. Years later, Paul discovers the truth and rescues her from the convent, whereupon he marries her and they move into his family's chateau in the south of France. At the chateau, Lydia unwittingly becomes the victim of Verity, who is in love with Paul; through a series of sinister tricks, she plots Lydia's 'accidental' death.

It was a calculated move, Margaret thought, on Rank's behalf to get revenge for *Roses for Her Pillow*. The studio could not understand Margaret's complaints, as she had not been saddled with the role of the villain. That role was given to Kathleen Byron; it also happened to be the most interesting part. And, like their onscreen characters, Byron herself disliked Margaret. She accused Margaret of flexing her muscles as the Queen Bee of the studio, demanding that Byron's close-ups 'be confined to those that showed her angular features distorted by frustration and anger'.[24] It was not only Byron who spoke of this side of Margaret: some (unnamed) actresses who were on the lower scale of the pecking order at Gainsborough and Rank claimed that she had a reputation for being a 'no nonsense woman [who was] very protective of her star image', and it was said that she 'liked to rule the roost'.[25]

However, Patricia Roc, having co-starred with Margaret three times, contradicted those anonymous claims. Far from being 'difficult', she said, 'Working with [Margaret] was a joy. I adored her.'[26] And Charles Bennett added, 'She was beautiful to work with, she was adorable. There was nothing you couldn't do with Margaret. I mean any inflection you wanted was always there, she was utterly divine. But the story was so awful.'[27]

Aside from Margaret's unhappiness with her character, she was also frustrated by the studio's makeover to transform her into the role of Lydia. The wardrobe was a poor imitation of Dior's New Look, which heralded longer hemlines – 'I hate longer dresses… I think they're ridiculous,'[28] she protested. She was not pleased, and it showed on film.

After fifty-five days of shooting on location in the south of France and at the Denham Film Studios, *Madness of the Heart* was screened for the Rank studio bosses. Upon viewing the rushes, they realised they had committed a grave error in casting Margaret in the film. They had completely misused their star; they had portrayed her as the pathetic victim rather than the protagonist who moved the story along. She was outshone by Kathleen Byron; and the makeover, they concurred, was far from flattering. To save themselves and their star's reputation, the film was not screened for critics, nor did it have a London premiere. Charles Bennett echoed Rank's reaction when he said: '*Madness of the Heart* was such a horrible thing... I wanted to throw up. Everything was right about it except the story, which was awful.'[29]

Instead, the film had a semi-official opening in Blackpool at the height of the 1949 holiday season. Fortunately for Margaret, earlier in the year, her public had rallied to *Cardboard Cavalier* in a bid to prove the critics wrong, transforming it from a critical disaster into a respectable commercial hit. And now they flocked to *Madness of the Heart*. Aware that her success relied upon the loyalty of her fans, Margaret repaid their kindness by travelling up to Blackpool to attend the premiere, where the crowds had lined the three-mile route from her hotel to the cinema.

To the studio's surprise, *Madness of the Heart* was a box office hit and far more successful than any of the Two Cities films of that period, including the Academy Award-winning *Hamlet*, directed by and starring Laurence Olivier, the year before.

However, it meant little to Margaret's career as a film actress. Her mind was already fixed on the theatre and its applause.

17
INTERVAL

FOLLOWING THE LACK of quality scripts being presented to her, Margaret made the decision to expand her horizons and explore the prospect of a theatrical career. She implored Herbert to find her a good stage play; and, although he was wary of the venture, he approached one of the West End's most successful impresarios, Henry Sherek.

A shrewd businessman, Sherek was renowned for taking risks, apparent in his production repertoire which often veered from the conventional. This approach benefited Margaret, for Sherek could see the potential where Herbert could not, and he instantly recognised the commercial possibilities of placing her name above a theatre marquee. Although he was aware of Margaret's ambition to reprise the role of Eliza Doolittle in a stage production of *Pygmalion*, he explained that it was out of the question. George Bernard Shaw's copyright limitations and Gertrude Lawrence's option on the play made it impossible for a production with Margaret to go ahead. When he broke the news to her during a lunchtime meeting at the Ritz, she was far from understanding. 'Then what the hell are we sitting here for?' she asked. 'We're wasting our time!'[1] He suggested that she telephone Gertrude Lawrence to gauge whether she would surrender her option on the play. 'She's very nice,' he told her. 'She won't mind.'[2] Lawrence 'did not mind', but her answer was a firm no.

However, it was not all bad news. Between them, Herbert and Sherek had come up with the idea of reviving Noël Coward's high-society comedy *Private Lives*, based on the real-life, turbulent marriage between Lord and Lady Castlerosse. A scandalous play when written in 1930, it remained a daring production for a 1940s audience. The plot revolved around Amanda and her new husband Victor, who are on honeymoon when she unexpectedly encounters her former husband, Elyot, and his new wife, Sybil. The divorced spouses run away together to Amanda's flat in Paris, where they not only reconcile but relive their past arguments which were fuelled by jealously and infidelity. It was a clever choice, they assured Margaret, for the flamboyant role of Amanda was 'virtually foolproof'. Though confident in her ability as an actress, they knew the character was not without its complexities: Amanda was spoilt, waspish, and, above all else, immoral. Won over by their idea, she readily made herself available for a long tour and the prospect of a West End run.

It had been thirteen years since Margaret last appeared in the theatre and, as her celebrity was attached to film acting, they agreed to judge the public's response by taking the play on a sixteen-week tour. If successful, it would have a West End opening. The biggest challenge, Herbert and Sherek discovered, was helping Margaret to forget the technique of film acting, which she had likened to a patchwork quilt, and to embrace the continuity of a play. Although she agreed with their constructive criticism, she began to question if she ought to do the play at all. 'I was risking my reputation,' she said of the venture. 'Would I be a flop? The thought worried me.' Recalling the experience, she wrote:

> I felt unsure as, on the morning of the first rehearsal, I drove to the theatre dressed in an old pair of slacks and hoping no one on earth would recognise me. As the stage door clicked behind me something happened. The narrow corridors, the faint musky smell from the fire curtain, the dusty wings, the empty, depressing gloom... they were all familiar. I walked towards the little group of people out there – waiting for me on the *stage*. How could I have stayed away from it so long? I felt as though I had come home again, and that was wonderful.[3]

The tour of *Private Lives* commenced in April 1949, opening at every prestigious theatre in towns and cities across Britain. As Sherek predicted, with Margaret's name above the marquee, the play sold out. It was reminiscent of a film premiere, with fans waiting outside the hotels where she stayed, lining the street in the hope of catching a glimpse of her, and besieging her at the stage door following each performance. On each opening night, at a new theatre, she found herself 'shaking like an aspen leaf', petrified at the thought of going on stage and facing a live audience. 'But how I loved the life,' she wrote. 'The fresh towns, the fresh theatres, the new audiences every night, and the camaraderie of working and travelling with the company.'[4]

Accustomed to the public's attention, Margaret appeared to take their enthusiasm in her stride, but privately she was elated; though, as she had learned from film acting, she could not please everyone and some cynical theatre-goers dismissed the production as 'a film actress having a "try out" on the stage'.[5] The majority of reviews were flattering, the box office receipts exceeded Henry Sherek's expectations, and Herbert was satisfied that the gamble had been worth it.

For the play's final performance in Brighton, Noël Coward graced the theatre with his presence. 'Charabancs of hate, dear, will descend on us now,' crowed her co-star, Peter Graves. That, Margaret knew, was theatre-talk for the fact that all of one's professional colleagues swoop down to Brighton when a well-known play with a well-known cast arrives, only to criticise it. She was right: for what Coward saw on stage did not please him, and he harboured a degree of resentment towards the leading lady. 'Margaret Lockwood looked charming but cannot act comedy,' he wrote in his diary. And, casting a critical eye over the production, he was further infuriated by the visual distortion of his work. The set was 'hideous', and he complained that 'the whole thing has all the chic of a whist drive in Tulse Hill'.[6] It did not quell his fury when the director, Daphne Rye, tampered with his dialogue. The original play had made reference to the Duke of Westminster's yacht and, at that moment, gossip columnists were reporting on Stewart Granger's yacht on which he was sailing around the Mediterranean. Thus, as a stylish joke for contemporary audiences, Rye substituted the Duke's name with Granger's. The audience roared with laughter at the topical reference, but Coward did not.

During the interval, Coward rushed backstage and berated Rye for taking liberties with his dialogue. Having left the director in no doubt of his feelings, he called on Margaret in her dressing room. To Margaret's disappointment, he advised her that it would be wise to avoid a West End opening. He did not elaborate on his reasoning, nor did he comment on her acting. And, as he departed, Coward warned Henry Sherek not to bring the play to London. Respecting Coward's wishes, Sherek broke the news to the cast. Despite the play being a commercial success, it was destined to close in Brighton. Margaret, who had been anticipating a West End opening, was bitterly disappointed.

Five months after the provincial tour of *Private Lives*, Margaret was offered 'an opportunity of a lifetime'. The role was that of Peter in the Scala Theatre's Christmas run of *Peter Pan*. Not many names could fill a two-thousand-seat theatre, let alone attract a sell-out audience for Sir James Barrie's slightly outdated, nineteen-year-old play. Having experienced her big break, or almost, as Margie Day in *Babes in the Wood*, the Scala held a special sentimentality for her, and she told Herbert to accept.

Immersing herself in the role of the immortal boy, Margaret ordered her hairdresser to cut her shoulder-length hair into a short, boyish style. With her makeover complete, she set out to learn the technicalities of taking off on a zip wire and landing gracefully on her marker. 'The first time you ever do it, it is simply marvellous, a most thrilling experience, quite as thrilling as seeing it,' she said. The choreography was made up of the Kirby's flying ballet, and, although a trained dancer, she found it to be the 'most physically demanding' role she had played.

The strain was not apparent, and Margaret triumphed in the role, breaking all box office records in the history of the play. With the success of *Private Lives*, regardless of Coward sabotaging a West End opening, and now *Peter Pan*, she had given her career and confidence a much-needed lift.

Another member of the Lockwood family was paving a stage career of her own. For some time, since they had shared their first scene together in *Hungry Hill*, and later *The White*

Unicorn, the idea of a stage career for Toots had not been far from Margaret's mind.[7] This had been confirmed when she brought Toots along to the rehearsals of *Peter Pan*, where the eight-year-old child watched in awe as her mother flew through the air. 'I could see myself in her all over again,' Margaret said.

A frequent visitor to the studios, as Toots grew older she came to accept them 'as quite ordinary places'.[8] But Stewart Granger heartily disagreed with Margaret inviting her daughter into her professional life. He accused her of 'ruining Toots's ideas of real values for life, if she accepts film studios as ordinary places now. Film studios, my dear Margaret, are not ordinary places. They are gilded palaces: they are sinks of iniquity; they are devoted to artifice and not reality'.[9]

Ignoring Granger's criticism, and seeing that Toots thrived in this type of environment, Margaret enrolled her as a full-time pupil at the Cone Dancing School, though by 1949 it had been renamed the Cone-Rippon School, later becoming the Arts Educational Schools. Its new name was the only difference, for the old spirit of the school still existed, and Miss Cone, Margaret's former dance teacher, continued to give lessons. 'Just for dancing lessons first…' Margaret warned Miss Cone. And, recalling how Margaret herself had started with *just* dancing lessons, Miss Cone mirthfully replied, 'Yes, just dancing lessons first, Margaret.'

As Miss Cone predicted, the dancing lessons extended to acting lessons, and Margaret realised that it was too late to stifle her ambitious daughter, for she showed genuine talent. However, she was to discover that Rupert was not enthusiastic about Toots pursuing a stage career at such a young age; and he found an unexpected ally, though from afar, in his estranged mother-in-law, for Margaret Evelyn, too, disapproved of Toots following in Margaret's footsteps: an ironic stance given her support when Margaret was a child performer. Perhaps, remembering how hard Margaret worked from a young age, she wished for Toots to enjoy her childhood. But, as Margaret pointed out, '[She] did not approve of anything I planned for Toots even to the smallest detail. She did not like the shoes I bought for her, the way in which I dressed her. And always, she said so.' [10]

*

After her success in the theatre, Margaret returned to the studio to film *Highly Dangerous*. The plot appeared to be the type of picture she had been begging Rank to let her try: a light, original comedy-thriller in the style of *The Lady Vanishes* and *Night Train to Munich*.

Scripted by 'master of the genre' Eric Ambler, it was a spoof of the popular BBC serial, *Dick Barton Special Agent*. A departure from her usual villainous roles and period pieces, Margaret played an entomologist who is recruited by the British government for a secret mission to an (unnamed) Eastern European communist country to investigate whether or not insects are being used for bacteriological warfare. Kidnapped and given a truth drug, she takes on the 'do-or die' hero, steals the insects, blows up the research plant and outruns a police chase. Her leading man, Dane Clark, had come over from Hollywood and, with this touch of international glamour, Margaret anticipated the film would be a sophisticated production and, more importantly, a hit.

With Margaret having been absent from films for eighteen months, and in spite of her stage successes, the press were sharpening their pens for a course of 'Lockwood-baiting'. Critics, too, fuelled speculation about her absence from the screen, claiming it had been due to the calibre of her recent film work. There was an ounce of truth in their assumption. Indeed, she longed for the type of reviews she had received from *The Stars Look Down* and *Night Train to Munich.*

One observant journalist pointed out that Margaret had been the victim of bad directing, rather than bad acting. Eve Patrick, an influential writer from the *Daily Express*, leapt to her defence when she wrote:

> I come not to bury Margaret Lockwood but to praise her. If there's any toe-stamping to be done in this column today, Miss Lockwood's already much-trodden toes are immune. Instead, this is aimed at all those who have been hurling unpleasantries at her ever since she graduated from a sweet young thing to Britain's No. 1 film star. For too long now has Miss Lockwood been a sitting target and general Aunt Sally for every would-be wisecracker. Too many personal appearances, too many guest spots in radio programmes, too many posed photographs. Her employers worked her too hard and too often in the wrong kind of pictures... But a word to those critics. When you gave her the rave reviews ten or more years ago they were for her performance in a film called *Bank Holiday*. The director of it was a young man named Carol Reed. Couldn't this imply that you've been shooting at the pianist instead of the offending singer? Isn't there a chance that Margaret Lockwood, well directed in a good picture, could yet prove herself acceptable to you critics as well as to the public?

While it was true that Rank was mishandling their star, Margaret and Herbert were not entirely blameless. Often erratic in their choice of scripts, their judgement was not always good. They were too cautious about her public image and too afraid to take risks. Her mentor at Gainsborough, Ted Black, once said in relation to her onscreen image: 'There is a tendency on the part of cinema-goers to think of stars in terms of the roles they play, i.e. whether the parts are sympathetic or not.'[11] This was certainly true when Margaret opted to decline the more recent roles she had been offered. They were Terrence Rattigan's *The Browning Version*, and *The Woman in Question*, both directed by Anthony Asquith. Jean Kent was cast in both, and in both she received the best notices of her career.

In hindsight, Margaret regretted her refusal to star in *The Woman in Question*. 'I was wrong to turn it down,'[12] she said. But at the time, she had more pressing matters to deal with. Rupert was suing her for divorce.

*

Before they had agreed to a separation, Margaret and Rupert had been living apart for nine years. Although Margaret had no intention of remarrying, she had sensed a divorce from Rupert would be a long time coming. However, as much as she welcomed it, she was worried how the surrounding publicity might affect Toots. She consulted with her lawyers, who advised her not to fight Rupert regardless of the grounds he cited (he was to claim desertion), pointing out that an undefended suit would not be reported in the newspapers. And then, her world came to a crashing halt: Rupert was also suing her for custody of Toots.

The divorce hearing, held at the High Court on 6th November 1950, was sufficiently handled and, as her lawyers predicted, it passed unnoticed as the press paid no attention to the petition named 'Leon versus Leon'. Granting Rupert a decree nisi, the judge postponed the custody hearing until a later date.

The following weeks were the worst of Margaret's life. In turmoil over the possibility of losing Toots, she worried about Rupert using her affair with Keith against her; she also recalled his disdain for her lifestyle and his recent disapproval of her encouraging Toots's career.[13] As much as her lawyers tried to console her that a child, if a girl, was normally placed with the mother, it did little to relieve her concerns.

In the middle of her legal woes, *Highly Dangerous* opened to dismal reviews. 'This film does little to add to Margaret Lockwood's reputation as one of Britain's first ladies of the screen,' criticised *The Advertiser*. It was a sentiment shared by many, including her loyal fans, who did not flock in their droves to support the film. It was a box office failure but its outcome did not worry her, for her mind was focused on her private life.

In the New Year of 1951, Margaret and Rupert met in the judge's chambers. She was prepared for the arguments Rupert would make against her, but she was unprepared when she heard the name of Mrs Margaret Evelyn Lockwood being admitted to the chambers. The presence of her mother, summoned by Rupert, pained Margaret as much as it baffled her. Why did she side with Rupert, a man she had openly detested for years? In order to get his mother-in-law on side, Rupert promised to fix her up in a house where she could live with Toots.[14] It was an arrangement that appealed to Margaret Evelyn, and the love she felt for her granddaughter surpassed any concern she may have had regarding the consequences of her actions.

When drawing on Margaret Evelyn's betrayal, Margaret herself had come to somewhat understand her mother's behaviour. Since the age of sixteen, Margaret Evelyn had borne the responsibility of taking care of others. She had been the parent figure to her own siblings, and then to her niece Betty; and she had raised her two children without the presence of her husband. By Margaret's admission, her mother demanded complete loyalty from her children, but that trust had been severed when she eloped with Rupert. However, with Toots, she had achieved that sense of love and stability in the form of her only grandchild. Her actions, as harmful as they were to Margaret as a mother, were done out of love for Toots. And perhaps, from her own puritanical point of view, Margaret Evelyn believed that she was doing the right thing; for, as she told Margaret several years before, the best place for Toots was with her.

Toots, as young as she was, felt torn between the three people that she loved most, who were fighting to gain custody of her. In her own words: she wanted to live with her mother, visit her father, and occasionally see her grandmother.

As Margaret listened to Margaret Evelyn testifying against her, all of the pain and resentment from her childhood played out that day in the chambers. Reflecting on her approach to motherhood, she said: 'The best mother is not necessarily the mother who is always with her child. It may be tough on the parent, but it's certainly better for the child. Look at it this way:

whether your parent is a film star or not, she may not be the best influence on you. She may adore you – but spoil you just for that reason. She may be over-anxious about you and build you up into a hypochondriac. I defend the female film star as a mother: she would probably like to see her child more than she does, but the child's all the better for having what I call disinterested attention. And, after all, a film star can at least afford to make sure her child has the best attention.'[15]

Ruling in Margaret's favour, the judge decided that Toots was to remain with her mother, and it was agreed that Rupert would still see her 'as often as he wanted'. Unlike Margaret Evelyn, who would have happily eradicated him from their lives before the custody hearing had taken place, Margaret never denied him a relationship with their daughter, and in turn he was devoted to Toots. With Rupert having settled in Chiswick, a short distance from Margaret's flat in Roehampton, Toots, who was close to her father, would spend the weekends at Rupert's house and part of her school holidays with him. When the ordeal was over, Margaret remarked that she felt 'like a small storm-tossed boat that has, at last, come safely into harbour'.[16]

As for Margaret Evelyn, the relationship between Margaret and her mother was dissolved in the judge's chambers. Returning to Delcott, the home her daughter had bought, maintained and signed over to her, she lived out the rest of her years on an income that Margaret paid into an account. Becoming something of a celebrity in the tiny community, she took a certain degree of pride in her status amongst the locals as 'Margaret Lockwood's mother', despite having no relationship with her famous daughter.

Three months after his decree nisi became absolute, Rupert remarried. Margaret, on her behalf, vowed never to marry again. 'I am dedicating my life to my daughter. She is all I have now. No woman can say she will never fall in love again. But for me it could never lead to marriage.'[17]

18
A New Venture

THE THEME FOR 1951 was a fresh start and, now parted from Rupert and Margaret Evelyn, Margaret asked to be released from her Rank contract eighteen months early. With no films lined up, or any career obligations to fulfil, for the first time in her life, since the age of eighteen, she would be free.

'Films have given me a raw deal,'[1] she said in an interview. But this was not entirely true. Films had provided Margaret with long-term financial security; and, having saved and invested her money wisely, she was in a position to become increasingly selective about future roles. She never had to resort to doing a film for the money – a luxury many of her contemporaries did not have. The departure from Rank occurred as the British studio system, much like Hollywood, was slowly dissolving. There were not enough roles to go round, and American stars had eclipsed the popularity of the British stars at home. And, from a business perspective, it was a wiser investment to cast an American star in a British production. The reality was that a lot of British stars, who once had the security of a studio system and frequent work, were now out of a job.

Without the obligation to Rank, Margaret had the chance to act in her dream theatrical role, that of Eliza Doolittle in

George Bernard Shaw's *Pygmalion*, at the Edinburgh Festival in August 1951. As it had been during the BBC live production, it was a 'severe test' for Margaret, intensified by her longing to play the part in a legitimate theatre – this production was to be staged at the Royal Lyceum Theatre. Her presence at the Festival, then in its infancy having only begun five years before, caused 'an atmosphere of mild crisis'[2] when the streets were crowded with fans who had come to watch her in the play. But critics wondered if the festival's 'artistic foundation' was as 'steady as it might be?' *The Spectator* wrote:

> This is the question that has been raised not so much by the musical programme (which must inevitably contain a great deal that can easily be heard in other capitals) as by the dramatic, and especially by the choice of *Pygmalion*, with Miss Margaret Lockwood playing Eliza, as the first play. It is certainly not the critics' idea of a 'festival play', whoever is to grace the production, and for that reason no doubt it is hard to resist the suspicion that the authorities had their eye on the box office rather than the ball, which in their case should be impeccable quality of matter and manner.

The pressure of giving a good performance in spite of the criticism troubled Margaret and, extremely nervous on the first night, it took several weeks before she got into her stride. Regardless of its uncertain start, the three-week-long production was not an unqualified success. The audience still demanded a curtain call, and she was well received by her fans. Critical response, however, was lukewarm. *The Spectator* wrote: 'If Miss Lockwood was a little stiff in the last act, a shade careful, a trifle stilted – why, this was admirable, turning those small errors of grammar and pronunciation into infinitely touching glimpses of the real world of passion and imperfection and poetry hidden away behind the smooth veneer of Shaw's icy comedy.'

When the festival ended, Margaret embarked on a five-month national tour with *Pygmalion*, lasting until the New Year of 1952. She played in the Midlands and all of the big northern cities, before the tour reached its conclusion in outer London.

*

During the years that Margaret reigned as 'queen of the screen', the newspapers and fan magazines had fabricated a professional rivalry between her and Anna Neagle. The fair-haired Neagle, renowned for her romantic comedies opposite Michael Wilding, was reported to have been Margaret's 'arch rival' in competing for the public's affection. Thus, it came as a surprise when Neagle's husband, the producer and director Herbert Wilcox, offered Margaret a two-year contract at his Elstree studios, dubbed the 'British Hollywood'. Reflecting the general belief that a real-life rivalry did exist, Neagle's secretary, Joyce Wright, recalled: 'Even in the studio there were people who expected the sparks to fly when Margaret Lockwood arrived.' Dismissing the rumours, Margaret and Neagle greeted one another warmly. 'These were highly professional, hard-working actresses. They never thought of themselves as rivals. That was just press talk.'[3] And, regardless of how many times they kissed one another on the cheek 'just to show there really was no enmity between us', the press continued with their speculation.

Impressed by Wilcox's 'no expense spared' way of running the studio, and attracted by the promise that she would have a say in the roles she was given, Margaret agreed to the contract. With the exception of Alexander Korda, she realised that Wilcox was the only British producer who had the pretensions to dare lay on the Hollywood glamour. 'He runs a film studio in the way most people outside the profession imagine a film studio is run. I'd never worked in such an atmosphere before,'[4] she said.

Elements of Wilcox's larger-than-life vision crossed over to his handling of the press when he announced that he was signing Margaret to a two-year contract. 'I am convinced that in Margaret Lockwood I have an actress of top world-star quality,' he told the press. When she signed her seven-year contract with J. Arthur Rank it had all of the echoes of wartime austerity,[5] but with Wilcox it was a gala occasion of bouquets, gifts and champagne (being a teetotaller she did not drink it), followed by a celebratory dinner. Enjoying the attention, Margaret recalled: 'From that day I was never allowed to forget I was a really bright and dazzling star on their horizon. They were going to look after me as no one else had done before.' She was also quick to acknowledge her former studio: 'I owe an awful lot to the Rank studios, but we have amicably agreed to part because of the difficulty in finding the right scripts for me over the past few years… I was not very happy about any of them.' However, there were suggestions that Margaret's age and brief hiatus from the screen could pose a threat to this revival of her film career. The *Daily Mirror* wrote: 'To be frank, thirty-five is a tricky age for a star to be out of films for two years. Let's face it: Margaret Lockwood is a controversial character. A lot of people like her, but a lot don't because they think she lacks warmth and ability on the screen.'

Margaret's first film under the guidance of Wilcox was to be *Trent's Last Case*. The script was adapted from E. C. Bentley's detective novel, first published in 1913, which had been filmed in 1920 and 1929. A whodunnit with a unique place in the detective canon as it was the first major send-up of the genre, it revolves around the murder of Sigsbee Manderson, a prominent international financier who is found dead at his Hampshire home. *The Record* newspaper assigns its leading investigative reporter, Philip Trent, to the case. In spite of the police cordon he gains entry to the house by posing as a relative, where he manages to learn a significant amount of information about the case from Inspector Murch, the Irish detective leading the investigation. Despite Murch's suggestion that the death is suicide, Trent is convinced that it was, in fact, murder. At the inquest, the coroner swiftly concludes that Sigsbee Manderson had killed himself. Trent, however, is given permission by his editor to continue his pursuit of the story, and his attention is drawn to Manderson's widow, Margaret, with whom he falls in love.

Directed by Herbert Wilcox, Margaret was cast as Margaret Manderson, with Anna Neagle's familiar co-star Michael Wilding starring as Trent, and Orson Welles was given the small but significant role of the murder victim. And making his film debut was Kenneth Williams in the part of Horace Evans, the junior gardener.

The wartime limitations of rationing, adhered to by Gainsborough, meant that costumes were often recycled from various productions. Margaret's oyster silk dressing gown from *The Lady Vanishes* appeared on her character in *Night Train to Munich*. And the costumes from *The Wicked Lady* ended up in a theatrical production, causing a mild panic when the American censors demanded it to be reshot. Thus, it came as a surprise when Anna Neagle announced: 'Margaret, darling, you're going to look more beautiful than ever before.' A Hollywood-style makeover was planned for her, and she was fitted for a wardrobe of tailored suits and chic evening dresses. 'I felt more beautiful than ever before,' she said. 'I have to grin when I think of this – but it was a fact.'[6]

However, the gaiety from pre-production became a distant memory as soon as filming began. Margaret's leading man, Michael Wilding, 'intoxicated and worse for wear', reported to the set to play the role of the detective, Philip Trent. Having only just returned from his eight-day honeymoon, he brought with him his new bride, the twenty-three-year-old Elizabeth Taylor, who stalked the set, her violet eyes possessively following her husband. 'He was on his knees,' Margaret recalled. 'He couldn't do a thing. He never turned up before noon and then he'd have to be given brandy or champagne to get him back on his feet. Poor chap, he was worn out.'[7] Wilding's blatant disregard for the cast and crew unnerved Margaret, and she was embarrassed by the newlywed's displays of affection, with Taylor 'keeping her hands off him only when he was called away for a take'.

With his production of *Othello* lingering in post-production and tempted by Wilcox's generous fee, Orson Welles reported for work and, as he had done in all of his roles, he insisted on wearing a false nose. Having not seen anything like it before, Margaret could barely conceal her laughter when they filmed together. But Welles could not laugh at himself, and he stalked off the set in a huff. 'He could be moody,' she said of her temperamental co-star. 'Some days he would just sit on his chair on the set and not say a word to anybody. No doubt he was worrying about his long-drawn-out production of *Othello*, which still awaited completion. Or maybe he was in love? At any rate, he was certainly very poor company at times.'[8] To compensate for Welles's absence, Wilcox planned to direct his double from behind, but the actor had outsmarted everyone and had taken his wardrobe with him.

The disturbances during production did not hinder the film's success, and *Trent's Last Case* was well received by the public upon its release in October 1952. However, critics remained divided in their praise of Margaret's performance and of the film itself. 'A placid, satisfying film,' reported the *Daily Herald*; 'British films are better than ever,'[9] wrote another. '*Trent's Last Case* is the first film where Margaret has quietly, calmly and painstakingly gone through her part and by sheer skilful acting made it hit right home,' wrote Leonard Mosley of the *Daily Express*. However, contradicting Mosley's appraisal, Richard Winnington of the *News Chronicle* ridiculed her appearance as 'glum suburban elegance untouched by the years'.

Still, as familiar as she was with the critics, Margaret admitted: 'Whenever I play in films there is always someone waiting to say something beastly, knowing only too well that it hurts, hurts, hurts.'[10] Regardless of the general feeling that it was 'a tasteful little comeback',[11] Margaret still had her admirers in high places. A few weeks before the film had its official premiere in London, it was screened at Balmoral Castle by command of one of Margaret's fans, the newly crowned Queen Elizabeth II.

After a brief holiday with Herbert de Leon and his wife, Margaret was given her next script for Wilcox. She was to star in *Laughing Anne*, a film adaptation of the Joseph Conrad short story *Because of the Dollars*, set in Paris and the Java Seas of the 1890s. An emotionally challenging role, unlike anything she had played before, it called for Margaret to portray a broken-down Parisian cabaret singer defunct in the tropics and torn between a crippled ex-prizefighter and a sea captain whose life she ruins.

Filmed in Technicolor, the harsh lights aided Margaret's character's ageing process; and, fitted with a red wig, the hairdressing department faded the colour until it ended up looking as ravished as her character. Reminiscent of *The Lady Vanishes*, the set was mostly confined to one space: a ship. Two American stars were cast in the film, Forrest Tucker as the prizefighter and Wendell Corey as the skipper, both of whom were contract players from Republic Studios in Hollywood. This decision, as opposed to using British actors, was made by Wilcox to give the production 'an international feel'.

The Breen Code closely monitored *Laughing Anne* and, as they had done with Margaret's previous films, they found fault. The offending piece of film was the sight of Margaret's naked back in a brief scene when her character sits up in bed. Prior to their objection, Wilcox had already cut a ten-second shot of Margaret swimming in the (implied) nude.

When *Laughing Anne* was released in the summer of 1954, the reviews 'shuttled between almost hysterical admiration on the one hand and sneers on the other'.[12] However, amongst the critiques were glowing notices for Margaret. 'She emerges as an actress of remarkable distinction,' praised the *News of the World*. 'The best acting of her career,' wrote *The Advertiser*.

*

Another career in the Lockwood household was beginning to flourish. The BBC television programme *The Shop Window*, in which a celebrity appears with a newcomer, had invited Margaret and Toots to guest star. Having spent hours rehearsing their double act, a producer queried: 'Oh, of course, she'll be twelve by the time the programme goes on, won't she?' Toots was only eleven and a half, and neither she nor Margaret had considered the 'wretched age limit' for child professionals. 'I do know how you feel. Remember how I've told you when I lost the part in *Babes in the Wood* and in *Alice*,' Margaret tried to lift her spirits. 'You'll get another chance.'[13] In due course Toots, who by then was twelve years old, did get another chance, and she received an offer to audition for the BBC serialisation of *Heidi* for the Children's Hour.

Margaret was also returning to television in George Bernard Shaw's *Captain Brassbound's Conversion*. With her own career in transition and Toots's just beginning, it was Margaret's turn to support her daughter. 'I loved the evenings when Toots and I curled up on the big settee in our sitting-room, me with a good supply of cigarettes, Toots with a packet of sweets and her beloved black cat, both of us working hard and having great fun at the same time.'[14]

To Margaret's delight and pride, Toots won the part of *Heidi*. 'You see,' she told Margaret, 'I was afraid I might not get it because you are my mother and they would have expected me to be much better than I was.'[15] Having auditioned alongside many talented children, Toots realised it was not an advantage to have a famous actress for a mother. Many were quick to assume that she had been given preferential treatment because of Margaret. But now Toots had the opportunity to prove that she could be an actress in her own right. Using the last name Lockwood, Toots was known professionally by her middle name, Julia.

The emergence of Toots's acting career inspired Margaret to reflect on her days as a child performer. Although Margaret Evelyn had always supported her career and accompanied her to auditions without complaining, Margaret could not help but recall her mother's method of offering criticism 'with the abruptness [she] used when she minimised everything with her favourite comment "rubbish".'[16] With this in mind, she adopted a gentler approach with Toots. 'Sometimes, naturally, she will give a better performance than others, and I reserve the right to be one of her sternest critics and greatest admirers.'[17] She also encouraged Toots to 'have her say', as she did not believe in the old-fashioned idiom 'little girls should be seen and not heard'. Margaret argued her point when she said: 'If you don't hear them, you cannot know what they are thinking and feeling, nor can you be as close to them as I believe every mother should be to her daughter.'[18]

Not entirely dismissive of Margaret Evelyn's influence during her childhood, Margaret said: 'It was my mother's constant care and perseverance that set me on the way to success. As I grew older it had been her intolerance and excessive possessiveness that had caused between us a rift which had only widened through the years.'[19]

Admitting that she was not 'one of those mothers who pretend to be modest about their child', if anyone asked Margaret how she felt about her daughter, she told them, 'To me, she's wonderful.' But Margaret realised that Toots had her faults, too. 'She is hideously untidy, she can't keep anything carefully for two minutes together. Put her in a new frock and she's climbing a tree in the next second; the dolls I had and treasured all my life were half wrecked after two days in her custody; and she can argue the hind leg off a donkey. She has what she and Nanny both call her "naughty temper" – but it is swift, tempestuous and over in a flash. She never sulks, she is never mean and whenever she is working she is always obedient and only too anxious to lend a hand to help.'[20] As much as she 'glowed with pride' when others complimented Toots, Margaret acknowledged that it was her own mother who was responsible for the early years of her life, and she could only take credit for the latter ones.

As rehearsals began on *Heidi*, Margaret spent her Sundays driving Toots to the set at Lime Grove studios. She did not interfere with Toots's work, and would discreetly watch a few scenes from the viewing room. 'I have stopped being nervous about Toots. When I went to the BBC and sat in the viewing room watching her in the first instalment with *Heidi*, I was almost violently sick with nerves.'[21] Confident that Toots knew what she was doing, Margaret no longer got 'into a secret panic every time she goes on the air' and would leave her to it, returning only to collect her.

Sensitive to how unforgiving the critics could be, Margaret anxiously awaited the reviews of *Heidi*. Rising the next morning to read the newspapers ahead of Toots, no one was more surprised than Margaret when she opened the newspaper and was greeted with: 'Move over, Margaret, your daughter has arrived'.[22]

*

As Margaret's contract with Herbert Wilcox came to an end, her third and final film would be *Trouble in the Glen*, in which she was cast as Marissa Mengues. Based on a story by Maurice Walsh, the film's plot was centred on an American ex-pilot, Major Jim 'Lance' Lansing, who returns to Scotland after the war to find much trouble in the glen due to the high-handed activities of the local laird. The laird, Sanin Cejador y Mengues, is a South American tycoon who, along with his daughter, Marissa, has returned to the land of his forefathers. Led by Lansing, the locals prevail upon Mengues to restore peace to the glen, but not before a fight between Lansing and Dukes, the Mengues foreman.

Modelled on John Ford's successful Irish-American production, *The Quiet Man* – also a story by Maurice Walsh – Wilcox promised his film would do for Scotland what Ford's had done for Ireland; although, certain that he had an advantage over *The Quiet Man*, which was filmed on a frugal budget on location in Ireland and at Republic studios in Hollywood, Wilcox spared no expense on his production.

Asking Walsh to assist with the location work, as he had done on *The Quiet Man*, Wilcox was taken aback when the author refused, citing that he disapproved of Frank S. Nugent's screenplay. Incidentally, Nugent had also adapted *The Quiet Man*. Having received a £4,000 fee for the story after two years of negotiations, and claiming that he wanted no part in the production, Walsh was further dismayed when he viewed the film, which he thought 'was not very good'.[23]

Wilcox announced that John Wayne was to star as Lansing; however, not entirely committed to the film, he dropped out before production began. Forrest Tucker, Margaret's leading man from *Laughing Anne*, replaced Wayne, and Orson Welles was cast as her father, Sanin Cejador y Mengues. As much as Welles and his false nose was a source of hilarity for Margaret, the sight of a white-haired, cigar-chomping Orson Welles in Scots kilts was far-fetched, to say the least. The critics agreed, and when released in December 1954, *Trouble in the Glen* failed to replicate the success of Margaret and Wilcox's previous efforts. 'A witless, muddled, inept comedy,' wrote *New York Life*. Shot in Trucolor – prone to give faces 'an orange peel look' – the cinematography also divided the opinions of the critics. Some found it superbly photographed, others thought it a clumsy attempt. One thing was certain: the public had unanimously avoided the film.

Having fulfilled her contract with Wilcox, and following the commercial failure of *Trouble in the Glen*, Margaret declined to renew their agreement. Reflecting on their partnership together, Wilcox said:

> I went to exceptional lengths in the three films we made together to find the deep, sympathetic understanding I had with Anna. Not Margaret's fault, I'm sure, but it did not come off. Perhaps Anna, with her fair loveliness, blue eyes and beautiful skin, plus her innate integrity as an actress, sublimated, both as woman and artist, my spiritual and physical needs and ideals, and I had subconsciously developed a blind spot for brunettes! It could well be.
>
> Whether the toughness of being at the top or the fear that the higher you go the harder you fall has any significance I cannot say, but seldom have I met a star, and particularly a woman star, who has enjoyed her success to the full and maintained a reasonable perspective.[24]

Wilcox's words, tinged with a degree of resentment, encouraged others to draw their own conclusion. Some (wrongly) sensed the animosity between Margaret and Anna Neagle was true, others viewed his words as 'edged with discourtesy' towards Margaret who had dutifully fulfilled her contract. Neagle's secretary, Joyce Wright, denied there had been any bitterness behind Wilcox's observation. 'Herbert and Anna were both great admirers of Margaret; I never heard anyone speak more highly of her than Anna. As far as any of us were aware it was a perfectly amicable agreement not to renew the contract.'[25]

Announcing her semi-retirement from films, Margaret once said of the critics who had the ability to make, and then break, a career: 'When you are in the "discovery" class they are wonderfully kind, gently demanding that you be given better chances and bigger roles, and in fact behaving almost like your press agents. But when you get to the top, beware. They bring a totally different set of rules to judge you by. They carp and criticise, and by this time are in full cry after another little Cinderella.'[26]

The deposed queen of the screen did not rest on her laurels, and Margaret occupied her time by setting a new record – for her sex as well as herself – in becoming the first woman to chair a panel on British television. *Down You Go* was a popular quiz show based on a crossword principle; and, being an avid crossword fan herself, it was a fitting venture. 'Margaret Lockwood conquers TV,' ran the headline on a *Daily Express* news story.

The series ended a few weeks later, and, for the first time in many years, Margaret took the summer off. She had lost interest in the film world, and although offers still reached her through Herbert de Leon, she turned them down. Where other actresses were hungry for work, she could afford to reject offers. With this freedom in mind, she looked to the theatre for her next role.

19
A Second Career

THE YEAR WAS 1954, and crime thrillers were *en vogue* on the West End stage. The force behind this latest theatrical trend was a relatively new producer, Peter Saunders, who had shunned his mother's practical advice to apply for a job in Harrods. His older brother, the director Charles Saunders, had worked as a location director on *The White Unicorn*; and, through his brother, Saunders began working as a studio cameraman, news reporter and press agent before launching a career in theatre production. Rising to fame two years before, he achieved success when he adapted Agatha Christie's novel *The Hollow* into a play. Following the critical acclaim with which the play was received, the author entrusted the theatrical rights of her works to him, and Saunders now had two of her plays – *The Mousetrap* and *Witness for the Prosecution* – running simultaneously in the West End.

An avid reader of whodunnits, Margaret cited Christie as her favourite mystery writer. Following his client's orders, Herbert approached Saunders and pitched the idea of commissioning Agatha Christie to write a play especially for Margaret. As Henry Sherek had done with *Private Lives*, Saunders could see the appeal of mixing celebrity with the theatre, and he agreed with Herbert that a collaboration between 'the queen of crime' and 'the wicked lady' was a clever marketing ploy.

At Saunders's request, Agatha Christie travelled from her home in Devonshire to London to meet with Margaret over lunch. They were mutual admirers of one another's work, and Margaret warmed to this gentle, silver-haired lady with vague blue eyes and a nervous voice. Christie, too, was charmed by Margaret and described her as a 'wonderful actress and a delightful person'. They spoke of Margaret's vision for a play, and she confided that her ideal genre would be that of comedy-thriller.

When Christie returned home, she began work on the play that would become *Spider's Web*. Modest in her approach to writing, the author, whose career had already spanned forty years, simply thought up the plot whilst doing the dishes. Although the inspiration had materialised during an ordinary task, Christie felt the full weight of her responsibility. It was the first time she had been commissioned to write a play for a specific star; so taken was she with Margaret, she also wrote a sizeable part for a fourteen-year-old girl, predicting that Toots might like to appear on stage with her mother.

Completed in the summer of 1954, the script of *Spider's Web* was presented to Margaret for her approval. Thrilled with the play, the character of Clarissa Hailsham-Brown – an upper-class woman 'with a vivid imagination who was not above exaggerating the truth' – had exceeded her expectations. White lies were the driving force of the plot, and they also provided the comedy, when Clarissa discovers the body of a man in her drawing room. Believing the murder must have been committed by her teenage stepdaughter (the role intended for Toots), she persuades two respectable elderly gentlemen and a young admirer to help her conceal the body, but none of them can foresee the danger and embarrassments that are in store.

To gauge the public's reaction, *Spider's Web* embarked on an eleven-week provincial tour, opening at the Theatre Royal in Nottingham. The northern cities gave the play a warm reception, and as it headed south to Oxford and Cardiff, the audience were calling for curtain speeches. Margaret travelled with her dresser, Gwen Bayliss, who methodically packed the star's wardrobe for the tour: evening gowns, winter coat, two hats, mink jacket, three pairs of slacks and shirts, three pairs of warm pyjamas, three hundred picture postcards ready for autograph hunters, hot-water bottles, influenza mixture in case she caught the cold, and half-a-dozen detective novels for her to read. Though Gwen appeared as 'a frail little creature' with her fair hair and slender figure, she guarded Margaret 'like a friendly dragon'. 'Now you'd better eat,' she would command Margaret; or 'You can't go out like that, you haven't enough warm clothes on,' or 'Those shoes aren't thick enough.'[1]

Although she had the company of Gwen, who ensured Margaret had her home comforts at whichever hotel she was staying during the eleven-week tour, she missed Toots. Remaining in London with her nanny, Toots was filming the television film *The Flying Eye* at Guildford, which called for her to leave home at six o'clock in the morning, not returning until seven o'clock at night. Worried that filming was too exhausting for Toots, Margaret asked Herbert and his wife to bring her along to a show. However, there was no reason for Margaret to worry: Toots was enjoying the work – 'no child could love her work more' – and she discovered it was her nanny who was flagging under the strain. Telephoning Margaret every other night, she complained: 'I'm not getting any housework done at all. And there seems so much delay that I'm wondering whether the film will be finished in time for [Toots] to go into her rehearsals.'[2]

The play was well received on tour, although, in spite of the audience's warm reception, the critics were not as enthusiastic as the public. Believing the audience had been blindsided by Margaret's fame, they were accused of overlooking the quality of the script, which the critics thought was not very good. *The Guardian* wrote:

> Tonight's audience evidently fell deeply for the wiles of Miss Lockwood. Artful finger on chin, or fluttering hands emphasising some particularly disingenuous point, she earns every word of the police inspector's tribute when he says, 'You haven't made things easy for us with your tall stories.'

Ignoring the critics, Saunders let the box office receipts decide the play's fate. And, ordering Christie to do a rewrite to reduce the flightiness of Margaret's character, he agreed to open *Spider's Web* in London.

It was a celebration for both actress and writer, for Christie had set a new record in the West End. Her three plays *Spider's Web*, *The Mousetrap* and *Witness for the Prosecution* were running simultaneously on the London stage. Her collaboration with Margaret was to run at the Savoy Theatre, and the casting of a film star in an Agatha Christie play had attracted a feverish response from the London press. The director of the West End run, Wallace Douglas, surrounded Margaret with a solid cast which included Felix Aylmer, her old co-star whom she famously murdered in *The Wicked Lady*. But for Margaret, the personal victory lay in her perseverance. For five years she had longed for a legitimate West End opening after the disappointment of *Private Lives*, which had folded on its provincial tour. She did not consider her turn as Peter Pan at the Scala Theatre as marking this milestone. And although she had fulfilled her ambition, she did have one regret: Toots was unable to appear in the play as she would be starring in the Christmas production of *Goldilocks and the Three Bears* at the Q Theatre.

As the opening night drew nearer, Margaret gave interviews to the press at her flat and at the Savoy Theatre during the play's dress rehearsal. Interviewing Margaret in her dressing room, there was little doubt that the play would be anything but a success, as every inch of the small room was filled with bouquets and telegrams, and Gwen surprised her with a huge pink-and-white iced cake. People were popping their heads around the door to wish her luck and, despite the first-night nerves, she seemed to be thoroughly in control of herself.

However, twenty minutes before her first call, stage-fright overwhelmed her: she could not remember her opening line, she did not remember her cue, and she fretted as she counted down the minutes until the curtain would rise. But, as soon as she stepped on stage, the first-night nerves vanished. She glimpsed Toots sitting with her nanny in the front row of the stalls, and she also peered at the audience to read their reaction. Finally, the curtain came down and the play was met with thunderous applause.

Margaret returned to an empty dressing room, where a moment later the door was flung open and a little figure in a white party dress and white fur wrap hurled towards her. 'Oh mummy, mummy, mummy, you were wonderful,'[3] said Toots; and then she burst into tears. Hardly had Margaret dried Toots's tears when Agatha Christie entered the room, fresh from the tribute the audience had paid to her as she left her box.

'What are you going to do now, Mrs Christie?' Margaret asked her.

'I'm going straight to the Savoy Hotel to consume vast quantities of food,' she chuckled. And, acknowledging their mutual feeling of first-night nerves, she confided, 'I haven't been able to eat a thing all day.'

Margaret and Toots had a similar plan of their own. Escaping through the crowd of fans waiting at the stage door, they drove to Les Ambassadeurs for a celebratory supper.

As much as the audience remained enthusiastic, the critics were contrary and could only muster a lukewarm response. 'As a whole [it] is the least exciting and not the most amusing of the three Agatha Christies now running in London,' *The Times* reported. However, a critic from *Theatre World* wrote: 'If this new Agatha Christie play achieves an equal success with her other two current record-breakers, it will be largely due to Margaret Lockwood... who dominates the scene with her unexpected comedy.' It was true that Margaret was the main draw of the play, or as *Picturegoer* put it: 'The public always spotted in her the magic qualities of a real top-liner.'

Commercial success aside, Margaret was gravely disappointed for herself and for Agatha Christie, who had taken a gamble with her career to write the play. She thought if the public were enthusiastic about her acting, then surely the critics would be too. Holding the view that they thrived on 'slapping her down', she said of their treatment: 'Persecution complex? I don't think so. I'm surprised I lasted as long as I did.'[4]

Sensing the critical response would upset Margaret, Herbert, who in such times acted as her friend first and agent second, asked whether she was disappointed. Answering as honestly as she could, Margaret told him that 'one is always disappointed when all the critics are not unanimous in their praise'. But she could not grumble; the play proved fruitful for both Margaret and Agatha Christie. The money invested had been repaid, and it launched Margaret's career on the West End stage.

*

Now an independent actress, Margaret was ready to accept film scripts that appealed to her. One project that initially caught her attention was *Murder Mistaken*, a screenplay adapted from Janet Green's successful play of the same title. However, after she read the screenplay, she added it to her pile of rejections without giving it a second thought. She did not care for the character of Freda Jeffries, a blowsy middle-aged barmaid, with her crass dialogue and blatant sexual attraction to a younger man, Edward 'Teddy' Bear. Edward, a pathological liar, murders his much older wife when he believes that she has disinherited him from her will. After escaping to a seaside hotel, he meets Freda and, having learned that she has come into money from the sale of her late husband's pub, he sets about manipulating her for monetary gain, without realising that she is falling in love with him.

Margaret was surprised, and flattered, when Rank's brightest new star, Dirk Bogarde – cast as Edward – pleaded with her to accept the role of Freda. After initially turning him down and advising him to approach Diana Dors instead, she relented and accepted the role.

Margaret was four months into the run of *Spider's Web* when *Murder Mistaken* – later retitled *Cast a Dark Shadow* – went into production at Elstree Studios. The early morning starts for filming, while also acting on stage at night, were reminiscent of her demanding schedule when she was making *Lorna Doone* for Basil Dean and acting in *Family Affairs* at the Ambassadors Theatre. At the age of nineteen, the ordeal had been tiring, but nothing she could not handle. Twenty years later, Margaret found it a gruelling task and one she did not wish to repeat. To restore her energy for her evening performance, she ferried around 'a comfortable stretcher bed' between takes, telling curious onlookers, 'I need every moment of my beauty sleep.'[5]

Cast a Dark Shadow opened in September 1955; and the critics, in a startling turn of events, lavished praise on Margaret. 'A first-rate salty piece of acting,' *London Calling* wrote. 'A commendable thriller,' reported *The Spectator*. Agreeing it was a 'brave performance', the *Evening Standard* wrote: 'The role is a triumph of talent over vanity. It reveals for the first time that inside the glittering star there is a real actress struggling to get out.' With her forty-fourth film, she had finally won the respect of the critics.

However, cinema-goers were not attracted to this less-than-glamorous image of Margaret, whom they found to be 'acting her age and looking it'. And, although the critics were lauding *Cast a Dark Shadow*, the public had avoided it. People were turning away from cinema in favour of television; and, despite the stardom associated with her name, Margaret was regarded as yesterday's film star. Regardless of the changing times, her peers still respected her and, in 1955, she was nominated for a BAFTA in the category of Best British Actress for *Cast a Dark Shadow*.

Such a response from the public would have troubled her a decade before, during the power struggle between herself and the studios, but not any more. She knew where her priorities lay. 'Now my home and my heart are centred on Toots. She comes first in all my thoughts.' [6]

In the midst of Margaret decreasing her workload, Herbert became Toots's agent and, under his management and her mother's careful guidance, she began to emerge as a star in her own right. 'I don't mind being known as mummy's daughter,' [7] she told a journalist. There was no rivalry in the Lockwood household, only generous support.

In the summer of 1955, Toots began work on *My Teenage Daughter*, a feature film that was to be produced and directed by Herbert Wilcox, and starring Anna Neagle as the widowed mother of two daughters. Viewed as a contemporary film which focused on social issues, it dealt with the generation gap and the prevalent issue of teenage rebellion. Sylvia Syms made her screen debut in the role of Neagle's delinquent daughter, Janet Carr, and Toots, now fourteen, was cast as the younger sister, Poppet. 'Everyone was terribly impressed with Julia; her charm, her professionalism, her beautiful manners. She was always making herself useful, running round the studio, fetching and carrying for people when she wasn't on call,' recalled Anna Neagle. And, full of admiration for Margaret as a parent, she added, 'I marvelled that Margaret managed to bring her up so beautifully while making such a fine career for herself at the same time.' [8]

Meanwhile, the press had been speculating that Margaret would take *Spider's Web* on tour in Australia and, whilst over there, she would also fulfil several theatrical engagements with a run of *Peter Pan*. Margaret herself told the press there was a ninety-nine per cent chance the tour would go ahead, but in spite of this she was not averse in expressing reluctance to go. When an interviewer asked if she was excited about performing in Australia, she replied: 'Oh, no, not particularly. In fact, I am extremely worried about the heat. I know one or two Australians and they've told me I simply couldn't stand the heat.'[9] The tour had only been informally agreed upon, and fortunately for Margaret, who privately regretted such an agreement, the deal fell through. In March 1956, *Spider's Web* closed after fifteen successful months at the Savoy Theatre.

Taking an opportunity to rest over the summer, Margaret returned to work in October when she revived the role of Freda Jeffries in *Cast a Dark Shadow* for the BBC under its original title, *Murder Mistaken*. When the production ended, Margaret and Toots went to the south of France for an extended holiday. With the intention of doing nothing for the foreseeable future, Margaret relaxed safe in the knowledge that Anne Crawford, the beautiful Rank star, had effortlessly replaced her in the new run of *Spider's Web*.

However, unbeknownst to Margaret, Crawford had accepted the role knowing that she was terminally ill with leukaemia, and within a few months she had succumbed to the disease, still acting on stage, at the age of thirty-six. Her understudy, Elizabeth Bird, stepped into the role and continued on with the West End run and the provincial tour. But in an unfortunate turn of events, Bird, too, had to resign from the role due to health problems.

With no other actress available to learn the part at such short notice, and unbeknownst to Peter Saunders, Herbert had telephoned Margaret in the south of France and explained the predicament to her. Always the professional, Margaret flew home immediately and offered her services to Saunders for the remaining weeks of the tour. 'I know of very few stars who would have done that,'[10] said an astonished, though grateful, Saunders. 'It was hardly the big time as the tour ended in Golders Green and Streatham.'[11]

When the tour ended, Saunders presented a new play, *Subway in the Sky*, to Margaret which he hoped would imitate the success of *Spider's Web*. Set in a New York penthouse and co-starring the American actor Zachary Scott as her leading man, Margaret played the role of an English tenant who shelters an American army officer deserter trying to clear his name for a murder he did not commit; and, having fallen in love with him, she begins to suspect him of being a killer. The play opened in Hull on 11th February 1957 and spent a week in Nottingham before opening at the Savoy Theatre to a 'warm and enthusiastic audience'.[12]

Indeed, there were elements of Clarissa Hailsham-Brown in the character, and the critics were quick to note that the play itself was a poor imitation of Agatha Christie's *Spider's Web*. '[She] skilfully suggests not only the attractiveness of the lady who has to lie her way from pillar to pillar but also a certain natural foolhardiness,' wrote the *Times*. Despite her leading man, Zachary Scott, being a Hollywood star, the play was only a moderate success; although, to the relief of Margaret – still determined to prove her mettle on the stage – the play garnered healthy box office receipts during its spring and summer run.

A new venture was on the horizon for Margaret, and this time it involved Toots as part of the act. Emerging as a professional mother-daughter team for the first time since they had shared a scene in *The White Unicorn*, they starred together in the BBC television play *Call It a Day*. Impressed by the high ratings, the BBC agreed to extend the role into a television series – one of the earliest examples of the television spin-off. Retitled *The Royalty*, it followed Margaret's character, Mollie Miller, a former Cochrane revue star running a small West End hotel while coping with the demands of bringing up her teenaged daughter, Carol, as played by Toots.

Acting in a television series was less demanding than a film and theatrical career, and the short turnaround in the production schedule gave Margaret time to write her autobiography, *Lucky Star*. Largely ghost-written with certain events misconstrued – presumably to fit with her public image – she ended the story on a confident note: 'Now I say to myself dramatically – I am the master of my own fate.'[13]

With this in mind, Margaret pondered her next career move, or indeed if she felt the need to pursue such a challenge. With her professional life in order, she reflected on her plans for 'Margaret-the-woman'. 'They were already coming true,' she decided, for she had made them a long time ago. 'I have built up a very comfortable and happy home life for myself and I am wholly contented with it.'

But the domestic affairs of Margaret-the-woman would have to wait. In the summer of 1950, when Toots had spent her school holidays at the Scala Theatre watching her mother rehearse for *Peter Pan*, she was made a promise that she had never forgotten. 'As soon as you're old enough,' Margaret told her, 'you shall play Wendy if we can arrange it – and I'll be Peter.' Seven years later, Margaret kept her word.

Although it was common for women to play the title role of Peter, never in the history of Sir James Barrie's play had a mother and daughter starred opposite one another. Margaret had accomplished her own record when she starred as Peter three times, more than any other actress had done at the time. It was 'an attractive performance' on Margaret's behalf, and the critics were quick to acknowledge 'tall, graceful' Toots's contribution to the role of Wendy, 'the little mother'; although *The Times* reported: '[She] makes rather more of that little mother than is sometimes done.'

Peter Pan would be Margaret's last stage work for a year. She was kept busy with numerous television offers and, although she had stepped away from film work, scripts still reached her through Herbert, and, as always, she refused them.

Theatre had become her passion, but the kind of theatre she was accustomed to was becoming unfashionable as the 1950s were drawing to a close. It would become the era of the 'Angry Young Men', a group of mostly working-class playwrights, in particular John Osborne, whose plays dominated the Royal Court theatre, which served as a catalyst for classical actors such as Laurence Olivier who adapted to this new wave of realism. But Margaret had no interest in adapting to anything, and she had no desire to become an ageing character actress. Thus, she chose to play it safe.

Peter Saunders respected Margaret as an actress, but he could not fail to notice the rut she was getting into. He thought Herbert did not always have the best judgement in scripts despite guiding Margaret to stardom; and, given that she was no longer Britain's number one film star, it was important that she remained current if she wished to be a bankable actress in the theatre, and to retain a mainstream interest.

He managed to persuade her to consider the script of Jack Popplewell's *And Suddenly It's Spring*, a different theme from what she was used to. It was forward-thinking and yet not too daring, as she felt her portrayal of Freda Jeffries in *Cast a Dark Shadow* was daring enough. It dealt with the story of a career woman who, at the age of thirty-five (Margaret was now forty-three), realises that love has passed her by. So, to make up for her lost youth, the character revamps her image with the hope of attracting a middle-aged lothario. Instead, she dazzles an American naval officer much younger than herself and discovers that she is falling in love for the first time.

Getting Margaret to agree to do the play was the easy part, as Saunders learned; however, trying to think up a clever marketing ploy was another matter. Rather than having a first night to debut the play, he came up with the concept of having a 'first afternoon'; and, far from being a gimmick, there was a reasonable explanation behind the bold move. Under ordinary circumstances, a first-night audience was made up of ticket sales representatives, critics and professionals who were attending by invitation. And since that audience was not reflective of the paying public, Saunders realised he had to attract the genuine public, on whom the commercial success of a play is dependent.

This unique plan only partly paid off, and the first afternoon of the play's premiere at the Duke of York's Theatre attracted a lot of valuable publicity in the newspapers. But, as Saunders confessed: 'To my horror, I saw the same first-night faces in the same seats and the thought that they might be a better audience was quickly dispelled. The play went through in near-silence. At the end, as the curtain came down, there was some modest applause, but as it went up again there was the loudest booing from the gallery I had heard in any theatre.'[14] The outcome came as no surprise to the principal cast. Margaret and her co-stars, Yolande Donlan and Frank Lawton, had been against Saunders's idea from the start; though, ever the esteemed professionals, they carried on and managed to turn a disaster into a moderately successful six-month run.

Turning her mind away from the disappointment of the play's disastrous opening, Margaret found her attention was drawn to the young actor playing her love interest. His name was John Stone; and, mirroring her character in the play, Margaret discovered that she, too, was falling in love.

20
New Beginnings

There was a time when Margaret thought that life for a woman who was not in love, or loved, or who had no one to take care of her, must be inadequate and incomplete.[1] When she was under contract to the studios she never had time, or many opportunities, for domesticity or companionship. The latter, she knew from experience, was vital in maintaining a happy marriage. 'I have never been used to cooking a man's breakfast, darning his socks or expecting to hear his key in the door at the end of the day.'[2] But now, with her career moving at a gentler pace, she had the time to devote to a relationship.

John Stone was an unconventional eight years younger than Margaret. Their age gap – she was forty-three and he was thirty-five – appeared to be the only uncommon factor between them. Born John Hailstone in Cardiff in 1924, his early childhood, like Margaret's, was spent in India where his father, Major Hailstone, had been posted soon after his son's birth. Their acting careers, too, had begun at the Q Theatre, and after several years in provincial repertory he debuted in the West End in 1948 with a small part in a long-running play, *One Wild Oat.*

Thereafter, he was never out of work; and, despite finding his name billed at the bottom of the cast list, he was steadily employed by theatrical producers. A reliable actor, who never reached the ranks of stardom, John had built up an impressive repertoire, including a part in the original British production of Arthur Miller's *A View from the Bridge*. Twice divorced, he had first married at the age of twenty-one to a woman called Elizabeth Taylor, known as 'Blackie'. That marriage ended in 1953 when he met the Chinese opera singer, Lian Shin Yang. After living together for six years, the two married in 1959; but, with the artistic temperament of her profession, Shin Yang proved too volatile for John, and marriage only served to intensify her jealousy. By the time John had joined *And Suddenly It's Spring*, Shin Yang had resorted to stalking him during the run of the play at the Duke of York's Theatre. On one occasion, she stormed through the stage door and, to escape her wrath, John ran out onto St Martin's Lane with his diminutive wife chasing after him, trying to beat him with her shoe.

No longer at the forefront of public life – though her fans still maintained an interest in her private life – Margaret embraced the modern aspect of her relationship with John. His lack of celebrity appealed to her, as did his temperament: he was strong 'in a quiet, unexceptional way' and everyone liked him. Lacking an 'actorish streak', he respected her as a great star but he was not awed by her; and, with a pithy sense of humour to match her quick wit, he made Margaret laugh.

Maintaining the promise she had made to herself to never marry again,[3] Margaret further shunned society's ideals on cohabitation when she invited John to move in with her. Toots, now eighteen, was still living at home, though she would soon move into her own flat at Dolphin Square.[4] This new domesticity of a shared household sat well with Margaret, and in due course she and John began to look for a home together.

With the exception of Delcott in Hampshire, Margaret had never invested in a home, she had always rented; and, now in her mid-forties and in a stable relationship, she decided to lay the foundations for her later years.

She was still considered a single woman by the press, however, and the presence of a man in her life was not detected from interviews Margaret gave at the time. Her sole interest, aside from her career, lay with Toots, and this was detected when both mother and daughter gave an interview to coincide with the release of Toots's film, *Please Turn Over.* Printed as a feature article, it focused on up-and-coming actresses who were the offspring of famous parents; the other young woman featured was Jane Fonda, who was treading the boards in her first Broadway play. Directing the attention away from herself, Margaret focused on Toots and her merits. 'Toots is in love with people and life itself,' she said. 'She gives a lot and that is why she gets such a lot back.' The reporter was quick to note: 'Margaret Lockwood remains her daughter's best friend.'[5]

Taking a break from house-hunting, Margaret persuaded Peter Saunders to produce *Milk and Honey*, a new play which had caught her eye, and she set about developing it into a family affair with parts for Toots and John. The play opened in Newcastle upon Tyne in February 1961; and, unfortunately for everyone involved, not least Saunders, it was a commercial failure. The lack of box office success killed any prospect of a national tour, and the play was quickly abandoned.

The disappointment of the play was quickly forgotten when Margaret and John found a house in Kingston upon Thames, located on the far side of Richmond Park, which had been her back garden for years. Built in 1929, the house was previously occupied by an elderly brother and sister, the Clarkes, who had died within six weeks of one another. Miss Clarke was completely blind; and her brother, Wallace Clarke, who was an art teacher at Tiffin School in Kingston, had lost an eye in an accident involving a starter pistol. Together, they had one working eye between them.

When Margaret and John moved in, he set about designing the garden, planting exotic and unusual trees and shrubs which still thrive there today, and replacing the rickety wooden fence which divided their house from the property next door (owned by the Harrisons) with a sturdy brick wall which 'guaranteed any film star the privacy they deserved'.[6]

Although they were happy together, John could find Margaret 'imperious' at times. Perhaps this trait was the product of the independent lifestyle she had maintained for years: it was, after all, a period in which society and women's lives were largely dominated by men. And to some, Margaret, with her career and money – achieved by her own merits – might have been viewed as an anomaly. She acknowledged this side of her personality when she told a reporter: 'Toots is always saying to me, "You frighten people." [She] says, "You've got this don't-come-near-me attitude. People are very frightened of it."' Disagreeing with the assessment, she added, 'I spend my life being frightened, I'm so reserved and shy.'[7] Could she have shared more similarities with Margaret Evelyn than she cared to admit?[8]

However, John knew how to take the heat out of any given situation with a raised eyebrow and a gentle mocking word or two. Their neighbour, Tim Harrison, recalled: 'John was urbane, reserved and softly spoken, while Margaret was louder and more theatrical, but they gave every appearance of being a very contented pair who went together extremely well.'[9] Their neighbours certainly never heard a row, or raised voices of any kind.

*

At forty-six, Margaret was fast approaching an age where most actresses, especially film stars, reached the end of their career. Stars renowned more for their beauty as opposed to their talent simply faded into oblivion; or they picked up a minor role here and there, but nothing that could capture the glory days of their youth. Some, who had lost their looks, settled into character roles, and others disappeared entirely. But not Margaret. Although not a vain woman, she was fortunate that age and her smoking habit had not withered her looks, and maintaining her brunette hair and youthful figure – 'I think it's a pity that some people allow their figure to go'[10] – she was still very much in demand.

In February 1962, Margaret's run of theatrical bad luck ceased when she broke away from Peter Saunders and accepted the leading role in *Signpost to Murder* at the Cambridge Theatre under the guidance of Emile Littler. Though the mechanics of the plot were formulaic, the audience found the play to be thrilling, and in turn it proved to be a success at the box office.

Saunders bore Margaret no grudge for opting to work with Littler, and in the absence of their partnership he had sourced 'the perfect play' for her. It was *Hostile Witness* and it contained the same formula of crime and comedy that had worked almost a decade before in *Spider's Web*. The main character, whom he wanted her to play, was a barrister who was on trial for murder. The idea of playing a barrister intrigued her, but she said it had to be a conventional barrister equipped with a wig and gown, and not one on the other side of the dock in civilian attire. There was no wig or gown, and because of this she rejected the play.

Instead, she convinced Saunders to produce *Every Other Evening*, a play adapted from a popular Parisian farce. A dated comedy, somewhat lost in translation, it was about a middle-aged man (played by Derek Farr) who moves into his mistress's apartment, whereupon his wife (Margaret) and teenage children, one of whom was played by Toots, promptly join him. Its theme of adultery did not go down well with the public or critics; Herbert Kretzmer of the *Daily Express* called it 'the dirtiest play now on view and so dull, too'. He went on to attack certain parts of the play, especially Toots's character, a seventeen-year-old girl, who 'describes her seduction by an American sailor, but reassures her parents it was quite all right since the sailor possessed a manual on contraception'. And he was offended by the 'proposal that two men should "swop" wives on alternate evenings'. His complaint lay with Saunders, whom he thought a hypocrite, since only three months previously he had attacked the Royal Shakespeare Company for 'sweeping London theatregoers into the sewers of the city'.[11] Despite its moments of controversy, the play failed to attract an audience and it closed after a brief run at the Phoenix Theatre.

Meanwhile, Saunders predicted *Hostile Witness* would be a success and he proceeded with the play, changing the female role into a male role in which he cast Michael Denison. In terms of her career, Margaret had made a foolish mistake: the play was a hit and it packed the Haymarket Theatre for a year.

*

For fifteen years there had been no reunion between Margaret and her mother. They had not spoken, nor did Margaret care to make the first move in reconciling with Margaret Evelyn following her betrayal during the custody hearing for Toots.

However, Toots made an attempt to welcome her grandmother back into her life when, in 1958 and performing in Bournemouth, she called on Margaret Evelyn at Delcott. Regardless of the long absence and the bitter feelings which had conspired to keep them apart, none of the adoration between grandmother and grandchild had disappeared.

In many ways, their reunion was a poignant one. During this period, Toots helped Margaret Evelyn to paint the rooms of the bungalow, and they went outside to an outbuilding at the bottom of the garden where her grandmother asked her to line the drawers with paper. As she did so, Toots discovered press clippings and notices from Margaret's career. Despite feeling that her mother had never been proud of her, since she had never openly praised her daughter, Margaret Evelyn had saved everything.[12]

Sensing that her mother and grandmother shared the same stubborn nature, Toots approached the topic of a reconciliation with Margaret, but the situation had reached a 'stalemate'.[13]

For years Margaret Evelyn's health had been failing, and in the final months of her life, Lyn, who had since divorced his wife, moved into Delcott to live with her. But it was not her son to whom she turned, but her niece, Betty Lait – who, since the death of her own mother, had become a surrogate daughter to Margaret Evelyn. Moving her into the home she shared with her husband and two children in Bourne End, Hertfordshire, she nursed her ailing aunt through repeated cerebral haemorrhages until she died on 6th January 1965, at the age of eighty-three.

In the end, there had been no reconciliation or contact between Margaret and her mother. And, perhaps, given the deep-rooted feelings of hurt and betrayal, and the events that prompted their estrangement, it was, as Margaret had once said, for the best.[14]

*

Two months after Margaret Evelyn's death, Margaret and Toots were presented with good news. They signed a contract with the BBC to appear in *The Flying Swan* – a spin-off from their earlier series, *The Royalty*, with Margaret's character Mollie Manning once again running a hotel, the namesake of the show. Toots was also back in the role of Carol, now grown up with a career as an air hostess.

Upon airing, the first episode was met with positive reviews and high ratings. The episodes which followed were each formed as a self-contained story, usually featuring a guest star. Scheduled during Saturday night's peak viewing time, the series replaced the BBC's then most popular drama, *Dixon of Dock Green*. The show ran for the next two years.

21
A Revival

In the summer of 1965, Margaret reached a milestone in her theatrical career when she was offered the chance to play a classical role on stage for the first time. Since her audition for RADA when she had read the part of Rosalind from *As You like It*, she had longed to play a classical role on stage, but producers and directors failed to pick up on the various hints she had given in interviews. Thus, when she was asked to play Mrs Cheveley in Oscar Wilde's *An Ideal Husband*, it seemed her ambitions were about to be fulfilled.

The casting idea had come not from a producer, but from Dulcie Gray, a long-time admirer of Margaret since she had made her own screen debut in the Gainsborough melodrama *A Place of One's Own*. 'Maggie had been tremendously kind to me then,' Gray said. 'I was very much the new girl at Gainsborough and she'd made me feel welcome. There was a distinct pecking order at the studios in those days. I was fairly low in it, Maggie was right at the top. She found out I was living at Dolphin Square and travelling to and from work by public transport. After that she insisted on giving me a lift home in her car every evening. I've always had the most affectionate feelings of warmth for her.'[1]

The 'distinct pecking order' of the studio days was over but a similar hierarchy existed in the theatre; and at the top was

Dulcie Gray, along with her husband, Michael Denison, whose run in *Hostile Witness* had come to an end. The Denisons were using their influence to help two producer friends through an unremarkable spell in their careers. Peter Donald, who had launched Gray's theatrical career and later teamed her with her husband professionally, had gone into partnership with Peter Bridge, a brilliant West End producer. That summer, business was slow for them, and the Denisons came up with the suggestion to produce *An Ideal Husband* headed by an all-star cast. Gray immediately thought of Margaret as the beautiful, blackmailing Mrs Cheveley who, in the words of Oscar Wilde, 'wore far too much rouge and not enough clothes… always a sign of despair in a woman'.

However, Margaret surprised the Denisons when she rejected the offer. 'She didn't think Cheveley was a very good part for her,' Dulcie Gray explained, 'because she didn't appear in the final scene, and Margaret was used to being on for the whole of a play.'[2] But, as Dirk Bogarde had done with *Cast a Dark Shadow*, the Denisons pursued Margaret until she relented.

Margaret was not the only individual who had reservations about the production, as many of Peter Bridge's contemporaries thought he was 'mad' to embark on such a venture. Ignoring his toughest critics, he went ahead and added Richard Todd, Roger Livesey and Ursula Jeans to the cast. His sceptics had not realised that Bridge booked his stars on a minuscule budget, with each star agreeing to take on the role for sixty pounds[3] a week plus a percentage of the profits. Three weekends into the tour, his gamble had paid off and the production recovered its costs and began to make money.

An Ideal Husband was described as Margaret's finest hour in the theatre when it opened at the Strand Theatre in December 1965. Her voice, deepened by heavy smoking, had developed an authoritative tone, her presence was commanding, and her movements and gestures were contrived with poise and grace, all working together to portray an inspiring interpretation of Wilde's character. The play, as a whole, failed to excite the critics, but Margaret shone. 'Who would have thought the day would come when she would sweep on board in a comedy dependent on bubble-light wit?' asked Mary Holland in *Plays and Players*. 'Here she seems to be the only one to have real control of her part from the moment she swaggers on resplendent in strapless velvet, beauty spot and wicked lady hair-do. She laughs with menace, glances murderously, relishes her lines and plays with a high gusto.' Margaret's deliberate air of high camp served to contradict Noël Coward's dismissive remark that she 'cannot act comedy'. Indeed, she *could* act comedy, and the play ran for almost eighteen months, transferring to the Garrick when it had outlasted its year-long span at the Strand Theatre.

As much as Margaret was revered by the critics and respected by her fellow actors, her behaviour backstage confused even those who were familiar with her reserved nature. Richard Todd recalled: 'Everyone remarked on her dress during rehearsals. It seemed curious that such a big star and such a glamorous one in public seemed to care nothing for her appearance out of the public's eye. She would wear very little make-up, trousers and very ordinary clothes. I always remember her wearing an old black balaclava when we were rehearsing *An Ideal Husband*. The next time we were in a play together, years later, she turned up at rehearsal in the same old balaclava. We often stayed in the same hotels on the *Ideal Husband* tour but the only times I ever seemed to see her outside the theatre was if I popped into the lounge for a pot of tea. She'd sometimes be sitting by herself at a table doing the *Times* crossword. But she'd never offer to join me or invite me to join her.'[4]

Margaret's introverted behaviour concerned the Denisons; and, although she did not appear in the final scene of *An Ideal Husband*, she had to remain in the wings for the curtain call. They noticed her apparent anxiety as she waited to leave the theatre, and they would often invite her to supper with them; but she declined the social invitation. As soon as the curtain came down, she rushed out of the stage door before the crowds had gathered. Dulcie Gray remarked: 'I always had the feeling she wasn't a very happy person.'[5] However, Margaret's neighbours, the Harrisons, did not detect an air of sadness from her. 'She was just a private person, initially very shy of strangers, who led a double life as an actress who could effortlessly come to life on the stage.'[6] And, as much as Margaret puzzled her co-stars, she was not acting out of character or veering from her normal behaviour. She arranged for a pair of free tickets to be set aside at the box office for her next-door neighbours, Edwin and Miriam Harrison. 'After the show we went around to see her in her dressing room, and Margaret drove us both home, with me holding her wig on a wooden head in my lap,' recalled Miriam. 'She drove herself to and from the West End for each performance, and always took her wig home.'[7] Her appearance, too, was not considered strange by her neighbours and those who knew the private Margaret. At home, she always dressed in trousers, shirt and headscarf: anything but the glamorous superstar. 'It meant she could go to the local shops in the pale-coloured Rover 2000 she and John kept in the carport,' explained Tim Harrison, 'and nobody would so much as glance at her, let alone recognise her.'[8]

During the West End run of *An Ideal Husband*, Peter Saunders approached Margaret to appear in *Justice is a Woman*, a play written by Ronald Kinnoch and Jack Roffey. This, he was certain, would evoke a positive answer from her, as it fulfilled Margaret's earlier ambition of playing a barrister, this time wearing a cap and gown. But surprisingly to Saunders, who was producing the play, Margaret declined the offer because she wished to remain with *An Ideal Husband* during its transfer to the Garrick Theatre.

Although disappointed by her response, Saunders continued with the play and cast Dame Flora Robson in the role intended for Margaret. But Dame Flora became ill and was forced to withdraw from the play three days before its opening night. The understudy stepped into the role, but, as good as she was, Saunders sensed the play needed a star to drive ticket sales. Remembering how Margaret had saved the revival of *Spider's Web* after Anne Crawford's death, he appealed for her to repeat the gesture.

Curious about the play, and whether or not she should consider Saunders's request, Margaret dispatched Herbert and several friends to watch it. This resulted in two contrasting reviews. Herbert was in favour of the play and he encouraged her to accept the role, but her friends warned against it. In a rare move, she overlooked Herbert's advice and declined the role. On this occasion, her instincts proved correct. Constance

Cummings stepped into the leading role and the play arrived in the West End to unexceptional reviews. It eventually folded after a brief run.

Although frustrated by Margaret's refusal to star in the theatrical run of *Justice is a Woman*, Saunders was not a man to admit defeat. A few months later, the allocation of licences for Independent Television companies came up for renewal and the Independent Broadcasting Authority considered bids for a new franchise to cover the Yorkshire area. As a member of the consortium awarded the licence, his first contribution to Yorkshire Television was to suggest that *Justice is a Woman* be adapted into a teleplay.

His second suggestion was that Margaret should star as the female barrister, Julia Stanford, who represents an innocent young man wrongly convicted of rape and murder. This time Margaret did not decline, and the teleplay would later serve a purpose in reviving her career.

For every script Margaret said yes to, she had turned down a dozen scripts worthy of her attention. True to form, she pondered the offer and then declined because her old concerns of what the public would think had come back to haunt her. Herbert was of no help in persuading Margaret to takes risks with her career, for he, too, shared her point of view.

'I'm not on the breadline yet and I don't have to do rubbish like that,' she would say after reading badly written Hollywood B-movie scripts. On this occasion Margaret's judgement had served her well. The script which had evoked such a reaction was *L'Avventuriero*. Rita Hayworth accepted the role and the film had one single screening in New York before it was canned.

Another script which Margaret had been offered was Joe Orton's black comedy, *Entertaining Mr Sloane*. She rejected it, having been shocked by the explicit tone of the play and its crude sexual innuendos. Furthermore, she was horrified at the thought of playing Kath, a middle-aged landlady who lecherously pursues a young lodger. One scene, in particular, had reinforced her decision to decline – the scene in which Kath, in full display of the audience, removes dentures from her mouth.

Turning her attention to provincial theatre, Margaret accepted the lead role in *The Others*, a two-character supernatural play which began its three-month tour in Glasgow in June 1967. The play, which she described as 'very eerie and spine-chilling',[9] was about a married couple marooned by a snowstorm in a remote cottage where the woman (Margaret) keeps hearing ghostly children's voices singing nursery rhymes. The play opened at the Strand Theatre and, described by critics as 'limpid and morbid', it folded as quickly as it had arrived.

Returning to the guidance of Peter Saunders, Margaret opened in *On A Foggy Day*, a play in which the mourners at a funeral reception 'peeled away the veils of their own stunted lives'. The reviews were far from good, with *The Times* writing: 'Margaret Lockwood, swinging between surface sympathy and granite self-interest, torturing her vowels with the relish of an old music-hall queen, gives a magnificently vulgar display of middle-aged sexual aggression.'

After reading the reviews, Saunders questioned whether or not he should take the play on tour. He telephoned both of his leading ladies, Margaret and Siobhan McKenna, to gauge their opinions. Margaret was happy to cut their losses and abandon the play, but McKenna was adamant they should 'battle on'. Battle on they did, and within a month they were all out of work.

*

More than ten years had passed since Margaret had starred in a film, but that did not detract from her appeal as a screen actress. An air of nostalgia was firmly attached to the name Margaret Lockwood; and what better endorsement could there be than a much-loved film star heading a television series aimed at the age group who, in their youth, had flocked to her films.

Having been impressed by Margaret's portrayal of Julia Stanford in *Justice is a Woman*, Yorkshire Television developed the teleplay into a television series 'so crisp it practically cracks down the middle'.[10] Margaret's character was renamed Harriet Peterson, and a love interest in the form of Dr Ian Moody, played by John Stone, was introduced. Each episode was a self-contained story, and the character of Harriet was loosely based on Rose Heilbron: a pioneering barrister from Liverpool who was the first woman to win a scholarship to Gray's Inn, one of the first two women to be appointed King's Counsel in England, the first woman Recorder, the first woman to lead a murder case, and the first woman judge to sit at the Old Bailey.

Margaret's portrayal of Harriet Peterson ('an independent tough-minded woman whose career is the greatest part of her life') was groundbreaking for 1970s television. 'Most of all women like it because it champions the female sex in a realistic way,' Margaret said at the time. 'We shouldn't write women off when they are forty… surely you must be more interesting when you have lived and had experience? I know I am.'[11]

However, others were quick to dismiss Harriet Peterson's modern views, especially the fictional relationship between herself and Dr Moody. Dr Moody, the *Daily Telegraph* wrote, was 'forever slaving over a hot stove or up to his armpits in detergent for Harriet's benefit as if he had been set a penance by Germaine Greer'. And, launching an attack on Harriet herself, a critic wrote: 'She's a sort of machine at work, a weakling at home. A domestic failure, she is divorced from her husband, and son Michael only occasionally calls; and collect at that.' [12]

The viewers overlooked any negative views the critics expressed; and, believing Margaret in the role of Harriet, they began to write to her to ask for legal advice. 'It's very flattering,' she said, 'but actually I'm just an actress playing a barrister and I can't possibly help you with your legal problems.' [13] This surge of topical fan mail was an ode to Margaret's talent, for as much as she revelled in the role of Harriet, the legal jargon synonymous with her character did not come naturally to her. 'One had to sit and learn it like a telephone directory,' she said. 'Often I didn't truly understand a word of it.'

The crew were equally impressed by Margaret's professionalism and dedication to the role. Christopher Hodson, director of the first series, remembered:

> Margaret was a delight to work with. Years of working on the film set had made her a professional to her fingertips, and a lovely lady. She was the first to know her lines – very rarely asked if she could change them – always hit her marks, and in spite of frequent costume changes, she never held us up; in fact in the days when we used to record everything a scene at a time, over about a three-hour period, when the lights went

> up on the set we were about to shoot on next, invariably she would be in her position waiting. I don't think we ever had to even send the call boy to tell her we were ready.

As the decade progressed, it was not only the character of Harriet Peterson who had enriched Margaret's life. In 1970, she became a grandmother for the first time when Toots gave birth to a son, Timothy – the name Margaret had chosen for the then unborn Toots when she thought her child would be a boy. And, more than ever, the pledge she had made to herself when Toots was fourteen became especially poignant. 'I have made one promise to myself which I may find very hard to keep,' she said in 1955. 'That no matter who Toots wants to marry, I will never let myself become an antagonist towards my child's husband.' The man who became Toots's husband was Ernest Clark, an actor of the stage and screen. The bride was thirty-one years old, and the groom, at the age of sixty, was four years older than his new mother-in-law. Despite the unconventional age difference, Margaret was determined to fulfil her promise. 'I would do anything rather than split my child's loyalty and affection between her mother and the man she might love.'[14]

To Margaret's disappointment, as it turned out, the third series of *Justice* would be its last as the producers agreed the final episode should end with Harriet's marriage to Dr Moody; characteristically, it was Harriet who did the proposing. Appealing to the show's producers to commission a fourth series, Margaret nurtured ambitious ideas for Harriet Peterson. She should enter politics, Margaret thought, and become a Member of Parliament, eventually becoming the first female

Prime Minister. 'I said at the time, you don't have to keep Harriet Peterson in the law. You can take her out and into politics. You can even take her into 10 Downing Street'.[15] Six years before Margaret Thatcher became Britain's first female Prime Minister, Margaret's ideas for her character's development were dismissed as 'unrealistic'.

It was a bitter disappointment when Margaret learned *Justice* was, indeed, over, and she gracefully said farewell to the character who had been part of her life for three years. The exposure from the series had revived Margaret's stock with prominent people in the film industry; and, after twenty years since her last film role in *Cast a Dark Shadow*, she was entertaining the idea of returning to the screen.

*

When Bryan Forbes embarked on his ambitious, and expensive, production of the retelling of *Cinderella*, he had only one person in mind who could play the Wicked Stepmother. Possibly with an element of irony, given her reputation for playing onscreen villains, Forbes contacted Herbert to see if Margaret would be interested. Knowing her response to previous requests, Herbert forewarned Forbes that the answer would more than likely be a firm no. Still, Forbes sent the script and awaited Margaret's response.

Pondering Herbert's advice that Margaret would reject his offer, Forbes had been refining his skills of persuasion. For him there was no one else in the industry who could do the part justice. And, surprisingly to Forbes, and most especially Herbert, Margaret had read the film script with great interest and was impressed by the part – though there had to be one minor adjustment before she would accept. In the credits, the word 'Wicked' had to be eradicated, leaving her billed simply as 'Stepmother'. For Forbes, it was a small sacrifice to make.

It was an ideal part for Margaret; her role was small yet flamboyant, and she did not have the pressure of carrying a film. She would be joining veteran actors such as Dame Edith Evans, who was cast as the Dowager Queen, Michael Hordern who played the King, and Kenneth More who appeared as Chamberlain; as well as contemporary actors who formed the principal cast: Gemma Craven (as Cinderella), Richard Chamberlain (as Prince Edward) and Annette Crosbie (as the Fairy Godmother). Viewing it as an experience rather than a job, Margaret arrived on her first day of filming at Pinewood Studios and announced: 'It feels as if I've never been away.' It was a poignant remark, for forty years had passed since her accidental film debut as the second female lead in *Lorna Doone*, an event that had gone unnoticed by her contemporaries. For Margaret, it was a private victory as she had wanted nothing more than to have a long career as an actress. 'I'm still passionately fond of acting. I would never willingly give it up,' she told an interviewer.

The two weeks she spent shooting on location in the Austrian Alps felt like a holiday for Margaret, though she admitted: 'I've always been attached to every place I've owned and I suffer from homesickness when I'm away.'[16] And, unlike her theatrical co-stars, who had found her reserved and somewhat stand-offish, her co-stars from *The Slipper and the Rose* found her a delight to be around. Sherrie Hewson, who played one of the stepsisters, recalled Margaret had taken her 'under her wing' and became a sort of 'surrogate mum'.[17] The younger, inexperienced cast were intrigued by her star status, and they were impressed by her work ethic. 'It turned out to be an inspired piece of casting,' Forbes said. 'She gave a glorious performance, without any hint of parody or pantomime, and it was my privilege to have her in the film.'[18]

In the spring of 1976, *The Slipper and the Rose* was chosen for the Royal Film Performance in the presence of Queen Elizabeth II and the Queen Mother. The events of her film career had come full circle for Margaret, as thirty years before it had been her own film, *The Wicked Lady*, that had had a royal premiere before Queen Mary. But, as Margaret modestly dismissed, 'That's old hat.' After forty-six films, it was to be her last.

22
A Downward Spiral

In September 1976, Margaret entered her sixties. She was settled in her private life, her career had experienced a new direction, and she had a contented family life which now included Toots's three young children. With her sights fixed on the future, Margaret toyed with the idea of doing a musical, joking that she 'might achieve my childhood ambition now I'm a senior citizen'.[1]

Those who knew Margaret were quick to remark on her youthful appearance. 'I don't take pills – tranquillisers or vitamins – I don't ever drink booze and except for cycling, I don't exercise either,' she said in an interview. Her trim physique, she said, was attributed to her new bicycling habit, inspired by her grandson, Tim. When he was old enough to stay overnight at Margaret's house, Tim asked if they could go bicycling in Richmond Park. 'I had a bicycle that I'd bought during the petrol crisis so I went with him,' she explained. 'I expected dreadful things would happen and that I'd ache all over and my thighs would seize up. But I was absolutely fine and now we ride together often.'[2]

John was still in Margaret's life, and, after seventeen years of living together, their relationship was as good as, if not better than, a successful marriage. They continued to act together when the opportunity arose, and their latest assignment was to be a tour of Noël Coward's romantic comedy, *Quadrille*. Produced by Richard Todd's company, Triumph Productions, Todd was also starring as Margaret's leading man.

Observing Margaret and John's rapport behind the scenes, Cheryl van Hoorn, who appeared in a minor role, remarked: '[Margaret] and John appeared to have a good relationship, friendly and relaxed. He tended to send her up a little, but in an affectionate way. Sometimes she would lay down the law a bit and he would just raise his eyebrows or make some amusing remark or other. She liked to think she was the boss... and he let her.'[3] However, some detected a restlessness in him and, perhaps owing to the imbalance of the couple's earning capacity and their age gap, an air of resentment too.[4] He gave the 'impression he was just hanging around and wanted to be moving on to bigger and better things.'[5]

When the tour reached its final stop at the Yvonne Arnaud Theatre in Guildford, John fell in love with the in-house wardrobe mistress, Patricia Wingfield. But, at first, his admiration appeared to be nothing more than a passing flirtation. 'We all realised, once we'd got to know him, that he had an eye for the ladies,' said Cheryl van Hoorn. 'It all seemed harmless. He obviously liked women and treated them in a very charming way.'[6]

The play ended three weeks later, and Margaret opted to take a rest. But John already had his next job lined up. He would be returning to the Yvonne Arnaud Theatre to play Friar Lawrence in *Romeo and Juliet*. During the three weeks of rehearsals and three more of performances, John and Patricia fell in love. It became an open secret amongst his colleagues, and a common joke given the title of the play.

At forty-seven, Patricia was younger than John, and she was married with a teenaged son. Prior to working in the theatre, she had been a seamstress at Debenham's department store in Guildford. Like John's two ex-wives and Margaret, Patricia possessed dark, 'almost gipsy-ish' looks, and although described by her colleagues as 'fairly large' and not conventionally beautiful, she cut a striking figure in her dramatic clothing. Men were said to find her strong personality attractive.

They continued to meet after the play had ended, with Guildford only a thirty-minute drive down the A3 from Kingston. At first, Margaret was not suspicious of John's comings and goings, but he eventually broke the news to her. Confessing that he was in love with another woman, he left the home he had shared with Margaret and moved into Patricia's flat in Guildford.

The news of his affair devastated Margaret. They had been together for more than seventeen years and she had every reason to believe that they would continue as a couple into the evening of their lives. The decision to leave was not an easy one; John loved Margaret, but her idea of their relationship petering out to that of companionship as she reached her old age did not appeal to him and for a while 'he did his best'. And as his unhappiness intensified, he came to realise that he 'had nothing'.[7]

However, his new-found happiness was not to last: soon after he set up home with Patricia she learned she had incurable cancer and, with only a few years left to live, John forfeited his career to care for her until her death in 1984 at the age of fifty-four. As for Margaret, the only explanation she would give was that he had 'found someone else'.[8]

At the age of sixty-two, Margaret did not foresee the prospect of rebuilding her life. In her solitary moments, she reflected on the outcome of her personal choices, and on the career she had given so much to. In her later years, she felt she had 'made a terrible mistake' in having an affair with Keith and instigating a divorce from Rupert.[9] But as much as she reflected on what might have been, it was her work to which she turned.

As the years progressed and Margaret continued to work, the press began to speculate that she had not retired due to financial problems. 'I've not been daft with my money,' she dismissed their claims, 'but no one has come up with a scheme to make me a fortune.'[10] Reacting to their false stories, Herbert defended the reasoning behind her enthusiasm to continue working. 'The amazing thing about Margaret is that in all these years she has never once asked me how much money she would be paid for a part. She is always so interested in the role itself that the fee does not seem to enter her head.'[11]

Richard Todd's Triumph Productions approached Margaret with the idea of having her co-star with Phyllis Calvert in a revival of Noël Coward's *A Suite in Two Keys.* Originally staged as three one-act plays, Coward's original title and production had a third key, though for this production it was pared down to two, hence the title. In the first play, *Come into the Garden, Maud*, Margaret played Maud Caragnani, a widowed Italian princess who encounters an American millionaire on the night that his wife is holding a dinner party and is persuaded to elope with him. In the second play, *A Song at Twilight*, she played Carlotta Gray, the long-time mistress of a writer, who is summoned to his deathbed so they can share their final hours together.

It was an inspired piece of casting on Todd's behalf, and, evoking an element of nostalgia, the two leading stars from the Gainsborough melodramas were reunited (on stage) playing love rivals. It also brought Phyllis back into Margaret's life, restoring their old friendship that began on the set of *The Man in Grey*. As the years passed and their careers went in different directions, Margaret and Phyllis, although they had remained on friendly terms, had fallen out of touch. Attempting to bring Margaret out of her introverted shell, Phyllis succeeded in lifting her spirits, and they fell into a pattern of reminiscing about their days at the studio, 'exasperated but amused by mutual attacks of amnesia'.[12]

The cast and crew were aware of the John Stone business, but they realised it was a forbidden topic of conversation. Margaret never talked about it, but her colleagues realised that things weren't going well for her. Sam Clarke, the assistant stage manager, was intrigued by Margaret's star quality which she felt a paradox to her private self. 'She would walk around the theatre in curlers, with a cigarette dangling from her mouth,' Clarke recalled. 'Anyone who didn't recognise her would have thought she was one of the cleaners. Then she'd come out on stage, the total star. She was magnificent. I remember how much I admired the way she kept up this front, always self-controlled, always the absolute professional, always pleasant to us all.'[13]

During the tour, Margaret began to feel unwell, and at first she decided it was provoked by the stress and upheaval she had endured. However, during the play's opening in Eastbourne, she suddenly became afflicted with debilitating dizzy spells, accompanied by whirring and whistling noises in her head.

After consulting various doctors, they eventually diagnosed her as suffering from a viral infection of the middle ear known as vestibulitis, thought to be caused by a virus she had picked up from the seawater during a recent holiday in Greece. It affected her balance and hearing, and occasionally caused vertigo; Margaret said: 'You go whirring off into space – it's ghastly.' For an actress performing on the live stage, the condition was a disruptive element in her work life. But, although she struggled with the tour, Margaret never missed a performance.

Antibiotics cured the virus but there was little the doctors could do to heal the after-effects, and as a result she lost the hearing in her left ear. 'God knows what was reported in the papers,' she said when the press ran stories, exaggerating her illness. 'As usual they got it all wrong – totally irresponsible – I'd like to sue them.'[14] Responding to the false reports about her health, Margaret received 'hundreds of letters from kind people all over the country who had read the lies'.[15] Despite putting on a brave face, it was evident that she was under strain. When the tour ended, she retreated to her house where she remained for the rest of the year.

Toots and Ernest did what they could to lift Margaret's spirits and, in the process of moving from London to Somerset, they invited her to live with them in the countryside, where she could remain independent by living in a granny flat. She deemed the 140-mile distance too far, and she declined the offer as she wished to stay in London. 'The children love it there,' she told a friend. But she felt their absence deeply: 'I wish they hadn't moved so far out.'[16]

By remaining in London, Margaret could maintain a social life, should she wish to. She knew the area and her neighbours well, and company, if she desired it, was close by. Herbert was on hand to offer support, and Theo Cowan was a willing companion. Phyllis Calvert, in particular, was only a short drive away in Barnes; and the ladies would go out for the day, usually shopping or to a garden centre, where invariably one of them would be recognised and asked for an autograph. Amused, they would ask, 'Wouldn't you like Margaret Lockwood's/Phyllis Calvert's as well?'[17]

*

Towards the end of 1979, Herbert sent Margaret the script of a new play with a powerful and challenging role for her to consider. *Motherdear*, written by Royce Ryton, spanned thirty-four years and explored the turbulent relationship between the beautiful Princess Victoria and her dominant mother, Queen Alexandra, to whom she had sacrificed her youth and marriage opportunities to remain her loyal companion.

Renowned for writing on the subject of royalty, Ryton's earlier work, *Crown Matrimonial*, dealing with the abdication crisis of 1936, had caused controversy with its portrayal, for the first time on stage, of living royals. Although it was a success when staged in 1972 and adapted for television, his latest efforts were deemed unfashionable by critics, and he was yet to replicate the success of *Crown Matrimonial*. Before *Motherdear*, he had written a contemporary play, *The Other Side of the Swamp*, in which he also starred as a washed-up actor who picks up a young man in a public lavatory. Despite favourable notices, it did not open in the West End.

Although he did not immediately think of Margaret when he was writing the play, Ryton knew he needed a charismatic actress to play the part of Queen Alexandra. It was when he completed the script that his mind turned to Margaret, whom he thought was 'ideal' for the part of 'a strong woman, all sweetness and charm to people who were not a threat to her but wilful and demanding with those closest to her'. Still harbouring the notion that he could, once again, write a hit play on a par with *Crown Matrimonial*, Ryton predicted it would give Margaret's career a lift. A burly man with orange hair and a preference for flamboyant clothing, often in red with glitter and frills, he did not shirk from expressing contempt towards his cast. Not even a star of Margaret's calibre was exempt, and he said: 'For the past twenty years she'd been too cautious, encouraged by Herbert, doing little else but thrillers and routine comedies. Her regular fans were ageing – old ladies in charabancs going to matinees of her latest whodunnit – and she hadn't made any new ones because, to be frank, she'd become predictable and boring.'[18]

With her confidence shaken by recent bouts of illness, Margaret was hesitant to commit to the play. Herbert agreed with Ryton's sentiments that it would benefit her career and, under his gentle coaxing, she agreed to consider it. But as preparations began on *Motherdear*, she suffered an unexpected blow when Herbert, whose health had been declining for some time, died suddenly at the age of seventy-four.

His death would have a lasting effect on her. For forty-five years, he had provided her with emotional support, managed her career, supervised her finances, and 'cushioned her against the pinpricks of everyday life'. More than an agent to her, she called him: 'My father, my guide, mentor, and dearest friend. I miss him every hour of my life.'[19]

Phyllis took the initiative and advised Margaret to sell her Kingston home and move into a service flat where she would not have to worry about the running of a household. And, unbeknownst to her, Phyllis had approached their old Gainsborough co-star, Peter Graves, who lived at Dolphin Square, and they discussed how Margaret could be persuaded to return there. Nothing came of it. Then, Phyllis took it upon herself to see that Margaret continued with *Motherdear*, even though she had no interest in proceeding with the play. 'Bullied and badgered', she reluctantly agreed to see it through.

In an attempt to retain some control over the situation that she felt forced into, Margaret requested certain conditions and stipulations. She insisted on and was granted the right to approve the director and cast, and she let it be known to Royce Ryton that their deal was off unless the director she wanted, Frith Banbury, was available. He was, and with that obstacle overcome, she then asked for the rehearsals to be held close to Kingston so she would not have to travel into central London. A rehearsal space was found in Richmond, and the rest of the company had to make their way from London. 'We didn't regard it as a case of her being "difficult"; rather, knowing what she had been through recently, we all wanted to make things as simple and easy as possible for her,'[20] Ryton explained. However, at the eleventh hour, Margaret announced that she would not be touring in the play. 'A pity for her sake; it would have given her more confidence,' he added. A compromise was agreed: they would open in Birmingham and then bring the play straight to the West End.

When it opened in Birmingham, *Motherdear* received a tepid response from the critics. 'Miss Lockwood is not one of nature's royal consorts. The petulance of a wicked lady is not precisely the tone needed for the arrogance of a princess,'[21] wrote Milton Shulman. As a play, the pace was slow and the events were drawn out over a passage of time spanning three decades. Margaret, in particular, aged thirty years on stage. Her co-star, Polly James, who played Princess Victoria, was also subjected to the tedious make-up alterations and wig changes in order to make the ageing characters believable. Alexandra's limp came under much speculation, and having incorporated it into the play without explaining its relevance to modern audiences, Ryton was approached by a critic who said: 'Oh dear, Miss Lockwood has hurt her foot. Isn't it brave for her to continue?'[22] A reference to Alexandra's famous limp, which had been imitated by her admirers, was written into the play.

The audience's confusion and the hasty alterations to the script during the play's run in Birmingham should have been a warning for what was yet to come. When *Motherdear* opened at the Ambassadors Theatre in May 1980, it was a commercial and critical disaster. 'Instead of Coronation Street it is a Coronation Crescent... Curiosity about the goings on at Sandringham might just be enough to keep this undistinguished play afloat for a while,'[23] Milton Shulman wrote. The critic of the *Independent Radio News* echoed this sentiment: 'I thought, the curtain rising will take my disbelief with it in order to suspend it. I was still clutching it uncomfortably when the red velvet swished up for the epilogue.'

With his refusal to accept that it was his sprawling script, filled with historical inaccuracies (as many critics pointed out), which had been the cause of the play's lack of success, Royce Ryton placed the blame on Margaret. 'She needed a tough young director who would storm down and beat the performance out of her,' he said. 'Frith Banbury showed too much respect for her stardom.'[24] However, *The Times* praised Margaret's performance as having 'complexity... ranging instantaneously from charm to tears, baring a loathing of sexuality, then turning flirtatious for gain'. *Motherdear* ran for six weeks, defeated in the end by an inflation-imposed box office slump in the West End.

At the age of sixty-four, Margaret took her final bow on stage. She never worked again.

*

The following year, a unique service to the stage and screen was recognised by the Queen, and Margaret was appointed a Commander of the Order of the British Empire in the New Year's Honours of 1981. 'Naturally we are all delighted,' she told a friend. 'Our only anxiety is, will Toots make it to the investiture?' At the time, Toots was expecting her fourth child. 'It wouldn't really do for he or she to arrive in the Throne Room!'[25] Margaret joked.

Two months later, Margaret journeyed to Buckingham Palace to collect the honour. It was a family affair with Ernest escorting Margaret, accompanied by her three grandchildren: Timothy, Nicholas and Lucy. Toots remained at home with her new baby, a girl she named Katharine. On that day nobody had any doubt about her star status; she was dressed in a fur hat and a fur-trimmed cape, looking as glamorous as she had done forty years previous during her feted publicity tours for Gainsborough. After the investiture she was told that the Queen, a long-time admirer of her work, had spoken longer to her than to anyone else she had invested that day. 'I couldn't hear a word,' Margaret said. 'It was like one of the early silent movies from my youth. It felt like my second childhood.'[26]

Flanked by her three grandchildren, Margaret was photographed outside the palace. It was to be her last public appearance. But she was far from forgotten: the publicity surrounding the CBE generated a torrent of fan mail, with hundreds of congratulatory letters (mainly addressed to Margaret Lockwood, actress, Kingston) arriving from across the country. To help her answer the quantity of letters, Margaret's neighbour, Miriam Harrison, went to her house to assist with the 'deluge of fan mail'. She recalled, 'Every day the postman arrived with another haul. It was clear Margaret was still very much in the public affection.'[27]

23
Curtain Call

In 1982, the British press reported that Michael Winner was to direct a remake of *The Wicked Lady*, starring Academy Award winner Faye Dunaway in the role of Barbara Skelton. A favourite film from his youth, Winner had originally purchased the rights to *The Wicked Lady* from Pinewood's chief, Cyril Howard, for £50 with a promise to pay him £30,000 on the first day of production. With the rights secured, Winner hired the Irish novelist Edna O'Brien to write the screenplay; but, upon reading the finished product, he thought it 'appalling'. Then he attempted to write it himself, an effort which O'Brien dismissed as 'terrible'. When the film was in pre-production, O'Brien went to the Writers Guild and accused Winner of plagiarising her work. The case was rejected; Winner had not 'nicked her work': he had, in fact, copied Leslie Arliss's 1945 screenplay word for word, scene for scene.

Within a month of Winner's announcement, the BBC aired the original film and overnight Margaret was inundated with fan mail. Without knowing of the explicit themes of Winner's script, Margaret revealed little about her opinion on the remake, though she remarked to a friend: 'I wonder what it will be like, and if the press will say as they did of the remake of *The Thirty-Nine Steps* and *The Lady Vanishes* – not as good as the original!'[1] And, drawing on her own happy memories of *The*

Wicked Lady, she told the press that a remake would be 'fun'. But she did not take kindly to the rumours circulating that Winner had persuaded her to appear in a cameo role in his film. 'In any case, what on earth could he expect me to play? One of the dotty old ladies in it? Nonsense,'[2] she said.

However, Winner himself was determined to include Margaret in his publicity campaign, regardless of whether she agreed to appear in the film or not. He contacted Herbert de Leon's widow who had been managing his clients since his death. Giving him Margaret's telephone number, Mrs de Leon warned him that Margaret would not attend the premiere, nor would she leave the house. Despite this game of cat and mouse, initiated by Winner, he claimed they 'became great telephone pals', and that Margaret 'clearly and emphatically agreed'[3] to come to the premiere. He invited her to his house to have dinner on the night of the Academy Awards; and, following her detailed directions on how to get from his house to hers, he sent a car to fetch her.

To Winner's amazement, she arrived 'looking very much like the Margaret Lockwood I knew and loved from the cinema in the 1940s'. They enjoyed a pleasant dinner before settling down to watch the Oscars on television. 'It was like watching them with an old-time movie star who was utterly disillusioned and bitter about everybody and about the fact that stardom had passed her by,' he recalled. 'She made caustic remarks about everybody who got an Oscar or was nominated, or just happened to be in the audience!' When the visit was over, he remembered Margaret as being 'great fun, but boy was she bitchy!'[4]

Given the several erroneous facts he related about Margaret in his memoirs, his claim of their visit together remains dubious. However, what can be certain is that Margaret had begun to ignore Winner's telephone calls. The premiere was approaching and construction of a stage was under way at Leicester Square, and Winner himself had, perhaps, reacted too hastily when he announced to the press that she would be there. 'The lady had vanished,' he said. Realising that her agreeing to dinner had been 'a miracle', he tried another tactic and drove to her house in his Rolls Royce with a bunch of flowers and a box of chocolates. During their phone calls Margaret had told him she never left the house, and that her neighbour did her shopping for her.

Arriving at Margaret's house, Winner stood outside in the rain, ringing her doorbell, and although he knew she was inside, she did not answer the door. Eventually, he tried the house next door, assuming it was probably the neighbour who did Margaret's shopping.[5] He gave Miriam Harrison the flowers and chocolates, and asked her to pass them on to Margaret and to try to persuade her to attend the premiere. He also invited Miriam to the premiere, and said he would send tickets. They never materialised. However, Miriam passed on the message and the chocolates to Margaret, but again she insisted she wanted nothing to do with 'that awful man'.[6]

Winner's proposal to invite Margaret to the premiere and to place her on a special dais of honour did not sit well with her. 'Like a fairground sideshow!' she said. 'Not, I think, in the best of taste.'[7] Margaret wisely avoided the premiere, and she distanced herself from the hype when *The Wicked Lady* opened in April 1983. The critics dismissed Winner's remake and applauded the Lockwood-Mason pairing. 'Living in retirement, Margaret Lockwood emerges as the most ladylike, conventional pioneer of modern movies. [The] staple selling line: wanton sexuality,' the *Daily Mail* wrote. It was an ironic statement, Margaret was quick to note, considering how the critics had rejected it at the time.

*

As the decade advanced, Margaret continued to receive scripts through Mrs de Leon. True to form, she contemplated each offer and then rejected it. 'Too much bother. It's not as though I need the money,' she would say. The *Daily Mail* suggested that she ought to play Joan Collins's mother in *Dynasty* – 'Now there's a thought!' Margaret quipped. 'Think about all that lovely lolly.'[8]

As Margaret increasingly retreated from public life, the British press bestowed on her the nickname, 'Britain's Greta Garbo'. Toots agreed with their assessment: 'My mother is a bit like Greta Garbo in a way… She won't even go out or give interviews.'[9] And, acknowledging the reports that she had become a recluse, Margaret began to refer to herself as such. 'Kind of you to remember the recluse,'[10] she wrote in a letter to a friend.

In her seventieth year, the famous brunette hair had turned white – she had developed an allergy to hair dye – and was covered by a chiffon headscarf; but the beauty spot still remained, painted high on her left cheekbone. Although her physical health was declining, she still continued to smoke – a habit she had never tried to quit.

She also maintained her sense of humour in spite of the personal tragedies she had suffered. The Harrisons recalled that a visit with Margaret always consisted of 'gales of laughter'.[11]

Every anecdote about film sets or encounters with other actors was accompanied by a raucous, coughing laugh. 'The laughter was powerful,' recalled Miriam. 'She blurred day and night, but seldom complained about anything. She was a remarkably contented soul, actually. Little things preoccupied her.'[12]

*

In the summer of 1990, Margaret's health had declined; and, in the morning of 15th July, she was taken by ambulance from her home to Cromwell Hospital in Kensington. That afternoon, *The Man in Grey* was screened on television, and, as always after an airing of one of her old films, her letterbox was overflowing with fan mail; but this time the letters remained unopened. Margaret died later that day with Toots by her side.

'I expect my next appearance on TV will be my funeral,' she had written in a letter before her death. 'You won't see me of course, but I'll be there.'[13]

By her own admission, all Margaret had wanted from life 'are those chances of justifying myself as a good mother, and a good actress… at the moment I have them. I pray I always shall.'[14] There was a familiar story of the three star dressing-rooms at the studios: one marked Miss Phyllis Calvert, one Miss Patricia Roc, and the third, Miss Margaret Lockwood. Opening Phyllis Calvert's door, you would have seen pots and pans, shopping lists, recipe books, dogs' leads and children's toys. If you opened Miss Roc's door you would have been greeted by a divan furnished with satin cushions, mascot dolls, cut-glass perfume bottles and flowers.

But if you opened Margaret Lockwood's door you would have found a picture of Toots.[15]

Afterword

Twenty-five years after her death, on 4th July 2015, Margaret Lockwood's family joined her fans, friends, and residents of Upper Park Road in Kingston upon Thames for the unveiling of her commemorative blue plaque. Given by the Heritage Foundation, it was erected at her former home, a place she loved so much she wanted to stay forever. In a way, she has been granted her wish. Surrounded by her own grandchildren, as Margaret had been at Buckingham Palace all those years ago, Toots did the honours and unveiled her mother's plaque.

Not only does it serve as a physical tribute to a great star, it is a reminder that Margaret Lockwood still commands an audience. As Alfred Hitchcock once told her, 'Great ladies never vanish.'

Select Bibliography

A Rose for Mrs Miniver: The Life of Greer Garson, Michael Troyan. The University Press, 1999

Behind the Laughter, Sherrie Hewson. Harper, 2011

Bernard Shaw and the BBC, L. W. Conolly. University of Toronto Press, 2008

Britain Can Take It: The British Cinema in the Second World War, Anthony Idgate and Jeffrey Richards. I. B. Tauris, 2007

British Stars and Stardom: From Alma Taylor to Sean Connery, Bruce Babington. Manchester University Press, 2001

Carol Reed, Peter Williams Evans. Manchester University Press, 2005

Dirk Bogarde: The Authorised Biography, John Coldstream. Hachette, 2011

Dolphin Square, A. P. Herbert. Richard Coatain Limited, 1935

Film and the Working Class: the Feature Film in British and American Society, Peter Stead. Routledge, 2013

Frankly My Dear: Gone with the Wind Revisited, Molly Haskell. Yale University Press, 2009

Heroines Without Heroes: Reconstructing Female and National Identities in European Cinema, 1945-1951, Sarah Street. A&C Black, 2000

Hitchcock's Partner in Suspense: The Life of Screenwriter Charles Bennett, Charles Bennett. University Press of Kentucky, 2014

In My Mind's Eye: An Autobiography, Michael Redgrave. Coronet Books, 1983
In the Footsteps of the Quiet Man: The Inside Story of the Cult Film, Gary McNee. Mainstream Publishing, 1990
Indicative Past: A Hundred Years of the Girls' Public Day School Trust, Josephine Kamm. Routledge, 1971
J. Arthur Rank and the British Film Industry, Geoffrey McNab. Routledge, 1993
Lucky Star, Margaret Lockwood. Oldhams Press, 1955
Memoirs of an Intelligence Officer, Rupert Leon. Amazon Media
My Life and Films, Margaret Lockwood. World Film Publications, 1948
Once a Wicked Lady, Hilton Tims. Virgin, 1989
Orson Welles in Italy, Alberto Anile. Indiana University Press, 2013
Patricia Roc: The Goddess of the Odeons, Michael Hodgson. AuthorHouse, 2013
Plain Tales from the Raj, Charles Allen. Abacus, 1975
Realism and Tinsel: Cinema and Society in Britain 1939-48, Robert Murphy. Routledge, 2003
Return of the B Science Fiction and Horror Heroes: The Mutant Melding of Two, Tom Weaver. McFarland, 2000
Sparks Fly Upward, Stewart Granger. Granada, 1981
Spellbound by Beauty: Alfred Hitchcock and his Leading Ladies, Donald Spoto. Random House, 2012
Structures of Desire: British Cinema, 1939-1955, Tony Williams. SUNY Press, 2000
Tales I Never Told, Michael Winner. Biteback, 2011

The Actor's Art: Conversations with Contemporary American Stage Performers, Jackson R. Bryer and Allan Richard (ed.). Rutgers University Press, 2001
The Dark Side of Genius: The Life of Alfred Hitchcock, Donald Spoto. Da Capo Press, 1999
The Dream Endures: California Enters the 1940s, Kevin Starr. Oxford University Press, 2002
The Espionage Filmography: United States Releases, 1898 Through 1999, Paul Mavis. McFarland, 2011
The Noël Coward Diaries, Graham Payn (ed). Da Capo Press, 2000
The Stars Look Down, A. J. Cronin. Gollancz, 1935
There's Always Tomorrow, Anna Neagle. W. H. Allen, 1974
Twenty-Five Thousand Sunsets: The Autobiography of Herbert Wilcox, Herbert Wilcox. Bodley Head, 1967
Wealth and Nobility: The Lockwood, Day and Metcalfe Families of Yorkshire and London, Robert Ward. Lulu, 2014
Women in British Cinema: Mad, Bad and Dangerous to Know, Sue Harper. A&C Black, 2001
Words into Images: Screenwriters on the Studio System, Ronald L. Davis. University Press of Mississippi, 2007

NOTES

Chapter 1: An Unfamiliar Place

1. As told to the author by Robert Ward and published in his book, *Wealth and Nobility: The Lockwood, Day and Metcalfe Families of Yorkshire and London* (Lulu, 2014) p108.
2. Graham Clews, grandson of John Alexander Ramsey/Lockwood.
3. Graham Clews.
4. 'Another Sad Suicide', *Western Mail*, Perth, 13th April 1907.
5. Graham Clews: 'My grandmother would not agree to a divorce…'
6. Graham Clews.
7. 'The handsomest man in the East they called him, my mother always said proudly.' Lockwood, Margaret, *Lucky Star* (Oldhams Press, London 1955) p10.
8. Margaret Evelyn was named after her two sisters, Margaret and Evelyn, who had died in infancy before her birth.
9. As told to the author by Margaret Lockwood's cousin Betty Elzea (née Waugh).
10. Lockwood, Margaret, *Lucky Star* (Oldhams Press, London 1955) p9.

Chapter 2: A Solitary Child

1. 'He was the quietest little boy I have ever known.' Lockwood, Margaret, *Lucky Star* (Oldhams Press, London 1955) p11.
2. As told to the author by Julia Lockwood-Clark.
3. Lockwood, Margaret, *Lucky Star* (Oldhams Press, London 1955) p12.
4. Lockwood, Margaret, *Lucky Star* (Oldhams Press, London 1955) p12.
5. Lockwood, Margaret, *Lucky Star* (Oldhams Press, London 1955) p13.
6. 'I sensed the disapproval from the other mamas, who thought my mother quite wrong in taking me and Lyn to the cinema so often, filling our heads with rubbish.' Lockwood, Margaret, *Lucky Star* (Oldhams Press, London 1955) p14.

7. Lockwood, Margaret, *Lucky Star* (Oldhams Press, London 1955) p15.
8. Kamm, Josephine, *Indicative Past: A Hundred Years of the Girls' Public Day School Trust* (Routledge, Oxfordshire 1971) p2.
9. http://www.sydenhamhighschool.gdst.net/about/history/
10. Lockwood, Margaret, *Lucky Star* (Oldhams Press, London 1955) pp17-18.
11. 'I thought the whole world had come to an end.' Lockwood, Margaret, *Lucky Star* (Oldhams Press, London 1955) p17.
12. 'But even this never cured me of being scared of Miss Hobson.' Lockwood, Margaret, *Lucky Star* (Oldhams Press, London 1955) p17.
13. Lockwood, Margaret, *Lucky Star* (Oldhams Press, London 1955) p17.
14. 'This resulted in her mother indignantly refusing to allow her daughter to play with me.' Lockwood, Margaret, *My Life and Films* (World Film Publications, London 1948) p19.
15. 'The Lockwoods didn't observe the protocol.' Lockwood, Margaret, *Lucky Star* (Oldhams Press, London 1955) p17.
16. Lockwood, Margaret, *Lucky Star* (Oldhams Press, London 1955) p17.
17. 'We were regarded as something between freaks and bohemians.' Lockwood, Margaret, *Lucky Star* (Oldhams Press, London 1955) p14.
18. Lockwood, Margaret, *Lucky Star* (Oldhams Press, London 1955) p18.

Chapter 3: Miss Margie Day

1. Lockwood, Margaret, *My Life and Films* (World Film Publications, London 1948) p20.
2. 'Mother had sent me to a little class where most of the other girls from my school went, but I didn't enjoy it. "It's not the right sort of dancing," I protested. "I want to learn the sort of dancing they do in pantomimes. I want to be a fairy in a pantomime."' Lockwood, Margaret, *Lucky Star* (Oldhams Press, London 1955) p18.
3. Lockwood, Margaret, *Lucky Star* (Oldhams Press, London 1955) p19.
4. Lockwood, Margaret, *Lucky Star* (Oldhams Press, London 1955) p19.
5. Lockwood, Margaret, *Lucky Star* (Oldhams Press, London 1955) p20.
6. Lockwood, Margaret, *Lucky Star* (Oldhams Press, London 1955) p21.
7. Lockwood, Margaret, *Lucky Star* (Oldhams Press, London 1955) p21.
8. Margaret's great-grandfather Henry Francis Lockwood married his first cousin Emma Dey (or Day) – their mothers were sisters – and their descendants were given the middle name Day. Margaret's name

has been given as Margaret Mary Lockwood Day (and Day Lockwood), but Day was used informally.
9. Lockwood, Margaret, *My Life and Films* (World Film Publications, London 1948) p21.
10. As told to the author by Betty Elzea.
11. Confirmed by Graham Clews.
12. Lockwood, Margaret, *Lucky Star* (Oldhams Press, London 1955) p23.
13. Lockwood, Margaret, *Lucky Star* (Oldhams Press, London 1955) p26.
14. According to Margaret's neighbour, Miriam Harrison, Margaret had told her that her father was a heavy drinker. This was partly why she would remain a devoted teetotaller all of her life.
15. Lockwood, Margaret, *Lucky Star* (Oldhams Press, London 1955) p24.
16. Lockwood, Margaret, *Lucky Star* (Oldhams Press, London 1955) p26.
17. Lockwood, Margaret, *Lucky Star* (Oldhams Press, London 1955) p27.
18. 'One day I'm going to be standing like that, at the front, making all those people happy.' Lockwood, Margaret, *Lucky Star* (Oldhams Press, London 1955) p27.
19. Tims, Hilton, *Once a Wicked Lady* (Virgin, London 1989) p27.
20. Julia Lockwood-Clark revealed the boy's identity to me.
21. 'Mummy, mummy, I've heard a bad word…' Lockwood, Margaret, *Lucky Star* (Oldhams Press, London 1955) p27.
22. Margaret Evelyn trained with Queen Alexandra's Nursing Corps before taking the post as nanny to Frank and Fay.
23. Lockwood, Margaret, *Lucky Star* (Oldhams Press, London 1955) p29.

Chapter 4: A Life That Can Be Splendid

1. 'My mother at once set about getting me into the Royal Academy of Dramatic Art.' Lockwood, Margaret, *My Life and Films* (World Film Publications, London 1948) p23.
2. Lockwood, Margaret, *My Life and Films* (World Film Publications, London 1948) p24.
3. 'I had my hair cut for the first time, because the Academy had ragged me.' Lockwood, Margaret, *Lucky Star* (Oldhams Press, London 1955) p32.
4. 'This time she cried a little. It isn't me you have to thank, my dear, it's yourself. You've worked so hard. We cabled the news to my father as first proof that it really had been worth while giving me the chance to

be an actress.' Lockwood, Margaret, *Lucky Star* (Oldhams Press, London 1955) p31.

5. Leon, Rupert, *Memoirs of an Intelligence Officer* (Amazon Media).
6. Leon, Rupert, *Memoirs of an Intelligence Officer* (Amazon Media).
7. Lockwood, Margaret, *Lucky Star* (Oldhams Press, London 1955) p33.
8. 'I never danced with anyone except Rupert. He wouldn't let me, and I regarded it quite natural to do as he said.' Lockwood, Margaret, *Lucky Star* (Oldhams Press, London 1955) p34.
9. Lockwood, Margaret, *Lucky Star* (Oldhams Press, London 1955) p34.
10. 'I was not optimistic when Mother met me afterwards. Mother said bluntly: "It was terrible, and I couldn't see you half the time."' Lockwood, Margaret, *Lucky Star* (Oldhams Press, London 1955) p35.
11. Lockwood, Margaret, *My Life and Films* (World Film Publications, London 1948) p25.
12. Lockwood, Margaret, *Lucky Star* (Oldhams Press, London 1955) p36.

Chapter 5: A Work in Progress

1. Coldstream, John, *Dirk Bogarde: The Authorised Biography* (Hachette, London 2011) p57.
2. *Saturday Night at the Mill*, BBC television, 19th April 1980.
3. 'But at least it broke the shock before she met her half-bald daughter.' Lockwood, Margaret, *Lucky Star* (Oldhams Press, London 1955) p39.
4. Approximately £760 in today's value. Bank of England Inflation Calculator: http://www.bankofengland.co.uk/education/Pages/resources/inflationtools/calculator/flash/default.aspx
5. Lockwood, Margaret, *Lucky Star* (Oldhams Press, London 1955) p.41.
6. 'And that is when the big money really began.' Lockwood, Margaret, *Lucky Star* (Oldhams Press, London 1955) p.41.
7. Lockwood, Margaret, *My Life and Films* (World Film Publications, London 1948) p35.
8. Approximately £32,000 in today's value. Bank of England Inflation Calculator: http://www.bankofengland.co.uk/education/Pages/resources/inflationtools/calculator/flash/default.aspx
9. Approximately £48,000 in today's value. Bank of England Inflation Calculator: http://www.bankofengland.co.uk/education/Pages/resources/inflationtools/calculator/flash/default.aspx

10. Approximately £640 in today's value. Bank of England Inflation Calculator: http://www.bankofengland.co.uk/education/Pages/resources/inflationtools/calculator/flash/default.aspx
11. Approximately £700 in today's value. Bank of England Inflation Calculator: http://www.bankofengland.co.uk/education/Pages/resources/inflationtools/calculator/flash/default.aspx
12. 'I began to realise that you have to educate them to expensive presents and at the same time learn that though they say they want this or that, they don't really, if they think it is beyond the range of their normal expenditure.' Lockwood, Margaret, *Lucky Star* (Oldhams Press, London 1955) p.42.
13. Lockwood, Margaret, *Lucky Star* (Oldhams Press, London 1955) p.43.
14. 'And that was a beautiful morning. Passing all the milk trucks and early morning workmen, Rupert and I built a wonderful shining dream for ourselves.' Lockwood, Margaret, *Lucky Star* (Oldhams Press, London 1955) p.43.

Chapter 6: Power Struggle

1. As told to the author by Betty Elzea.
2. *The Mail on Sunday*, 7th September 1986.
3. *Saturday Night at the Mill*, BBC television, 19th April 1980.
4. As told to the author by Julia Lockwood-Clark.
5. Lockwood, Margaret, *Lucky Star* (Oldhams Press, London 1955) p.45.
6. Lockwood, Margaret, *Lucky Star* (Oldhams Press, London 1955) p.44.
7. Lockwood, Margaret, *Lucky Star* (Oldhams Press, London 1955) p.44.
8. Lockwood, Margaret, *Lucky Star* (Oldhams Press, London 1955) p.45.
9. Lockwood, Margaret, *Lucky Star* (Oldhams Press, London 1955) p.45.
10. 'The meaning was certainly not lost upon my admirer, whose spirits drooped appreciably.' Lockwood, Margaret, *My Life and Films* (World Film Publications, London 1948) p26.
11. *Daily Mail*, 21st November 1975.
12. 'This was the first time I had worked for a well-known director, and I was terrified.' Lockwood, Margaret, *Lucky Star* (Oldhams Press, London 1955) p.46.
13. 'One never got to know these giants of the film world well… I never dreamed of calling any director by their Christian names.' Lockwood, Margaret, *Lucky Star* (Oldhams Press, London 1955) p.46.

14. Lockwood, Margaret, *Lucky Star* (Oldhams Press, London 1955) p.48.
15. Lockwood, Margaret, *Lucky Star* (Oldhams Press, London 1955) p.49.
16. 'Stars were the great ones like Chevalier himself, who simply terrified me.' Lockwood, Margaret, *Lucky Star* (Oldhams Press, London 1955) p.49.
17. 'I think she thought I was enjoying her discomfiture.' Lockwood, Margaret, *Lucky Star* (Oldhams Press, London 1955) p50.
18. Lockwood, Margaret, *Lucky Star* (Oldhams Press, London 1955) p51.
19. Lockwood, Margaret, *Lucky Star* (Oldhams Press, London 1955) p51.
20. When Henry's children gathered to settle his estate, Margaret met her eldest half-brother, John Alexander Lockwood (the son of Jessie Ramsey), for the first time. For obvious reasons relating to her career, Margaret never openly acknowledged this half-brother or spoke of her father's complicated past. Source: Graham Clews.
21. Lockwood, Margaret, *Lucky Star* (Oldhams Press, London 1955) p52
22. 'It took me a long time to live it down with him.' Lockwood, Margaret, *My Life and Films* (World Film Publications, London 1948) p37.

Chapter 7: Mrs Leon

1. Lockwood, Margaret, *Lucky Star* (Oldhams Press, London 1955) p53.
2. Lockwood, Margaret, *Lucky Star* (Oldhams Press, London 1955) p53.
3. Approximately £252,500 in today's value. Bank of England Inflation Calculator: http://www.bankofengland.co.uk/education/Pages/resources/inflationtools/calculator/flash/default.aspx
4. 'But in his heart Rupert knew it would not be all right. He had realised how indomitable my mother could be.' Lockwood, Margaret, *Lucky Star* (Oldhams Press, London 1955) p55.
5. 'Darling, kind Rupert. He had waited for me for four years. Waited all hours of the night and morning just to see me for a few minutes each day... Now he was even willing to marry me and "give me up" the next day, as long as I was happy and he could spare me the dreaded quarrel with my mother.' Lockwood, Margaret, *Lucky Star* (Oldhams Press, London 1955) p56.
6. Related by Carol Reed: 'She looked considerably confused, giggled a great deal in a way that seemed to me entirely unlike the Margaret Lockwood I knew, and generally convinced me that something unusual

was afoot.' Lockwood, Margaret, *My Life and Films* (World Film Publications, London 1948) p52.

7. Lockwood, Margaret, *My Life and Films* (World Film Publications, London 1948) p51.
8. Approximately £1,260 in today's value. Bank of England Inflation Calculator: http://www.bankofengland.co.uk/education/Pages/resources/inflationtools/calculator/flash/default.aspx
9. Approximately £2,525 in today's value. Bank of England Inflation Calculator: http://www.bankofengland.co.uk/education/Pages/resources/inflationtools/calculator/flash/default.aspx
10. Lockwood, Margaret, *Lucky Star* (Oldhams Press, London 1955) p60.
11. Lockwood, Margaret, *Lucky Star* (Oldhams Press, London 1955) p60.
12. Approximately £128,000 in today's value. Bank of England inflation calculator: http://www.bankofengland.co.uk/education/Pages/resources/inflationtools/calculator/flash/default.aspx
13. Herbert, A. P., *Dolphin Square* (Richard Coatain Limited, London 1935).
14. 'He literally squirmed in his seat with embarrassment.' Lockwood, Margaret, *Lucky Star* (Oldhams Press, London 1955) p65.

Chapter 8: Leading Lady

1. *The Pittsburgh Press*, 27th November 1939. 'Margaret Lockwood best of Hitchcock's trio…'
2. Babington, Bruce, *British Stars and Stardom: From Alma Taylor to Sean Connery* (Manchester University Press, Manchester 2001) p94.
3. Lockwood, Margaret, *My Life and Films* (World Film Publications, London 1948) p51.
4. Macnab, Geoffrey, *Searching for Stars: Stardom and Screen Acting in British Cinema* (A&C Black, London 2000) p155.
5. 'Star was a dirty word, a word that represented a sellout and a prostitute.' Bryer, Jackson R. and Davison, Richard Allan (ed.) *The Actor's Art: Conversations with Contemporary American Stage Performers* (Rutgers University Press, New Jersey 2001) p165.
6. Spoto, Donald, *The Dark Side of Genius: The Life of Alfred Hitchcock* (Da Capo Press, Boston 1999) p186.
7. 'Actors are cattle,' [Hitchcock] tells Truffaut. *The Guardian*, 12th May 2015.

8. Redgrave, Michael, *In My Mind's Eye: An Autobiography* (Coronet Books, London 1983) p120.
9. Redgrave, Michael, *In My Mind's Eye: An Autobiography* (Coronet Books, London 1983) p123.
10. '... I had done a number of films for Carol Reed, and he was quite meticulous by contrast.' Spoto, Donald, *Spellbound by Beauty: Alfred Hitchcock and his Leading Ladies* (Random House, New York 2012) p54.
11. Spoto, Donald, *The Dark Side of Genius: The Life of Alfred Hitchcock* (Da Capo Press, Boston 1999) p174.
12. Mavis, Paul, *The Espionage Filmography: United States Releases, 1898 through 1999* (McFarland, North Carolina 2011) p170.
13. Lockwood, Margaret, *Lucky Star* (Oldhams Press, London 1955) p66.
14. Spoto, Donald, *The Dark Side of Genius: The Life of Alfred Hitchcock* (Da Capo Press, Boston 1999) p176.
15. Lockwood, Margaret, *Lucky Star* (Oldhams Press, London 1955) p67.
16. Leon, Rupert, *Memoirs of an Intelligence Officer* (Amazon Media).
17. 'This was supposed to be a honeymoon holiday, and I thought him unnecessarily gloomy.' Lockwood, Margaret, *Lucky Star* (Oldhams Press, London 1955) p67.
18. Lockwood, Margaret, *Lucky Star* (Oldhams Press, London 1955) p67.
19. Approximately £360,700 in today's value. Bank of England inflation calculator: http://www.bankofengland.co.uk/education/Pages/resources/inflationtools/calculator/flash/default.aspx
20. 'Older villagers remember Delcott as little more than a hut.' Tims, Hilton, *Once a Wicked Lady* (Virgin, London 1989) p.88.
21. *Saturday Night at the Mill*, BBC television, 19th April 1980.
22. Lockwood, Margaret, *Lucky Star* (Oldhams Press, London 1955) p69.
23. 'I had nothing against Shirley, except that I knew too well she would always out-star any adult playing with her, who, at the most, could only hope for an insipid supporting role.' Lockwood, Margaret, *Lucky Star* (Oldhams Press, London 1955) p69.
24. 'I had no time to think about homesickness. I had so many things to do.' Lockwood, Margaret, *Lucky Star* (Oldhams Press, London 1955) p70.

Chapter 9: Hollywood

1. 'Director William Seiter congratulated Miss Lockwood on winning the Scarlett O'Hara role. She was embarrassed because she doesn't believe she resembles Miss Leigh very much.' *Herald Journal*, 14th February 1939.
2. 'She's striking, but not dazzling, pretty in an exquisite Margaret Lockwood way.' Haskell, Molly, *Frankly My Dear: Gone with the Wind Revisited* (Yale Univeristy Press, Yale 2009) p72.
3. Troyan, Michael, *A Rose for Mrs Miniver: The Life of Greer Garson* (The University Press of Kentucky, Lexington 1999) p77.
4. Hilton Tims gives the hotel as the St Moritz in his 1989 book *Once A Wicked Lady* (Virgin, London 1989). In *Lucky Star*, Margaret wrote that it was the Barbazon [sic]. I have chosen to use Margaret's information as the Barbizon fits within the time period and it had a reputation of being used by film studios for their up-and-coming stars.
5. 'This was a gaffe on my part.' Lockwood, Margaret, *Lucky Star* (Oldhams Press, London 1955) p71.
6. 'I was frigid, with a mixture of their cold climate and colder reception. I could only stare blankly at the man.' Lockwood, Margaret, *Lucky Star* (Oldhams Press, London 1955) p71.
7. Lockwood, Margaret, *My Life and Films* (World Film Publications, London 1948) p49.
8. 'A sort of chic place in those days.' Weaver, Tom, *Return of the B Science Fiction and Horror Heroes: The Mutant Melding of Two* (McFarland, Jefferson 2000) p261
9. 'It was [Robert] Benchley who said: "I've got to get out of these wet clothes and into a dry martini." ' Starr, Kevin, *The Dream Endures: California Enters the 1940s* (Oxford University Press, Oxford 2002) p300.
10. Lockwood, Margaret, *Lucky Star* (Oldhams Press, London 1955) p72.
11. Designed by Alla Nazimova to remind her of her beloved Crimea.
12. *Nine Five*, BBC Radio Wales, 1978.
13. Lockwood, Margaret, *Lucky Star* (Oldhams Press, London 1955) p75.
14. *San Jose News*, 8th February 1939.
15. Lockwood, Margaret, *Lucky Star* (Oldhams Press, London 1955) p76.
16. Lockwood, Margaret, *Lucky Star* (Oldhams Press, London 1955) p76.

Chapter 10: Wartime

1. Cronin, A. J., *The Stars Look Down* (Gollancz, London 1935).
2. Tims, Hilton, *Once a Wicked Lady* (Virgin, London 1989) p97.
3. Lockwood, Margaret, *Lucky Star* (Oldhams Press, London 1955) p76.
4. Lockwood, Margaret, *My Life and Films* (World Film Publications, London 1948) p52.
5. http://www.flickeringmyth.com/2009/10/great-reed-carol-reed-profile-part-1.html
6. Stead, Peter, *Film and the Working Class: the Feature Film in British and American Society* (Routledge, Oxfordshire 2013) p113.
7. Leon, Rupert, *Memoirs of an Intelligence Officer* (Amazon Media).
8. Lockwood, Margaret, *My Life and Films* (World Film Publications, London 1948) p52.
9. As told to the author by Betty Elzea.
10. Lockwood, Margaret, *Lucky Star* (Oldhams Press, London 1955) p.81.
11. *Nine Five*, BBC Radio Wales, 1978.
12. Lockwood, Margaret, *Lucky Star* (Oldhams Press, London 1955) p.83.
13. Lockwood, Margaret, *Lucky Star* (Oldhams Press, London 1955) p.84.
14. Lockwood, Margaret, *Lucky Star* (Oldhams Press, London 1955) p.85.
15. Lockwood, Margaret, *Lucky Star* (Oldhams Press, London 1955) p.85.

Chapter 11: Toots

1. 'There was so much compensation. And to me, at any rate, a baby seemed utterly to defy bombs and horror and fighting.' Lockwood, Margaret, *Lucky Star* (Oldhams Press, London 1955) p92.
2. Lockwood, Margaret, *Lucky Star* (Oldhams Press, London 1955) p.86.
3. Leon, Rupert, *Memoirs of an Intelligence Officer* (Amazon Media).
4. Lockwood, Margaret, *Lucky Star* (Oldhams Press, London 1955) p.84.
5. Margaret Evelyn was infuriated that Rupert had a say over Margaret's health and her reaction was a reflection of that. *Lucky Star* (Oldhams Press, London 1955) p.88.
6. Lockwood, Margaret, *Lucky Star* (Oldhams Press, London 1955) p.89.
7. Lockwood, Margaret, *Lucky Star* (Oldhams Press, London 1955) p93.
8. Lockwood, Margaret, *Lucky Star* (Oldhams Press, London 1955) p93.

9. 'He seemed a little bewildered about the prospect of becoming a father, of having to give his permission for an operation, and generally, I think, with all this complicated business of bringing children into the world.' Lockwood, Margaret, *Lucky Star* (Oldhams Press, London 1955) p.88.
10. Lockwood, Margaret, *Lucky Star* (Oldhams Press, London 1955) p95.
11. Lockwood, Margaret, *Lucky Star* (Oldhams Press, London 1955) p95.
12. 'With my earning capacity I was the bread, and perhaps I should say cake, winner of the family.' Lockwood, Margaret, *Lucky Star* (Oldhams Press, London 1955) p95.

Chapter 12: All Change

1. *Western Herald*, 26th November 1943.
2. *The Telegraph*, 22nd May 1943.
3. *The Glasgow Herald*, 21st September 1942.
4. Lockwood, Margaret, *Lucky Star* (Oldhams Press, London 1955) p138.
5. 'With the long separations enforced upon us by the war, the continuous tension of my mother's inability to accept him, and my memories of his aloofness during the months before Toots was born, we were both aware of a sense of estrangement between us.' Lockwood, Margaret, *Lucky Star* (Oldhams Press, London 1955) p97.
6. The information on whether Margaret wanted to play Hesther or not is conflicting. In *My Life and Films* (World Film Publications, London 1948, p62.) and in *Lucky Star* (Oldhams Press, London 1955, p98) she wrote that it was the part of Clarissa which appealed to her and she was hesitant to accept the part of Hesther who was 'downright wicked'. However, in various cinema books it is related that Margaret wished to play Hesther and had to convince Maurice Ostrer that it was a good idea.
7. Lockwood, Margaret, *Lucky Star* (Oldhams Press, London 1955) p98.
8. Lockwood, Margaret, *Lucky Star* (Oldhams Press, London 1955) p98.
9. Granger, Stewart, *Sparks Fly Upward* (Granada, London 1981) p61.
10. Lockwood, Margaret, *Lucky Star* (Oldhams Press, London 1955) p100.
11. Hodgson, Michael, *Patricia Roc: The Goddess of the Odeons* (Authorhouse, Milton Keynes 2011) p72.
12. Lockwood, Margaret, *Lucky Star* (Oldhams Press, London 1955) p101.
13. Lockwood, Margaret, *Lucky Star* (Oldhams Press, London 1955) p127.

14. Stewart Granger's remark was provoked by an incident which occured in post production. He had refused to film the scene where his character dives into the sea with Margaret's character, thus Leslie Arliss was forced to hire a stand-in. During a private screening of the film he realised that his stand-in was bow-legged and this infuriated him. Hodgson, Michael, *Patricia Roc: The Goddess of the Odeons* (Authorhouse, Milton Keynes 2011) p70.
15. Approximately £7,900,000 in today's value. Bank of England inflation calculator: http://www.bankofengland.co.uk/education/Pages/resources/inflationtools/calculator/flash/default.aspx

Chapter 13: The Wicked Lady

1. 'We had been leading such vastly different lives and our letters were getting fewer and fewer and more non-committal.' Lockwood, Margaret, *Lucky Star* (Oldhams Press, London 1955) p102.
2. Lockwood, Margaret, *Lucky Star* (Oldhams Press, London 1955) p104.
3. This information was related by Margaret in *Lucky Star*. Given the period in which the book was published it appears that Margaret romanticised Keith's background. Julia Lockwood-Clark told me that Keith did not have a (steady) job, nor was he in the army. However, in *Once a Wicked Lady* (Virgin, London 1989) Hilton Tims wrote that Keith was in the RAF. p122.
4. Author's original research.
5. As told to the author by Julia Lockwood-Clark. Further research indicates that Keith worked at the Rank Organisation during the time in which Margaret's future friend and colleague Theo Cowan worked there, as Cowan claimed he knew Keith. Although speaking in the past tense, this suggested Cowan knew of Keith before he (Cowan) met Margaret. It also appears that Keith left Rank shortly after meeting Margaret.
6. Lockwood, Margaret, *Lucky Star* (Oldhams Press, London 1955) p105.
7. Lockwood, Margaret, *Lucky Star* (Oldhams Press, London 1955) p106.
8. Letter from Margaret to Wendy Maunder, 26th January 1949.
9. Lockwood, Margaret, *Lucky Star* (Oldhams Press, London 1955) p108.
10. Lockwood, Margaret, *Lucky Star* (Oldhams Press, London 1955) p108.
11. Macnab, Geoffrey, *Searching for Stars: Stardom and Screen Acting in British Cinema* (A&C Black, London 2000) p165.

12. Tims, Hilton, *Once a Wicked Lady* (Virgin, London 1989) p120.
13. *Saturday Night at the Mill*, BBC television, 19th April 1980.
14. The *New York Times*, circa 1939.
15. Lockwood, Margaret, *Lucky Star* (Oldhams Press, London 1955) p113.

Chapter 14: Sound and Fury

1. *Pebble Mill at One*, BBC 1, 1978.
2. Tims, Hilton, *Once a Wicked Lady* (Virgin, London 1989) p128.
3. *Pebble Mill at One*, BBC 1, 1978.
4. Tims, Hilton, *Once a Wicked Lady* (Virgin, London 1989) p129.
5. *Australian Women's Weekly*, 4th May 1946.
6. Tims, Hilton, *Once a Wicked Lady* (Virgin, London 1989) p131.
7. *Saturday Night at the Mill*, BBC television, 19th April 1980.
8. Leonard Mosley, the *Daily Express*.
9. The *New York Times*, circa 1946.
10. *Daytona Beach Morning Journal*, 1st October 1946.
11. *Nine Five*, BBC Radio Wales, 1978.
12. *Daily Mail*, 7th September 1990.
13. Tims, Hilton, *Once a Wicked Lady* (Virgin, London 1989) p134.
14. Thanks to Tania Todd for sharing with me her informative leaflet on Margaret's make-up transformation.
15. Murphy, Robert, *Realism and Tinsel: Cinema and Society in Britain 1939-48* (Routledge, Oxfordshire 2003) p116.
16. *The Age*, 27th March 1948.

Chapter 15: The Merits of Success

1. Leon, Rupert, *Memoirs of an Intelligence Officer* (Amazon Media).
2. 'I sat down to write to my husband. I told Rupert, as honestly and as simply as I could, that I had fallen in love with someone else.' Lockwood, Margaret, *Lucky Star* (Oldhams Press, London 1955) p117.
3. As told to the author by Julia Lockwood-Clark.
4. Lockwood, Margaret, *Lucky Star* (Oldhams Press, London 1955) p114.
5. 'All I wanted now was to be able to marry [Keith], and then, I thought, I could expect no further measure of happiness.' Lockwood, Margaret, *Lucky Star* (Oldhams Press, London 1955) p116.

6. Murphy, Robert, *Realism and Tinsel: Cinema and Society in Britain 1939-1948* (Routledge, Oxfordshire 2003) p110.
7. Lockwood, Margaret, *Lucky Star* (Oldhams Press, London 1955) p121.
8. He was not the only one who thought Margaret's dramatic look was unncessary. Jympson Harman, a critic, wrote: 'I do wish Margaret Lockwood would do something about her lipstick. They tell me that the heavy make-up is her own idea. But there is no reason why such a pretty girl should do a Joan Crawford with her mouth.' Tims, Hilton, *Once a Wicked Lady* (Virgin, London 1989) p145.
9. Lockwood, Margaret, *Lucky Star* (Oldhams Press, London 1955) p122.
10. 'I hated to hurt him but he helped me considerably by making our meeting a very sensible and unemotional one.' Lockwood, Margaret, *Lucky Star* (Oldhams Press, London 1955) p122.
11. Lockwood, Margaret, *Lucky Star* (Oldhams Press, London 1955) p122.
12. Lockwood, Margaret, *Lucky Star* (Oldhams Press, London 1955) p123.
13. 'It did not seem that I was going to be able to get a divorce. Even if I could, as Rupert had seriously warned me, it would risk endangering my legal rights of having my little daughter in my care.' Lockwood, Margaret, *Lucky Star* (Oldhams Press, London 1955) p124.
14. Lockwood, Margaret, *Lucky Star* (Oldhams Press, London 1955) p124.
15. As told to the author by Julia Lockwood-Clark.
16. 'My mother and I had long outgrown that companionable stage when I could rush home and tell her the odd, everyday things, some comic, some irritating, some interesting, which happen to all of us in the course of a day's work. This had ceased when Rupert and I had got our own home. Rupert was never very interested in my work, we had never talked about it much.' Lockwood, Margaret, *Lucky Star* (Oldhams Press, London 1955) pp125-126.
17. 'I can't come back to be so near and not to see him.' Lockwood, Margaret, *Lucky Star* (Oldhams Press, London 1955) p127.
18. It appears he lived for the rest of his life in Australia.
19. As told to the author by Julia Lockwood-Clark.
20. As told to the author by Julia Lockwood-Clark.
21. Leon, Rupert, *Memoirs of an Intelligence Officer* (Amazon Media).
22. As told to the author by Julia Lockwood-Clark.
23. Lockwood, Margaret, *Lucky Star* (Oldhams Press, London 1955) p129.

Chapter 16: Severing Ties

1. *The New Yorker*, 26th July 1947.
2. Official Canadian box office poll for 1948.
3. Lockwood, Margaret, *Lucky Star* (Oldhams Press, London 1955) p130.
4. Conolly, L. W., *Bernard Shaw and the BBC* (University of Toronto Press, Toronto 2008) p134.
5. Conolly, L. W., *Bernard Shaw and the BBC* (University of Toronto Press, Toronto 2008) p141.
6. Tims, Hilton, *Once a Wicked Lady* (Virgin, London 1989) p154.
7. Tims, Hilton, *Once a Wicked Lady* (Virgin, London 1989) p154.
8. Tims, Hilton, *Once a Wicked Lady* (Virgin, London 1989) p153.
9. Holmes, Su, *British Television and Film Culture in the 1950s: Coming to a TV Near You* (University of Chicago Press, Chicago 2005) p59.
10. Aldgate, Anthony and Richards, Jeffrey, *Britain Can Take It: The British Cinema in the Second World War, Second Edition* (I. B. Tauris, London 2007) p159.
11. Tims, Hilton, *Once a Wicked Lady* (Virgin, London 1989) p144.
12. Tims, Hilton, *Once a Wicked Lady* (Virgin, London 1989) p155.
13. Lockwood, Margaret, *Lucky Star* (Oldhams Press, London 1955) p131.
14. Film Stars' Brains Trust, 1949.
15. *The Mail*, 26th July 1947.
16. Film Stars' Brains Trust, 1949.
17. Lockwood, Margaret, *Lucky Star* (Oldhams Press, London 1955) p135.
18. *The Courier-Mail*, 8th May 1948.
19. Lockwood, Margaret, *Lucky Star* (Oldhams Press, London 1955) p136.
20. Approximately £410,300 in today's value. Bank of England inflation calculator: http://www.bankofengland.co.uk/education/Pages/resources/inflationtools/calculator/flash/default.aspx
21. Lockwood, Margaret, *Lucky Star* (Oldhams Press, London 1955) p138.
22. Lockwood, Margaret, *Lucky Star* (Oldhams Press, London 1955) p138.
23. Lockwood, Margaret, *Lucky Star* (Oldhams Press, London 1955) p141.
24. Kathleen Byron's obituary. *The Guardian*, 19th January 2009.
25. Hodgson, Michael, *Patricia Roc: The Goddess of the Odeons* (Authorhouse, Milton Keynes 2011) p69.
26. Hodgson, Michael, *Patricia Roc: The Goddess of the Odeons* (Authorhouse, Milton Keynes 2011) p70.

27. Davis, Ronald L., *Words into Images: Screenwriters on the Studio System* (University Press of Mississippi, Jackson 2007) p14.
28. *The Mirror*, 18th October 1947.
29. Davis, Ronald L., *Words into Images: Screenwriters on the Studio System* (University Press of Mississippi, Jackson 2007) p15.

Chapter 17: Interval

1. Tims, Hilton, *Once a Wicked Lady* (Virgin, London 1989) p156.
2. Lockwood, Margaret, *Lucky Star* (Oldhams Press, London 1955) p146.
3. Lockwood, Margaret, *Lucky Star* (Oldhams Press, London 1955) p147.
4. Lockwood, Margaret, *Lucky Star* (Oldhams Press, London 1955) p147.
5. *The Glasgow Herald*, 20th May 1949.
6. Payn, Graham (ed.), *The Noël Coward Diaries* (Da Capo Press, Boston 2000) p64.
7. 'Already I was thinking of a stage career for Toots, and Rupert was entirely against this.' Lockwood, Margaret, *Lucky Star* (Oldhams Press, London 1955) p124.
8. Film Stars' Brains Trust, 1949.
9. Film Stars' Brains Trust, 1949.
10. Lockwood, Margaret, *Lucky Star* (Oldhams Press, London 1955) p138.
11. Lockwood, Margaret, *My Life and Films* (World Film Publications, London 1948) p53.
12. Tims, Hilton, *Once a Wicked Lady* (Virgin, London 1989) p162.
13. 'I was remembering Rupert's earlier opposition to a theatrical career for Toots. Supposing he raised this as an objection. I had no knowledge of what he would do. I recalled his unyielding dislike of my wearing make-up and smoking.' Lockwood, Margaret, *Lucky Star* (Oldhams Press, London 1955) p156.
14. As told to the author by Julia Lockwood-Clark.
15. Film Stars' Brains Trust, 1949.
16. Lockwood, Margaret, *Lucky Star* (Oldhams Press, London 1955) p157.
17. Tims, Hilton, *Once a Wicked Lady* (Virgin, London 1989) p164.

Chapter 18: A New Venture

1. *The Age*, 21st June 1955.

2. *The Spectator*, 24th August 1951.
3. Tims, Hilton, *Once a Wicked Lady* (Virgin, London 1989) p168.
4. Tims, Hilton, *Once a Wicked Lady* (Virgin, London 1989) p168.
5. 'And while they looked after you well enough they certainly did not spoil you.' Lockwood, Margaret, *Lucky Star* (Oldhams Press, London 1955) p160.
6. Lockwood, Margaret, *Lucky Star* (Oldhams Press, London 1955) p161.
7. Tims, Hilton, *Once a Wicked Lady* (Virgin, London 1989) p169.
8. Anile, Alberto, *Orson Welles in Italy* (Indiana University Press, Bloomington 2013) p259.
9. *News*, 31st March 1953.
10. Leonard Mosley, the *Daily Express*.
11. The *Sunday Chronicle*.
12. *The Mail*, 20th May 1954.
13. Lockwood, Margaret, *Lucky Star* (Oldhams Press, London 1955) p165.
14. Lockwood, Margaret, *Lucky Star* (Oldhams Press, London 1955) p165.
15. Lockwood, Margaret, *Lucky Star* (Oldhams Press, London 1955) p165.
16. Lockwood, Margaret, *Lucky Star* (Oldhams Press, London 1955) p176.
17. 'Margaret Lockwood's Day Diary', *TV Mirror*, 11th September 1954.
18. Lockwood, Margaret, *Lucky Star* (Oldhams Press, London 1955) p176.
19. Lockwood, Margaret, *Lucky Star* (Oldhams Press, London 1955) p176.
20. Lockwood, Margaret, *Lucky Star* (Oldhams Press, London 1955) p177.
21. 'Margaret Lockwood's Day Diary', *TV Mirror*, 11th September 1954.
22. Tims, Hilton, *Once a Wicked Lady* (Virgin, London 1989) p172.
23. McNee, Gary, *In the Footsteps of the Quiet Man: The Inside Story of the Cult Film* (Mainstream Publishing, Edinburgh 1990)
24. Wilcox, Herbert, *Twenty-Five Thousand Sunsets: The Autobiography of Herbert Wilcox* (Bodley Head, London 1967) p168.
25. Tims, Hilton, *Once a Wicked Lady* (Virgin, London 1989) p173.
26. *The Australian Woman's Weekly*, 15th November 1947.

Chapter 19: A Second Career

1. Lockwood, Margaret, *Lucky Star* (Oldhams Press, London 1955) p183.
2. Lockwood, Margaret, *Lucky Star* (Oldhams Press, London 1955) p184.
3. Lockwood, Margaret, *Lucky Star* (Oldhams Press, London 1955) p187.
4. Letter to Denis Gilding.
5. *Mirror*, 14th May 1955.

6. Lockwood, Margaret, *Lucky Star* (Oldhams Press, London 1955) p189.
7. *Sydney Morning Herald*, 29th September 1960.
8. Neagle, Anna, *There's Always Tomorrow* (W. H. Allen, London 1974) p192.
9. *The Age*, 13th September 1955.
10. Tims, Hilton, *Once a Wicked Lady* (Virgin, London 1989) p179.
11. As quoted by Peter Saunders. Date and publication of the article is unknown. Author's private collection.
12. Davis, Ronald L., *Zachary Scott: Hollywood's Sophisticated Cad* (University Press of Mississippi, Jackson 2009) p171.
13. Lockwood, Margaret, *Lucky Star* (Oldhams Press, London 1955) p189.
14. Tims, Hilton, *Once a Wicked Lady* (Virgin, London 1989) p182.

Chapter 20: New Beginnings

1. 'Then I thought that life for a woman who was not in love, or loved, a woman who had no one to take care of her, must be inadequate and incomplete. But I did have someone to love, and someone to love me – my child.' Lockwood, Margaret, *Lucky Star* (Oldhams Press, London 1955) p189.
2. Lockwood, Margaret, *Lucky Star* (Oldhams Press, London 1955) p189.
3. 'I would never stick my head into that noose again.' *The Times*, 17th July 1990.
4. 'Soon – when she's had her tonsils removed – she'll be taking the giant step towards independence by moving into a bachelor-girl flat in London's Dolphin Square.' *The Sydney Morning Herald*, 29th September 1960.
5. *The Sydney Morning Herald*, 29th September 1960.
6. As told to the author by Tim Harrison.
7. *Daily Mail*, 27th November 1975.
8. Margaret's cousin, Betty Elzea, told me that Margaret had a lot of Margaret Evelyn's mannerisms and turn of phrase, although their voices were not similar as Margaret Evelyn's was influenced by her Anglo-Indian upbringing.
9. As told to the author by Tim Harrison.
10. *Mail on Sunday*, 7th September 1986.
11. *Daily Express*, 11th November 1964.
12. As told to the author by Julia Lockwood-Clark.

13. As told to the author by Julia Lockwood-Clark.
14. 'I constantly regret we do not see more of her, I think this arrangement is possibly the best solution.' Lockwood, Margaret, *Lucky Star* (Oldhams Press, London 1955) p139.

Chapter 21: A Revival

1. Tims, Hilton, *Once a Wicked Lady* (Virgin, London 1989) p188.
2. Tims, Hilton, *Once a Wicked Lady* (Virgin, London 1989) p188.
3. Approximately £1,000 in today's value. Bank of England Inflation Calculator: http://www.bankofengland.co.uk/education/Pages/resources/inflationtools/calculator/flash/default.aspx
4. Tims, Hilton, *Once a Wicked Lady* (Virgin, London 1989) p190.
5. Tims, Hilton, *Once a Wicked Lady* (Virgin, London 1989) p190.
6. As told to the author by Tim Harrison.
7. As explained to the author.
8. Author's interview with Tim Harrison.
9. Letter to Dorothy Hodge.
10. *Ottawa Citizen*, 16th June 1972.
11. *Daily Mail*, 12th November 1975.
12. *Ottawa Citizen*, 16th June 1972.
13. *Nine Five*, BBC Radio Wales, 1978.
14. Lockwood, Margaret, *Lucky Star* (Oldhams Press, London 1955) p176.
15. *Daily Mail*, 21st November 1975.
16. Interview with Catherine Olsen, circa 1977.
17. Hewson, Sherrie, *Behind the Laughter* (Harper, London 2011) p98.
18. Tims, Hilton, *Once a Wicked Lady* (Virgin, London 1989) p197.

Chapter 22: A Downward Spiral

1. Letter to Dorothy Hodge.
2. Interview with Catherine Olsen, circa 1977.
3. Tims, Hilton, *Once a Wicked Lady* (Virgin, London 1989) p198.
4. 'It was as though his style was being cramped.' Interview with Cheryl van Hoorn. Tims, Hilton, *Once a Wicked Lady* (Virgin, London 1989) p199.
5. Interview with Cheryl van Hoorn. Tims, Hilton, *Once a Wicked Lady* (Virgin, London 1989) p199.

6. Interview with Cheryl van Hoorn. Tims, Hilton, *Once a Wicked Lady* (Virgin, London 1989) p199.
7. As told to the author by Julia Lockwood-Clark.
8. *The Mail on Sunday*, 7th September 1986.
9. As told to the author by Julia Lockwood-Clark.
10. *Daily Mail*, circa 1986.
11. Interview with Catherine Olsen, circa 1977.
12. Tims, Hilton, *Once a Wicked Lady* (Virgin, London 1989) p201.
13. Tims, Hilton, *Once a Wicked Lady* (Virgin, London 1989) p201.
14. Letter to Wendy Blanchard.
15. Letter to Wendy Blanchard.
16. Letter to Wendy Blanchard.
17. Tims, Hilton, *Once a Wicked Lady* (Virgin, London 1989) p202.
18. Tims, Hilton, *Once a Wicked Lady* (Virgin, London 1989) p203.
19. Letter to Denis Gilding.
20. Tims, Hilton, *Once a Wicked Lady* (Virgin, London 1989) p205.
21. *Evening Standard*, 13th May 1980.
22. *Round Midnight with Brian Matthew*, Radio 2, 1980.
23. *Evening Standard*, 13th May 1980.
24. Tims, Hilton, *Once a Wicked Lady* (Virgin, London 1989) p205.
25. Letter to Dorothy Hodge.
26. From a copy of Margaret Lockwood's obituary. Publication is unknown. Author's own collection.
27. Interview with Miriam Harrison.

Chapter 23: Curtain Call

1. Letter to Audrey Haylerbrown.
2. Tims, Hilton, *Once a Wicked Lady* (Virgin, London 1989) p207.
3. Winner, Michael, *Tales I Never Told* (Biteback, London 2011).
4. Winner, Michael, *Tales I Never Told* (Biteback, London 2011).
5. 'Lucy spotted him walking up the garden path, and shouted through to the kitchen: "Mummy, Michael Winner's at the door!" Miriam and Lucy asked him in for tea, and after he explained *The Wicked Lady* situation, they told him firmly, "Margaret doesn't want to see anybody."' Author's interview with Tim Harrison.
6. As told to the author by Miriam Harrison.

7. Letter to Denis Gilding.
8. Letter to Audrey Haylerbrown.
9. 'Where Are They Now?' magazine feature, circa 1990.
10. Letter to Wendy Blanchard.
11. As told to the author by Miriam and Tim Harrison.
12. As told to the author by Miriam Harrison.
13. Letter to Wendy Blanchard.
14. Lockwood, Margaret, *Lucky Star* (Oldhams Press, London 1955) p190.
15. As related in *Lucky Star* (Oldhams Press, London 1955) p191.

CW01659192

Enid Blyton®

В СЕРИИ

«ПЯТЬ ЮНЫХ СЫЩИКОВ И ПЁС-ДЕТЕКТИВ» ВЫХОДЯТ:

Тайна сгоревшего коттеджа

•

Тайна пропавшей кошки

•

Тайна секретной комнаты

•

Тайна анонимных писем

•

Тайна жемчужного ожерелья

•

Тайна зловещего дома

•

Тайна ограбления в театре

•

Тайна вора-невидимки

•

Тайна исчезнувшего принца

•

Тайна красной перчатки

•

Тайна украденной мебели

•

Тайна похищенной картины

Энид Блайтон

Пять юных сыщиков

Тайна пропавшей кошки

Перевод с английского
Ольги Пановой

Художник
Александр Кукушкин

Москва
«Махаон»

УДК 821.111-312.4-93
ББК 84(4Вел)
Б68

Enid Blyton
The Find-Outers
THE MYSTERY OF THE DISAPPEARING CAT

Enid Blyton and Enid Blyton's signature are registered trademarks of Hodder & Stoughton Limited.
Text and illustrations © Hodder & Stoughton Limited.
All rights reserved.

First published in Great Britain in 1943

Блайтон Э.
Б68 Тайна пропавшей кошки : прикл. повесть / Энид Блайтон ; пер. с англ. О. Пановой ; худож. А. Кукушкин. – М. : Махаон, Азбука-Аттикус, 2022. – 256 с. : ил. – (Пять юных сыщиков и пёс-детектив).

ISBN 978-5-389-15890-0 *(рус.)*
ISBN 978-1-444-93078-8 *(англ.)*

Пять юных сыщиков снова собираются вместе на летних каникулах. В этот раз они расследуют таинственное исчезновение дорогой сиамской кошки – питомицы леди Кэндлинг, новой соседки Пипа и Бетси. Полицейский А-ну-ка-разойдись и сварливый садовник мистер Склокинг уже готовы обвинить в краже помощника садовника Люка, но сыщики отказываются верить, что этот добродушный паренёк – вор. Кто же тогда украл кошку?

УДК 821.111-312.4-93
ББК 84(4Вел)

© Панова О. Ю., перевод на русский язык, 2022
© Кукушкин А. И., иллюстрации, 2022
© Издание на русском языке, оформление. ООО «Издательская Группа «Азбука-Аттикус», 2022
Machaon ®

ISBN 978-5-389-15890-0 *(рус.)*
ISBN 978-1-444-93078-8 *(англ.)*

Глава первая

Парень по соседству

Бетси была сама не своя от волнения. Её старший брат Пип наконец-то возвращается домой на летние каникулы! Его не было дома три месяца – это же целая вечность! И вот теперь они снова увидятся.

– Завтра приезжает Пип, а послезавтра – Ларри и Дейзи! – радостно сообщила она маме. – Мамочка, как же я соскучилась по ним! Наконец-то мы опять соберёмся вместе!

Ларри и Дейзи, друзья Пипа, тоже были старше Бетси, но обычно принимали её в свою компанию и разрешали ей участвовать в разных играх и затеях. На весенних каникулах они вместе с Фатти – соседским мальчиком, хозяином симпатичного пёсика, играли в сыщиков. Им удалось раскрыть загадочное преступление – они узнали, кто поджёг коттедж в саду мистера Хика.

– Ах, мамочка, вот если бы и в этот раз произошло какое-нибудь таинственное преступление, чтобы клуб сыщиков снова смог что-нибудь расследовать! – мечтательно произнесла Бетси.

Но мама только снисходительно улыбнулась:

– Уж не думаешь ли ты, Бетси, что ты и твои друзья и впрямь стали сыщиками? Брось эти фантазии! Действительно, вам тогда удалось догадаться, кто поджёг коттедж, но вышло это совершенно случайно. Давай-ка лучше одевайся поскорей, нам пора идти встречать Пипа!

И вот Пип снова дома! Он обошёл весь сад вместе с сестрёнкой, и ему казалось, что он не был здесь несколько лет. Бетси непрерывно щебетала, как неугомонная птичка-синичка: она была на седьмом небе от счастья, хотя старший брат не особо обращал на неё внимание.

– Ах, Пип, послушай, Пип! Завтра приезжают Ларри и Дейзи! – Бетси просто задыхалась от радости. – Пип! Слушай, Пип! А мы ведь будем снова играть в сыщиков, правда?

– Ну конечно же, если будет что расследовать. Кстати, Бетси, забыл тебе сказать: Фатти тоже будет здесь на каникулах! Его родителям так понравилось у нас в Петерсвуде, когда они гостили тут весной, что они купили небольшой домик, и Фатти скоро приедет сюда вместе с мамой и папой.

Услышав эту потрясающую новость, Бетси запрыгала от восторга.

– Ах, Пип, как же это чудесно! Фатти ведь приедет не только с мамой и папой, но и с Бастером?

– Ну разумеется! – кивнул Пип.

– Значит, мы снова соберёмся все вместе! Фатти ужасно милый! Он всегда был так добр ко мне! И пёсик у него такой славный! Я так полюбила их обоих! Скорей бы они приехали! А откуда ты узнал, что Фатти будет здесь?

– Он написал мне, – ответил Пип и достал из кармана смятый листок. – На, прочти его письмо. Между прочим, он передаёт тебе привет.

Бетси торопливо раскрыла листок линованной бумаги. На нём твёрдым, аккуратным почерком было написано:

Дорогой Пип,

Пишу тебе, потому что у меня есть важная новость: мои родители купили дом неподалёку от вашего, так что скоро мы встретимся. Я приеду в Петерсвуд на каникулы вместе с мамой и папой. Хорошо бы летом снова произошло какое-нибудь таинственное происшествие, чтобы мы ещё раз стали сыщиками. В прошлый раз у нас отлично получилось!

Передай от меня привет Бетси. Я зайду к вам, как только мы приедем в Петерсвуд.

Твой Фредерик Алджернон Троттвиль

– Интересно, почему он не подписался просто «Фатти»? Разве это не глупо – подписываться «Фредерик Алджернон Троттвиль»?

– Фатти иногда ведёт себя глупо, – пожал плечами Пип. – Надеюсь, он стал меньше задаваться.

Ларри и Дейзи прибыли на следующий день – и, едва успев выпить чаю, помчались к Пипу и Бетси. Наконец-то друзья снова были вместе! Когда они все уселись в беседке, старшие принялись обсуждать уроки, учителей и школьных приятелей, и Бетси почувствовала себя лишней: в школу она ещё не ходила и не могла поддержать разговор. Вздохнув про себя, она в который раз подумала: «Ну почему мне всего лишь восемь?

Ларри целых тринадцать лет, Пипу и Дейзи – двенадцать... Скорей бы стать взрослой!»

Между тем, пока они болтали и смеялись, вдруг раздался скрип калитки, потом цоканье коготков по садовой дорожке – и вот уже маленький чёрный скотчтерьер с радостным лаем пулей влетел в беседку.

– Бастер! Это же Бастер! Иди скорей ко мне, голубчик! Какой же ты умница и красавец! Скучал по нам, Бастер?! – наперебой кричали ребята.

Пёс вскочил на колени к Ларри, дал лапу Дейзи и лизнул Бетси в нос. Все так обрадовались Бастеру, что даже не заметили его хозяина, который появился на садовой дорожке вслед за своей собакой. Первой увидела его Бетси и с радостным визгом бросилась к своему дорогому другу и крепко обняла его. Фатти просиял от радости: Бетси была его любимицей. Остальные ребята, улыбаясь, помахали ему из беседки и крикнули:

– Привет, Фатти!

А Ларри спросил:

– Как твои успехи в школе? Всё в порядке?

– Ещё бы! – приосанившись, ответил Фатти. – Я был в отличной форме!

– Фатти в своём духе! – усмехнулся Пип. – Отличник отличился отличной формой. Скромности тебе не занимать!

– Завидуешь, старина? – рассмеялся Фатти. – Бьюсь об заклад, что ты был хорошим хорошистом – а до отличника не дотянул.

Как чудесно было, растянувшись на зелёной травке, греться в тёплых солнечных лучах и знать, что впереди целых два месяца совершенно свободного времени! Никаких уроков. Никаких контрольных. Никаких домашних заданий. Что может быть лучше летних каникул?!

– Какие новости, Бетси? – поинтересовался Фатти. – Как насчёт загадок, таинственных происшествий и расследований? Сыщики снова в сборе и готовы к новым свершениям!

Бетси вздохнула и покачала головой:

– Никаких загадок, тайн и происшествий... Представь себе, я уже месяц не видела нашего А-ну-ка-разойдись.

Ребята дали такое прозвище деревенскому полицейскому мистеру Гуну, который чуть что сразу всех разгонял. Он терпеть не мог детей, потому что они «вечно путаются под ногами», и дети платили ему той же монетой.

– Да, похоже, ничего интересного в Петерсвуде всё это время не происходило, – развёл руками Пип, но Бетси вдруг радостно воскликнула:

– Вспомнила! Всё-таки есть новости! У нас появилась новая соседка.

Ребята заинтересовались: дом по соседству пустовал уже много лет. Кто же там поселился?

– Новая соседка? – переспросил Пип. – Кто же она? А дети у неё есть?

– Нет... Кажется, нет. Пару раз я там видела какого-то мальчишку, но он, кажется, приходил поливать цветы и полоть грядки в саду. Я слышала, как он насвистывал какую-то песенку – у него получалось очень красиво. О, кстати, у этой соседки живут кошки – очень много кошек.

– Неужели? – удивился Пип, а Бастер, услышав хорошо знакомое слово, навострил уши и глухо заворчал. – И что это за кошки?

– У них длинные тёмные мордочки, лапки и хвостики, – ответила Бетси, – а шёрстка красивого кремового цвета.

– Похоже, это сиамские кошки, – решил Ларри. – А глаза у них какого цвета? Наверное, голубые?

– Не знаю, – пожала плечами Бетси. – Я видела их только издалека и не заметила, какие у них глаза. Вообще-то у кошек они обычно зелёные...

– А вот у сиамских кошек они голубые, – сказал Фатти. – Я точно это знаю, потому что у моей тёти сиамская кошка – очень красивая, по кличке Парвати. Эти кошки породистые и очень дорогие.

– Хотелось бы на них как-нибудь взглянуть, – заинтересовалась Дейзи. – Кремовая шкурка, тёмные лапки, голубые глаза – наверное, они очень симпатичные. Бетси, а как зовут их хозяйку?

– Кажется, леди Кэндлинг. Я её ни разу не видела. Говорят, она часто уезжает, дома почти не бывает.

Дети смолкли. Солнышко пригревало всё жарче, всех разморило, глаза слипались. Бастер, который вначале прыгал возле ребят и пытался лизнуть то одного, то другого в лицо, тоже успокоился и улёгся на травке. Вдруг из-за забора послышался красивый, мелодичный свист.

– Это тот самый мальчишка, – прошептала Бетси. – Как хорошо он насвистывает, правда?

Ларри поднялся, подошёл к забору, залез на большой цветочный горшок и заглянул в соседский сад. Возле грядки стоял мальчик лет пятнадцати – румяный, круглолицый, синеглазый. Он удивился, увидев над забором голову Ларри. Некоторое время они молча смотрели друг на друга.

– Привет! – наконец сказал Ларри. – Ты тут работаешь? Ты садовник?

Паренёк белозубо улыбнулся:

– Нет, я только помогаю садовнику мистеру Склокингу. Это такой старый ворчун, нос крючком, вечно всем недоволен.

Ларри подумал, что этот садовник, судя по всему, малоприятный тип и такая фамилия ему очень подходит.

– Слушай, а можно нам как-нибудь зайти взглянуть на кошек леди Кэндлинг? Это ведь настоящие сиамские кошки?

– Да, сиамские. Они очень красивые. Посмотреть на них можно, но только когда мистера Склокинга не будет поблизости. Он почему-то считает этот дом и сад своими и распоряжается тут как хозяин. Заходите завтра после обеда, можно прямо через забор. Склокинг завтра не собирался приходить, а девушка, которая присматривает за кошками, не будет против. Её зовут мисс Хармер.

– Отлично! Договорились! А тебя как зовут?

Но прежде чем паренёк успел ответить, из-за кустов раздался сердитый голос:

– Люк! Эй, Люк! Ах ты, бездельник! Почему здесь до сих пор валяется этот мусор? Я ещё вчера велел тебе убрать его!

Люк испуганно оглянулся, положил тяпку на грядку и прошептал:

– Это он, Склокинг! Пойду узнаю, чем он недоволен. До завтра! – И он поспешно скрылся в глубине сада.

Ларри спрыгнул с цветочного горшка и вернулся к друзьям.

– Я поговорил с этим пареньком. Он помощник садовника. Зовут его Люк. По-моему, он славный малый.

– А мы и вправду сможем посмотреть на кошек? – Бетси захлопала в ладоши. – Я слышала, он сказал, чтобы мы приходили завтра после обеда!

– Да, завтра мистера Склокинга не будет в саду. Мы перелезем через забор и пойдём смотреть на кошек. Только Бастера не будем брать с собой, а то от кошек останутся только лапки и хвостики!

Бастер снова заворчал при слове «кошки». Кошки! Вот ещё не хватало! Несносные, вредные звери: когтистые, шипящие, трусливые. Никакого от них нет толку, всякий уважающий себя пёс знает, что годятся они только для одного – чтобы гонять их по двору!

Глава вторая

Пренеприятнейшее знакомство с мистером Склокингом

На следующий день сразу после обеда ребята отправились к соседям. Подойдя к забору, Ларри влез на большой садовый глиняный горшок и свистнул, подавая сигнал Люку. Тот вынырнул из гущи кустов и широко улыбнулся.

– Всё в порядке, мистера Склокинга нет. Заходите скорей!

Ребята один за другим быстро перелезли через забор. Фатти помог малышке Бетси. По ту сторону остался только бедняга Бастер, который страшно огорочился, что друзья бросили его одного. Он то отчаянно лаял, то жалобно скулил и царапал забор. Бетси стало ужасно жалко пёсика.

– Не расстраивайся, Бастер! Мы скоро придём! – ласково произнесла она.

– С собаками сюда нельзя, – предупредил Люк. – Здесь же кошки. Они породистые, очень дорогие, участвуют в выставках и уже собрали кучу призов. Так говорит мисс Хармер.

Ребята направились по тропинке, которая вела к теплицам.

– Ты здесь живёшь? – спросил Ларри нового знакомого.

– Нет. Я живу с отчимом. А мама у меня умерла. Братьев и сестёр нет. Я только что пошёл на работу. Это моя первая работа, и я не хочу потерять её. Меня зовут Люк Браун. Мне пятнадцать лет.

– А я – Лоренс Дейкин, мне тринадцать. А это Маргарет, моя сестра, ей двенадцать. Мы зовём её Дейзи. Ещё с нами наш друг Фредерик Алджернон Троттвиль. Ему тоже двенадцать лет, и мы дали ему прозвище Фатти.

– Вообще-то я предпочитаю, чтобы меня звали Фредерик, – хмуро сказал мистер Троттвиль. – И мне непонятно, почему всякий встречный-поперечный должен звать меня Фатти!

– Ты ведь не всякий встречный-поперечный, правда? – сказала Бетси Люку. – Наоборот, ты встречный-сговорчивый, потому что сразу же разрешил нам посмотреть на кошек!

Люк звонко рассмеялся и легонько хлопнул Фатти по плечу:

– Ну, раз я такой сговорчивый, так и быть, не стану тебе перечить и буду звать тебя Фредерик!

– А меня можно звать просто Бетси, хотя вообще-то меня зовут Элизабет Хилтон, и мне восемь лет, – Бетси поторопилась представиться, боясь, что Ларри забудет про неё. – А вот мой брат Филипп, которого мы все зовём Пип! Ему двенадцать лет.

Ребята рассказали Люку, где они живут, а Люк рассказал, что он живёт в старом домике-развалюхе прямо у реки. Так, дружески беседуя, они миновали теплицы и оказались у великолепного розария, за которым виднелся небольшой домик, выкрашенный в зелёный цвет. Люк показал на него пальцем.

– Вот тут и живут сиамские кошки, – сообщил он. – А вот и мисс Хармер.

Возле кошачьего домика ребята встретили женщину лет двадцати в брюках и твидовом жакете.

– Добрый день! – поздоровалась она, удивлённо осматривая детей. – Откуда вы взялись?

– Добрый день, мисс Хармер! Мы взялись из-за забора, – вежливо ответил Ларри. – Вы позволите нам взглянуть на кошек? Говорят, они у вас какие-то особенные?

– Да, такие кошки – большая редкость, – кивнула мисс Хармер. – Взгляните сами!

Ребята заглянули в кошачий домик. Кошек было много, и они действительно были необычайной красоты – бежевые и кремовые с тёмно-коричневыми мордочками, ушками, лапками

и хвостами. Кошки смотрели на незваных гостей большими сверкающими ярко-голубыми глазами и мяукали на разные голоса.

– Что за прелестные кошечки! – восхитилась Дейзи.

– А по-моему, они очень смешные! – пожал плечами Пип.

– Неужели это и вправду кошки? – удивилась Бетси. – Они больше похожи на обезьянок.

Все дружно рассмеялись.

– Протяни-ка руку – и сразу почувствуешь, что это кошки, а вовсе не обезьянки! – усмехнулась мисс Хармер. – Все эти кошки постоянно ездят на выставки и уже принесли хозяйке кучу денег.

– А которая из них выиграла самый большой приз? – поинтересовалась Бетси.

– Во-о-он та. – Мисс Хармер показала на кошку, сидевшую в отдельном маленьком вольере. – Принцесса! Принцесса! Ах ты наша красавица! Иди-ка сюда, пусть гости полюбуются тобой!

Большая сиамская кошка подошла к стенке вольера и с громким мурлыканьем стала тереться о прутья.

– Принцесса – это наша гордость, – сказала мисс Хармер, ласково поглаживая кошку. – Она только что получила огромный приз на престижной выставке. Такая кошка стоит целое состояние.

Принцесса смирно стояла возле стенки вольера, слегка покачивая тёмно-коричневым хвостом. Некоторое время Бетси внимательно разглядывала её, а потом воскликнула:

– Ах, посмотрите-ка! У неё на кончике хвоста шёрстка не коричневая, а бежевая!

– Верно, – кивнула мисс Хармер. – Когда она ещё жила вместе со всеми в большом вольере, её покусала одна из кошек, на месте укуса выросли светлые волоски. Но это не страшно, они потом потемнеют. Как вам наша Принцесса?

– По-моему, она ничем не отличается от остальных кошек, – пожала плечами Дейзи. – Они все так похожи, что их и не отличишь друг от друга.

– Да, они похожи, – согласилась мисс Хармер. – Они все одной расцветки и вроде бы все одинаковые. Но это только на первый взгляд. Я всегда сумею отличить их друг от друга, никогда не перепутаю одну кошку с другой.

– Не могу представить себе, что кошка может стоить целое состояние! – воскликнул Фатти, разглядывая Принцессу, которая тоже смотрела на него блестящими голубыми глазами. – Люк, а ведь у тебя глаза точь-в-точь как у сиамских кошек! Точь-в-точь как у Принцессы!

Все рассмеялись, а Люк смущённо улыбнулся.

– А вы не могли бы на минуточку выпустить Принцессу из вольера? – попросила Дейзи. Ей очень хотелось взять кошку на руки. – Она ведь домашняя и не боится людей?

– Они все домашние и охотно общаются с людьми, – ответила мисс Хармер. – Мы держим их в клетке только потому, что это очень дорогие, породистые кошки. Нельзя позволить им свободно бродить по дому и по саду – за ними будет трудно уследить, они могут сбежать или их могут украсть.

Мисс Хармер сняла с гвоздика ключ, отперла дверцу и вынула из клетки Принцессу. Дейзи осторожно погладила красавицу-кошку, и та прыгнула прямо на руки девочке.

Дейзи восхищённо вздохнула:

– Что за прекрасная кошечка! И какая ласковая!

Вдруг послышался громкий лай – это Бастер каким-то чудом прорвался в сад. Пёсик стремительно пронёсся по дорожке и с радостным тявканьем бросился к Фатти. В тот же миг Принцесса выгнула спину, зашипела, вырвалась из рук Дейзи и стремглав нырнула в заросли кустов у дорожки. От удивления Бастер смолк, но ненадолго: в следующее мгновение он с оглушительным лаем ринулся за пушистой беглянкой. Что тут началось!

Мисс Хармер пронзительно визжала, Люк в панике озирался по сторонам, кошки хором принялись мяукать, а Фатти закричал что было мочи:

– Бастер! Бастер!! Фу!!! Ко мне!!! КО МНЕ!!!

Но не тут-то было! Бастер и ухом не повёл. Ещё бы! Настоящий охотник за кошками никогда не останавливается на полпути! Бастер моментально оказался возле кустов, засунул туда нос и взвизгнул от боли: куст оказался очень колючим. Однако боль не уменьшила его охотничьего азарта: уши у него стояли торчком, глаза блестели, а хвост так и ходил ходуном вправо-влево.

Следом за Бастером к кустам подскочила мисс Хармер.

– Где Принцесса?! – пронзительно крикнула она. – Она потерялась? Какой ужас! Несносный пёс! Брысь! То есть фу! Пошёл вон!

Бетси разрыдалась: она испугалась, что кошечка потеряется. Ей почудился шум в кустах, и она бросилась прямо в густые заросли, в надежде отыскать Принцессу.

Вдруг с другой стороны сада послышались шаги, и из-за деревьев показался какой-то человек. Это был мистер Склокинг собственной персоной! Завидев его, Люк от страха лишился дара речи.

– Что тут происходит? – грозно спросил садовник. – Кто вы такие и что вы делаете в моём саду?

– Это вовсе не ваш сад! – дерзко возразил ему Фатти. – Это сад леди Кэндлинг! Я с ней хорошо знаком – она дружит с моей мамой.

Услышав такое, мистер Склокинг окончательно вышел из себя. Он давно уже считал этот сад своей вотчиной и был убеждён, что каждая травинка, каждый кустик, каждый цветок здесь – его собственность. И вот пожалуйста: в этот райский уголок ворвались дети и собаки – целая орава вандалов! Мистер Склокинг терпеть не мог детей и собак.

– А ну марш отсюда! – загремел он, размахивая граблями. – Убирайтесь! Живо! Если я ещё раз увижу вас у себя в саду, я надеру вам уши и сообщу вашим родителям! Пусть они вас как следует выпорют! Мисс Хармер, в чём дело? Мне надоело ваше хныканье!

– Принцесса! Где Принцесса? Принцесса сбежала! – простонала мисс Хармер, опасливо поглядывая на мистера Склокинга. Похоже, она не меньше Люка боялась сварливого садовника.

– Сбежала? Что ж, очень хорошо! Надеюсь, теперь вас наконец-то выгонят с работы! Может, выпустить всех остальных кошек? Кому они нужны? Бесполезные твари. Терпеть их не могу!

– Мисс Хармер, давайте мы поможем найти Принцессу, – предложила Дейзи.

Но тут раздался рёв мистера Склокинга:

– А ну убирайтесь отсюда! Чтобы через минуту духа вашего здесь не было!

От ярости его крючковатый нос покраснел, как помидор, а соломенная шляпа съехала на затылок. Он угрожающе сжимал тяжёлые кулаки и яростно топал ногами. Дети решили бежать. Они заметили, что Бетси исчезла, но подумали, что она уже перелезла через забор.

Фатти позвал Бастера, но садовник схватил пса и крикнул:

– Собака останется здесь! Я запру её в сарай, чтобы вам было неповадно водить псов в мой сад!

– Не смейте трогать Бастера! Это не ваша собака! Я сейчас прикажу ему, и он вас укусит! – крикнул Фатти, но садовник, не слушая его, бросил пса в сарай, запер дверь на ключ, положил ключ в карман и направился прямо к Фатти. Мальчик бросился наутёк, а за ним и все остальные.

Ребята перелезли через забор, добежали до беседки и упали на траву, чтобы отдышаться. Люк и мисс Хармер остались по ту сторону забора –

и Бетси тоже. Впрочем, они думали не о Бетси, а о бедняжке Бастере, запертом в сарае.

– Какой негодяй! – сквозь слёзы пробормотала Дейзи.

– Просто свинья! – бросил сквозь зубы Фатти.

– Бедный наш Бастер! – вздохнул Пип.

Все прислушались. Из соседского сада донёсся пронзительный вой. Ларри оглянулся.

– Где же Бетси? Куда она подевалась? Эй, Бетси! Отзовись!

Ответа не было.

– Может быть, она уже дома? – пожал плечами Пип. – Как же нам теперь быть? Надо вызволить Бастера. Мы не можем бросить его там одного.

– Бедный Бастер! – всхлипнула Дейзи. – И бедная Принцесса! Хоть бы она нашлась... Интересно, как Бастеру удалось пробраться в соседский сад? Не мог же он перемахнуть через забор?

– Нет, конечно, – отозвался Фатти. – Он, должно быть, пораскинул мозгами и понял, что надо выбежать на улицу, подойти к соседской двери, подлезть под неё – и готово дело! Бастер – исключительно умный пёс. Однако что же нам делать? Как нам освободить его? Проклятый мистер Склокинг! Этого я ему никогда не прощу!

Бедняга Люк... Подумать только, этот Склокинг им командует! И как только Люк это терпит?

– Пойду-ка я поищу Бетси, – решил Пип. – Малышка, должно быть, так перепугалась, что спряталась где-то в доме. Надо её найти.

Пип зашёл в дом и через несколько минут снова вернулся в сад.

– Её нигде нет! – тревожно сказал он. – Куда она подевалась? Она же не могла остаться там, за забором, правда? Такого быть не может!

Но дело обстояло именно так. Бетси осталась за забором, в саду леди Кэндлинг. Она не могла перелезть через забор сама, без помощи старших, и она не могла выбраться на улицу через садовую калитку, потому что её обязательно заметил бы страшный мистер Склокинг.

Глава третья

Люк приходит друзьям на помощь

Бетси в поисках Принцессы бросилась в заросли кустов, но увидела там только большого чёрного дрозда, который тут же улетел.

– Кис-кис-кис, – звала Бетси, как вдруг, подняв голову, она увидела два сверкающих ярко-голубых глаза. Это была Принцесса, которая, усевшись на дереве, обозревала окрестности. Бетси подпрыгнула от радости. – Ах, Принцесса! Вот ты где! Как хорошо, что я тебя нашла!

Когда первая радость прошла, Бетси задумалась: пожалуй, не стоит снимать Принцессу с дерева, пока из сада не уведут Бастера. На дереве кошка будет в безопасности. Бетси ласково улыбнулась Принцессе, и кошка замурлыкала в ответ. Ей понравилась эта маленькая девочка.

Бетси удалось залезть на дерево. Она добралась до ветки, на которой сидела Принцесса, и стала гладить кошку по спинке. Принцесса, громко мурлыча, принялась тереться своей коричневой мордочкой о руки Бетси.

В этот момент неподалёку раздался хриплый голос мистера Склокинга. Господи! Неужели он вернулся? Или он вообще не уходил? Садовник что-то злобно кричал, и напуганная Бетси не решилась выйти из укрытия, чтобы вместе с остальными ребятами покинуть сад. Замерев от страха, она тихонько сидела рядом с Принцессой и прислушивалась, пытаясь понять, что же там происходит. Вскоре Бетси стало ясно, что все убежали, бросив её одну. Девочка уже приготовилась слезть с дерева, отыскать мисс Хармер и сказать ей, что Принцесса нашлась, как вдруг совсем рядом послышались чьи-то шаги. Выглянув из-за густой листвы, Бетси увидела мистера Склокинга, который держал за шиворот своего юного помощника.

– Ах ты, негодник! Вздумал приводить своих приятелей в мой сад! – рычал садовник, встряхивая беднягу Люка как тряпичную куклу. – За что тебе платят деньги, спрашивается? Сегодня будешь работать ещё два часа сверхурочно. И смотри у меня! В следующий раз так легко не отделаешься!

Наконец садовник отпустил мальчика и ушёл в глубину сада. Люк взял тяпку и побрёл в другую сторону. И тут Бетси тихонько окликнула его:

– Люк!

От неожиданности мальчик уронил тяпку и испуганно огляделся. Вокруг никого не было.

– Люк! – снова позвала Бетси. – Это я! Я тут, на дереве, и со мной рядом Принцесса!

Мальчик наконец увидел и Бетси, и кошку, примостившихся на дереве. Бетси бесшумно спрыгнула вниз.

– Люк, помоги мне, пожалуйста, перелезть через забор, – попросила она.

Люк был еле жив от страха, его щёки раскраснелись, в глазах стояли слёзы. Бетси тоже была насмерть перепугана.

– Если мистер Склокинг заметит, то выгонит меня с работы, – прошептал он.

– А-а... Тогда лучше не надо. Я не хочу, чтобы ты из-за меня потерял работу, – сказала Бетси. – Я уж как-нибудь сама...

Однако Люк, хоть и был напуган, решил помочь малышке. Они сняли Принцессу с дерева и крадучись пошли по тропинке, всё время озираясь. Наконец они очутились возле кошачьего домика. Люк посадил Принцессу в клетку и закрыл дверцу.

– То-то обрадуется мисс Хармер! – шепнул он Бетси. – Сейчас пойду скажу ей, только сначала помогу тебе выбраться из сада.

Они побежали к забору. Люк подсадил Бетси, и вскоре она уже сидела на ограде.

– Давай скорей! – торопливо шепнул Люк. – Я слышу шаги мистера Склокинга!

От испуга Бетси спрыгнула с забора, ободрав ладони и коленки. Задыхаясь, она помчалась к беседке, возле которой на травке расположились её друзья, и упала рядом с ними, не в силах произнести ни слова.

– Бетси! Где ты пропадала?! – воскликнул Пип.

– Ты что, осталась там одна? Ох, только взгляните! У неё же все ноги в крови! – всплеснул руками Фатти.

– И руки тоже, – пробормотала Бетси дрожащим голосом.

Фатти вынул носовой платок и аккуратно вытер ободранные ладошки и коленки.

– Как же тебе удалось перелезть через забор? – спросил он.

– Мне помог Люк, хотя ему было очень страшно. Если бы мистер Склокинг увидел, Люк потерял бы работу.

– Молодец! – одобрительно заметил Ларри. Все остальные были того же мнения.

– Люк мне очень понравился, – сказала Бетси. – Он очень хороший. Жаль, что мы так его подвели. Он согласился пустить нас в сад и показать нам кошек, а мы...

Она не успела закончить – из соседского сада вдруг послышался заунывный собачий вой. Бетси удивлённо прислушалась, а потом оглянулась вокруг.

– А где же Бастер? – спросила она. Сидя в кустах, она слышала шум и крики, но конечно же не могла видеть, как садовник утащил пса и запер в сарае.

Ребята рассказали ей, что произошло. Бетси была вне себя от возмущения.

– Мы должны освободить его! – со слезами на глазах твердила она. – Пошли, Фатти! Мы перелезем через забор и заберём Бастера!

Однако Фатти не горел желанием снова очутиться лицом к лицу со злобным садовником. Кроме того, он знал, что Склокинг забрал с собой ключ от сарая, где сидел арестованный Бастер.

– Бедненький наш Бастер! Он снова завыл. Давайте пойдём к забору и посмотрим, что там происходит. Если увидим Люка, попросим его заглянуть в окошко сарая и подбодрить Бастера.

Ребята на цыпочках подкрались к забору. Ларри встал на глиняный горшок и оглядел соседский сад. Никого не было видно. И вдруг они услышали, как кто-то вдалеке насвистывает мелодию. Ну конечно же это был Люк! Ларри пару раз свистнул в ответ. Наступила пауза, а потом мелодичный свист повторился. Ларри повторил мелодию. Послышался шелест кустов и звук приближающихся шагов. Вскоре из зарослей показался краснощёкий Люк.

– В чём дело, ребята? – прошептал он. – Мне нельзя болтать с вами. Мистер Склокинг ходит рядом.

– Мы беспокоимся о Бастере, – ответил Ларри тоже шёпотом. – Не мог бы ты заглянуть в окошко сарая и сказать ему что-нибудь ласковое? Например: «Бастер! Хороший пёс! Держись, Бастер!» Это бы его подбодрило.

Люк кивнул и ушёл в глубину сада. Оглядываясь по сторонам, он направился было к сараю, но тут же увидел Склокинга, который собирался поработать и для этого снял куртку, повесив её на гвоздь, вбитый в стенку теплицы.

Заметив Люка, садовник сердито закричал:

– Ах ты, лодырь! Ты что, всё ещё не вскопал эту грядку? Ах, уже вскопал? Тогда иди сюда, подвязывай помидоры!

Люк что-то крикнул ему в ответ и исчез в ближайших кустах. Оттуда он увидел, как Склокинг направился к огороду и, задержавшись на минуту, чтобы распутать листья пальмы, скрылся за зелёной калиткой.

И тут Люк решился на отчаянный поступок. Выскочив из кустов, он подбежал к куртке садовника, вытащил из кармана ключ и помчался к сараю. По плану, который он придумал, надо было взять Бастера на руки, отнести его к забору и перекинуть на другую сторону. Но едва он отпер дверь, как Бастер проскочил у него между ног и бросился наутёк.

Люк торопливо запер замок, побежал обратно к теплице, где висела куртка садовника, и опустил ключ в карман. Затем он поспешил в огород, надеясь, что Бастеру хватит ума самому выбраться из сада.

Однако надежды его не оправдались. Бастер, похоже, заблудился. Обежав сад, он неожиданно появился в огороде и радостно тявкнул, увидев своего спасителя. Мистер Склокинг недоумённо уставился на пса.

– Опять этот пёс! – с досадой проворчал он. – Как же он умудрился выбраться из сарая? Ведь я же запер его на ключ! И ключ должен лежать у меня в кармане.

– Ну конечно же вы заперли дверь на ключ, сэр, – заверил его Люк. – Наверное, это какая-то другая собака. А та всё ещё сидит взаперти.

Мистер Склокинг завопил не своим голосом и принялся размахивать руками, как ветряная мельница. Бастер тут же включился в игру и поскакал по грядкам, радостно топча морковку и капусту. Люк был уверен, что пёс нарочно дразнит своего мучителя. От попыток поймать собаку Склокинг весь побагровел и едва переводил дух.

– Пошёл вон! – завопил он, хватая грабли.

Бастер звонко тявкнул и стал яростно раскапывать грядку. Свёкла и морковка полетели вверх тормашками.

Склокинг побелел от ярости. Он бросился спасать овощи, а Бастер, перепрыгнув через несколько грядок, принялся за зелёный лук и укроп. Наконец игра ему надоела, и он выбежал из огорода через зелёную калитку, промчался по садовой дорожке и выскочил на улицу. Там он сразу нашёл дорогу к дому Пипа и вскоре был среди ребят, которые кинулись гладить, обнимать и целовать его и хором загомонили:

– Бастер! Бастер! Умница! Молодец! Как же ты выбрался оттуда? Ты цел? Не ушибся? С тобой всё в порядке?

Бастер, страшно довольный, катался по траве с боку на бок, размахивал лапами, радостно тявкал и колотил хвостом по земле.

– Ай да пёс! – Фатти погладил его по тёплому круглому животику. – Жаль, что ты не можешь рассказать нам, как тебе удалось вырваться оттуда!

Ребята лежали на лужайке возле беседки, дожидаясь, когда Люк закончит работу и отправится домой. Обычно он освобождался в пять, но сегодня Склокинг решил проучить его и заставил работать до семи. Люк был крепкий и сильный мальчик, но к концу дня сильно устал. Наконец он вышел на улицу. Ребята тут же окружили его.

– Знаешь, Люк, а Бастер-то выбрался из сарая! – сообщил ему Пип.

Люк кивнул в ответ:

– Знаю, конечно. Это я его выпустил. Мне удалось вытащить ключ из куртки Склокинга. Вы бы видели его физиономию, когда Бастер вдруг появился в огороде! Его чуть удар не хватил.

– Люк, дружище, так это ты освободил Бастера? Слушай, ты просто герой! Даже не знаю, как тебя благодарить! – На радостях Фатти изо всех сил хлопнул Люка по плечу. – Мы так волновались за него! Как же ты не побоялся его выпустить? Тебе, наверное, было очень страшно?

– Это точно, – подтвердил Люк. Он почесал в затылке и живо припомнил, как он дрожал, когда вытаскивал ключ из куртки садовника. – Но пёс ведь ни в чём не виноват! И потом, я представляю, как вы за него волновались.

– Ах, Люк, какой же ты хороший! – восхищённо сказала Бетси и крепко пожала руку мальчика. – Ты помог мне перелезть через забор, а потом освободил Бастера. Теперь мы – твои друзья.

– Ты выручил нас из беды, и, если ты попадёшь в беду, ты всегда сможешь рассчитывать на нас!

– Спасибо, ребята! Но надеюсь, вам не придётся вступаться за меня, – улыбнулся Люк. – Я бы не хотел доставлять вам хлопот. А у меня к вам просьба: не лазьте больше через забор, а то я точно потеряю работу.

– Обещаем! – ответил за всех Фатти. – И помни, если понадобится, мы всегда готовы прийти на помощь!

Глава четвёртая

Мисс Тримбл оправдывает своё прозвище

Люк оказался отличным другом. Он не умел читать и писать, но зато знал много такого, о чём ребята и не подозревали.

Он делал свистульки из полых стеблей для Бетси. Он научил её свистеть на разные лады – чудеса, да и только! Он знал каждую птичку в лесу, знал, где они гнездятся, какие у них яйца и как они поют. Ребята часто ходили гулять с Люком, слушали его рассказы и без конца восхищались своим новым другом.

– Откуда он всё это знает? Ведь он не умеет ни читать, ни писать! – удивлялся Пип. – А как ловко он вырезает из дерева животных и птиц! Смотрите, какую он мне подарил белку!

– А мне он обещал сделать фигурку Принцессы, – объявила Бетси. – Люк раскрасит её, и она будет совсем как живая, с бежевой полоской на хвостике и ярко-голубыми глазами!

Через два дня Люк действительно сделал деревянную фигурку Принцессы. Дети услышали из соседского сада свист и поспешили к забору. Там их ждал Люк. Он вручил Бетси фигурку – и ребята с восторгом стали рассматривать её. Это был верх искусства! Даже Фатти, который считал себя непревзойдённым художником, не скрывал своего восхищения.

– Какая красота! – воскликнул он. – А какие краски! Тёмно-коричневые ушки, лапки, хвост, блестящие ярко-голубые глаза – и даже бежевая полоска на хвосте, там, где её укусила другая кошка. Вылитая Принцесса!

– Да, у Принцессы бежевая полоска на хвосте, но скоро на этом месте вырастет тёмная шерсть. Мисс Хармер говорит, что это ничуть не повредит ей на кошачьих соревнованиях.

– А как поживает старина Склокинг? – поинтересовался Пип.

– Лучше не вспоминай про него, – вздохнул Люк. – Врагу не пожелаю такого начальника. Чуть что – сразу в крик. Но ещё хуже, когда он жалуется на меня отчиму. Отчим и так меня терпеть не может...

Ребята сочувствовали Люку. Жизнь у него была не сахар, а ведь он заслуживал лучшей доли. Он был хорошим, добрым, щедрым, в любой момент был готов прийти на помощь. Он любил малышку Бетси и всегда защищал её, если Пип начинал поддразнивать или строго воспитывать её.

Бастер тоже обожал Люка.

– Он благодарен тебе за то, что ты спас его от Склокинга, – сказал как-то раз Фатти, наблюдая, как пёс пытается забраться на колени к Люку и лизнуть его в нос.

– Славная собака! – ответил Люк. – Я вообще люблю собак. И кошек тоже люблю – они такие красивые, правда?

– Мы видели сегодня у вас в саду какую-то леди, – сказал Ларри. – Средних лет, волосы собраны в пучок, сама она очень худая, с красным носом, и с этого носа очки всё время падают. Это не леди Кэндлинг?

– Нет, это её компаньонка мисс Тримбл. Я зову её Трусиха – потому что она жутко боится Склокинга. Она должна украшать дом цветами, и каждый раз, когда она идёт в сад, чтобы срезать свежие цветы и сделать букеты, Склокинг так и ходит вокруг неё кругами и ворчит, как злобный пёс, – того гляди, укусит! «Не срезайте розы, а то весь куст засохнет!», «Не вздумайте рвать маки – они осыпятся!», «Нельзя трогать цветы на жаре – они сразу завянут!». Бедная Трусиха вся трясётся от страха как осиновый лист.

– Похоже, все трясутся от страха при виде мистера Склокинга, – хмыкнула Дейзи. – Жуткий тип! Ну да ничего, рано или поздно он получит по заслугам!

– Пошли, Люк, я тебе покажу мой садик, – сказала Бетси, потянув его за рукав. – У меня там как раз цветёт львиный зев.

Люк пошёл за ней. Бетси отгородила себе маленький участок, где посадила шиповник, маленький куст крыжовника, львиный зев и алые маки.

– Красота! – воскликнул Люк. – А крыжовник ты уже собирала?

– Нет, ни разу, – вздохнула Бетси. – А ещё в прошлом году я посадила две клубнички – зарыла в землю две красные спелые ягодки и всё ждала, что они вырастут, но они так и не взошли. Так обидно! А я-то надеялась, что в начале лета у меня будет своя клубника...

Люк звонко рассмеялся:

– Ха-ха-ха! Нет, Бетси, чтобы вырастить клубнику, не надо сажать в землю ягоды. Тут нужна рассада. У клубники есть усы – длинные побеги, которые отходят от кустиков. Их-то и надо посадить, чтобы они дали корни. Знаешь, давай-ка я дам тебе клубничную рассаду из нашего сада. Я сейчас как раз расчищаю грядки, и у меня полным-полно этих усов. Я собирался их выкинуть, но, если хочешь, пойдём со мной, выберем тебе несколько штук.

– А можно? – нерешительно спросила Бетси. – Они действительно никому не нужны? Ты и вправду собирался их выкинуть?

– Да, я собирался сжечь всю эту кучу! – кивнул Люк. – Завтра у нашего приятеля Склокинга выходной, так что ты смело можешь перелезть через забор. Я покажу тебе, где растут усы, и у тебя будет клубничная рассада.

На следующий день Пип помог Бетси перелезть через забор, а Люк встретил её с другой стороны, привёл на клубничную грядку и показал ягодные кустики, которые выросли из усов, взятых от прошлогоднего урожая.

– Какая умница эта клубника! Старые кустики дают и ягоды, и новые побеги! – восхищённо всплеснула руками Бетси. – А вот эти ты собираешься выбросить? – поинтересовалась она, указав на груду вырванных кустов. – Сколько мне взять?

– Возьми штук пять-шесть, – предложил Люк. Он выбрал самые лучшие, крепкие и длинные усы и отдал их Бетси.

– Ой, кто это? – вдруг спросила девочка, завидев вдалеке какую-то фигуру.

– Это мисс Тримбл. Не бойся её. Она и мухи не обидит.

Мисс Тримбл подошла к детям, приветливо улыбаясь, однако Бетси она совсем не понравилась: худющая, кожа да кости, странные очки без оправы, которые всё время падали с её носа и висели на короткой цепочке. «Интересно, сколько раз они упадут?» – подумала Бетси.

– Ах, какая славная маленькая девочка! Как её зовут? – прощебетала мисс Тримбл, по-птичьи склонив набок голову. Очки тут же соскочили с её носа, и она привычным жестом водрузила их на место.

– Меня зовут Бетси, я живу по соседству, – отрекомендовалась Бетси.

– А что это у тебя такое? – спросила мисс Тримбл, показывая на кустики клубники, которые Бетси зажала в кулачке. – Золото? Драгоценные камни?

– Нет, – ответила Бетси. – Это всего-навсего клубничные усы.

Очки мисс Тримбл опять упали и повисли на цепочке, так что ей снова пришлось их надевать.

– Усы? Ты хочешь их посадить? Не боишься, что вырастет борода? – Мисс Тримбл громко рассмеялась над собственной, скажем прямо, не самой удачной шуткой и снова поправила очки, которые никак не хотели держаться на месте.

Бетси улыбнулась из вежливости, хотя «бородатая» шутка вовсе не показалась ей смешной.

– Почему у вас очки всё время падают? – поинтересовалась девочка. – Наверное, у вас слишком тонкий нос?

– Какая смешная малышка! – хихикнула мисс Тримбл. – До свидания, крошка! Мне надо заняться делами.

Она ушла, и Бетси вздохнула с облегчением.

– Очки у неё упали шесть раз! – сказала девочка.

– Неужели ты считала? – усмехнулся Люк. – Надеюсь, она не скажет мистеру Склокингу, что видела тебя здесь.

Однако Люк просчитался. Мисс Тримбл выдала их садовнику – хоть и без всякого злого умысла. Она даже не знала, что пару дней назад Склокинг выгнал ребят из сада.

Это случилось на следующий день. Мисс Тримбл вышла в сад за розами. Едва она принялась срезать цветы, как рядом с ней словно из-под земли вырос Склокинг. Он не сводил с неё глаз, и бедная леди была сама не своя. Она очень боялась грубого, злобного садовника.

Мисс Тримбл взглянула на него и, насилу выдавив из себя улыбку, произнесла:

– Чудесное утро, не правда ли, мистер Склокинг? И чудесные розы!

– Чудесно было бы, если бы вы не трогали их! – рявкнул мистер Склокинг.

– О! Я не причиню им вреда! Я умею срезать розы! – попыталась возразить мисс Тримбл.

– Умеете? Не смешите меня! Вы, голубушка, как дитя малое! – проворчал садовник, довольный тем, что ему удалось в очередной раз запугать бедняжку.

Мисс Тримбл воспользовалась случаем и попыталась перевести разговор на другую тему:

– Между прочим, вчера Люк привёл сюда прелестное дитя. Такая очаровательная малышка!

Лицо Склокинга стало чернее тучи.

– Что-о-о-о? Этот негодник Люк опять привёл сюда девчонку? Где этот бездельник? Я с него шкуру спущу! Я запретил ему пускать в сад детей! Люк! Эй! Где ты? Ну, погоди! – И Склокинг, размахивая кулаками, ушёл на поиски своего помощника.

Мисс Тримбл задрожала от страха. Её очки в очередной раз соскочили с носа и запутались в кружевном воротничке, так что бедняжке пришлось изрядно повозиться, чтобы извлечь их оттуда.

– О, какой ужас! Этот садовник – настоящее чудовище! – бормотала она себе под нос. – Похоже, я подвела бедного Люка. Вот досада! Такой милый мальчик! Остаётся надеяться, что всё обойдётся...

Однако, увы, не обошлось. Склокинг налетел на него как коршун. Его серые стальные глаза под кустистыми седыми бровями так и буравили Люка.

– А ну, признавайся, кто к тебе приходил вчера? – прошипел садовник. – Девчонка из соседнего дома? Что ей было надо?

– Мы ничего плохого не делали, мистер Склокинг! Эта девочка очень славная.

– Я спросил, ЧТО ЕЙ БЫЛО НАДО?! – заревел Склокинг. – Маленькая воровка! Небось таскала из нашего сада персики или сливы!

Люк горячо вступился за Бетси:

– Ничего подобного! Эта малышка – наша соседка. Она ничего не брала без спроса! Я сам дал ей немножко клубничных усов, чтобы она посадила их у себя. Эти усы мы всё равно собирались сжечь!

У Склокинга был такой вид, будто его вот-вот хватит удар. Подумать только! Этот мошенник Люк раздаёт рассаду направо и налево! С какой стати мальчишка хозяйничает в его саду? (Склокинг считал, что сад принадлежит ему, а вовсе не леди Кэндлинг. Ему и в голову не пришло, что настоящая хозяйка сада охотно подарила бы девочке клубничные усы. Леди Кэндлинг очень любила детей.)

Склокинг был вне себя от ярости. Он направился к забору, явно намереваясь устроить скандал соседям. Люк был уверен, что ребят там нет – он слышал, как они выкатили на улицу велосипеды и уехали, весело смеясь. Наклонясь над грядкой, он снова принялся за работу, но мысль о мисс Тримбл не давала ему покоя. «Трусиха! Ну конечно же это она выдала Бетси!» – думал он.

Ребята действительно уехали кататься на велосипедах. Только Бетси осталась дома с Бастером. Как же это обидно, когда ты на целых пять лет младше всех остальных! Как досадно, когда говорят, что ты слишком мала для такой далёкой прогулки! Вечно исключают из самых интересных игр, не хотят брать с собой и бросают одну-одинёшеньку!

– Бастер, иди ко мне! Садись поближе, я почитаю тебе сказку про кроликов, – позвала пёсика Бетси.

Услышав слово «кролики», Бастер подбежал к ней, думая, что они отправятся на прогулку. Но вместо этого Бетси села под дерево, достала книгу и принялась читать:

– «Жил да был большой, толстый кролик, и звали его Уофли. Однажды он...»

Бастеру сразу же стало скучно. Он выбежал из сада и потрусил вниз по улице – навстречу ребятам. Бетси осталась одна. Вдруг за её спиной раздался шум. Бетси обернулась и... о ужас! Она увидела страшного садовника, мистера Склокинга. Лицо его было перекошено от ярости, глаза метали молнии. Он уже почти перелез через забор. Помощи ждать было неоткуда.

Глава пятая

Склокинг, Бастер и мистер Гун

Бетси оцепенела от ужаса. Она была не в силах ни бежать, ни даже подняться с земли. Она оглянулась в поисках Бастера, но его нигде не было.

– Это ты взяла мои клубничные усы?! – прикрикнул мистер Склокинг. – Где они? Покажи их мне, живо!

Бетси пришлось отвести его в свой садик. Увидев аккуратно посаженные и политые кустики, мистер Склокинг наклонился и вырвал их – все до одного. Потом он разорвал их на мелкие кусочки и швырнул в костёр, который тлел неподалёку. Бетси горько заплакала.

– Скверная девчонка! – топнул ногой мистер Склокинг. – Учти, если ты ещё хоть раз сунешься в мой сад, я вызову моего старого друга, полицейского мистера Гуна. Он всё расскажет твоему отцу, и тебе как следует надерут уши!

С этими словами мистер Склокинг направился к забору, однако уйти целым и невредимым ему не удалось. В сад вихрем влетел Бастер. Он услышал плач Бетси, учуял запах Склокинга и сразу понял, что к чему. Не зря Бастер славился сообразительностью!

Он с рычанием бросился на Склокинга и вцепился зубами в его левую штанину.

Садовник завопил от ужаса:

– А-а-а-а! Проклятье! Убери свою бешеную собаку!

Бетси стала звать пса:

– Нельзя, Бастер! Фу! Ко мне!

Но не тут-то было! Бастер твёрдо решил показать Склокингу, как обижать его друзей.

– Р-р-р-р-р!

Перепуганный Склокинг попытался выдернуть штанину из пасти грозного зверя, как вдруг – кр-р-р-ах! – ткань с треском разорвалась и изрядный кусок брюк остался в зубах у Бастера. Пёс с видом победителя улёгся под кустом и с наслаждением принялся терзать свою добычу. Воспользовавшись передышкой, Склокинг потрусил было к забору, но Бастер с рычанием выскочил из засады и впился в лодыжку незваного гостя. Склокинг издал душераздирающий вопль и перемахнул через забор, оставив в зубах у Бастера кусок другой штанины.

Бетси не знала, плакать ей или смеяться. Она обняла пёсика:

– Бастер, дружок, ты был просто великолепен!

– Р-р-р-р! – откликнулся Бастер, дожёвывая кусок штанины.

Немного успокоившись, Бетси уселась на траву и задумалась. Ей очень хотелось пойти пожаловаться маме, чтобы та обняла и приласкала её. Но она боялась, что мама расскажет обо всём леди Кэндлинг и та вызовет к себе Склокинга, который всё свалит на Люка. А если Склокинг и впрямь пойдёт в полицию и в дело вмешается мистер Гун?

«А мистер Гун нас терпеть не может ещё с тех пор, как мы разгадали тайну сгоревшего коттеджа, – думала Бетси. – Что же делать? Надо посоветоваться с ребятами. Когда же они наконец вернутся?!»

Едва друзья вошли в сад, Фатти сразу же заметил, что Бетси чем-то огорчена.

– Что случилось? Ты с кем-то поссорилась? – спросил он участливо.

– Вы не представляете, что тут произошло... Это был такой ужас! – всхлипнула Бетси и поделилась пережитым с друзьями, рассказав всё, что случилось – по порядку, во всех подробностях.

Мальчишки были вне себя от ярости. Мерзкий Склокинг! Да как он смел так обращаться с малюткой Бетси! Дейзи крепко обняла её и погладила по голове.

– Бедняжка Бетси! – приговаривала она. – А потом? Что было дальше?

Бетси рассказала о том, как Бастер героически защищал её и как он порвал брюки Склокинга. Дети хохотали до слёз. Они наперебой кинулись гладить Бастера.

– Молодчина, Бастер, умница! – похвалил его Пип. – Задал трёпку этому склочному Склокингу! Будет ему хороший урок!

Фатти обнял Бетси и постарался утешить её.

– Ты правильно сделала, что не стала говорить маме, – подумав, сказал он. – Не нужно, чтобы взрослые знали об этом. Мы же не хотим, чтобы у Люка были неприятности, правда?

– Ну что за человек! Как он мог вырвать и выбросить клубничные кустики! – негодовал Пип. – Эх, был бы я взрослым, я бы взгрел его как следует за это! Долго бы он меня помнил!

Все засмеялись. На самом деле Пип выразил общее настроение: все почувствовали то же самое, когда узнали, как Склокинг обидел малышку Бетси, как он уничтожил её драгоценную клубничную рассаду. Бастер тявкал, виляя хвостом, и явно был солидарен со всей компанией.

– Он говорит, что опередил Пипа и как следует взгрел противного Склокинга! – улыбнулась Дейзи.

Ребята постарались утешить Бетси и развлечь её. Ларри сбегал домой и попросил у родителей несколько клубничных усов. Те конечно же дали, и Ларри, очень довольный, принёс их Бетси. Он помог девочке посадить их, и она совершенно успокоилась насчёт рассады.

Фатти преподнёс ей книжку с картинками. Он истратил на этот подарок все свои карманные деньги и устоял перед искушением похвастаться этим – что для него было настоящим подвигом.

Дейзи подарила ей свою старую куклу, которая давно нравилась Бетси. Даже Пип, которому вечно было недосуг возиться с сестрёнкой, усадил её с собой на велосипед и пару раз прокатил по деревне. Ребята как могли старались порадовать девочку, и она была им очень благодарна!

Всё было бы хорошо, если бы не Люк. Ребята волновались: удалось ли ему избежать неприятностей? Услышав наконец знакомый свист, дети помчались к калитке, чтобы встретить Люка на улице.

– Люк! Как дела? Всё обошлось? Тебя не выгнали с работы? Как же Склокинг узнал про то, что Бетси взяла клубничную рассаду? Ты уже знаешь, что он налетел на Бетси, вырвал и сжёг все кустики?

– Бедняжка Бетси, – вздохнул Люк. – Я ведь не знал, что она осталась дома, а то бы перелез через забор вслед за Склокингом! Я думал, что вы все уехали на великах – я слышал, как вы проехали по улице. Когда Склокинг вернулся и рассказал мне, что он «проучил эту девчонку», я еле сдержался, чтобы не броситься на него с кулаками. Да и что было толку драться с ним? Он бы заявил на меня в полицию и отдал на растерзание мистеру Гуну.

– Тебе снова досталось от Склокинга? – жалобно спросила Бетси. – И как он вообще узнал про клубничную рассаду?

– Думаю, ему проболталась эта бестолковая Трусиха! – сердито ответил Люк. – Склокинг задал мне сегодня жару, я ещё никогда столько не работал. Как бы я хотел уйти от него!

– А почему ты не уйдёшь? – спросил Ларри. – Зачем ты терпишь всё это?

– Видишь ли, я ведь только начал работать. Плохо, когда человек сразу же вылетает с первого места работы, – объяснил Люк. – Склокинг выгонит меня с волчьим билетом, лишь только заподозрит, что я ищу другую работу. Если он даст мне плохую рекомендацию, меня вряд ли возьмут на какое-то приличное место. А отчим! Он выйдет из себя, если узнает, что я потерял работу. Я ведь отдаю ему половину своей зарплаты.

– Да, положение сложное... – задумалась Дейзи. – Если бы только мы могли тебе помочь!

– Вы мне и так помогаете, – заверил Люк. – Я делюсь с вами своими бедами, и это большое облегчение. Раньше мне приходилось всё носить в себе и не с кем было поговорить. Ух ты! Вон идёт наш деревенский детектив! Только его нам не хватало!

Действительно, по улице размашисто шагал толстый, краснолицый, пучеглазый мистер Гун.

– Куда это он? Надеюсь, не к Склокингу? – тревожно спросила Бетси.

– Кто его знает, – пожал плечами Люк. Ему явно было не по себе. Люк побаивался мистера Гуна и старался не попадаться ему на глаза.

– Вот увидите, сейчас он завопит: «А ну-ка разойдись!» – шепнула Дейзи. – Помните, как он всё время кричал на нас, когда мы были здесь весной?

Мистер Гун медленно приближался к детям, которые не сводили с него глаз. Бастер сердито заворчал. Ребята ждали, что полицейский сейчас закричит и затопает на них ногами, но он сделал вид, что не замечает их. После того как «эти несносные дети» раскрыли тайну сгоревшего коттеджа, которую он сам так и не смог разгадать, Гун всячески старался забыть об их существовании.

И тут Бастер с оглушительным лаем набросился на мистера Гуна. Он не пытался укусить его, а просто решил облаять врага, но полицейский всё-таки порядком испугался.

– А ну-ка разойдись... гхм! То есть брысь! То есть фу! – гаркнул он на собаку. – Негодная шавка!

– Бастер, ко мне! – для порядка позвал собаку Фатти, однако строгости в его интонации явно не хватало, так что Бастер и ухом не повел.

День складывался исключительно удачно для маленького храброго скотчтерьера. Сначала он задал трёпку этому грубияну Склокингу, а теперь – вот удача! – ему подвернулся зловредный А-ну-ка-разойдись.

– А НУ-КА РАЗОЙДИСЬ! – заревел мистер Гун, пытаясь отпихнуть собаку.

Но не тут-то было! Бастер, ловко уклоняясь от пинков, тявкал всё яростнее и громче. Люк, глядя на эту битву моськи и слона, не выдержал и залился звонким смехом.

– Эй, ты! – рявкнул А-ну-ка-разойдись. – Решил посмеяться над законом, щенок? До добра это тебя не доведёт! Что ты здесь делаешь?

– Это наш друг, не трогайте его, – сказал Фатти. – Бастер! Ко мне!

Услышав шум, лай и крик, из сада вышел мистер Склокинг. Он сразу узнал Бастера.

– Надо составить протокол на пса! – обратился садовник к полицейскому. – Он порвал мне брюки – вот взгляните! – и пытался укусить! Негодная шавка, точно вы сказали!

Тут он заметил Люка и напустился на него:

– А ты что здесь болтаешься? Марш домой!

Люк торопливо зашагал прочь: ему вовсе не нужна была ещё одна стычка со Склокингом, да ещё в присутствии мистера Гуна.

Бастер ретировался с поля боя и побежал к хозяину. Фатти взял его на руки.

– Мерзкая шавка! – повторил мистер Склокинг и повернулся к полицейскому: – Вы будете составлять протокол, сэр? Я могу сообщить вам все подробности!

Но мистер Гун вовсе не горел желанием составлять протокол на Бастера. Он отлично понимал, что заявление попадёт к инспектору Дженксу, который дружит с ребятами и всячески опекает их. Однако для острастки он решил сделать вид, что собирается составить протокол, в котором будет сказано, что Бастер – злобный и неуправляемый зверь, опасный для окружающих. Полицейский достал свой большой чёрный блокнот и принялся что-то записывать в него толстым коротким карандашом.

Ребята не на шутку встревожились и поспешили укрыться в саду у Пипа. Бетси была в ужасе. Она смотрела на Бастера полными слёз глазами.

– Теперь они посадят Бастера в тюрьму? – пробормотала она.

Услышав это, все покатились со смеху, а Бетси облегчённо вздохнула.

– Да нет, конечно! – успокоил её Фатти. – Люди пока ещё не додумались до собачьих тюрем. Не беспокойся о Бастере! Арест ему точно не грозит.

Глава шестая

Исчезновение Принцессы

С того дня события стали развиваться стремительно, так что скоро юные сыщики смогли наконец начать расследование новой загадочной и запутанной истории. Дело и впрямь оказалось первоклассное!

Следующим утром ребята играли в салочки в саду у Пипа. Как всегда, было шумно и весело, но в конце концов малышка Бетси устала и они перешли к более тихим и спокойным играм.

Меж тем мама Пипа, миссис Хилтон, отправилась на чай к своей подруге леди Кэндлинг, которая только что вернулась домой после короткого отдыха на море.

– Можешь устроить пикник в саду для своих друзей, – сказала миссис Хилтон Пипу. – А ты, Дейзи, проследи, пожалуйста, чтобы все вели себя хорошо. Если не хватит еды, сходи на кухню и попроси кухарку сделать ещё бутербродов. Только не забудь сказать ей «пожалуйста» и «спасибо»!

– Да, миссис Хилтон! Большое спасибо! – ответила довольная Дейзи.

Ровно в полчетвёртого дети увидели, как нарядная и красивая миссис Хилтон прошествовала по дорожке и вышла из сада. Ребята радовались, что им не надо переодеваться и идти в гости, а можно пить чай в саду, прямо на траве, в стареньких шортах и майках.

Всё было очень вкусно! На свежем воздухе у всех разыгрался аппетит, и Дейзи пришлось дважды бегать на кухню за бутербродами. Каждый раз она очень вежливо просила добавки, за что кухарка дала ей ещё сладких спелых слив. Словом, пикник удался на славу.

Вскоре вернулась миссис Хилтон. У неё был очень расстроенный вид. Не заходя в дом, она прямиком направилась к детям:

– Вы уже знаете, что случилось у соседей? Пропала Принцесса, самая красивая, породистая и ценная кошка-медалистка. Бедная леди Кэндлинг! Это была уникальная кошка, второй такой нет. Но хуже всего то, что Принцессу, видимо, украл Люк, тот самый мальчик, подручный садовника.

– Мама, как ты можешь такое говорить! – возмутился Пип. – Люк наш друг. Он никогда в жизни не сделал бы ничего подобного!

– Никогда! Ни за что! – со слезами воскликнула Бетси.

– Миссис Хилтон, – очень серьезно произнёс Фатти. – Я уверен, что вы напрасно подозреваете Люка.

– Я же не утверждаю, что это он. Я только сказала, что Люк вполне мог это сделать. Во всяком случае, у него были для этого все возможности.

– Нет-нет, он не мог! Никак не мог! – поддержала ребят Дейзи. – Он честный человек! Скорее всего, кошку украл этот мерзкий Склокинг!

– Мистера Склокинга не было в саду. В это время он встречался с мистером Гуном. Похоже, они приятели, – ответила миссис Хилтон. – Так что он никак не мог украсть Принцессу.

Дети озадаченно уставились на миссис Хилтон, не зная, что и думать.

Наконец Фатти проявил инициативу и медленно заговорил, взвешивая каждое слово:

– Люк – наш добрый друг. Он не раз выручал нас. Если он попал в беду, теперь наш черёд прийти ему на помощь. Я совершенно уверен, что он не имеет никакого отношения к исчезновению Принцессы. Не могли бы вы, пожалуйста, рассказать нам всё по порядку? Похоже, пять юных сыщиков должны взяться за это дело.

– Мой милый Фредерик, ты слишком высокопарно выражаешься, – усмехнулась миссис Хилтон и, покачав головой, с явным неудовольствием заметила: – Не вздумайте вмешиваться в это дело, вас оно, к счастью, совершенно не касается. То, что вам удалось докопаться до истины в том запутанном деле с пожаром, ещё не даёт вам права всё время совать нос в чужие дела.

Фатти вспыхнул от негодования. Он терпеть не мог, когда его публично отчитывают словно первоклашку!

– Мама, пожалуйста, расскажи, как всё случилось, – попросил Пип.

– Дело было так. Утром, накормив кошек и вычистив их клетки, мисс Хармер уехала в город. Принцессу она в тот день посадила в большую клетку к остальным кошкам. Мисс Хармер села на десятичасовой автобус. Около часа дня леди Кэндлинг и мисс Тримбл пришли взглянуть на кошек и удостовериться, что у них всё в порядке, и мистер Склокинг показал им, где сидит красавица Принцесса. В самом деле чудесная кошка!

Дети согласно кивнули.

– А что было дальше? – спросил Пип. – Это был последний раз, когда видели Принцессу?

– Нет. В четыре часа, перед тем как мы пошли пить чай, мисс Тримбл повела меня взглянуть на кошек. Принцесса была в клетке с остальными кошками.

– Как же ты её узнала? – удивился Пип. – Они ведь все одной породы, все похожи как две капли воды.

– Я знаю, что у Принцессы на хвосте растёт несколько бежевых волосков. Они выделяются на тёмно-коричневом фоне. Мисс Тримбл показала мне эту кошку, и я хорошо разглядела

светлую бежевую полоску у неё на хвосте. Так что в четыре часа Принцесса сидела в клетке и была цела и невредима.

– А дальше? – нетерпеливо спросил Пип.

– Мистер Склокинг вернулся в пять вместе с мистером Гуном, – продолжала свой рассказ миссис Хилтон. – Он показал Гуну свои помидоры, за которые недавно получил приз, а затем повёл его смотреть кошек. Тут-то и обнаружилось, что Принцесса пропала.

– Ах вот как! – воскликнул Фатти. – Значит, кошка исчезла между четырьмя и пятью, так, миссис Хилтон?

– Именно так, – подтвердила мама Пипа. – И поскольку только Люк был в это время в саду, боюсь, его-то и заподозрят в краже. Он знал, что эти кошки очень дорогие. Склокинг сказал, что на днях мальчишка уже стащил у него что-то – клубничную рассаду, кажется, или ещё какой-то пустяк.

Бетси залилась краской, слёзы выступили у неё на глазах. Опять эта клубника, будь она неладна! Она собралась уже рассказать маме, как всё было на самом деле, но Фатти пристально посмотрел на неё, нахмурился и отрицательно покачал головой.

– Ну вот и вся история, – закончила свой рассказ миссис Хилтон, снимая перчатки. – Боюсь, у вашего приятеля Люка будут серьёзные неприятности. Как раз между четырьмя и пятью вечера его никто не видел. Он вполне мог посадить кошку в корзину и вынести из сада.

– Мама, Люк очень хороший, добрый и честный! – Бетси всё-таки не выдержала и расплакалась. – Знаешь, какие он мне сделал свистульки? И ещё прекрасную деревянную фигурку Принцессы! Вот она, посмотри!

– Бетси, ты ещё слишком мала, чтобы разбираться в людях. И вот ещё что: советую вам держаться от него подальше, пока вся эта история не закончится.

Миссис Хилтон направилась к дому и скрылась за дверью. Дети, расстроенные и подавленные, молча переглянулись.

– Как она может так говорить! «Держитесь от него подальше»! – негодующе воскликнул Фатти. – Нет уж, дудки. Мы должны помочь нашему другу. Сколько раз он выручал нас – и Бастера! Теперь наша очередь.

Все были согласны. Ребята уселись в кружок на траве, чтобы хорошенько обдумать и обсудить услышанное.

– Нет сомнений, что это кража, – начал Фатти, – и всё сделано так, что подозрение падает на Люка. Но мы-то совершенно точно знаем, что это не он. Кто же тогда вор?

– Надо искать улики! – радостно выпалила Бетси, вспомнив, как сыщики расследовали тайну сгоревшего коттеджа.

– Нет, давайте сначала составим список подозреваемых, – предложила Дейзи. – Как в прошлый раз, помните?

– Да, это дело для клуба сыщиков, – с важным видом изрёк Фатти. – Я предлагаю...

– Эй, Фатти! – перебил его Ларри. – Ты, кажется, забыл, кто здесь главный сыщик? Я, а не ты!

– Ах так? Ну и ладно! – надулся Фатти. – Давай действуй. Только учти, что я соображаю получше тебя. Я был в отличной форме в этом учебном году...

– Ой, хватит! Опять ты за своё! Перестань задаваться, Фатти! – наперебой закричали ребята.

Только Бетси промолчала: она никогда не критиковала Фатти. А тот так разобиделся, что уже хотел встать и уйти. Но дело было такое интересное и увлекательное, что дулся он недолго, и вскоре вся компания друзей взволнованно обсуждала план расследования.

– Надо всё хорошенько обдумать, – повторила Дейзи. – Что нам известно? Мы знаем, что Принцесса сидела в клетке с другими кошками до четырёх часов дня. Её видели мисс Тримбл и мама Пипа. Но уже в пять, когда

А-ну-ка-разойдись и Склокинг пришли смотреть кошек, её в клетке не было. Значит, между четырьмя и пятью кто-то зашёл в кошачий домик, открыл клетку, взял кошку, снова запер клетку и унёс Принцессу. Вор либо отдал её кому-то, либо где-то спрятал.

– Правильно, Дейзи, ты всё очень чётко изложила, – одобрительно кивнул Ларри.

– Но главный вопрос – кто мог украсть кошку? Есть ли у нас подозреваемые? – вставил Пип.

– Давайте подумаем. Вот, к примеру, мисс Тримбл. Она могла незаметно проскользнуть в кошачий домик и вытащить из клетки кошку. Но это, конечно, маловероятно. Она ведь собственной тени боится. Но мы должны иметь в виду каждого, у кого была хоть какая-то возможность украсть Принцессу.

– Я составлю список подозреваемых. – Ларри достал блокнот. – Итак, мисс Тримбл – номер один. А как насчёт леди Кэндлинг?

– Зачем же ей воровать собственную кошку? Глупость какая-то, – фыркнула Дейзи.

– Не такая уж это и глупость, – возразил Ларри. – Принцесса могла быть застрахована, и в этом случае леди Кэндлинг получила бы по страховке кучу денег. Мы не должны это сбрасывать со счетов. – И Ларри вписал в свой блокнот имя леди Кэндлинг – под номером два.

– Склокинг! – выпалила Бетси.

Но Ларри отрицательно покачал головой:

– Нет, Бетси. Я бы с огромной радостью внёс его имя, но, если он провёл весь день вместе с Гуном, у нас нет оснований его подозревать. А мисс Хармер? Не могла ли она незаметно вернуться и похитить Принцессу? Уж кто-кто, а она-то знала ей цену!

Эта неожиданная мысль всех поразила. Ребятам было трудно представить себе улыбчивую и приветливую мисс Хармер в роли похитительницы кошки. Но тем не менее её тоже внесли в список подозреваемых.

– Хорошо бы узнать, где мисс Хармер находилась сегодня между четырьмя и пятью часами, – задумчиво сказал Пип.

– А ну, давайте! Кто ещё? – подгоняла ребят Дейзи. – У нас в списке уже есть мисс Тримбл, леди Кэндлинг и мисс Хармер. А повар и горничная в доме леди Кэндлинг? У них ведь тоже была возможность зайти в кошачий домик и украсть кошку, правда?

– Я никогда не видел ни кухарки, ни горничной в этом доме, – пожал плечами Пип. – Надо бы о них разузнать. Ну что же, у нас получается неплохой список! Есть над чем подумать.

– Гадкий, мерзкий мистер Склокинг! Он больше всех подходит на роль грабителя! А мы даже не можем его подозревать! – сердито топнула ножкой Бетси. – Так что же, всё? Больше нет подозреваемых?

– Мы обязаны внести в список Люка, – сказал Ларри. – Конечно, мы его не подозреваем, но Склокинг утверждает, что Люк мог украсть кошку, так что нам придётся включить его в число подозреваемых. Мы не можем вычеркнуть его из этого списка только потому, что нам так хочется.

Итак, Люк тоже оказался в списке. Бедняга Люк! Всё-таки ему не удалось избежать неприятностей.

– Пойдёмте свистнем ему, – предложил Ларри. – Думаю, он ещё не ушёл домой. Если бы он собрался уходить, то обязательно свистнул бы нам и рассказал, что там случилось.

Ребята подошли к забору и стали вызывать своего друга. Но сколько они ни свистели, Люк так и не отозвался. Интересно почему?

Глава седьмая

Люк попадает в беду

Ребята залезли на забор, а Бастер остался внизу – ему ничего другого не оставалось, как скулить и царапать кирпичи. Никто не знал, что предпринять.

– Уже четверть шестого, – сказал Пип, взглянув на часы. – Может, Люк ушёл домой?.. Да нет, сначала он обязательно поговорил бы с нами.

– Может быть, его уже допрашивает А-ну-ка-разойдись? – предположил Фатти.

Ребята решили проверить, так ли это.

Фатти пришла в голову отличная идея:

– Слушай-ка, Пип, *ты* можешь узнать, что там делается!

– Почему я?

– А кто же ещё? Ведь твоя мама только что была в гостях у леди Кэндлинг! Давай ты перелезешь через забор и разведаешь обстановку. А если тебя увидят и спросят, что тебе надо, просто скажи, что твоя мама, которая только что была здесь, потеряла где-то в саду свой носовой платок.

– Ничего она не теряла! – возразил Пип. – Помнишь, она доставала платок из сумки, когда разговаривала с нами?

– Конечно, помню! – с досадой ответил Фатти. – Эта история про платок – только предлог пойти туда, как ты не понимаешь?! В конце концов, вовсе не обязательно говорить, что она потеряла платок, раз ты не хочешь врать. Можно просто спросить: «Вы случайно не находили здесь платочек моей мамы?» Это уж точно нельзя считать обманом.

– Молодчина, Фатти! – воскликнул Ларри. – Думаю, под этим предлогом действительно можно проникнуть в соседский сад без подозрений, так что у Гуна и Склокинга не будет повода прогнать тебя. Смелей, Пип! Сходи узнай, что там происходит. Как же нам повезло, что твоя мама только что пила чай с леди Кэндлинг!

Пипу, конечно, тоже не терпелось узнать, что делается у соседей. Однако он побаивался встречи со Склокингом и А-ну-ка-разойдись. Поколебавшись немного, он наконец решился, спрыгнул с забора и, помахав на прощание друзьям, скрылся за кустами.

Пип отправился на поиски Люка, но того нигде не было. Он дошёл до кошачьего домика, но Люка и там не оказалось. Пип подошёл к домику и заглянул в клетку, где некоторое время назад вместе с другими кошками сидела исчезнувшая Принцесса. Увидев Пипа, кошки дружно замяукали. Пип пошёл дальше по тропинке мимо теплиц и, услышав неподалёку голоса, спрятался в кустах. Сквозь листву он стал разглядывать собравшихся на лужайке.

«Вот леди Кэндлинг, – подумал Пип. – А там – мисс Тримбл. Какой у неё огорчённый вид! Мистер Склокинг – куда же без него! Так и раздувается от важности. Интересно, что это он так сияет? Чему это он так рад? Ну и старина А-ну-ка-разойдись, наш деревенский бобби*. Ух ты! Да это же Люк! Бедняга! Похоже, он крепко влип!»

Все обступили бедного Люка, который затравленно озирался и был, судя по всему,

---

* Бобби – прозвище полицейских в Англии.

страшно напуган. Прямо возле него, держа в руках свой чёрный блокнот, грозно возвышался полицейский. Он допрашивал мальчика, и Люк, устрашённый его рыком, весь дрожа и заикаясь, робко отвечал на его вопросы.

Сзади стояли две незнакомые Пипу женщины. Он решил, что это, вероятно, кухарка и горничная. Они перешёптывались и подталкивали друг друга локтями.

Пип тихонько подкрался поближе к лужайке. Теперь ему были хорошо слышны вопросы, которыми мистер Гун засыпал мальчика:

– Что ты делал во второй половине дня?

– Я б-б-был... я выкапывал старый горох на большой грядке, – пробормотал Люк.

– На той самой грядке, что возле кошачьего домика?

– Д-д-да, сэр, – едва слышно произнёс мальчик.

– Значит, после обеда ты всё время болтался возле кошек... Так-так... Ну и что ты видел? Кто-нибудь ещё приходил туда?

– Мисс Т-т-тримбл приходила около ч-ч-четырёх часов с какой-то леди, – отвечал Люк, приглаживая свои непокорные вихры. – Они были в домике минут пять и ушли.

– А что сам-то ты делал с четырёх до пяти? – рявкнул мистер Гун.

– Н-н-ничего, сэр… я… к-к-копал, копал г-г-грядку рядом с кошачьим домиком. А больше никого там не было, ни души, пока вы и мистер Склокинг не пришли смотреть кошек…

– И тут-то мы и обнаружили, что Принцесса исчезла! – злобно прошипел садовник. – Что же, мистер Гун, дело ясное, не так ли? Принцесса пропала как раз между четырьмя и пятью вечера. Парень сам сознался, что никто не подходил к кошкам в это время, только он околачивался там, один-одинёшенек, без свидетелей. Уж конечно, это он украл кошку – больше некому! Вытащил её из клетки и продал кому-то из своих приятелей за ломаный грош. Этот парень – обманщик и воришка.

– Нет, мистер Склокинг! Вовсе я не воришка! И не обманщик! – Люк от обиды даже забыл про страх. – Я никогда не брал чужое. Я всегда честно трудился и всё терпел от вас! Никто не стерпел бы такого. Вы отлично знаете, что я никогда не стал бы воровать кошек, и наговариваете на меня…

– Перестань! Хватит! – гаркнул мистер Гун.

– Мистер Склокинг, – негромко, но решительно произнесла леди Кэндлинг, – вы не можете обвинять Люка, пока не прояснятся все обстоятельства этого загадочного происшествия.

У Склокинга был обескураженный вид: давно его никто так не осаживал. Он так увлёкся, что совершенно забыл о присутствии хозяйки. Люк повернулся к леди Кэндлинг.

– Пожалуйста, мэм, – умоляюще заговорил он, – очень прошу вас, пожалуйста, не верьте мистеру Склокингу и мистеру Гуну. Я не брал Принцессу. Я не знаю, куда она подевалась. Я никогда ничего не брал из вашего сада, честное слово!

– Враньё! – торжествующе воскликнул Склокинг. – А клубничная рассада?

– Отпустите его, – спокойно сказала леди Кэндлинг, – и прекратите допрос. В конце концов, он всего лишь мальчик пятнадцати лет. Я прошу вас покинуть мой сад, мистер Гун. Люк, ты можешь идти домой.

Мистер Гун был явно недоволен тем, что не может спрашивать с Люка как со взрослого. Полицейский ни за что бы не отпустил его домой, если бы не леди Кэндлинг. Кстати, почему эта дама приказывает ему, служителю закона, да ещё и выпроваживает его с места преступления? Он громко кашлянул, бросил презрительный взгляд на леди Кэндлинг, захлопнул свой блокнот и напустил на себя важный вид.

– Да-да, иди домой, а я пойду с тобой. Мне придётся сказать пару слов твоему отчиму, –

сообщил он Люку, который, услышав это, побелел как мел.

– И я! И я пойду с вами! – встрял мистер Склокинг. – Отец мальчишки наверняка расскажет нам, кому из приятелей этот воришка мог продать кошку.

Бедный Люк побрёл домой под конвоем мистера Гуна и мистера Склокинга. Ух, как же Пип ненавидел эту парочку! Как ему было жаль Люка! Силы были слишком неравны, и, похоже, Люку не выпутаться...

Пип поздно заметил, что они направляются прямо к его укрытию. Он собрался было отступить, но зоркий Склокинг увидел Пипа, затаившегося за кустом рододендрона.

– Что ты здесь делаешь? – рявкнул он. – Это один из соседских мальчишек, мистер Гун, – пояснил он, обернувшись к удивлённому полицейскому. – Вечно они лазят здесь повсюду, никакого нет с ними сладу! Давайте-ка я отведу его к хозяйке, пусть разберётся с ним.

Люк разинул рот от удивления, увидев Пипа. Меж тем садовник, ухватив незваного гостя за шиворот, вытащил его на дорожку. Леди Кэндлинг, услышав шум, вернулась на лужайку посмотреть, что ещё там произошло.

– Отпустите меня! – сердито крикнул Пип. – Уберите руки!

Вскоре оба они предстали перед леди Кэндлинг, которая несказанно удивилась, увидев у себя в саду ещё одного мальчика.

– Этот засел в кустах возле лужайки, – доложил Склокинг. – Один из шайки Люка. Всё время шныряют тут, только успевай их вылавливать.

– Что ты делаешь у меня саду? – строго спросила леди Кэндлинг.

– Добрый вечер, леди Кэндлинг! – вежливо ответил Пип. – Моя мама сегодня приходила к вам пить чай. Вы не видели здесь её платка? Кажется, она его случайно обронила у вас в саду...

– Ах, так ты Филипп, сын миссис Хилтон? – улыбнулась леди Кэндлинг. – Твоя мама рассказывала мне о тебе и о твоей сестрёнке. Её, кажется, зовут Бетси?

– Да, именно так, – ответствовал Пип, тоже сладко улыбнувшись в ответ. – Бетси очень милая. Я бы с радостью вас с ней познакомил.

– Конечно же! Буду рада, – сказала леди Кэндлинг. – Склокинг, вы напрасно набросились на этого мальчика. Это сын моей подруги, миссис Хилтон, он искал платок, который она сегодня потеряла у меня в саду.

Склокинг был мрачнее тучи. Всё шло совсем не так, как ему бы хотелось!

– Если мы найдём платок миссис Хилтон, то обязательно пришлём его вам, – пообещала Пипу леди Кэндлинг. – И не забудь, что ты собирался познакомить меня со своей сестрёнкой. Приводи её как-нибудь в гости. Я очень люблю маленьких девочек.

– Мистер Склокинг нас выгонит, если мы придём, – жалобно сказал Пип.

– Ни в коем случае! – твёрдо заявила леди Кэндлинг. – Склокинг, эти дети могут приходить сюда, когда захотят. Это мой приказ.

Склокинг побагровел и, казалось, готов был взорваться, но не посмел спорить с хозяйкой. Резко повернувшись, он направился к мистеру Гуну и Люку, которые ждали его чуть поодаль.

Пип попрощался с леди Кэндлинг, поблагодарил её и отправился вслед за Склокингом.

– Люк! – обратился он к своему приятелю. – Эй, Люк! Не отчаивайся! Мы тебя не бросим. Мы знаем, что ты ни в чём не виноват!

– А ну-ка разойдись! – завопил не на шутку рассвирепевший мистер Гун. – Вечно эта мелюзга всюду лезет, всюду суёт нос! А ну-ка разойдись!

Но Пип не внял требованию мистера Гуна «а ну-ка разойтись». Держась на безопасном расстоянии, он перебегал от дерева к дереву и подбадривал Люка, чем окончательно взбесил полицейского и садовника. Вдруг он услышал, как мистер Гун сказал Склокингу, что собирается сегодня вечером «как следует изучить место преступления».

«Ах вот как! – подумал Пип. – Ясно, что он собирается искать улики против Люка. Мы должны опередить его. Пойду расскажу всё ребятам».

Прокричав ещё несколько ободряющих слов Люку, Пип помчался к забору, моментально перемахнул через него и поспешил к товарищам. Он хотел быстрее рассказать им всё, что ему удалось узнать. Да, дело об исчезнувшей кошке становилось всё интереснее и интереснее!

Глава восьмая

Улики

– В чём дело? Куда ты пропал? – едва завидев Пипа, Ларри накинулся на него с вопросами.

Пип уселся на траву рядом с друзьями и Бастером.

– В общем, ребята, А-ну-ка-разойдись и Склокинг уверены, что кошку украл Люк! – сказал он. – Бедняга!

– Почему они так считают? – спросила Дейзи.

– Да потому, что кошка исчезла между четырьмя и пятью вечера и в это время возле кошачьего домика не было никого, кроме Люка, –

объяснил Пип. – Люк сам признался в этом и подтвердил, что больше там никто не появлялся.

– Как же так? – растерянно оглядела всех Бетси. – Вы что-нибудь понимаете? Мы точно знаем, что Люк не крал Принцессу, а всё, как нарочно, выглядит так, будто это сделал он. Мне кажется, тут какая-то тайна.

– Точно, – кивнул Фатти. – По-моему, даже нет смысла расспрашивать наших подозреваемых, потому что главный подозреваемый, то есть Люк, сам признался, что только он был возле кошачьего домика в то время, когда произошла кража. Но... знаете, я просто ПОВЕРИТЬ НЕ МОГУ, что Люк украл кошку. Он никогда не решился бы на это, даже если бы ему в голову пришла такая мысль (а такая мысль, разумеется, ему в голову и не приходила!).

– Интересно, где сейчас Принцесса? – задумалась Бетси.

– Да, если бы удалось её отыскать, нам было бы легче выяснить, кто её украл, – отозвался Ларри. – Ведь тот, у кого она сейчас, – или сам похититель, или его друг и сообщник. Ну и ну! Настоящая головоломка.

– А может быть, нам поискать улики? – предложила Бетси. Она надеялась, что удастся найти что-то такое, что поможет оправдать Люка.

– О! Совсем позабыл! – встрепенулся Пип. – Я слышал, как А-ну-ка-разойдись говорил садовнику, что сегодня вечером будет обследовать место преступления. Наверняка он надеется найти улики против Люка.

– Мы должны опередить его! Давайте пойдём прямо сейчас! – решительно сказал Фатти и вскочил на ноги.

– Да вы что? Нельзя сейчас лезть через забор! – воскликнул Ларри. – Мы опять получим нагоняй.

– Не получим, – заверил его Фатти. – Мы сто раз успеем вернуться обратно, пока в саду снова появятся Склокинг и А-ну-ка-разойдись. Им сейчас спешить некуда. Они же собирались объяснить бедному отчиму, какой негодяй его пасынок – а на это нужно время.

– Ну ладно. Тогда идём, – согласился Ларри. – Надеюсь, мы найдём какие-нибудь улики, хотя кто знает, что нас там ждёт. Вперёд, ребята!

– Пожалуй, нам лучше не брать Бетси, – предложил Пип. – Она ещё маленькая и опять попадёт в какую-нибудь историю.

– Вот ещё! – негодующе воскликнула Бетси. – Перестань меня обижать, Пип! Я пойду с вами! Я не хуже других умею искать улики. Только помогите мне, пожалуйста, перелезть через забор. Вот увидите, я вам пригожусь.

– Конечно, Бетси! – Фатти, как всегда, поддержал девочку. – Пип, она пойдёт с нами. Представь, каково ей будет сидеть здесь одной, пока мы будем там расследовать преступление.

В итоге было решено, что Бетси пойдёт вместе со всеми. А вот Бастера сыщики с собой не взяли, больше того: его ещё и заперли в сарае, чтобы он не смог выбежать на улицу и проникнуть в сад леди Кэндлинг.

Все, включая Бетси, которую подсадил Фатти, перелезли через забор. В саду, казалось, никого не было. Дети осторожно пробрались к кошачьему домику. Кошки лениво растянулись в своём

домике, глядя на сыщиков немигающими голубыми глазами.

– Ну, теперь за работу! Ищите улики, – скомандовал Ларри.

– Какие улики? – прошептала Бетси.

– Пока не знаю, посмотрим, – ответил Ларри. – Первым делом надо осмотреть землю вокруг домика. Смотрите! Здесь, наверное, и работал Люк. – Ларри показал на тачку, наполовину заполненную сорняками. В землю была воткнута лопата, а рядом, на дереве, висела куртка Люка.

– Он копал вон ту грядку, – заключил Фатти. – Она ближе всего к кошачьему домику. Уж конечно, он заметил бы любого, кто попытался бы подойти к кошкам.

Дети подошли к тому месту, где работал Люк. Отсюда хорошо просматривалась каждая кошка в клетке. Было совершенно ясно, что никто не мог вынести Принцессу и запереть домик незаметно от Люка.

Но факт оставался фактом – кошку украли, и Люк клянётся, что это сделал не он. А если не он – то кто же похитил Принцессу?

– А вдруг Принцесса сама сбежала из клетки? – предположил Ларри. – Давайте обойдём вокруг кошачьего домика и проверим мою версию.

– Отличная мысль! – шепнул Фатти.

Они обошли вокруг и тщательно обследовали крепкий, добротно сколоченный деревянный домик, который стоял на высоких толстых балках и чем-то напоминал курятник.

– Здесь кошке просто негде вылезти, – вздохнул Пип. – Ни дырочки, ни щёлочки! Тут и мышь не прошмыгнёт. Нет, Принцессу определённо украли.

– Но ещё в четыре она была здесь, когда сюда подходили твоя мама и мисс Тримбл, – сказала Дейзи. – А уже в пять, когда явились А-ну-ка-разойдись и Склокинг, кошки не было. И всё это время Люк работал прямо возле домика. Я не понимаю, как же так? Чудеса, да и только!

– Может, это и в самом деле чудо, – серьёзно произнесла Бетси. – Чудеса ведь бывают не только в книжках...

Ребята покатились со смеху, а Бетси покраснела от досады.

– Да, это может быть чудо! – настойчиво повторила она. – Чудесное исчезновение кошки! А может, всем только мерещилось, что кошка сидит в клетке...

– Бетси, что за детские фантазии! Мама сказала, что своими глазами видела Принцессу, – ей это не могло померещиться, – сурово осадил сестрёнку Пип и вдруг вскрикнул: – Ой, смотрите, что это там? – Он показывал на клетку, в которой сидели кошки.

И тут все увидели, что там на полу что-то лежит. Сыщики прижались носами к прутьям, пытаясь разглядеть странный предмет.

После короткого молчания Фатти поджал губы, поднял брови и почесал затылок.

– Вот это да! – удивился он. – Я, кажется, знаю, что это такое. Это одна из тех свистулек, которые Люк смастерил для Бетси.

Да, именно так – Фатти угадал. Свистулька лежала на полу клетки – самая явная и самая бесспорная улика! Как она могла туда попасть? Ответ был только один – Люк открыл дверцу клетки, зашёл к кошкам и выронил её. Дети переглянулись. Они были озадачены и расстроены.

– Нет-нет! Всё равно это не он! Это не Люк! Он не мог, не мог! – твердила Бетси со слезами на глазах. – Мы все знаем, что это не он!

– Да, конечно, мы это знаем, но вот первая улика: в клетке лежит свистулька, которую мог выронить только Люк, – покачал головой Фатти. – Вот уж действительно чудеса!

– Фатти, если мистер Гун найдёт свистульку, он тут же воспользуется этим, чтобы доказать, что Люк украл Принцессу! – взволнованно проговорила Бетси.

Фатти кивнул:

– Конечно! Это Наиважнейшая и Совершенно Неопровержимая Улика для нашего деревенского детектива.

– Но для тебя же она не такая непове... невержи... то есть не-по-ро-вре-жимая, ведь правда, Фатти? – не сдавалась Бетси. – Ты же не думаешь, что это Люк залез в клетку и потерял там свистульку?

– Если вам интересно знать, то я скажу, что думаю, – важно произнёс Фатти. – Кто-то подбросил сюда эту свистульку нарочно, чтобы навести подозрение на Люка! Вот что я думаю.

– Ого! Пожалуй, ты прав, – задумчиво сказал Ларри. – Дело всё больше запутывается. Для начала надо решить, оставим ли мы эту улику мистеру Гуну? Если мы совершенно уверены, что это ложная улика, то...

– Правильно! – кивнул Пип. – Я за то, чтобы вынуть отсюда эту улику и забрать с собой.

Пятеро сыщиков молча смотрели на свистульку, лежавшую в клетке. Клетка была заперта, ключа у них не было. Как же достать улику? Фатти отчаянно всплеснул руками:

– Надо поторопиться! А-ну-ка-разойдись может явиться в любой момент. О господи! Как же её достать?

Никто не знал, что делать. Если бы свистулька лежала возле сетки, можно было бы попытаться подцепить её палкой или веткой. Но она была далеко, у задней стенки.

И всё же Фатти нашёл выход. Это было одно из тех решений, которые осеняют человека в безвыходной ситуации – когда помощи ждать неоткуда. Он поднял маленький камешек и бросил его в клетку, целясь в свистульку. Камушек покатился к задней стенке, и одна из кошек тут же спрыгнула с полки, заметив новую игрушку. Она тронула камушек лапкой, слегка зацепив и сдвинув с места свистульку.

Дети следили за ней затаив дыхание. Кошка вновь ударила лапой камушек и погналась за ним. Потом она повернулась к свистульке и уставилась на неё, ожидая, когда та шевельнётся. Наконец устав дожидаться, она осторожно протянула к свистульке передние лапки, подхватила её и несколько раз подбросила в воздух – раз, два... три! На третий раз свистулька приземлилась прямо возле сетки.

– Ура! Ура! Ура! – шёпотом прокричал Фатти, выуживая из кармана моток проволоки. Карманы Фатти были просто кладезем полезных вещей! Он отмотал немного, соорудил на конце небольшую петлю и просунул проволоку через сетку.

Все внимательно следили за его действиями. Вот проволока коснулась свистульки, и Фатти постарался подцепить игрушку петлёй, проявляя большую ловкость и терпение. Кошка, которая играла с камушком и свистулькой, следила за происходящим с неменьшим интересом. Вдруг она игриво ухватила проволоку, дёрнув петлю вверх, – и точно насадила проволоку на свистульку.

– Ай да киска! Вот спасибо! – с облегчением выдохнул Фатти. Он осторожно потянул на себя проволоку, пока свистулька не оказалась прямо у сетки, а потом резко дёрнул её.

Свистулька проскочила между прутьев и упала прямо возле Бетси. Девочка быстро подхватила её.

– Готово! – сказал Фатти, осматривая добычу. – Да, это одна из тех свистулек, которые вырезал Люк. Как хорошо, что мы её достали. А-ну-ка-разойдись придётся обойтись без этой улики. По крайней мере мы хоть избавили Люка от новых неприятностей.

– Какой же ты умный, Фатти! – восхищённо воскликнула Бетси.

– Да! Ловко ты это проделал, Фатти! – добавил Пип.

Фатти тут же начал надуваться от гордости как индюк.

– Да это ещё что, – завёл он опять свою шарманку. – Бывали у меня идеи и получше. Вот, помню, как-то раз...

– Фатти, прекрати! – дружно оборвали его Ларри, Дейзи и Пип.

Фатти умолк и сунул свистульку в карман.

– Пошли искать дальше, – сказал Пип. – Давайте проверим, там в клетке ничего больше нет?

Все снова прижались носами к сетке, пытаясь как можно лучше рассмотреть, нет ли там ещё чего-нибудь интересного. Бетси сморщилась.

– Пахнет очень неприятно, – заявила она.

– От животных всегда идёт запах, когда они сидят в клетке, – ответил Ларри.

– Нет, это не животные. Это совсем другой запах, – возразила Бетси. – То ли бензин, то ли керосин.

Сыщики принюхались.

– Это скипидар, – объявил Фатти. – Теперь я тоже чувствую, хоть запах и слабый. Однако, Бетси, я тебя разочарую: это не улика. Видимо, мисс Хармер пользуется скипидаром для чистки клеток. Ну что же, найдём мы ещё что-нибудь сегодня?

Увы, больше ничего обнаружить не удалось, хотя сыщики тщательно осмотрели всё внутри клетки и вокруг неё.

– Безобразие! – буркнул Фатти. – Ничегошеньки! Ладно, хотя бы нашли эту свистульку до Гуна и Склокинга. Я совершенно уверен, что кто-то специально подбросил её сюда, чтобы навести подозрение на Люка. Кому пришла в голову такая подлость?

– Раз улик нет, мы вполне можем их создать – пусть наш друг А-ну-ка-разойдись поломает голову над этим! – предложил Пип.

Сыщики одобрительно закивали. Идея всем пришлась по вкусу.

– Красота! – воскликнул Фатти, жалея, что сам не додумался до этого.

– Давайте! – радостно потёр руки Ларри. – Накидаем в клетку всякой всячины – и ничего такого, что бы указывало на Люка. Пусть А-ну-ка-разойдись попотеет, разбираясь со всеми этими уликами!

Ребята засмеялись.

– У меня есть мятные леденцы, – хихикнул Пип. – Один из них пусть полежит в клетке.

– А я брошу обрывок ленты для волос, – решила Дейзи. – У меня как раз утром порвалась лента – вот она, у меня в кармане.

Ларри тоже стал исследовать свои карманы:

– А вот и мой вклад – новенький коричневый шнурок.

– А ты, Фатти? – спросила Бетси.

На глазах у изумлённых сыщиков Фатти извлёк из кармана кучку недокуренных сигар.

– Зачем они тебе? – спросил наконец Ларри.

– Папа оставил их вечером в пепельнице в гостиной, а я забрал на всякий случай – вдруг пригодятся? Одну я брошу на пол возле клетки, а вторую просуну к кошкам. Думаю, кошки не станут её жевать – не хотелось бы, чтобы они заболели из-за меня. Надеюсь, мне удастся свести мистера Гуна с ума!

Тихо и торжественно пятеро сыщиков разложили в кошачьем домике свои улики. Пип просунул в клетку большой круглый мятный леденец, запах которого явно не понравился кошкам, Дейзи – затёртый обрывок голубой ленты для волос, Бетси – маленькую синюю пуговицу от кукольного платьица, Ларри – новый коричневый шнурок, Фатти – окурки сигар.

– Ну вот, теперь нашему деревенскому детективу есть чем заняться! – заявил Фатти. – Думаю, он уже скоро явится сюда.

Глава девятая

Мистер Гун сбивается с толку

– Слушайте, – сказала вдруг Дейзи, глядя, как на полу клетки её ленточка подрагивает от лёгкого сквозняка. – Я надеюсь, никто не подумает, что это я украла Принцессу. Мама ведь узнает мою ленту, если ей покажут этот обрывок.

– Надо же! Мне это и голову не пришло. Вот балда! – сокрушённо развёл руками Пип.

– Всё в порядке, – ободрил друзей Фатти. – У меня с собой большой конверт. Мы сложим в него то же, что набросали в клетку. Я положу два окурка, Дейзи – оставшийся обрывок ленты.

Вслед за Дейзи и Фатти Бетси положила в конверт ещё одну синюю пуговицу от кукольного платья, Ларри – второй коричневый шнурок, а Пип – мятный леденец. Фатти аккуратно сложил конверт и засунул его в карман.

– Если кого-нибудь из нас попробуют обвинить в краже, мы предъявим содержимое этого конверта и скажем, что просто пошутили.

Из-за забора раздался голос миссис Хилтон: она звала Бетси.

– Эх, мне пора спать, – с тяжёлым вздохом сказала Бетси. – Как же не хочется идти домой!

– Нет уж, Бетси, давай беги скорей. Вчера тебе и так попало за то, что ты поздно легла. – Пип погрозил сестрёнке пальцем. – Эх, дорого бы я дал, если бы можно было остаться тут и полюбоваться на физиономии Склокинга и А-ну-ка-разойдись, когда они обнаружат наши «улики»!

– Слушайте, давайте и вправду останемся и дождёмся их? – предложил Ларри.

– А я? Как же я? Я тоже останусь! – захныкала Бетси, чувствуя, что её опять исключают из игры.

Пип толкнул её локтем в бок:

– Бетси, быстро домой! Мама опять позвала тебя. Слышишь?

– Ах так? – сердито топнула ножкой Бетси. – Тогда идём вместе. Слышишь? Мама и тебя зовёт тоже. Пошли, иначе ты не успеешь к ужину!

Пип, конечно, знал, что ему тоже придётся вернуться. Ларри вздохнул. Он понимал, что это касается и их с Дейзи, тем более что до дома им было гораздо дальше, чем Пипу и Бетси.

– Нам тоже пора, – сказал Ларри. – А ты, Фатти? Может, ты останешься и посмотришь, что будет? Твои родители ведь не требуют, чтобы ты так рано возвращался домой.

– Конечно, я останусь! – ответил Фатти. – Я залезу на дерево и спрячусь в листве. Сверху мне всё будет отлично видно, а меня никто не заметит.

– Ладно, пошли, Бетси, – уныло сказал Пип. Ему так не хотелось идти домой! Он страшно завидовал Фатти: вот будет потеха, когда Гун найдёт улики.

Вдруг у входа в сад послышались голоса. Дети переглянулись.

– Это Склокинг и А-ну-ка-разойдись, – шепнул Ларри. – Бежим скорей!

– Пока, Фатти, до завтра, – тихонько сказал Пип.

Вчетвером ребята помчались к забору. Пип подсадил Бетси и осторожно переправил её на ту сторону. Вслед за девочкой перелезли остальные. Фатти остался один в саду леди Кэндлинг. Он ловко вскарабкался на дерево, устроился на длинной толстой ветке и осторожно раздвинул листья – и тут же увидел Склокинга и Гуна, которые направлялись к кошачьему домику.

– Ну что ж, – говорил Гун, – сейчас мы тут всё обыщем, мистер Склокинг. Никогда нельзя знать заранее, какие улики могут обнаружиться. Частенько случалось так, что я находил явную и бесспорную улику, которая выводила меня прямо на преступника.

– Ну разумеется, – поддакнул Склокинг. – Я вам полностью доверяю, дорогой мистер Гун.

Этот бездельник Люк наверняка оставил какие-то улики. Он вполне мог додуматься, как стащить ценную кошку, но вряд ли у него хватило сообразительности как следует замести следы.

Полицейский с садовником принялись за поиски. Они долго рыскали вокруг кошачьего домика, к изумлению кошек, которые не сводили с беспокойной парочки своих ярких голубых глаз. Кошки были явно озадачены тем, что возле их домика постоянно бродят толпы двуногих. А сверху Фатти, спрятавшись среди листьев, с интересом наблюдал за усилиями горе-детективов.

Наконец мистер Гун нашёл сигару, брошенную возле клетки. Он бросился к ней, быстро поднял и с торжествующим видом продемонстрировал находку Склокингу.

– Что это? – удивился тот.

– Окурок сигары! – важно объявил мистер Гун. Постепенно его торжество сменилось недоумением: он снял шлем и озадаченно почесал затылок.

– А что, этот парень, Люк, курит сигары? – спросил он.

– Что за ерунда! – раздражённо бросил мистер Склокинг. – Ну конечно же нет! Разве это улика? Просто кто-то из гостей леди Кэндлинг, разглядывая кошек, курил здесь и бросил на землю окурок.

– Хм... – задумчиво протянул мистер Гун, изучая окурок. – Не знаю, не знаю... Это ещё предстоит обдумать...

Фатти тихонько хихикнул. Поиски продолжались. Наконец Склокинг, кряхтя, выпрямился и объявил:

– Похоже, тут больше ничего нет. Ну что, будем осматривать кошачий домик?

Мистер Гун с минуту колебался. Покачав головой, он сказал:

– Скорее всего, и там мы ничего не найдём. Но для порядка надо бы взглянуть. Где ключи, мистер Склокинг?

Мистер Склокинг снял ключи, висевшие на гвоздике, который был прибит к задней стене кошачьего домика. И не успел он отпереть клетку, как мистер Гун издал оглушительный вопль: он не смог сдержать изумления, увидев на полу клетки кучу каких-то странных предметов. Где это видано, чтобы место преступления так и кишело уликами!

– Что там? – спросил Склокинг.

– Вы только посмотрите! Видите? Вон там шнурок от ботинка, – воскликнул мистер Гун. – Это важнейшая улика! Кто-то здесь был и потерял шнурок.

Мистер Склокинг с недоумением уставился на злосчастный шнурок – и вдруг заметил рядом синюю пуговку, а ещё чуть дальше обрывок голубой ленты. От изумления у него перехватило дыхание. Он молча вставил ключ в замок и отпер дверцу клетки. Вместе с Гуном они собрали улики, чтобы изучить их.

– Значит, наш подозреваемый был в ботинках с коричневыми шнурками, – важно заявил мистер Гун. Он был явно очень доволен такой кучей улик. – И взгляните на эту пуговицу – она оторвалась от чьей-то куртки.

– А это что? – возмущённо спросил мистер Склокинг, тыкая в мятный леденец.

Мистер Гун тщательно обнюхал улику.

– Это мята, – заключил он. – Значит, этот Люк любит мятные леденцы?

– Пожалуй, – ответил Склокинг. – Все мальчишки – сладкоежки. Но ленточек в волосах он точно не носит. О! А вот ещё один окурок – точно такой же, как и тот, что валялся возле клетки.

Восторг мистера Гуна постепенно сменился недоумением. Полицейский заметно скис. Он в задумчивости разглядывал улики.

– Итак, если судить по всем этим вещам, вор курит сигары, сосёт мятные леденцы, носит голубую ленту в волосах, куртку с синими пуговицами и ботинки с коричневыми шнурками... – пробормотал он. – Но это... это же ерунда какая-то!

Фатти давился от смеха, с восторгом наблюдая за тем, как мистер Гун и мистер Склокинг ломают головы, пытаясь разобраться в уликах, которые любезно оставили для них юные сыщики.

Полицейский осторожно лизнул леденец.

– Ну да, так и есть – мятный леденец, – пробормотал он. – Чудеса, да и только! Множество улик, но совершенно неясно, кому могут принадлежать все эти вещи? Вы нашли что-нибудь ещё, мистер Склокинг?

Садовник вернулся в кошачий домик и снова тщательно осмотрел всё вокруг.

– Решил ещё раз проверить, на всякий случай – вдруг мы чего-то не заметили, – ответил он.

Но как он ни старался, ничего больше отыскать не удалось.

Наконец Склокинг вышел из домика, весь растрёпанный и злой.

– Всё. Больше ничего нет, – сказал он. В голосе его явно слышалось разочарование. – Я уверен, мистер Гун, что вы сможете доказать вину Люка. Конечно же воришка – это он. А все эти предметы – никакие не улики, они случайно оказались в клетке.

– Ну, знаете, мятный леденец вряд ли попал в клетку по недоразумению! – сердито отозвался мистер Гун. – Я должен взять улики с собой и обдумать всё как следует.

Фатти посмеивался про себя, глядя, как полицейский старательно складывает свои «улики» в чистый белый конверт. Гун заклеил конверт, что-то написал на нём, аккуратно положил в карман и обернулся к садовнику:

– Всего доброго, мистер Склокинг. Спасибо вам за помощь. Я абсолютно уверен, что это Люк. Его рук дело. Завтра я устрою ему допрос с пристрастием и, если не выжму из него признание, не будь я Теофиль Гун!

С этими словами старина А-ну-ка-разойдись прошествовал по дорожке к выходу – с полным конвертом загадочных «улик» и в полном недоумении от такого набора. Голубая лента – что бы это значило? Синяя пуговка – странно, странно... Коричневый совершенно новый шнурок – кто бы мог подумать... Мятный леденец – к чему бы это? И целых два окурка... Чудеса в решете, да и только!

Фатти хотелось поскорее слезть с дерева и попасть домой. Он вдруг понял, что страшно проголодался. Раздвинув листья, он снова посмотрел вниз – и увидел, что садовник всё ещё не ушёл. Склокинг снова зашёл в кошачий домик и тщательно обыскал там каждый уголок. Спустя некоторое время он, обескураженный, вышел из домика, запер клетку и уныло побрёл по дорожке. Когда его шаги затихли, Фатти осторожно спрыгнул с дерева и пробрался к выходу. Обернувшись, он ещё раз на прощание взглянул на голубоглазых кошек и нащупал в кармане деревянную свистульку. «Хорошо, что мы вынули её из клетки. Вот это была бы улика!» – подумал он и прыснул, вспомнив гору «улик», которую озадаченно разглядывал Гун.

«Ну что ж, завтра повидаем Люка и узнаем, какие у него новости, – думал Фатти по дороге домой. – Интересный завтра будет день!»

И день действительно выдался интересный, полный самых неожиданных и захватывающих событий.

Глава десятая

Пип и Бетси наносят визит соседям

Ранним утром Фатти примчался к Пипу: ему не терпелось поскорее рассказать всем, как мистер Гун и садовник обнаружили фальшивые улики. В то же время в саду появились Ларри с Дейзи, и скоро вся компания хохотала над рассказом Фатти.

– Представляете, и тут старина А-ну-ка-разойдись спрашивает Склокинга: «Разве Люк курит сигары?» – Фатти так похоже изобразил полицейского, что дети не могли сдержаться от смеха. – Я чуть с дерева не свалился, когда услышал это!

– Мы сегодня уже несколько раз свистели Люку, – сказал Пип. – И никакого ответа. И у забора он не появлялся. В чём дело? Может, он боится?

– Да, может быть, – кивнул Фатти. – Нам надо обязательно поговорить с ним и рассказать о свистульке, которую мы нашли в клетке, да и про наши «улики» тоже. Пойду-ка свистну ему ещё разок.

Но даже на громкий и заливистый посвист Фатти Люк не отозвался. Тогда сыщики решили дождаться обеденного перерыва и поймать Люка у калитки, когда тот пойдёт домой.

Друзья ждали его до десяти минут второго, но Люк так и не появился, и дети отправились по домам, где родители ждали их к обеду.

– Слушайте, а может быть, его уже уволили? – предположил Фатти. – Если так, то он больше не появится в саду у леди Кэндлинг.

– Бедный Люк! – вздохнула Бетси. – Неужели леди Кэндлинг запретила ему сюда приходить?

– Надо бы проверить это, – задумчиво произнёс Ларри.

– Может, спросить у Склокинга?.. – робко предложила Дейзи.

Все с удивлением посмотрели на неё.

– Попробуй. Представляю, что он тебе ответит, – фыркнул Ларри.

Сыщики задумались.

– Я знаю, что делать, – вдруг сказал Пип. – Леди Кэндлинг приглашала меня и Бетси в гости. Вот мы и навестим её сегодня – и попробуем выяснить, что случилось с Люком.

– Отличная мысль! – одобрил идею Фатти. – Я и сам об этом подумал. И заодно хорошо бы выяснить (как бы между прочим), где была и что делала сама леди Кэндлинг в тот день с четырёх до пяти. Попробуйте узнать, была ли у неё возможность незаметно проникнуть к кошкам и утащить свою Принцессу?

– Я уверен, она этого не делала! – воскликнул Пип. – С первого взгляда ясно, что ей такое и в голову не могло бы прийти. И кроме того, мы уже решили, что нет смысла спрашивать об этом наших подозреваемых – ведь Люк был у кошачьего домика в это время и обязательно заметил бы, если бы там кто-то появился. А он говорит, что никого не видел.

– Да, действительно, невозможно было выкрасть кошку перед носом Люка, – согласился Фатти. – А он клянётся, что не отлучался ни на минуту.

– Ладно, ребята, нам пора домой, – сказала Бетси. – Пошли, Пип, а то нам опять влетит от родителей. Потом встретимся, и мы расскажем, как сходили в гости к леди Кэндлинг.

Друзья расстались – каждый пошёл к себе домой, где их ждали к обеду. Все очень переживали за Люка. Похоже было, что леди Кэндлинг и впрямь его уволила, иначе он бы обязательно пришёл на работу.

В половине четвёртого Пип и Бетси вышли из дома. Их встретила Дейзи. Она критически осмотрела помятое платьице Бетси и грязные штаны Пипа:

– А вам не кажется, что раз вы идёте к леди Кэндлинг, то стоило бы одеться поприличнее? Особенно тебе, Пип: такое впечатление, что это не Люк, а ты работаешь помощником садовника и целыми днями возишься в земле.

– Вот ещё не хватало! Может, мне ещё крахмальные манжеты нацепить, как девчонке? – мрачно буркнул Пип, который терпеть не мог наряжаться.

– Но будет некрасиво заявиться в гости в грязной одежде, – возразила Дейзи, и Пип с Бетси, тяжело вздохнув, отправились переодеваться.

В прихожей они сразу столкнулись со своей мамой, которая поинтересовалась, почему они не играют с друзьями и зачем пришли домой.

– Мамочка, мы пришли, потому что нам надо умыться и надеть что-нибудь красивое и чистое, – объяснила Бетси.

– Что-о-о? – Мама не поверила своим ушам. – Что это с вами случилось? Вы что, собрались куда-то?

– Да, мамочка, мы идём в гости к леди Кэндлинг, – выпалила Бетси, прежде чем Пип успел её остановить.

– К леди Кэндлинг? – Изумлению миссис Хилтон не было предела. – Зачем? Кажется, она вас не звала. Или вы решили явиться к ней без приглашения?

И тут Пип так толкнул Бетси, что малышка едва устояла на ногах. Она застыла с раскрытым ртом, не успев ответить маме. Она наконец-то поняла, что проболталась о чём-то таком, что маме знать не следовало.

– Ну, в чём дело, Бетси? Ты язык проглотила? – недовольно сказала миссис Хилтон. – Пип, может быть, ты объяснишь мне по-человечески, что всё это значит? С каких это пор ты начал наносить визиты нашим соседям? Может, решил обучить Бетси великосветским манерам?

– Дело в том, мамочка, что вчера я видел леди Кэндлинг. Она рассказала мне, что вы с ней говорили про Бетси, и попросила меня как-нибудь познакомить её с моей сестрёнкой. Оказывается, леди Кэндлинг очень любит маленьких девочек.

– Ах, вот как? А где и когда ты видел леди Кэндлинг? – поинтересовалась миссис Хилтон. – Впрочем, я догадываюсь. Ты, верно, снова без спроса лазил в соседский сад. Когда ты перестанешь досаждать взрослым?

– Ну что ты, мамочка! – проговорил Пип, скромно опустив глаза и переминаясь с ноги на ногу. – Я и не думал досаждать соседям. Но если ты против, мы конечно же никуда не пойдём. Правда, я ведь обещал леди Кэндлинг... она обидится и решит, что я обманщик... да и Бетси давно мечтала с ней познакомиться...

– Ну хорошо, идите, – разрешила миссис Хилтон и, покачав головой, строго добавила: – Только ведите себя как подобает воспитанным детям из хорошей семьи!

– К тому же, мамочка, мы подумали, что нужно выразить сочувствие миссис Кэндлинг, раз у неё пропала любимая кошка, и спросить, не отыскалась ли она, – с невинным видом добавил Пип.

Мама пристально взглянула на сына и покачала головой:

– С каких это пор, друг мой, ты стал таким вежливым и предупредительным? Что-то здесь не так. По-моему, вы опять затеваете какие-то каверзы. Если это так, то я выведу вас на чистую воду и как следует накажу тебя, Пип, имей в виду!

Брат с сестрой отправились мыться и переодеваться. Бетси ужасно боялась, что Пип устроит ей взбучку за то, что она сболтнула лишнего, но, как ни странно, он не сказал ей ни слова.

Вскоре оба снова появились в саду – уже при полном параде, чинно вышли из калитки на улицу и прошествовали в сад леди Кэндлинг. Там они увидели мистера Склокинга, который подравнивал ножницами живую изгородь. Он злобно покосился на детей, когда те проходили мимо.

– Здравствуйте, мистер Склокинг! Сегодня чудесный день, не правда ли? – произнёс Пип светским тоном – точь-в-точь как миссис Хилтон. – Впрочем, наверное, всё же пойдёт дождь. Что же, без дождя никак не нельзя – растениям в саду он пойдёт на пользу.

Склокинг заворчал в ответ и принялся яростно кромсать кусты. Пип подумал, что садовник с удовольствием прошёлся бы ножницами по ним с Бетси. Он сладко улыбнулся Склокингу и направился прямо к дому, держа за руку сестрёнку.

Дети подошли к двери и позвонили. Им открыла молодая приветливая горничная.

– Добрый день! Скажите, пожалуйста, леди Кэндлинг дома? – осведомился Пип.

– Кажется, она в саду, – ответила горничная. – Я провожу вас на веранду, и вы сможете сами пройти к ней. Она, наверное, срезает розы.

– А кошка всё ещё не нашлась? – поинтересовался Пип, пока горничная вела их через весь дом на залитую солнцем веранду.

– Нет, – вздохнула девушка. – Мисс Хармер просто в отчаянии. Как-то всё это странно, не правда ли? Неужели это действительно Люк? Ведь только он один был возле кошачьего домика как раз между четырьмя и пятью вечера в тот злосчастный день.

– А в тот день всё было как обычно? Вы ничего странного не заметили? Не появлялся ли в саду после обеда какой-нибудь незнакомый человек? – спросил Пип, решив, что нужно воспользоваться случаем и как следует расспросить горничную.

– Нет, я никого не видела, – отвечала девушка. – Понимаете, леди Кэндлинг вчера устраивала чаепитие. Были гости – девять или десять человек, так что и я, и кухарка были очень заняты. Мы вообще не выходили в сад между четырьмя и пятью, нам было некогда. Если кто-нибудь из нас оказался бы там, мы могли бы застать вора на месте преступления. Вообще, надо сказать, что вор выбрал самый удобный день для кражи: мисс Хармер уехала, Склокинг отлучился, мы с кухаркой хлопотали по хозяйству, а леди Кэндлинг принимала гостей.

– Да, – согласился Пип. – Похоже, вор знал это и хорошо спланировал преступление.

– Вот потому-то мы и думаем, что это Люк, – сказала девушка. – Честно говоря, мне этот паренёк всегда нравился. Ему не хватало сноровки, но он был такой славный и добрый! А этот мистер Склокинг совершенно замучил его.

– Вы тоже не любите Склокинга? – спросила Бетси.

– Конечно! Старый грубиян! – подтвердила горничная. – Но пожалуйста, не передавайте никому мои слова. Мы с кухаркой ничуть бы не удивились, если бы оказалось, что это он украл кошку. Однако мы уже пришли. Идите в сад – там вы и найдёте леди Кэндлинг.

Пип и Бетси вышли на солнечную веранду и по ступенькам спустились в сад.

– Из того, что сказала горничная, ясно, что её саму, кухарку и леди Кэндлинг можно спокойно исключить из списка подозреваемых, – подытожил Пип. – А вот и мисс Тримбл! – прошептал он, подталкивая локтем Бетси.

Мисс Тримбл действительно шла по дорожке им навстречу.

– Пип, давай считать, сколько раз очки упадут у неё с носа, – хихикнув, шепнула Бетси.

– Милые крошки! – проворковала мисс Тримбл, сладко улыбаясь. – Вы, наверное, ищете леди Кэндлинг? А с этой маленькой девочкой мы, кажется, уже знакомы. Не та ли это малышка, от которой убежали побеги клубники? Ну-ну, не хмурьтесь! Это просто шутка, хи-хи-хи!

Она засмеялась, очки тут же слетели у неё с носа и, качаясь, повисли на тоненькой цепочке. Мисс Тримбл привычным движением водрузила их на место.

– Да, это я, та самая девочка, – ответила Бетси. – Мы пришли в гости к леди Кэндлинг.

– О! Как жаль! Она только что ушла, – произнесла мисс Тримбл. – Боюсь, пока вам придётся довольствоваться моим обществом.

Она захихикала, и очки снова свалились у неё с носа.

– Два... – пробормотала Бетси.

– А вы не знаете, где Люк? – спросил Пип, подумав, что было бы неплохо отыскать его, если он в саду.

– Не знаю. Его сегодня не было. Мистер Склокинг весьма недоволен этим, – сказала мисс Тримбл.

– Скажите, мисс Тримбл, а леди Кэндлинг не уволила его? – спросила Бетси.

– Нет, не думаю, – ответила мисс Тримбл. – Какая жалость, что наша прелестная кошечка пропала! А ведь ещё в четыре часа я её видела – она была на месте.

– Да, вы приходили вместе с моей мамой смотреть кошек, – кивнул Пип. – Вы говорили, что около кошачьего домика никого не было, кроме Люка?

– Никого, – подтвердила мисс Тримбл. – Люк действительно был неподалёку, он усердно копал грядки. Мы с твоей мамой пробыли там пару минут, а потом я проводила её назад, гости собирались пить чай. У меня было столько хлопот! Ни секунды свободной, пока не закончилось чаепитие.

– Ну, в таком случае вы уж точно вне подозрений, – усмехнулся Пип.

Мисс Тримбл подпрыгнула от неожиданности, а очки спрыгнули с её носа, который стал не просто красным, а багровым.

– Что за глупые шутки?! – пробормотала она, пытаясь отцепить очки от своего кружевного воротничка. – Я никогда в жизни не смогла бы ничего украсть! Я бы сто раз умерла от страха при одной мысли о краже!

– А можно нам пойти посмотреть на кошек, мисс Тру… Тримбл? – спросила Бетси.

– Конечно же можно. А как вы меня назвали? Меня зовут мисс Тримбл! Пожалуйста, потрудитесь запомнить! Ну, идёмте же, мои дорогие. Там мы увидим мисс Хармер – она только что пошла к кошачьему домику.

Она засеменила по дорожке, и через пару шагов её очки снова свалились с носа.

Бетси воскликнула:

– Четыре!

– Четыре? Но, дорогая, нас только трое! – сказала мисс Тримбл, обернувшись к девочке и сладко улыбнувшись. Очки попытались снова соскользнуть с её носа, но она успела указательным пальцем вернуть их на место.

– Это я считаю, сколько раз у вас упали с носа очки, – объяснила Бетси. – Пожалуйста, не ловите их в следующий раз, ладно?

– Хи-хи! Какая забавная маленькая девочка! – проговорила мисс Тримбл, пытаясь скрыть досаду. Она сняла очки и пошла дальше, держа их в руке.

Бетси разочарованно прошептала: «Ну-у-у, так нечестно!»

Вскоре они очутились у кошачьего домика. Там была мисс Хармер, которая собиралась кормить кошек. Она ласково кивнула гостям, но её круглое добродушное лицо было печальным и озабоченным.

– Здравствуйте, дети! Пришли взглянуть на моих кошечек? – спросила она.

– Да, если можно, – ответила Бетси. – Ах, мисс Хармер, как жаль, что украли Принцессу! Ведь это случилось, когда вас не было?

– Ужасное происшествие! – тяжело вздохнула мисс Хармер, раскладывая корм по мискам. – Не надо было мне уезжать! Надо было взять только полдня – а не целый день. Мистер Склокинг вызвался присмотреть за кошками, чтобы отпустить меня. Я поблагодарила его и уехала. И вот теперь никак не могу себе простить этого!

– Как вы сказали? Мистер Склокинг вызвался присмотреть за кошками? – Пип не мог поверить, что садовник оказал кому-то услугу. – Что-то на него не похоже!

– Действительно, это не в его правилах, – рассмеялась мисс Хармер. – Мне очень надо было съездить домой, а успеть за полдня просто невозможно: я ведь живу очень далеко. Кстати, вы не собираете железнодорожные билеты? Вчера контролёр почему-то не забрал у меня обратный билет. Можете взять его, если хотите.

Пип действительно коллекционировал железнодорожные билеты и, поблагодарив, взял подарок мисс Хармер. Он положил билет в карман, думая о том, как будет завидовать ему Ларри, который тоже собирал билеты.

– Как вы считаете, мисс Хармер, это Люк украл кошку? – продолжил разговор Пип.

– Нет, не думаю. Пусть он не блещет умом, но он хороший, честный мальчик. А вот его друг, циркач, запросто мог стащить Принцессу. Кажется, его зовут Джейк.

Дети переглянулись. Ну и новости! Люк никогда не говорил ребятам ни про какого Джейка. Значит, у него есть друг, который работает в цирке! Как интересно! Почему же Люк ни слова не сказал об этом?

– А этот Джейк живёт у нас в деревне? – спросил Пип.

– Нет-нет. Просто цирк, в котором он работает, сейчас приехал в соседний городок, в Фарринг, – объяснила мисс Хармер. – Так что Джейк сейчас где-то неподалёку. Между прочим, Принцесса отлично могла бы выступать в цирке! Она очень хорошо поддавалась дрессировке. Я уже научила её нескольким трюкам.

Мисс Тримбл начала проявлять нетерпение, так как близилось время вечернего чая. Пару раз она вежливо кашлянула, отчего её очки незамедлительно соскочили с носа.

Наконец Пип сказал:

– Мы, пожалуй, пойдём, мисс Хармер. Спасибо, что показали нам кошек. Нас можно не провожать. Мы перелезем через забор без посторонней помощи.

– По-моему, не стоит вам лезть через забор, – возразила мисс Тримбл. – Почему бы не выйти из калитки и не пройти по улице? Идёмте, я вас провожу.

– Там мистер Склокинг, – сказала Бетси.

Услышав имя грозного садовника, мисс Тримбл вздрогнула, и очки опять сорвались с её носа.

– Ну что ж, если вы непременно хотите лезть через забор, не стану вам мешать, – вздохнула она. – До свидания, милые дети. Я передам леди Кэндлинг, что вы заходили в гости.

– Они упали восемь раз! – торжествующе сообщила Бетси, пока Пип подсаживал её на забор. – И всё-таки странно, что Люк никогда не рассказывал нам о Джейке, правда, Пип?

Глава одиннадцатая

Поход в цирк-шапито

В тот день друзья собирались попить чай дома у Ларри и Дейзи. Перед этим они все вместе встретились на улице.

Пип начал рассказывать новости:

– Люк сегодня не пришёл на работу, и это очень странно, потому что леди Кэндлинг его не увольняла. И ещё меня удивило, что он нам никогда ничего не говорил о Джейке.

– Я сомневаюсь, что он уговорился с этим Джейком, встретился с ним и передал украденную кошку, – недоверчиво ответил Ларри. –

В общем... я хочу сказать... словом, мы ведь по-прежнему верим Люку, так? Или... что скажете?

Впервые ребята засомневались. Почему Люк ни разу не упомянул Джейка? Ведь им было бы интересно послушать рассказы про человека, который работает в цирке. И в конце концов, Люк был единственным, кто находился возле кошачьего домика в то время, когда произошла кража.

– Нет, я всё-таки не верю, что кошку украл Люк или его друг Джейк, – решительно заявила Бетси. – Не верю – и всё!

– И я не верю, – поддержала её Дейзи. – Однако дело всё больше запутывается...

– В прошлый раз нам повезло больше, – уныло сказал Ларри. – Надо ещё раз обдумать всё, что нам удалось разузнать от наших подозреваемых.

– Кстати, насчёт подозреваемых, – подхватил Пип. – Мы можем смело вычеркнуть из списка всех, кого мы туда внесли. За те полчаса, что я провёл у соседей, я выяснил, что никто из них не мог украсть Принцессу.

– И как же ты это выяснил? – поинтересовался Фатти.

– В тот вечер леди Кэндлинг устроила чаепитие, у неё были гости. Она не могла бросить их одних и отправиться воровать собственную кошку. У кухарки и горничной было полно хлопот, поскольку в доме принимали гостей, так что они тоже исключаются. Мисс Тримбл постоянно была с гостями, и леди Кэндлинг уж наверняка заметила бы её отсутствие, если бы та отлучилась даже на несколько минут.

– Ясно, Пип, – сказал Фатти. – Ларри, где наш список подозреваемых? Давай вычёркивать их всех по очереди.

– Мы можем вычеркнуть и мисс Хармер, – продолжал Пип. – Вчера она ездила домой, в Лэнгстон, это далеко отсюда. Она мне подарила свой обратный билет, который у неё не стал забирать кондуктор.

– Ну что ж, в списке остался один Люк, – произнёс Ларри. – Вот беда! Всё выглядит так, будто кошку мог и в самом деле украсть тот самый Джейк. Он пробрался в сад, вытащил из клетки кошку, подмигнул Люку и скрылся – зная, то Люк его не выдаст. Нам надо найти Люка и расспросить его о Джейке.

– Я знаю, где Люк, – вдруг заявил Пип. – Держу пари, он отсиживается у своего приятеля и, наверное, задумал сбежать вместе с цирком.

Эта версия показалась сыщикам убедительной. Люк и впрямь вполне мог скрываться у Джейка.

– Давайте-ка после чая возьмём велики и съездим в Фарринг, – предложил Фатти. – Найдём цирк-шапито, а может, и Люка, если он действительно там.

– Отлично! Так и сделаем! – радостно откликнулись все, предвкушая необычайные приключения. – Давайте скорей выпьем чаю – и в путь!

Миссис Дейкин, мама Ларри и Дейзи, была очень удивлена скорости, с которой дети пили чай и поедали печенье и конфеты.

– Вы куда-то спешите? Или вы так проголодались? – заботливо спросила она. – Такое впечатление, что вы сегодня не обедали и не завтракали.

– Мы действительно немножко торопимся, миссис Дейкин. – Фатти пытался отвечать очень вежливо, что было трудновато с набитым ртом. – Мы решили после чая прокатиться на велосипедах.

– До Фарринга и обратно, – уточнила Бетси и тут же получила два толчка справа и слева – от Пипа и от Ларри. Мальчишки испугались, что Бетси снова наговорит лишнего.

– А почему вы решили ехать в Фарринг? – удивилась миссис Дейкин. Она не знала, что туда приехал цирк. – Там не очень-то живописные виды.

– На велосипеде будет в самый раз – не очень далеко, но и не близко, – сказал Ларри первое, что пришло в голову. – Мы поедем прямо сейчас, пока ещё не поздно, хорошо? Спасибо за чай, мамочка!

Фатти, Пип и Бетси отправились за своими велосипедами. Бетси была счастлива, что ей разрешили прокатиться вместе со всеми: Фарринг находился неподалёку. Наконец сыщики отправились в путь.

Вскоре ребята заметили впереди ещё одного велосипедиста – высокого грузного мужчину в тёмно-синей форме.

– Глядите-ка, да это наш старый друг А-ну-ка-разойдись! – воскликнул Пип. – Только этого не хватало! Как-то не хочется, чтобы он нас заметил... Может, он скоро свернёт с дороги, и тогда мы прибавим скорость и быстренько доберёмся до Фарринга.

Но А-ну-ка-разойдись и не думал никуда сворачивать. Скоро ребятам стало ясно, что он тоже направляется в Фарринг.

– Слушайте, неужели он тоже ищет Джейка? – с досадой спросил Фатти. – Наверное, он заставил Люка выложить всю правду о его друге-циркаче. Вот незадача! Нельзя допустить, чтобы Гун опередил нас. В конце концов, именно Джейк может сильно помочь нам в этом деле!

То, что произошло дальше, было для ребят полной неожиданностью. Мистер Гун вдруг соскочил с велосипеда и, чертыхаясь, стал осматривать колёса. Сыщики увидели, что у него спустило заднее колесо. Пыхтя и отдуваясь, полицейский отволок велосипед на обочину, а ребята с ветерком промчались мимо, причём Фатти приветственно помахал рукой и участливо поинтересовался:

– Что случилось, мистер Гун? Велосипед подвёл? Примите наши соболезнования!

Полицейский поднял голову, и удивление на его лице сменилось раздражением: пятёрка сыщиков стремительно удалялась в сторону Фарринга. Гуну предстояло обнаружить и заклеить прокол, так что у ребят было как минимум четверть часа, чтобы добраться до города и отыскать Джейка.

Они въехали на холм, с которого открывался вид на город.

– Вот он, цирк-шапито! – крикнула Бетси. – А там разноцветные фургончики и клетки со зверями. Как здорово!

Зрелище действительно было необычное. Семь великолепных вороных лошадей скакали по полю рядом с цирком – это была репетиция конного аттракциона. Трубы на разноцветных фургонах дымили. Пахло чем-то очень вкусным.

– Рыбу жарят. – Бетси потянула носом.

– Нет, колбасу, – возразила Дейзи.

Фатти тоже принюхался.

– Это бекон! – уверенно объявил он.

– Как будем действовать? – спросил Ларри, спрыгнув с велосипеда. – Будем искать Люка или сразу Джейка?

– Лучше не бродить там всей толпой, – ответил Фатти. – Давайте я схожу сам и постараюсь осторожно разведать, где мы можем найти Джейка.

– Нет уж. Я главный сыщик, я и пойду, – заявил Ларри.

– А вот и нет! – вмешался Пип. – Это была моя идея – поехать в Фарринг. Я пойду и отыщу Люка или Джейка.

– Хватит вам препираться, – сердито прервала их спор Дейзи. – Скоро сюда нагрянет А-ну-ка-разойдись!

– Ладно, пошли все вместе, кроме Бетси, – предложил Ларри. – Лучше держаться вместе, чем бродить тут поодиночке. А Бетси останется и посторожит наши велики.

– Ну уж нет! – Бетси возмущённо топнула ногой. – Почему это я должна сторожить велики? Я тоже хочу посмотреть на цирк!

– Да потому что ты боишься тигров, слонов и других зверей, – сердито ответил Пип. – Ты даже на ослике не захотела кататься, когда мы с родителями ходили в зоопарк.

– Ах так? Ну что ж, ладно. Я останусь тут. И пусть вам будет стыдно, что вы бросили меня здесь одну! – всхлипнула малышка. Она, конечно, побаивалась и слонов, и тигров, и лошадей, но всё-таки было бы справедливо, если бы кто-нибудь остался вместе с ней и посторожил велосипеды.

Меж тем ребята перелезли через изгородь и двинулись к шапито. Очутившись у фургонов, они разделились и стали спрашивать каждого

встречного, где найти Джейка. Удача улыбнулась Пипу. Он спросил у девушки, где Джейк, и она показала ему на рослого мужчину, который поил лошадь из большого ведра. Пип направился к нему. Мужчина удивлённо взглянул на мальчика:

– Что вам тут нужно?

– Простите, пожалуйста, – начал Пип. – Я ищу своего приятеля, его зовут Люк. Мне ему нужно кое-что передать. Он ведь где-то здесь?

– Нет, – коротко ответил мужчина. – Я его уже сто лет не видел.

Пип приуныл:

– А вы не знаете, как его найти? Мне очень нужно с ним поговорить. У вас нет его адреса?

– Нет, – отрезал мужчина. – От меня вы ничего не получите. Идите-ка отсюда и не суйте любопытный нос, куда вас не просят.

Фатти, заметив, что Пип беседует с незнакомым мужчиной, подошёл поближе.

– Это Джейк? – спросил он.

Пип кивнул:

– Он уверяет, что давным-давно не видел Люка.

– Послушайте, мы и вправду его добрые друзья, – сказал Фатти проникновенным тоном. – Честное слово! Нам надо только поговорить с ним.

– Я же сказал, что не знаю, где он, – повторил мужчина. – Уходите отсюда, повторяю: я его уже сто лет не видел!

А бедная Бетси стояла у велосипедов, наблюдая, как остальные сыщики расспрашивают прохожих. Кроме того, она время от времени оглядывалась по сторонам, чтобы проверить, не появился ли А-ну-ка-разойдись. Ей вовсе не хотелось, чтобы он заметил её и стал допытываться, что она тут делает. Наконец Бетси решила спрятаться от посторонних глаз за изгородью, чтобы её не видно было с дороги. Перебравшись через ограду, она растянулась на траве неподалёку от ярко-красного фургона. Девочка некоторое время разглядывала его – как вдруг... Нет, не может быть! Бетси не поверила своим глазам. Она вгляделась повнимательнее... Неужели не показалось? Бетси поднялась и подошла поближе к фургону. Из маленького окошечка, спрятавшись за полупрозрачной кружевной занавеской, прямо на неё смотрел Люк!

Глава двенадцатая

Люк появляется снова

Бетси замерла затаив дыхание. Тем временем занавеска медленно отодвинулась, осторожно приоткрылось окно – и из него выглянул Люк.

– Привет, малышка Бетси! – тихо произнёс он. – Зачем ты пришла? Хотела посмотреть на цирк?

– Вовсе нет, – так же тихо отвечала Бетси. – Мы узнали, что у тебя здесь есть друг, и подумали, что ты можешь быть у него. Поэтому пришли сюда, чтобы отыскать тебя и поговорить.

– Это мой дядя, – объяснил Люк. – Я его не очень-то люблю, но больше мне не к кому пойти. Знаешь, я ужасно испугался, что все решат, будто это я украл Принцессу, и меня посадят в тюрьму. Поэтому я убежал и прячусь здесь.

– Но ведь ты же не крал Принцессу, правда?

– Конечно же нет! Я не вор! А ты одна или с ребятами?

– Мы все здесь, – ответила Бетси. – Остальные отправились искать Джейка, чтобы расспросить о тебе.

– Вот как? Между прочим, я ничего не говорил дяде о своих неприятностях, о краже Принцессы. Я подумал, что, если всё это выложу ему, он не разрешит мне остаться здесь. Поэтому я только рассказал, что поссорился с отчимом, не хочу возвращаться к нему и думаю уйти вместе с цирком. Джейк пообещал спрятать меня, а потом взять с собой. Ему как раз нужен помощник – крепкий паренёк вроде меня.

– А отчим сильно на тебя разозлился? – сочувственно спросила Бетси. – Бедный Люк! Трудное у тебя сейчас время! Надеюсь, что ребята тоже ничего не скажут Джейку про кражу кошки. Они только хотели узнать у него, не здесь ли ты, и попросить передать тебе записку.

– Хорошо, если так, а то он меня точно не возьмёт, если всплывёт эта история с Принцессой, – вздохнул Люк. – Циркачи терпеть не могут полицейских и стараются с ними не связываться. Слушай, Бетси, ты ведь никому не скажешь, что видела меня? Я должен тихо сидеть здесь и не высовывать носа, пока цирк не отправится дальше.

– Конечно! Я буду молчать как рыба! – заверила его Бетси. – Скажу только мальчишкам и Дейзи. Ты можешь полностью доверять нам. А как ты думаешь, Люк, кто мог украсть кошку? Это случилось с четырёх до пяти вечера. Ты ведь всё время был там. Может, ты всё-таки кого-нибудь видел?

– Нет, ни души! – развёл руками Люк. – Чудеса, да и только! Ума не приложу, как всё это могло случиться.

– Да, вот ещё что. Знаешь, тут такое дело... – начала было Бетси, вспомнив о свистульке, найденной в кошачьей клетке. Но продолжить ей не удалось: невдалеке вдруг послышались голоса. Люк тут же поспешно захлопнул окно и задёрнул занавеску.

Однако это были всего лишь ребята, которые возвращались после неудачных переговоров с Джейком. Вид у них был грустный и подавленный.

– Ничего у нас не вышло, Бетси, – грустно сказал Фатти. – Джейка мы нашли, но он нам ни слова не сказал о Люке. Только твердил, будто бы сто лет не видел его.

– И всё-таки я уверен, что Джейк видел Люка и знает, где он, – сердито произнёс Пип. – Вот досада! Зря только время потратили!

– А что это с нашей Бетси? – спросил Фатти, внимательно глядя на девочку. – Щёки красные, глаза горят, и вот-вот лопнет от нетерпения – похоже, у неё важные новости! А ну-ка, малышка, выкладывай, в чём дело? Что тут произошло?

– Да ничего особенного, – скромно опустив глазки, ответила Бетси. – Кроме того, что я знаю, где Люк, – только и всего.

Дети изумлённо уставились на Бетси, пытаясь понять, шутит она или говорит серьёзно.

– В чём дело, Бетси? Ты нас разыгрываешь, что ли? – наконец не выдержал Пип. – Если ты действительно знаешь, где Люк, так скажи нам!

Бетси оглянулась по сторонам, показала пальчиком на красный фургон и тихо произнесла:

– Он там, прячется в этом фургоне. Я его видела. Он выглянул в окошко, и мы поговорили.

– Ничего себе! – рассмеялся Ларри. – Мы бродим по цирку, всюду ищем Джейка, наконец чудом находим его, пытаемся выспросить у него, где Люк, возвращаемся ни с чем – а в это время наша малышка Бетси, не сходя с места, находит того, кого мы искали! Похоже, наша девочка далеко пойдёт – и скоро мне придётся передать своё звание главного сыщика.

Бетси раскраснелась от радости и гордости. Конечно, ей просто повезло, что она решила перелезть через изгородь и расположиться возле красного фургона. И всё-таки как приятно было хоть ненадолго оказаться в центре внимания!

– Кстати, вы ничего не говорили Джейку о Принцессе? Люк не хочет рассказывать ему о краже: боится, что если Джейк узнает про эту историю, то не станет прятать его и откажется взять с собой. Люк сказал ему, что поссорился с отчимом и сбежал от него.

– Ну разумеется, мы ни слова не сказали о кошке! – ответил Пип. – Интересно, а получится у нас поговорить с Люком? Где его окошко, Бетси? Покажи-ка ещё раз.

Бетси снова показала, где прячется Люк, и Пип тихонько свистнул. Это был условный свист, и Люк знал его. Занавеска слегка шевельнулась, и за ней мелькнул профиль Люка. Потом окно медленно открылось.

– Привет, Люк! – прошептал Фатти. – Мы ничего не сказали Джейку об этом деле с кошкой. Слушай, ты и в самом деле собираешься уйти с цирком?

– Собираюсь, – кивнул Люк.

– Вот тогда-то все и подумают, что это ты украл Принцессу и ударился в бега, – покачал головой Ларри. – По-моему, прятать голову в песок и скрываться от проблем – не лучший способ.

И тут вдруг со стороны дороги послышалось шуршание велосипедных шин, а потом кто-то спрыгнул с велосипеда и, тяжело дыша, потопал к ограде. Дети быстро переглянулись и обернулись к изгороди...

Увы, случилось именно то, чего они боялись! Это был А-ну-ка-разойдись. Он наконец починил свой велосипед и нагнал сыщиков.

– Это ваши велосипеды? – спросил мистер Гун. – Что вы тут делаете?

– Приехали посмотреть на цирк, – любезно поклонившись, ответствовал Фатти. – Какие у них милые тигры, мистер Гун!

Полицейский сердито засопел.

– А ну-ка разойдись! Столпились тут, так что пройти невозможно! Небось уже отыскали тут этого вашего приятеля, воришку Люка?

– Как вы сказали? Люка? – Фатти изумлённо уставился на краснолицего полицейского. – А где он? Мы думали, он трудится в саду у леди Кэндлинг. Если вы скажете, где он, будем премного благодарны. Нам бы хотелось с ним кое о чём потолковать.

Полицейский фыркнул, как полковая лошадь. Фатти завистливо хмыкнул: ему очень нравилось фырканье мистера Гуна. Если бы он научился фыркать так же звучно и смачно, все мальчишки в классе умерли бы от зависти!

– А ну-ка разойдись, я сказал! – прорычал мистер Гун, садясь на велосипед. – Всюду лезете, всюду суёте свои сопливые носы! Предупреждаю в последний раз: не шутите с законом!

С этими словами полицейский покатил к шапито. Дети решили, что не стоит рисковать, снова вызывая Люка. Они перелезли через ограду и подошли к велосипедам.

А мистер Гун тем временем уже успел расспросить кого-то из циркачей и направился к Джейку, который всё ещё поил лошадей.

– Ну вот, так мы и думали, – сказал Фатти. – Гун тоже разнюхал про Джейка. Одна надежда, что тот не выдаст ему Люка, когда узнает о краже Принцессы.

– Давайте-ка побыстрей уносить ноги отсюда, – предложил Пип. – Старина Гун не очень-то быстро соображает, но если мы будем здесь и дальше околачиваться, то он может в конце концов смекнуть, что это неспроста.

Ребята вскочили на велосипеды и поехали обратно, оставив бедного Люка отсиживаться в красном фургоне. Им очень хотелось хоть чем-то ему помочь. Но чем? Оставалось только надеяться, что Люк незаметно покинет эти места вместе с Джейком, не попавшись своим преследователям на глаза.

– Да-а-а... – протянул Ларри, – похоже наш друг попал из огня да в полымя. Не думаю, что с этим мрачным Джейком ему будет лучше, чем с отчимом или с садовником Склокингом...

Наступил уже поздний вечер, когда они вернулись в Петерсвуд. Бетси пора было ложиться спать, да и остальных ждали родители.

– Пожалуй, на сегодня всё. Пора по домам, – сказал Ларри, затормозив возле своего дома. – Спокойной ночи! До завтра!

– Спокойной ночи. – Ребята простились с Ларри и Дейзи и поехали дальше.

– Ну вот и твой дом, Фатти, – сказал Пип. – Какая, однако, досада, что мы ни на шаг не продвинулись к разгадке этой тайны! Теперь Люк уйдёт с цирком, Гун в итоге прекратит расследование, и мы останемся ни с чем.

– Да, похоже, тайна так и останется нераскрытой, – согласился Фатти. – Неужели мы никогда не узнаем, кто украл Принцессу?

– Пока, Фатти! Спокойной ночи! – Бетси и Пип помахали рукой на прощание другу.

Через минуту они подкатили к дому – и тут же услышали, что мама зовёт Бетси.

– Мы вернулись как раз вовремя, – с облегчением сказал Пип. – Обойдётся без выговоров и нотаций. Приятных сновидений, Бетси!

Бетси пошла умываться и чистить зубы, а Пип поднялся в свою комнату, чтобы переодеться. Доставая чистую одежду, он принялся насвистывать – и вдруг поймал себя на том, что выводит трели и рулады, которым его научил Люк. «Бедняга Люк! – подумал Пип, натягивая свежую майку. – Боюсь, мы больше его не увидим. На память останутся только свистульки, которые он смастерил для Бетси».

Пип поужинал и пошёл в сад отмывать велосипед. Он был уже совсем взрослым и ложился не раньше полдевятого, так что у него была ещё уйма времени до сна. Покончив с велосипедом, он взял книжку и уселся в беседке.

Едва он начал читать, как вдруг рядом раздался чуть слышный шорох. Пип оторвался от книги и огляделся, пытаясь определить, откуда доносится звук. Однако снова стало тихо. Решив, что это, должно быть, птица шуршит в листве или пробежала в траве полевая мышь, Пип снова погрузился в книгу. Вскоре часы на площади пробили полдевятого. Пип встал, захлопнул книгу и пошёл в дом. Пожелав родителям спокойной ночи, Пип поднялся к себе и сразу же улёгся в постель. Он страшно устал.

Ему снился какой-то тревожный бессвязный сон: вначале А-ну-ка-разойдись гнался за ним верхом на Бастере, как вдруг из-за угла выехал Джейк, оседлавший тигра. Потом откуда-то появился Люк: его тащил за шиворот садовник Склокинг. И тут раздался мелодичный свист – их с Люком условный сигнал.

Пип тяжело вздыхал и ворочался во сне. Нелепый сон продолжался: в нём всё время был Люк и отчётливо слышался мелодичный звонкий посвист. Он звучал всё громче и настойчивее.

Вдруг кто-то схватил Пипа за плечо. Спросонья Пип подскочил с постели и сдавленно вскрикнул. Весь дрожа, он сел на кровать, с трудом приходя в себя.

– Тсс! Это я, Пип, – послышался шёпот Бетси. – Тихо! Не шуми...

– В чём дело, Бетси? – возмутился Пип. – Ты меня заикой хочешь сделать? Ты меня так напугала, что у меня чуть сердце не выпрыгнуло!

– Слушай, Пип, в саду кто-то свистит, – прошептала Бетси. – Похоже на свист, каким мы обычно зовём друг друга. Может, это Люк? Может, ему надо с нами срочно поговорить?

Пип проснулся окончательно. Он открыл было рот, чтобы ответить Бетси, но тут снова послышался тот же свист, который он слышал во сне, – и Пип понял, что это ему вовсе не приснилось, а было наяву.

– Молодец, Бетси! – сказал он, соскочив с постели. – Да, это, должно быть, Люк. Наверное, ему пришлось уйти из цирка, и он вернулся сюда. Надо узнать, что с ним и что ему нужно. Я пошёл, а ты жди здесь!

– Я тоже пойду, – насупилась Бетси. – Я услышала свист, а не ты! Я пойду!

– Ты сейчас споткнёшься в темноте на лестнице или что-нибудь уронишь, разбудишь родителей...

– Ничего я не уроню! И не споткнусь! – топнула ногой Бетси.

– Тихо ты! – Пип толкнул её локтем. – Сейчас всех перебудишь! Ладно, так и быть, идём, только осторожней.

Они даже не стали надевать халаты: ночь была тёплой и безветренной. На цыпочках дети прошли по коридору и стали спускаться по лестнице. Вдруг Пип споткнулся и кубарем покатился вниз по ступенькам, цепляясь за перила. Затормозить ему удалось только на полпути вниз.

– Как ты, Пип? – с тревогой спросила Бетси. – Не ушибся?

– Ничего, цел! – шепнул тот. – Наткнулся в темноте на кошку! Только бы никто не услышал...

Брат с сестрой примостились на нижней ступеньке и с минуту напряжённо прислушивались, не проснулись ли родители. Однако всё было тихо. Кошка уселась рядом. В темноте яркими зелёными огоньками горели её глаза.

– Она, как нарочно, подвернулась мне под ноги! – разозлился Пип. – С тех пор как здесь появился Бастер, она всё время вредничает. А ну брысь!

Кошка мяукнула и скрылась в темноте. Дети ощупью двинулись дальше к выходу. Пробравшись к входной двери, они вышли в ночной сад. Бетси изо всех сил вцепилась в брата. Она побаивалась темноты.

Вновь раздался знакомый свист. Пип прислушался.

– Это в той части сада, – показал он. – Скорей! Пойдём по траве, а то гравий очень хрустит.

Осторожно ступая, дети пересекли лужайку, прошли мимо грядок и обогнули большую мусорную кучу. У беседки мелькнула чья-то тень. Они пригляделись. Это действительно был Люк! Неужели он и впрямь вернулся?

Глава тринадцатая

Верные друзья

– Люк! Это ты? – прошептал Пип. – Что случилось? Ты ушёл из цирка?

Он схватил Люка за руку, втащил в беседку и усадил посередине, между собой и Бетси.

– Да, пришлось уйти, – тяжело вздохнув, отвечал Люк. – Этот полицейский отыскал моего дядю и рассказал ему и про украденную кошку, и про то, что в краже подозревают меня. Он всё допытывался, известно ли дяде что-нибудь об этом деле.

– И когда Джейк всё узнал, он тебя выгнал, да? – сочувственно спросил Пип.

Люк снова вздохнул.

– Спасибо, что он не выдал меня полицейскому! Дядя сказал, что ничего не слышал ни о кошке, ни обо мне и слышать не желает. Я уверен, что полицейские устроят в цирке обыск. Гун думает, что Принцессу спрятали там.

– Думаю, они стали бы искать и тебя, – прошептала Бетси.

– Пожалуй, – согласился Люк. – В общем, дядя подождал, пока Гун скрылся из виду, пришёл ко мне и велел мне убираться восвояси. Он сказал, что взял бы меня с собой, если бы дело было только в отчиме, но раз у меня неприятности с полицией, он не собирается мне помогать.

– Неужели тебе придётся вернуться обратно к отчиму? – спросил Пип. – Не думаю, что тебя ждёт ласковый приём.

– Это точно, – уныло ответил Люк. – А что делать? Куда мне деваться? Я вот пришёл сюда к вам ночью, думал, может, вы дадите мне поесть? У меня с утра маковой росинки во рту не было.

– Бедный Люк! – воскликнула Бетси. – Сейчас я принесу тебе что-нибудь. Я видела на кухне пирог с мясом и сливовый торт.

– Стой, Бетси! Ты что? – возмутился Пип, схватив её за руку. – Как ты думаешь, что скажет мама утром, обнаружив, что на кухне нет ни пирога, ни торта? Лгать ты не умеешь, а если попытаешься сделать вид, что первый раз об этом слышишь, тебя быстро выведут на чистую воду. Тебе всё равно придётся признаться, начнутся расспросы, кому и зачем ты отдала пирог и торт, и в конце концов выяснится, что их съел Люк.

– А что же тогда мы дадим ему? – спросила Бетси.

– Хлеба с маслом, – ответил Пип. – И тогда никто ничего не заметит. К тому же в саду полным-полно слив.

– Отлично! Спасибо вам большое! – Люк был очень благодарен ребятам.

Бетси побежала на кухню и принялась собирать скромный ужин для Люка. Пару раз она споткнулась о кошку, но, к счастью, не упала и, тихонько выскользнув из дома, вернулась к мальчишкам. Люк в мгновение ока расправился с угощением.

– Так-то лучше! – сказал он. – Я всегда говорю, что голодать – последнее дело.

– А где же ты собираешься сегодня ночевать? – спросил Пип.

– Не знаю. Где-нибудь под забором, – развёл руками Люк. – Я ведь стал бездомным бродягой...

– Нет, ни в коем случае! – решительно заявила Бетси. – Ты останешься у нас. Мы устроим тебя в этой старой беседке. Сейчас я принесу матрас, который стелют в кресло-качалку, мы положим его на лавку, и получится что-то вроде кровати.

– И есть будем приносить тебе каждый день, пока что-нибудь не придумаем, – радостно добавил Пип. – Вот здорово!

– Я не хочу, чтобы из-за меня у вас были неприятности, – запротестовал было Люк.

– Ничего нам за это не будет! – возразил Пип. – Побудешь пока здесь, в саду, а мы постараемся раскрыть тайну исчезновения Принцессы. Когда всё уладится, ты сможешь вернуться на работу.

– Я пошла за матрасом! – объявила Бетси и помчалась к дому.

Глаза уже немного привыкли к темноте, и она без труда нашла качалку. Пип помог ей: вместе они притащили в беседку матрас и устроили на скамейке постель для Люка. Пип принёс из гаража старый плед.

– Ночь сегодня тёплая, ты не замёрзнешь, – сказал Пип. – А утром мы принесём что-нибудь на завтрак.

– А как же ваш садовник? – с тревогой спросил Люк. – Когда он приходит на работу?

– Он заболел, – ответил Пип. – Его не будет ещё несколько дней. Мама очень переживает за овощи. Всё твердит, что им нужна вода, и пытается заставить нас с Бетси поливать их. Но я терпеть всё это не могу!

Люк облегчённо вздохнул:

– Вот и хорошо! Значит, я здесь в полной безопасности. Спокойной ночи! Спасибо вам!

Пип и Бетси вернулись в дом и неслышно проскользнули каждый в свою комнату. Засыпая, они думали о ночном приключении. Интересно, что завтра скажут остальные, когда узнают, что Люк ночевал у них в беседке? Бетси была счастлива, что ей удалось помочь Люку – он такой славный и хороший товарищ. Теперь и они могут что-то сделать для него.

Как волнительно было проснуться с утра, зная, что в беседке прячется Люк. Интересно, как он там? Пип сел в кровати и стал думать, что можно добыть Люку на завтрак. Вот бы мама дала сосиски! Можно было бы незаметно спрятать одну и отнести в беседку. С яйцами этот номер не пройдёт. В крайнем случае всегда можно опять отнести ему хлеб с маслом.

Бетси думала о том же самом. Она быстро оделась и спустилась вниз, в надежде, что успеет намазать хлеб маслом и вынести еду в сад, пока на кухне никого нет. Она отрезала толстенный ломоть хлеба и положила на него огромный шмат сливочного масла, направилась к выходу – и в столовой столкнулась с мамой, которая удивлённо взглянула сначала на свою дочь, а потом на тарелку с едой.

– В чём дело, Бетси? – спросила она. – Ты что, умираешь от голода? Боишься не дожить до завтрака? Такой кусок под стать обжоре Робину-Бобину!

Бетси пришлось положить ломоть хлеба с маслом себе на тарелку и, давясь, жевать его, заедая кашей. Наконец с овсянкой было покончено. И тут – ура! – на столе появилось блюдо с сосисками. Глаза у ребят заблестели, они радостно переглянулись. Теперь нужно только улучить момент – и дело будет сделано!

– Мам, а можно мне сегодня две сосиски? – с невинным видом попросил Пип.

– И мне тоже! – поспешила добавить Бетси.

– Бетси, тебя будто бы не кормили неделю! – пожала плечами миссис Хилтон, но положила им обоим по две сосиски.

Отец, как обычно, уткнулся в газету и ничего не замечал вокруг себя, но мама не сводила с них глаз. Как же изловчиться и спрятать хотя бы по одной сосиске? Когда они почти совсем отчаялись, в столовую вдруг вошла горничная Энни.

– Миссис Хилтон, там пришли из больницы, собирают пожертвования, – сказала она. – Мисс Лэси ждёт в прихожей.

– Ах да, конечно! – Миссис Хилтон поспешно встала со стула и стала подниматься вверх по лестнице, чтобы взять из своей комнаты кошелёк.

Оставшись одни, дети подмигнули друг другу и принялись за дело. Пип вынул из кармана чистый носовой платок и быстро завернул в него сосиску. Платок Бетси не блистал чистотой, но делать было нечего. Раз! – и сосиска оказалась в кармане у Бетси. Осталось прихватить только хлеба с маслом.

К возвращению мамы Пипа и Бетси вся еда уже перекочевала в карманы детей. Миссис Хилтон изумлённо обозрела пустые тарелки.

– Бетси! Пип! Как в вас столько помещается? Каждому досталось по миске овсянки, по две сосиски и ещё несколько кусков хлеба с маслом. Боюсь, у вас случится несварение желудка от обжорства!

Бетси, не удержавшись, тихонько хихикнула и тут же получила пинок под столом от брата. До конца завтрака утащить им больше ничего не удалось: они постоянно ловили на себе испытующий и недоверчивый взгляд матери.

Люк с удовольствием уплетал хлеб с маслом и сосиски. Пип и Бетси захватили в беседку стакан с водой. Пока Люк завтракал, друзья обсуждали ближайшие планы.

– На обед мы тоже что-нибудь принесём, – обещал Пип. – А пока ты можешь угощаться сливами прямо с деревьев.

Люк кивнул, допил воду и отдал ребятам стакан. Вдруг неподалёку послышалось уханье совы – и Бетси радостно захлопала в ладоши.

– Это Фатти! А с ним Бастер! – воскликнула она. – Фатти, эй! Мы здесь, в беседке!

Фатти вошёл в сад. За ним семенил чёрный скотчтерьер. Увидев ребят, он вихрем ворвался

в беседку, заливаясь радостным лаем. Люк потрепал его по голове.

Следом за пёсиком к беседке подошёл Фатти и, увидев Люка, так и застыл с открытым ртом. Бетси, взглянув на него, звонко рассмеялась.

– Он пока побудет у нас, – объяснила она. – Мы носим ему еду. Это так интересно! Настоящее приключение! Ах, Фатти, как было бы хорошо, если бы мы поскорее раскрыли тайну пропавшей кошки. Тогда Люк мог бы ничего больше не бояться. Давайте расследуем это дело – и поскорей.

Фатти выслушал длинный рассказ о ночных событиях. Потом пришли Ларри и Дейзи, и всё началось снова: удивление, радость, расспросы, рассказы... Словом, утро удалось на славу!

– А где та свистулька, которую мы нашли в клетке? – спросил Пип.

Свистульку достали и показали Люку.

– Она валялась в кошачьей клетке, – пояснил Фатти. – Было понятно, что мистер Гун найдёт её, а мистер Склокинг скажет, что она твоя, поэтому мы решили вытащить её из клетки и спрятать. А вместо неё накидали туда всяких фальшивых улик. Ты умер бы со смеха, увидев, что там валялось, когда мы уходили. Я оставил там два окурка от сигар, один засунул в клетку, а другой бросил на пол, рядом.

Услышав это, Люк присвистнул:

– Ого! Теперь ясно, почему мистер Гун стал сам не свой, когда увидел, что мой дядя курит сигары. А я-то и не понял, в чём дело. Дядя сказал, что полицейский весь побагровел от волнения, когда он достал сигару и закурил. Джейку показалось, что мистера Гуна удар хватит.

Ребята дружно расхохотались, представив эту картину. А Люк меж тем рассматривал свистульку, которую друзья нашли в клетке.

– Да, это моя, – наконец сказал он. – Я потерял её в саду. Как же она могла попасть в клетку к кошкам? Я сделал её месяц тому назад.

Все стали опять обсуждать эту загадку, но так и не придумали никакого объяснения. Люк по-прежнему уверял, что, пока он работал возле кошачьего домика в тот злосчастный вечер, вокруг не было ни души. Но если это было так, как и куда могла исчезнуть Принцесса?

Теперь сыщики все вместе стали кормить Люка. Во время обеда они хитрили как могли, чтобы спрятать и вынести что-нибудь вкусненькое из дома. Дейзи попалась на месте преступления: мама застукала её, когда девочка засовывала в карман кусок пирога с вареньем. Дейзи ничего не оставалось, кроме как изобразить, что она по рассеянности перепутала пирог с носовым платком, но провести маму ей не удалось.

– Всё понятно! – строго сказала миссис Дейкин. – Ты тайком таскаешь со стола еду для собаки вашего друга Фредерика. Не смей его закармливать – он и так весьма упитанный пёс!

– Что ты, мамочка, я вовсе и не думала угощать Бастера! Честное слово! – отвечала Дейзи, не покривив душой. Ведь еда и в самом деле не предназначалась пёсику.

Друзья притащили Люку кучу еды, принесли ему ведро с водой, мыло и старое полотенце. Каждую ночь они устраивали ему постель в беседке. А Люк в благодарность за это работал в огороде, когда поблизости не было миссис Хилтон. Он старательно поливал овощи, полол грядки, мотыжил землю. Огород был далеко от дома, и Люка никто не видел.

– Мне так хочется отплатить вам за вашу доброту, – повторял он.

Три дня Люк скрывался в саду у Пипа и Бетси, и за это время ребята ещё больше привязались к своему новому другу. А потом события снова приняли неожиданный оборот.

Глава четырнадцатая

Мистера Гуна одолевают подозрения

Миссис Хилтон, мама Пипа и Бетси, прогуливалась в саду и заглянула в огород – и была поражена тем, что все овощи как следует политы и тщательно прополоты. Походив между грядок и полюбовавшись на такое диво, она позвала детей и ласково сказала:

– Какие же у меня растут замечательные дети! Послушные, прилежные – на радость маме. Я была уверена, что наши овощи погибнут без садовника, а вы и поливали их, и пололи. Какие молодцы! Спасибо вам, мои дорогие!

Бетси раскрыла было рот, чтобы сказать, что они тут ни при чём, но Пип состроил такую угрожающую физиономию, что девочка тут же прикусила язычок. Пришлось им с Пипом, заливаясь краской от стыда, выслушивать мамины похвалы и принимать незаслуженную благодарность. Оказалось, что это гораздо хуже, чем получать нагоняй за то, в чём ты не виноват. Пип подумал про себя: «Вот незадача! Надо было мне и Бетси хоть чуть-чуть поработать в огороде, хоть пару раз полить эти несчастные овощи. Тогда было бы не так стыдно слушать, как нас хвалят ни за что».

Вскоре Люк с удивлением застал ребят в огороде: Пип, раздуваясь от гордости, поливал из шланга грядки, а Бетси прилежно выдёргивала сорняки.

– Молодцы, ребята! – крикнул им Люк. – Вот только Бетси выдернула салат-латук, приняв его за сорняк. Но это сущие пустяки, не расстраивайся, Бетси! На соседней грядке есть ещё латук, так что без салата ваша мама не останется.

Как-то мистер Гун встретил Фатти с Бастером и остановил их.

– Позвольте сказать вам пару слов, господин Фредерик, – церемонно обратился он к мальчику, раздуваясь от важности и доставая свою большую чёрную записную книжку.

– Боюсь, я сейчас занят, – вежливо ответил Фатти. – Я иду на прогулку с Бастером.

– Стоять! Смирно! – рявкнул мистер А-ну-ка-разойдись. – Ты что, не слышал? Молчи и слушай, что я тебе скажу! Где же это?.. Ах, вот тут, конечно, – пробормотал он, отыскав наконец нужную страницу в своей записной книжке. – Так вот, пятого числа сего месяца вы, господин Фредерик, и ещё четверо несовершеннолетних были замечены возле цирка. Следствие располагает данными, что вы вступали в контакт с подозреваемым Джейком.

– Какие же выводы сделало следствие? – вежливо осведомился Фатти.

– Не торопитесь, молодой человек! – буркнул мистер Гун, буравя взглядом мальчика.

Тот не отвёл глаз и дружелюбно улыбнулся полицейскому. Да, Фатти был сама невинность! А его джентльменская вежливость и выдержка всегда доводили Гуна до белого каления.

– Так что вы хотели мне сказать, господин полицейский? Я был бы благодарен, если бы вы как можно скорей перешли к делу. Я мог бы беседовать с вами хоть целый день, но терпение Бастера на исходе.

– Гав! – подтвердил пёсик, сердито покосившись на Гуна.

– Так вот, слушай. – Мистер Гун наклонился к Фатти, жарко дыша ему прямо в лицо: – Признавайся: ведь в тот день Люк прятался где-то там, у циркачей? Ведь так? Не вздумай отпираться! Мне всё известно!

– В самом деле? Зачем же спрашивать меня о том, что вам и так известно? Раз вы всё знаете, ваше дело поймать его и арестовать. Я-то зачем нужен?

– Фокус в том, что сейчас его там уже нет! Но это ничего, я его найду, этого Люка, этого кота в мешке...

– Кота в мешке? – Фатти удивлённо поднял брови. – Вы имеете в виду Принцессу? Так это вы засунули её в мешок? Зачем? И где она сейчас?

– Придержи язык! – рявкнул Гун. – «Кот в мешке» – это твой приятель, от которого непонятно чего ждать. То, что он прятался у циркачей, я точно знаю – мне призналась в этом одна девчонка-акробатка. Я обыскал весь их табор, но парня и след простыл!

– М-да... не повезло, – посочувствовал Фатти.

Услышав это, Гун так рассвирепел, что Фатти попятился:

– За что вы так сердиты на меня, многоуважаемый мистер полицейский? Я, по-моему, ничего обидного вам не сказал в отличие от вас.

Вы не очень-то похожи на джентльмена, а ещё требуете уважения к старшим!

Гун снова наклонился к Фатти, заглянув ему прямо в глаза:

– Есть у меня подозрение, что ты и твои дружки знаете, где скрывается этот Люк. Понятно, к чему я клоню? Так вот, я вас предупреждаю: если вы прячете его или знаете, где он прячется, и не сообщаете полиции, вы рискуете нажить себе крупные неприятности. Да-да, очень крупные неприятности.

Фатти встревожился. Почему мистер Гун заподозрил их в том, что они прячут Люка?

– Почему вы считаете, что мы его прячем? – спросил он. – Не думайте, будто мы рассчитываем что-то скрыть от вас, мистер Гун. Такой проницательный полицейский, как вы, знает всё!

– Гм, – буркнул мистер Гун. – Поверь мне, дружок, я знаю гораздо больше, чем ты думаешь.

Было ясно, что разговор закончен. Мистер Гун звонко захлопнул свою записную книжку и зашагал прочь, а Фатти пошёл вниз по улице, думая о том, что имел в виду А-ну-ка-разойдись. «Должно быть, Склокинг заглянул через забор и заметил Люка в соседском саду... или просто вбил себе в голову, что Люк отсиживается у Пипа и Бетси, – размышлял Фатти. – Вот досада! Не хотелось бы неприятностей с полицией. Но что же нам делать с бедным Люком? Может, дать ему немного денег и отправить куда-нибудь?»

Выслушав рассказ Фатти, сыщики встревожились. Бетси совсем расстроилась.

– Не надо никуда отправлять Люка! – попросила она. – Мы ведь рано или поздно расследуем это дело, и тогда он сможет вернуться на работу к леди Кэндлинг.

– Мы не сможем раскрыть эту тайну, – мрачно ответил Фатти. – Мы воображали, что мы самые умные, а оказалось, что нам надо быть скромнее. Держу пари, даже инспектор Дженкс не справился бы с этим загадочным делом!

– О-о-о! – воскликнула Дейзи, сразу вспомнив дружелюбного и приветливого инспектора Дженкса, который помог им, когда на прошлых каникулах они раскрыли дело о сгоревшем коттедже. – Инспектор Дженкс! Я совсем забыла о нём. А что, если мы свяжемся с ним и расскажем всё про нашего бедного Люка? Я уверена, что он не станет сажать Люка в тюрьму ни за что. Он не выдаст наш секрет и поможет нам в расследовании.

– Ты так считаешь? – спросил Ларри. – Думаю, ты права. Похоже, другого выхода нет. Если А-ну-ка-разойдись начнёт обыскивать сад Пипа и найдёт Люка, будет хуже и ему, и нам. Давайте действительно расскажем обо всём инспектору. Он ведь сказал тогда, что он наш друг и будет всегда готов прийти к нам на помощь.

– Да, он мне тоже очень понравился! – вставила Бетси.

– Да тебе все вокруг нравятся, – снисходительно заметил Пип.

– Неправда! Мне совсем не нравятся мистер Склокинг и А-ну-ка-разойдись. Давайте и вправду всё расскажем инспектору. Он всё поймёт и поможет нам!

– Я позвоню ему, – сказал Фатти.

Все посмотрели на него с уважением. Ну разве это не замечательно – вот так запросто взять и позвонить «большому полицейскому начальнику».

Фатти сдержал слово. Он вернулся домой, дождался момента, когда рядом никого не было, и набрал номер полицейского участка в ближайшем городе, где служил инспектор.

Фатти повезло – инспектор был на месте. Он сам подошёл к телефону:

– А, Фредерик Алджернон Троттвиль, это вы? Надеюсь, у вас всё в порядке? Да-да, конечно, я помню, как на Пасху вы с ребятами раскрыли дело о сгоревшем коттедже – и очень нам помогли. Вы очень ловко провели расследование – это была отличная работа! Что, есть какое-то новое интересное дельце?

– Да вот, сэр, тут случилась ещё одна история, но мы никак не можем в ней разобраться, – сказал Фатти, ободрённый дружеским тоном инспектора. – У нас ничего не получается. Может быть, вы слышали об этом? Пропала очень ценная кошка.

Наступила пауза. Инспектор, видимо, задумался, а потом его голос снова раздался в телефонной трубке:

– Да, у меня уже есть рапорт об этом деле. Я вспомнил. Думаю, что наш друг мистер Гун уже расследует это загадочное происшествие.

– Боюсь, он не считает себя нашим другом, – признался Фатти. – А тот, кого он подозревает в краже, как раз наш друг! Поэтому я и решил вам позвонить. Похоже, мы совершенно запутались. Может быть, вы могли бы помочь нам советом?

– Очень хорошо, что вы обратились ко мне, – ответил инспектор. – Как раз завтра я буду проезжать мимо вашей деревни. Может быть, выпьем вместе чаю и всё обсудим? Буду рад, если вы позовёте меня на пикник на берегу реки.

– О, конечно! – обрадовался Фатти. – Это просто замечательно! Там и поговорим.

– Договорились! – сказал инспектор. – Я заеду около четырёх. Рад буду снова повидать вас.

– И мы тоже! – ответил Фатти. – До завтра, сэр. Большое спасибо!

Фатти положил трубку и помчался к дому Пипа. Он был очень взволнован и торопился сообщить приятные новости. Ребята были в саду.

– Всё отлично! Я договорился с инспектором, – сообщил Фатти. – Он приезжает к нам завтра на чай, предложил устроить пикник на берегу реки. Тут-то мы ему всё и расскажем.

– Ух ты! Вот это да! Здорово! Фатти, он правда приедет? Ты пригласил его на чай? – загалдели друзья.

Фатти, весь сияя и раздуваясь от гордости, завёл свою шарманку:

– Да уж, кто, кроме меня, смог бы всё устроить? Я в таких делах незаменим, так что смело можете положиться на меня. Для меня позвонить инспектору – сущие пустяки...

– Опять?! А ну прекрати! – хором крикнули Ларри и Пип.

Впрочем, долго сердиться на хвастунишку они не могли. Всех занимала завтрашняя встреча с большим, умным и добрым инспектором. Больше всех волновалась Бетси: он так понравился ей в прошлый раз! Дженкс всё сразу понял и помог ребятам довести расследование до конца. Может, он и в этот раз найдёт правильное решение?

– Вот что, ребята, – сказала Дейзи, – раз мы собираемся устраивать пикник с инспектором, надо сказать об этом родителям, и они конечно же дадут нам всё что нужно. Полицейских инспекторов уважают все – даже взрослые!

Дейзи оказалась права. Когда мамы ребят узнали, что к ним на чай пожалует инспектор Дженкс собственной персоной, они приготовили великолепное угощение.

– У нас шоколадные кексы и сэндвичи с огурцом! – радовалась Дейзи.

– А наша мама сделала имбирное печенье и торт с чёрной смородиной! – похвастался Пип.

– А я принёс джем и пиццу с помидорами, – добавил Фатти. – Вкуснятина!

Дети взяли сумки с угощением, вышли на улицу, столпились у калитки и стали ждать инспектора. И тут вдруг к ним на велосипеде подкатил А-ну-ка-разойдись.

– Мне надо поговорить с вами, – торжественно провозгласил он.

– Простите, но нам некогда – мы собираемся на пикник, – ответил Ларри. – Думаю, вы с удовольствием присоединитесь к нам, и мы все отлично проведём время.

Мистер Гун с удивлением посмотрел на сумки, набитые едой.

– Вы что, собираетесь всё это съесть сами? – подозрительно спросил он.

Фатти понял, что Гун, видимо, счёл, что еда приготовлена для Люка.

– Нет, что вы! Тут хватит не только нам, – поддразнил он полицейского. – У нас будут гости, а кто – мы вам не скажем. Это секрет.

– Гм, – хмыкнул мистер Гун. Подозрения его усиливались с каждой минутой. – А где вы затеваете этот свой пикник? – поинтересовался он.

– Мы идём на речку, – ответила Бетси.

Мистер Гун взгромоздился на велосипед и укатил. Видно было, что он изрядно озадачен.

Фатти прыснул:

– Он, конечно, думает, что мы несём еду Люку – туда, где он прячется. Ему и в голову не пришло, что мы устраиваем пикник для инспектора Дженкса. Вот будет здорово, если он решит нас выследить и накрыть с поличным, но вместо Люка с нами будет инспектор!

– Вот мы посмеёмся! – хихикнула Дейзи. – Ой, смотрите скорей, вот и инспектор!

Действительно, это был инспектор Дженкс. Он подъехал на элегантной чёрной полицейской машине, поставил её к Пипу в гараж и учтиво поздоровался с каждым из ребят за руку.

– Очень рад нашей встрече! – сказал он, ослепительно улыбаясь. – Итак, все в сборе? Пять юных сыщиков и пёс-детектив? А кстати, где собака? Ах, вот она! Славный пёс и большой умница!

Вся компания направилась к реке. Бетси крепко держала дорогого гостя за руку. Инспектор был высокий, сильный мужчина. В его глазах светился ум и играли весёлые искорки, широкая белозубая улыбка часто озаряла его лицо. Ему очень шла полицейская форма. Бетси шла вприпрыжку и радостно щебетала, рассказывая ему, сколько всякой всячины мамы наготовили для пикника.

– Ну что, для начала перекусим? – предложил инспектор. – У меня уже слюнки текут. Надо найти удобное местечко.

Глава пятнадцатая

У мистера Гуна неприятности

Они нашли укромное место у воды под обрывом, на котором густо росли деревья. Там, в спокойной обстановке, укрытые от посторонних глаз, они могли обсудить все важные вопросы.

Но вначале все радостно набросились на еду. Инспектор не отставал от детей. Бастер удобно расположился возле него на траве и на лету ловил разные вкусности, которые время от времени перепадали ему от пирующих.

– Ну что же, – начал инспектор, когда почти всё было съедено, – поговорим теперь о нашем деле? Я просмотрел рапорт об этом происшествии с кошкой и знаю все подробности. Теперь мне очень хотелось бы послушать вас. Вы говорите, этот мальчик Люк – ваш друг?

Дети стали наперебой рассказывать инспектору всё, что знали, умолчав только о ложных уликах, которые они подбросили Склокингу и Гуну. Почему-то никто не захотел об этом говорить.

Они поведали инспектору о том, как обнаружили Люка в цирке, и о том, как он ночью пришёл к Пипу и Бетси.

– С тех пор он прячется у нас в саду: спит в беседке, и мы носим ему еду, – закончил рассказ Пип. – Вот только А-ну-ка-разойдись... ой, извините, я хотел сказать, мистер Гун, похоже, догадался, что мы прячем Люка, и мы боимся, что дело кончится плохо и для него, и для нас.

– Вы правильно поступили, что обратились ко мне, – сказал инспектор. – Вам, конечно, не надо прятать Люка. Если он пустился в бега и прячется от полиции – это расценивается как косвенное доказательство его вины. Так поступать нельзя ни в коем случае. Но в тюрьму его не посадят, не беспокойтесь. Во-первых, ему только пятнадцать лет, а во-вторых, мы не сажаем никого за решётку, если вина полностью не доказана. А его вина пока не доказана, хотя действительно всё складывается против него. Вы согласны со мной?

– Да. Мы тоже так думаем, – кивнул Фатти. – И это нас очень настораживает. Знаете, инспектор, мы все знаем Люка и любим его, и мы не представляем себе, как такой парень, как Люк, мог совершить кражу. Он скромный и даже робкий, очень уважает старших. И он очень-очень добрый! Но мистер Склокинг и мистер Гун ополчились на него и уверены, что он преступник.

– Вот что: я смогу убедить Люка, что ему надо перестать прятаться и вернуться на работу, – предложил инспектор. – Но только... э-э... как бы это сказать... мне кажется, ему не стоит рассказывать, где он был и кто его прятал. Это никому не нужно.

– Но тогда Люку придётся вернуться к отчиму, – заговорила Бетси. – Вы даже не представляете себе, инспектор Дженкс, какой он злой, его отчим. Люк очень его боится. Он отругает Люка или даже накажет его!

– Нет-нет, он его и пальцем не тронет, – заверил друзей инспектор. – Я с ним поговорю и строго-настрого велю ему оставить Люка в покое. Обещаю вам, что сам займусь этим делом и, возможно, смогу пролить свет на загадочные события. Сейчас, после того что вы мне рассказали, эта история кажется мне весьма интересной.

– Ах, господин инспектор, вы просто чудо! – восхитилась Бетси и взяла за руку мистера Дженкса. – Как бы я хотела, чтобы именно вы – и никто другой! – расследовали моё преступление, если я его совершу!

Все дружно рассмеялись.

– Надеюсь, что ты всё-таки не станешь совершать преступлений, моя дорогая Бетси! – улыбнулся инспектор, глядя девочке прямо в глаза. – У тебя такое хорошее, открытое лицо! Ты совсем не похожа на злоумышленника.

– Слышите? Что это творится с собакой? – вдруг воскликнул Фатти.

Пёс, оказывается, уже давно покинул дружескую компанию. Сверху послышались его заливистый лай и сердитое рычание. Вдруг оттуда же донёсся знакомый голос:

– А ну-ка разберись со своим псом! Уберите собаку, а то я составлю на неё протокол!

– Это старина А-ну-ка-разойдись! – злорадно прошептала Дейзи. – Он таки выследил нас! И он, конечно, уверен, что мы здесь прячем Люка. Бастер, наверное, услышал, как он крался к нам, и решил задать ему перцу.

– Заберите собаку! – снова послышался грозный крик полицейского.

Фатти поднялся наверх, пробрался через густой кустарник и подошёл к разъярённому полицейскому.

– Эй! А ну-ка разберись со своей собакой! Я знаю, что вы все там, внизу, а с вами кое-кто ещё.

– В таком случае вам бы следовало быть немного повежливее, – невозмутимо заявил Фатти.

– Повежливее?! Ты, щенок, будешь меня манерам учить?! – заорал мистер Гун. – Попались, голубчики? Накрыл я таки вас с поличным! Укрываете преступника? Встали на пути у закона? Ну погодите, сейчас я спущусь и арестую этого воришку, да и вам, его подельникам, тоже как следует достанется!

Фатти не удержался и громко прыснул. Он свистнул Бастера, взял его за ошейник и посторонился, любезно пропуская мистера Гуна вперёд. Полицейский с шумом продрался сквозь кусты и спрыгнул с обрыва, собираясь «накрыть с поличным» четырёх изрядно перепуганных ребят и смертельно перепуганного «воришку» Люка.

Однако вместо всего этого, он, к своему ужасу и удивлению, обнаружил под обрывом инспектора Дженкса. Мистер Гун просто не поверил своим глазам. Они и без того всегда были выпучены, а тут и вовсе вылезли из орбит. Он застыл на месте, уставившись на инспектора, не в силах вымолвить ни слова.

– Добрый день, Гун! – приветствовал его инспектор.

– З-з-з-з... – Гун застрял на первом же слове и, нервно сглотнув, набрал воздуха в грудь и начал снова: – З-з-з-з... з-д-д-дравствуйте, сэр! Я... гм... н-н-никак не ожидал вас здесь встретить...

– Кажется, мне послышалось, что вы собирались арестовать меня? – осведомился инспектор.

Гун снова сглотнул, дёрнул воротник рубашки, который вдруг стал его душить, и попытался выдавить из себя улыбку.

– Я просто пошутил, сэр, – пробормотал он дрожащим голосом. – Я... гм... думал найти здесь кое-кого.. но не вас, сэр! Какой сюрприз – встретить вас тут, сэр...

– Ничего удивительного. Я встречался с детьми, которые любезно посвятили меня в некоторые детали происшествия с кошкой, – пояснил инспектор. – Садитесь, Гун. Буду рад выслушать вашу версию случившегося. Судя по всему, расследование движется не очень-то быстро?

– Да, сэр... То есть я хочу сказать, сэр... Зато у меня очень много улик по этому делу! Мне бы очень помогли ваши советы, сэр... – угодливо добавил полицейский, надеясь завоевать расположение инспектора.

Мистер Гун вынул из кармана белый конверт, раскрыл его и извлёк два окурка, голубую пуговицу, ленту для волос, мятный леденец и коричневый шнурок от ботинок. Теперь удивился инспектор. Он с недоумением уставился на всё это добро.

– Это всё улики? – наконец спросил Дженкс.

– Да, сэр, – отрапортовал Гун. – Обнаружены на месте преступления, сэр, прямо в кошачьем домике.

– Вы действительно обнаружили всё это в кошачьем домике? – недоверчиво спросил инспектор, с любопытством разглядывая находки. – И этот леденец тоже оттуда?

– Да, сэр, это всё оттуда. Никогда раньше не обнаруживал сразу столько улик, сэр, – произнёс мистер Гун, наслаждаясь изумлением инспектора.

– Признаться, я тоже, – пожал плечами инспектор. Он взглянул на пятёрку сыщиков, которые, конечно, до смерти перепугались, когда Гун предъявил инспектору свои находки. Лукавые искорки промелькнули в глазах мистера Дженкса. – Отлично, Гун! – сказал он. – Вас можно поздравить с удачей! А вы, ребята, ничего не нашли на месте преступления?

Фатти извлёк из кармана конверт, куда они сложили дубликаты всех «улик», обнаруженных Гуном, и с серьёзным видом вскрыл его. Бетси едва сдерживала смех, но не решалась нарушить торжественность момента.

– Не знаю, можно ли считать всё это уликами, сэр, – с расстановкой произнёс Фатти. – Скорее всего, нет. Мы тоже не склонны рассматривать эти находки как улики, сэр.

По мере того как Фатти неспешно доставал из своего конверта полный набор тех же самых «улик», Гун бледнел и менялся в лице, так что, когда на свет был извлечён последний предмет, полицейский окончательно уподобился гипсовой статуе с отвисшей челюстью.

– Один мятный леденец! – звонко объявил Фатти.

Далее последовала лента для волос.

– Обрывок ленты!

Дейзи не удержалась и громко хихикнула.

– Один коричневый шнурок! От ботинка. А также синяя пуговица и целых две (представьте себе!) недокуренные сигары!

– Две недокуренные сигары? – еле слышно пробормотал Гун. – Как же так? Что за вздор?...

– Да, всё это, мягко говоря, чрезвычайно странно, – произнёс инспектор. – А вы что думаете? Согласны со мной? – обратился он к детям.

Те молча кивнули. А что они могли сказать? Даже Фатти не вымолвил ни слова, хотя мысленно аплодировал инспектору Дженксу за то, что тот обо всём догадался, но и виду не показал и ничем не выдал их.

– Ну что же, – продолжал инспектор, – давайте сложим эти улики обратно по конвертам, хотя я не очень понимаю, как они помогут нам в расследовании. Как вы считаете, Гун?

– Да, сэр! Совершенно согласен, сэр! – невпопад брякнул мистер Гун.

Он снова побагровел от досады и недоумения. Подумать только – у этих мальчишек оказались точно такие же замечательные улики! Что всё это значит? Бедняга Гун! Только ночью, когда он лежал без сна, ломая голову над этой загадкой, его вдруг осенило, в чём тут дело. Гун наконец всё понял, но жаловаться инспектору не пошёл, зная, что тот на стороне ребят.

– А теперь, Гун, предлагаю навестить этого мальчика, Люка, и сказать ему, чтобы он заканчивал свою игру в прятки, – продолжал инспектор деловым тоном. – Не думает же он неделями скрываться от нас?

От удивления мистер Гун уже в третий раз за день разинул рот – и снова закрыл его, так и не найдя что сказать. Навестить Люка, который играет в прятки с полицией? Откуда инспектор узнал про это? Гун метнул на детей яростный взгляд. Вот назойливая мошкара! Всюду лезут, путаются под ногами!

– Как прикажете, сэр, – пробормотал он, с трудом поднимаясь на ноги.

– Пошли, ребята! – обратился инспектор к юным сыщикам. – Надо поговорить с этим загнанным в угол мальчуганом. Поговорить по-доброму, по-хорошему.

Глава шестнадцатая

Большая неожиданность

Инспектор, широко шагая, прошёл через луг, свернул в деревню и двинулся вверх по улице к дому Пипа. Бетси семенила рядом, крепко вцепившись в его руку, следом быстрым шагом двигались остальные четверо сыщиков. За ними маршировал Гун, а Бастер замыкал шествие, время от времени прихватывая зубами форменные брюки полицейского. Гун был так подавлен, что даже не пытался крикнуть пёсику своё любимое «а ну-ка разойдись!».

Надо сказать, дети не ожидали, что инспектор примет такое решение – немедленно извлечь Люка из укрытия и вернуть его домой и на работу. Они пытались угадать, что будет с Люком, когда он увидит перед собой не просто полицейского, а инспектора.

Маленькая процессия шествовала по центральной улице Петерсвуда. Фатти старался поддерживать с мистером Гуном светскую беседу, но полицейский только скрежетал зубами и бросал на мальчика злобные взгляды.

– И всё же, что может быть приятней, чем пикник на берегу реки, не правда ли, мистер Гун? – щебетал Фатти. – Пожалуй, и вы не отказались бы как-нибудь принять участие в таком пикнике – может быть, на выходных? Или вы работаете без выходных?

Мистер Гун издал звук, похожий на скрип несмазанных петель, и метнул на мальчика испепеляющий взгляд.

– Как забавно, что мы нашли точно такие же улики, как и вы, правда, мистер Гун? – Фредерик Алджернон Троттвиль продолжал как ни в чём не бывало свою непринуждённую болтовню. – Удивительное совпадение!

Дейзи разразилась смехом. Полицейский снова заскрежетал зубами, выпучив от злости глаза.

– Прекрати, Фатти, а то его сейчас хватит удар, – шепнул Ларри на ухо приятелю.

Фатти ухмыльнулся и замолк, одобрительно поглядывая на своего пёсика, который пытался добраться до щиколоток полицейского.

– Вот сюда, – сказал Пип, когда они подошли к его дому.

Вся компания зашла в сад Хилтонов, но, едва за ними закрылась калитка, Пип остановился и взглянул на инспектора.

– Можно мне всё-таки предупредить Люка, что вы хотите поговорить с ним? Я передам ему, что вы сказали, что он может перестать прятаться и вернуться на работу. Бедняга ужасно напуган.

– Отличная мысль, – одобрил предложение Пипа инспектор Дженкс. – Только я думаю, что поговорить с ним должен я. А остальные пока подождут здесь. Не волнуйся, дружок, я знаю, как говорить с такими ребятами, как ваш Люк.

Гун снова скрипнул зубами от досады и злости. Кто, как не он, местный полицейский, лучше всех умеет беседовать по душам с несовершеннолетними преступниками – такими, как этот мошенник Люк? Инспектор слишком мягко обращается с ними. Всегда старается войти в положение. Никогда никого не считает виноватым, пока не получит неоспоримых доказательств. Как будто тут нужны какие-то доказательства! Случай-то яснее ясного – кто, как не Люк, стащил эту кошку? Больше некому!

Но инспектор был большим начальником, и Гун не мог выложить ему всё что думал. Поэтому он молча уселся на садовую скамейку и принялся что-то записывать в свою книжку, не обращая внимания на детей.

Инспектор прошёл с Пипом в глубь сада к беседке. Однако Люка там не оказалось.

– Вот же он, смотрите. – Пип указал в сторону огорода, где Люк вскапывал грядки. – Он говорит, что просто не может сидеть без дела. И ещё он говорит, что, поливая наш огород и пропалывая наши грядки, он старается хоть немного отплатить нам за нашу доброту.

– И правильно говорит, на мой взгляд, – сказал инспектор, внимательно наблюдая за Люком.

– Позови его, пожалуйста, сюда, скажи, что я ему друг, а не враг, и оставь нас наедине, – попросил инспектор.

– Эй, Люк! – крикнул Пип. – Я привёл к тебе одного нашего доброго друга. Иди сюда, он хочет поговорить с тобой.

Люк обернулся и увидел огромного полицейского инспектора в синей форме. Бедняга побелел как мел и чуть не упал в обморок.

– Я не брал эту кошку... честное слово... – насилу пробормотал он, испуганно уставившись на инспектора.

– Давай-ка поговорим, – предложил инспектор. – Пойдём сядем в беседке, и ты мне всё расскажешь.

Он твёрдо взял Люка под руку и повёл к беседке, где ребята столько раз обсуждали таинственное исчезновение Принцессы. Люк весь дрожал как осиновый лист.

Пип ободряюще улыбнулся ему и побежал к ребятам. Заслышав его шаги, мистер Гун оторвался от записной книжки.

– Эй, ты! – прикрикнул он. – И где же этот парень скрывался от правосудия? У тебя в саду? А почему вы не сказали об этом мне? Зачем было сразу всё докладывать инспектору? Вы изо всех сил пытаетесь очернить меня перед начальством!

– Что вы, мистер Гун! – елейным голосом заговорил Фатти. – Как же можно? Чтобы вас очернить, не хватит чёрной краски, даже если собрать все наши наборы для рисования.

Гун снова рассвирепел.

– Помолчи, негодник! – загремел он. – Скверный мальчишка! Как ты смеешь мне дерзить? На месте твоего отца я бы тебя хорошенько выпорол!

– Ох, опять вы разгорячились, мистер Гун! Не хотите ли освежиться? Вот, возьмите-ка этот мятный леденец, – любезно предложил Фатти, доставая леденец из конверта. – В качестве улики он нам вряд ли пригодится, так что можно смело наслаждаться свежим мятным вкусом.

Гун скрипнул зубами и снова уткнулся в записную книжку. Что толку тратить пыл на эту мелюзгу? А Ларри, слушая перепалку Фатти и Гуна, подумал, что вежливостью можно добиться большего, чем упрямством и ссорами. «Попробую-ка я этот метод в школе с учителями», – решил он.

Все страшно переживали за Люка и пытались угадать, как пройдёт разговор с инспектором. Говорили они довольно долго. Но вот наконец послышались приближающиеся шаги. Гун захлопнул книжку, вскочил со скамейки и встал по стойке «смирно». Вскоре на дорожке появились инспектор и Люк. Мальчик явно повеселел, а инспектор улыбался своей неизменной белозубой улыбкой. Бетси бросилась к ним:

– Люк может больше не прятаться? Всё в порядке? Что ему теперь делать?

– Рад сообщить вам, что Люк очень разумно отнёсся к моим доводам и согласился, что ему будет лучше вернуться на работу, а не прятаться от полиции, – сообщил инспектор.

– А как же быть с его злым отчимом? – спросила Дейзи, которой было не по себе от мысли, что Люку придётся вытерпеть дома.

– Ах да! – вспомнил инспектор. – Я ведь обещал уладить этот вопрос. Мне, конечно, нужно было бы с ним поговорить, но, к сожалению, у меня больше нет времени. Мне нужно срочно ехать назад. Гун, ступайте к отчиму мальчика и передайте ему, чтобы он не смел третировать своего пасынка. Потом вы отправитесь к садовнику мистеру Склокингу и скажете ему, что леди Кэндлинг разрешила Люку вернуться на работу, так что пусть мальчик трудится у неё в саду.

Мистер Гун совершенно растерялся. Только что он убеждал и отчима Люка, и мистера Склокинга «всыпать по первое число этому мошеннику» – и вот теперь ему предстояло оправдывать перед ними мальчишку.

Фатти внимательно посмотрел на инспектора. «Держу пари, он специально дал Гуну это поручение за то, что тот совсем запугал беднягу Люка», – подумал он.

Инспектор, в свою очередь, пристально посмотрел на мистера Гуна.

– Вы поняли приказ, Гун? – проговорил он. Голос его звучал по-прежнему спокойно, но сейчас в нём послышались металлические нотки.

Мистер Гун поспешно кивнул.

– Так точно, сэр, – отрапортовал он. – Я должен пойти к отчиму мальчика, сэр. По фамилии Браун. После этого я должен побывать у садовника Склокинга, сэр.

– Надеюсь, вы понимаете, что, если будут хоть какие-нибудь жалобы на плохое обращение с несовершеннолетним Люком, вся ответственность ляжет на вас, Гун, – предупредил инспектор. – Я полагаю, вы сумете довести до сведения этих джентльменов, что это мой приказ. Напомню, что вашей обязанностью является проследить за точным выполнением моих распоряжений. Вы поняли меня, Гун?

– О да, сэр, так точно, сэр, – щёлкнул каблуками мистер Гун. – А... гм... как же насчёт пропавшей кошки? Что с этим делом, сэр? Мы, значит, закрываем его? Больше никаких допросов и расследований?

– Ну что ж, можно, конечно, и дальше изучать ваши улики в надежде, что они прольют свет на это дело, – сурово сказал инспектор, но в глазах его снова промелькнули озорные искорки.

Мистер Гун промолчал. Инспектор повернулся к детям и торжественно пожал каждому руку.

– Был очень рад снова повидать пятерых юных сыщиков и пса-детектива, – весело

сказал он. – До свидания – и спасибо за пикник. Давно меня так вкусно не угощали, как здесь. До встречи!

Инспектор сел в свою блестящую чёрную машину, помахал рукой ребятам, и вскоре шум мотора затих вдалеке.

– Я иду к мистеру Склокингу, – мрачно сказал полицейский, искоса взглянув на Люка и сыщиков. – Но не рассчитывайте на то, что дело закрыто и забыто. Как бы не так! Я буду продолжать расследование, несмотря на то что инспектор отнёсся к моим доводам без должного внимания. И я найду вора. Вот увидите!

Он бросил на Люка угрожающий взгляд, и мальчик понял, что с него по-прежнему не сняты подозрения. Мистер Гун направился к дому леди Кэндлинг, и Люк мрачно посмотрел ему вслед.

Ребята окружили своего друга.

– Люк, тебе понравился наш инспектор? О чём вы говорили? Расскажи нам скорей!

– Он был так добр ко мне, – отвечал Люк, – и ни капли не похож на нашего полицейского. Мистер Гун только кричит и угрожает! Но я напрасно согласился вернуться к отчиму и снова выйти на работу... Зачем я это ему пообещал? Когда мы с ним говорили, мне казалось, что всё будет хорошо, а теперь я вдруг сдрейфил...

Такого слова ребята ещё не слышали. Бетси недоумённо взглянула на Люка.

– Что значит «сдрейфил»?

– Ну... вот сдрейфил – и всё тут! – растерянно повторил Люк. – Сдрейфил, потому что они такие страшные – и мистер Склокинг, и мистер Гун. И мой отчим тоже.

– А! Я понял! Ты дрейфуешь, как корабль, который не может пристать к берегу из-за волнения на море, – объяснил Фатти, который обожал книжки о мореплаваниях. – Хорошее словечко! Оно из морского жаргона. Буду теперь тоже так говорить.

– Я часто дрейфую... или дрейфлю, – призналась Бетси. – Прошлой ночью я дрейфовала или дрейфила во сне, когда мне приснилось что-то страшное. И сегодня я сдрейфила, когда А-ну-ка-разойдись заявил, что хочет с нами поговорить.

– Бедный Люк тоже дрейфит, – сказала Дейзи, сочувственно глядя на мальчика, на его растрёпанные волосы, на его загорелый лоб. – Как нам помочь ему набраться храбрости?

– Единственный способ – это найти украденную кошку, – вздохнул Пип. – Тогда у Люка не будет причин дрейфить. Он дрейфит потому, что его подозревают в краже. Я бы тоже дрейфил на его месте.

В это время в кустах послышался шорох. Бастер навострил уши, звонко тявкнул и ринулся в кусты. Раздался жуткий визг, шипение и фырканье, а потом кто-то вспрыгнул на дерево. Дети побежали смотреть, что произошло.

Ну и сюрприз ожидал их! На дереве восседала породистая сиамская кошка и не мигая смотрела на них сверху вниз. У неё были ярко-голубые глаза и шкурка кремово-шоколадного цвета.

Люк вдруг схватился за голову и закричал во весь голос:

– Да ведь это же Принцесса! Смотрите, у неё светлое колечко на хвосте! Принцесса нашлась! Ну и чудо!

Все сразу увидели кремовую полоску на тёмном кошачьем хвосте, который так и ходил вправо-влево. Сиамская красавица явно нервничала, пристально глядя на беснующегося под деревом пса.

– Фатти, убери Бастера, – поспешно сказал Ларри. – Он напугает Принцессу, она снова удерёт, а виноват опять будет Люк – мистер Гун уж постарается.

Негодующего Бастера заперли в сарае. Пёс яростно лаял и царапал дверь, пытаясь выбраться на волю. Принцесса же сразу успокоилась, поудобнее устроилась на дереве и замурлыкала.

– Ох, как же она отощала! – воскликнула Дейзи.

– А грязная-то какая! – подхватил Ларри. – Шерсть свалялась, вся в колтунах. И где, интересно, её носило? Давайте отнесём Принцессу к мисс Хармер. Вот это будет сюрприз!

Глава семнадцатая

Дела Люка идут на лад

Принцесса позволила Дейзи осторожно снять себя с дерева, и пятеро сыщиков вместе с Люком направились к соседям. По дороге к кошачьему домику они встретились с леди Кэндлинг, которая, увидев кошку на руках у Дейзи, удивлённо подняла брови:

– В чём дело, дети? Кто вам разрешил взять мою кошку из клетки?

– Леди Кэндлинг, да это же Принцесса! – радостно сообщил хозяйке Ларри. – Мы только что нашли её в саду у Пипа. Представляете себе? Вот мисс Хармер обрадуется!

– Не может быть! – изумилась леди Кэндлинг. Она внимательно осмотрела кошку и сразу же заметила на её хвосте светлое колечко. – Да, это действительно моя красавица! Моя Принцесса! Где же она пропадала?! Боже мой, на кого она похожа?! Вся исхудала, бедняжка!

– Жаль, что кошки не умеют разговаривать, а то она рассказала бы нам, что с ней приключилось и где она была, – сказала Бетси, поглаживая мурлыкающую Принцессу. – Леди Кэндлинг, с нами Люк. Мы всё это время прятали его у себя, потому нам было его очень жалко. Вы ведь примете его обратно на работу, правда?

– Ну конечно! – заверила их леди Кэндлинг. – Инспектор Дженкс только что звонил мне. Люк, ты можешь спокойно приступать к работе. Ну и чудеса! Принцесса отыскалась! Она цела и невредима!

– Мы собирались отдать её мисс Хармер, – сказал Ларри. – Хотели обрадовать её.

– Я пойду с вами, – решила леди Кэндлинг. – О, а вот мисс Тримбл! Мисс Тримбл, представьте себе – нашлась наша Принцесса!

– О! Ах! Неужели?! – засуетилась мисс Тримбл, и очки тут же слетели с её носа. – Откуда она взялась? Кто её принес?

Дети рассказали обо всём, и мисс Тримбл, водрузив очки на положенное место, выслушала их с нескрываемым удивлением.

Потом они все вместе направились к кошачьему домику, где мисс Хармер гладила двух своих самых любимых кошек. Увидев Принцессу на руках у Дейзи, она от изумления лишилась дара речи. Беглянка охотно пошла к хозяйке: уютно устроившись у неё на руках, кошка принялась громко мурлыкать и тереться об неё головой.

– Ну и радость! – воскликнула мисс Хармер. – Где же ты пропадала, голубушка? Какое счастье, что ты вернулась!

Ребята, перебивая друг друга, рассказали мисс Хармер, как они обнаружили Принцессу в саду у Пипа, а та слушала их, нежно поглаживая сиамскую красавицу.

– Она так отощала! Бедненькая моя! Шёрстка свалялась, и какая она грязная! Посмотрите, её лапки все в репьях. Наверно, она сбежала от похитителя и отыскала дорогу домой. Должно быть, ей пришлось преодолеть много миль, по лесам и полям...

– Кошки очень умные, – сказал Фатти. – Бедная Принцесса! Изрядно ей досталось. Как хорошо, что всё позади и она снова дома!

В это время возле лужайки показались мистер Склокинг и мистер Гун. Было ясно, что полицейский передал своему приятелю приказ инспектора: вид у Склокинга был унылый. Он бросил злобный взгляд на Люка, а потом увидел Принцессу и переменился в лице.

– Да-да, это она! – торжествующе произнесла Бетси. – Принцесса нашлась! Вот радость, правда, мистер Склокинг?

Склокинг был потрясён. Он не мог поверить своим глазам. Долго и пристально он разглядывал кошку, потом взял её за хвост и стал вертеть его, рассматривая светлую метку. Гун застыл как вкопанный, с раскрытым от изумления ртом и выпученными, как у рака, глазами.

Немного придя в себя, он выхватил свою записную книжку и ручку.

– Надо составить рапорт инспектору об этой неожиданной находке, – важно сказал он. – Необходимо прояснить некоторые обстоятельства. Леди Кэндлинг, вы были здесь, когда обнаружили кошку?

Дети в четвёртый раз повторили свою историю о том, как они нашли Принцессу. Гун с важным видом запротоколировал их рассказ. Склокинг единственный из всех не выказал ни малейшей радости по поводу возвращения Принцессы. Напротив, он злобно воззрился на бедное животное – и было непонятно, чем кошка ему не угодила.

– Очень хорошо, что вы здесь, мистер Склокинг. Мы с инспектором Дженксом говорили о Люке, – сказала леди Кэндлинг своим нежным, но властным голосом. – Мальчик завтра же снова выйдет на работу. Я приняла такое решение, и мистер Гун, я уверена, уже сообщил вам о нём. Надеюсь, что я не услышу от Люка жалоб на то, что вы плохо обращаетесь с ним.

– Что ж, раз вы и инспектор считаете, что можно брать на работу всяких мошенников... – сварливо начал садовник, но леди Кэндлинг резко оборвала его:

– Я не собираюсь обсуждать это с вами. Извольте выполнить моё распоряжение. Разговор окончен! – С этими словами леди Кэндлинг удалилась, и мисс Тримбл засеменила за ней, страшно довольная, что грубиян садовник получил выволочку от хозяйки. От восторга её очки снова спрыгнули с носа и запутались в кружевном воротничке.

– Ух ты! – выдохнул Фатти. – Как она его припечатала!

– А теперь марш отсюда! А ну-ка разойдись! – рявкнул Гун.

– Да, пожалуй, – дерзко ухмыльнулся Фатти. – Пошли, ребята! Не будем мешать мистеру Гуну – он сейчас займётся поиском новых улик. Мало ли что может обнаружиться на месте преступления? Огрызок яблока, ириска, шоколадка... Кстати, мистер Гун, как вам мятный леденец? Хорошо освежает дыхание, правда?

Глаза мистера Гуна налились кровью как у бешеного быка. Ребята не стали ждать, когда разразится буря, и с хохотом помчались к забору. Пожалуй, на сей раз Фатти хватил через край!

Сыщики перелезли через забор, и Фатти первым делом выпустил из сарая охрипшего от лая Бастера. И тут миссис Хилтон позвала Бетси домой: ей пора было ложиться спать.

Малышка тяжело вздохнула:

– Ну вот, всё как всегда! Почему меня вечно отправляют спать в самый неподходящий момент? Не хочу я спать! Слушайте, ну и день сегодня! Сколько всего интересного произошло!

– Точно, – согласился Пип. – Пикник с инспектором, выход Люка из укрытия, возвращение Принцессы... Что ж, дело об исчезнувшей кошке теперь закрыто?

– Э-э-э-э нет! Мы ведь так и не выяснили, кто украл Принцессу, – возразил Ларри. – Может, она каким-то чудом сама сбежала из клетки, а Люк и не заметил, как она удрала. Может, забыли запереть дверцу клетки... Кто знает!

– Не думаю, – откликнулся Фатти, – хотя очень соблазнительно принять эту версию. Нам не удалось найти разгадку тайны, и теперь мы пытаемся сделать вид, что никакой тайны и не было. Якобы Принцесса сбежала сама – и сама же вернулась, устав бродить по окрестностям.

Ребята честно признались себе, что им не очень-то верится в это. Они были недовольны собой: на сей раз им не удалось оправдать гордое звание сыщиков.

А Люк тем же вечером вернулся домой. Удивительное дело: отчим не только не стал его наказывать, но даже не повысил на него голос.

Наутро Люк пришёл в сад на работу. Он со страхом ждал встречи со Склокингом, но тот, как ни странно, ни разу не прикрикнул на него: садовник не мог ослушаться хозяйки, потому что ему вовсе не хотелось потерять хорошую работу.

Люк был страшно рад, что нашлась Принцесса. Казалось, жизнь налаживается! Он трудился не покладая рук, и дети слышали, как он, весело насвистывая, катит свою тачку вдоль дорожки и мотыжит грядки. Ребята влезли на забор и стали наблюдать за его работой.

– Привет, Люк! – сказала Бетси. – Как хорошо, что ты снова здесь!

Люк кивнул:

– Да, правда хорошо! Теперь всё в порядке. Я ведь не из тех, кто любит болтаться без дела. Ребята, не знаю, как вас отблагодарить за то, что вы для меня сделали. Вы меня приютили, когда мне было некуда идти, кормили и поддерживали меня. И главное – вы мне верили. Спасибо вам большое!

– Да не за что! – сказал Ларри. – Мы рады, что нам удалось тебе помочь.

– Хотите, я каждому подарю свистульку? – на радостях предложил Люк. – Я сделаю хорошие, большие свистульки, больше, чем у Бетси, и раскрашу их в разные цвета.

– О, вот это будет здорово! – обрадовался Пип. – У тебя они отлично получаются. Но когда же ты их будешь мастерить? У тебя полно работы!

У Люка действительно было много дел, но он хотел сделать что-то и для своих верных друзей – и для Бастера тоже, но собаке свистульки были ни к чему.

Люк светился счастьем. Отчим и садовник больше не обижали его (хотя Склокинг порой по привычке покрикивал на своего подручного). Леди Кэндлинг ласково обращалась с ним, а ребята часто встречали его после работы.

Так и шёл день за днём – тянулись летние каникулы. Дети ходили друг к другу в гости, устраивали пикники, катались на велосипедах, купались в речке, а Бастер охотился на кроликов.

– Кажется, прошла целая вечность с тех пор, как мы пытались раскрыть тайну исчезнувшей кошки, – как-то сказал Фатти. – И с чего мы решили, что тут какая-то тайна? Дураки же мы были. Тайна, тайна! Ну и где там была тайна? Подумаешь, кошка сбежала из клетки! Сбежала – а потом нашлась. Наверняка это дело яйца выеденного не стоит.

– И всё-таки мы должны были раскрыть это дело, – сказала Бетси. – Иначе с какой стати мы назвались сыщиками? Сыщикам полагается что-нибудь расследовать. Как бы я хотела, чтобы за время каникул случилась ещё какая-нибудь таинственная история!

– Когда чего-то очень хочется, обычно это не сбывается, – сказал Фатти.

Однако на сей раз он ошибся. Вскоре случилось нечто такое, что пятерым сыщикам пришлось снова взяться за расследование. Принцесса снова исчезла – уже во второй раз!

Глава восемнадцатая

Принцесса исчезает вновь

О новом происшествии дети узнали от Люка. Около половины пятого он появился в саду у Пипа, бледный, дрожащий, не похожий на себя. Дети решили, что Склокинг снова взялся за старое – но оказалось, что дело обстоит куда хуже.

– Что стряслось? – спросила его Дейзи.

– Принцесса опять пропала, – еле слышно ответил мальчик. – И опять прямо у меня из-под носа, точно как в прошлый раз!

– Как же так? – изумился Фатти. – Не может быть! Сядь и расскажи всё по порядку.

– Значит, так, – начал Люк, усевшись на лужайке рядом с ребятами, – после обеда я расчищал дорожки вокруг кошачьего домика. Прошлой ночью шёл сильный дождь, и мне сказали привести дорожки в порядок. Я прошёлся по ним метёлкой – вверх-вниз, и пока я махал метлой, кто-то стащил Принцессу. И главное, опять рядом не было ни души!

– А как же ты узнал, что она пропала? – спросил Ларри.

– У мисс Хармер снова был выходной, – стал объяснять Люк. – Она уехала в десять и вернулась минут пятнадцать назад. Первым делом она пошла проверить кошек, и, когда она заглянула в кошачий домик, я услышал крик. Мисс Хармер выбежала из домика и сообщила, что Принцесса опять пропала.

– С ума сойти! – хором воскликнули ребята. – А ты проверил клетки?

– Да! Я заглянул в домик и увидел своими глазами, что все кошки на месте, а Принцессы нет. Её опять украли прямо у меня из-под носа!

– А почему ты решил, что она пропала именно тогда, когда ты мёл дорожки возле домика? – спросил Фатти. – Может быть, она исчезла раньше?

– Нет, не раньше, – ответил Люк. – Леди Кэндлинг теперь каждый день навещает кошек около трёх дня. Приходит посмотреть на своих красавиц и поболтать с мисс Хармер. В три, как всегда, леди Кэндлинг посещала кошек, и Принцесса была на месте.

– Но мисс Хармер-то не было? Значит, она кошек не видела?

– Нет, конечно! Сегодня хозяйку сопровождал мистер Склокинг – как и в прошлый раз. Когда нет мисс Хармер, леди Кэндлинг отдаёт ему всякие распоряжения, которые он передаёт мисс Хармер. Я сам слышал, как Склокинг сказал: «А вон там, сзади, прямо возле стенки, сидит Принцесса – видите, мадам? У неё светлое колечко на хвосте». Это было в три часа дня.

– А ты после трёх никуда не отлучался от кошачьего дома – до самого появления мисс Хармер, которая вернулась и обнаружила, что Принцесса пропала? – уточнил Ларри.

Люк кивнул, тяжело вздохнул и обречённо проговорил:

– Вы же понимаете, что опять во всём обвинят меня. Всё было точь-в-точь как в прошлый раз! Я снова был там один. Но клянусь, я не притрагивался к Принцессе!

– А как мисс Хармер обнаружила пропажу? – спросил Фатти, очень заинтригованный рассказом Люка.

– Как только она вернулась домой, Склокинг встретил её и сказал, что одной из кошек нездоровится. Потом, прямо у меня на глазах, пока мисс Хармер шла к домику, он вошёл в кошачий домик и взял кошку, ту, которую он счёл больной. Потом они вместе с мисс Хармер вошли вовнутрь. Тут-то она и закричала, что опять пропала Принцесса.

– А не мог Склокинг выпустить её случайно, когда заходил внутрь? – спросил Ларри.

– Нет, – уверенно ответил Люк. – Я не видел, что делал Склокинг в домике, но кошка из домика не выбегала. Дверь была плотно закрыта, пока Склокинг был там.

Ребята замолчали. Всё это действительно было просто невероятно. Принцесса опять пропала перед самым носом у Люка – пока он один работал возле кошек. Странно. Очень странно.

– Слушай, а ты сам решил, что надо расчистить дорожки у кошачьего домика? – спросил Фатти.

– Конечно нет! – ответил мальчик. – Я вообще ничего не делаю по своему усмотрению. Поручения мне даёт Склокинг. Он и велел мне после обеда подмести дорожки.

– В прошлый раз ты был в этом самом месте и в это же время – точь-в-точь как сегодня, – задумался Пип. – В прошлый раз у мисс Хармер тоже был выходной – как и сейчас. В прошлый раз именно Склокинг входил к кошкам, и в тот раз он тоже был первым, кто обнаружил пропажу Принцессы. В прошлый раз он заходил в домик с мистером Гуном, а в этот раз – с мисс Хармер. Многовато совпадений! Всё это странно. Очень странно...

– Есть и ещё совпадение: ни в тот, ни в этот раз я не трогал кошку! – воскликнул Люк. – Я это помню совершенно точно! Если бы это я её выпустил из клетки, я, наверное, запомнил бы это. Я ещё не сошёл с ума! Кажется, у меня ещё не бывало провалов в памяти.

– Не волнуйся, Люк! Никто из нас тебя ни в чём не подозревает. Конечно, случается, что люди делают что-то в беспамятстве, а потом не могут вспомнить, что с ними было. Но к тебе это не относится.

– Это самая таинственная из всех тайн! Никогда не слышал ничего подобного! – воскликнул Фатти, вскочив на ноги. – Давайте-ка я наведаюсь к кошачьему домику и постараюсь разнюхать, что к чему. Помните, что мы нашли в клетке в прошлый раз? Одну из свистулек Люка. Раз мы насчитали столько совпадений, бьюсь об заклад, что мы снова обнаружим там одну из его поделок.

– Глупости! – пожала плечами Дейзи. – Это просто случайность, мало ли бывает совпадений.

– Совпадений, кстати, многовато, – глубокомысленно произнёс Фатти. – Так вот: если я найду свистульку в клетке и на этот раз, мы должны будем признать, что это не случайность. Что её подбросили туда нарочно. Вот сейчас пойду и посмотрю.

Конечно же всем тоже захотелось сходить и проверить версию Фатти. Сыщики перебрались через забор – и Люк вместе с ними. Мальчик отчаянно «дрейфил», но оставаться в одиночестве не хотел. В саду у Пипа остался только Бастер, которого Фатти привязал к дереву. Пёс яростно лаял и грыз поводок, тщетно стараясь вырваться на свободу.

Незаметно подкравшись к кошачьему домику, сыщики настороженно осмотрелись. Вокруг никого не было. Склокинг и мисс Хармер отправились докладывать о происшествии леди Кэндлинг. Только кошки не мигая смотрели на ребят ярко-голубыми глазами. Бетси сосчитала их. Кошек было семь.

– Смотрите, – сказал Фатти, показывая на клетку. – Опять свистулька Люка. А вы не верили!

Люк в изумлении уставился на свою поделку. Он подошёл к своей куртке, которая висела рядом на дереве, и стал нервно обшаривать карманы.

– Похоже, свистульку вытащили отсюда, – растерянно пробормотал он. – Я положил её в карман... Она была почти готова – осталось только покрасить. Это для Пипа... А кто-то взял её...

– ...и подкинул в клетку, чтобы навести на тебя подозрение! – заключил Фатти, ухмыльнувшись. Он стал рассматривать свистульку, напряжённо о чём-то раздумывая.

– Нам, наверное, надо вытащить её из клетки, как в прошлый раз? – предложила Дейзи.

– Нет, не успеем, – ответил Фатти. – Посмотрите вокруг, может, найдём ещё какие-то улики. Скорей!

Дети стали внимательно рассматривать всё вокруг, а Бетси засунула нос в клетку и принюхалась.

– Тот же запах, что и в прошлый раз! – сообщила она.

Фатти прижался носом к прутьям клетки и втянул носом воздух.

– Точно, опять скипидар! – удивлённо воскликнул он. – Чудеса! Всё точно, как в тот раз: и свистулька на полу, и запах скипидара. Нет, это самая таинственная тайна из всех, какие я встречал в своей жизни!

– Фатти, я думаю, это не улика, но всё-таки посмотри. – Бетси показала на камешек возле дорожки. На нём отчетливо виднелась маленькая круглая капелька краски.

Фатти взглянул на находку.

– Да, не думаю, что это улика... – сказал он, поднимая камень и разглядывая пятно. – Наверное, это Люк капнул краской. Ты здесь красил свои свистульки, Люк?

– Ни разу, – решительно ответил Люк. – Я всегда крашу в сарае, где хранятся банки с краской. И потом, я не пользуюсь бежевым цветом. Я беру яркие цвета – красный, синий, зелёный.

– Вряд ли это улика, – заключил Фатти, но на всякий случай спрятал камень в карман.

В это время послышались шаги, и на дорожке показались леди Кэндлинг, мисс Тримбл, мисс Хармер и мистер Склокинг. Садовник важно вышагивал впереди. Остальные были очень подавлены, а очки мисс Тримбл от огорчения сваливались с носа каждые две секунды.

Все по очереди заглядывали в клетку, тщетно надеясь увидеть там Принцессу. Вдруг мисс Хармер пронзительно вскрикнула.

– Что случилось? – спросила леди Кэндлинг.

Мисс Хармер показала на пол клетки.

– Что это? – спросила она.

Все столпились возле клетки.

– Ага! – злорадно закричал Склокинг. – Это же одна из свистулек, которые делает Люк! Интересно, как она туда попала?

Мисс Хармер взяла ключи и открыла дверцу клетки. Склокинг вытащил свистульку и показал её леди Кэндлинг.

– Это твоя свистулька, Люк? – спросила леди Кэндлинг.

Люк кивнул. От страха он побелел как мел. Тщетно бедняга ломал голову, пытаясь понять, как Принцесса могла опять пропасть у него из-под носа и как его свистулька могла оказаться в клетке.

– У каждого из нас есть свистульки, которые делает Люк, – сказал Фатти, вытаскивая свою из кармана. – Он дарит их всем подряд. Та, что оказалась в клетке, могла быть одной из тех, что он подарил кому-нибудь.

– Но как она очутилась в клетке? – удивлённо покачала головой леди Кэндлинг.

– Мадам, это ясно как дважды два, – вмешался Склокинг. – Этот парень залез в клетку, чтобы взять кошку – точно так же, как он проделал это в прошлый раз, и сам не заметил, как случайно обронил свистульку. Потом он запер дверцу, ключ положил на место и скрылся вместе с Принцессой.

– Я даже не знаю, где хранятся ключи, – возразил Люк.

– Они всегда у меня в кармане, – сказала мисс Хармер. – А когда у меня выходной, я отдаю ключи мистеру Склокингу. А вы где их храните, Склокинг?

– Держу их у себя в кармане, точно так же, как и вы, – ответил садовник. – Но как раз сегодня днём я оставил куртку где-то здесь, так что Люк легко мог взять ключи. Помяните моё слово, Принцессу он спрятал поблизости, чтобы потом, улучив момент, незаметно вынести из сада. Я же говорил вам, мадам, вы напрасно приняли этого парня обратно. И я не ошибся. Сколько раз я говорил мистеру Гуну...

– Меня не интересует, что вы говорили мистеру Гуну, – прервала его леди Кэндлинг. – Думаю, на сей раз мы обойдёмся без него и обратимся напрямую к инспектору Дженксу. Надо немедленно позвонить ему!

Дети очень обрадовались, услышав, что леди Кэндлинг хочет сообщить обо всём инспектору, но его, к сожалению, не оказалось на месте, так что пришлось всё же вызвать мистера Гуна, который не замедлил явиться. Раздуваясь от важности, он принялся за поиски улик и допрос свидетелей.

Для начала он недоверчиво оглядел пятерых сыщиков, потом обследовал кошачий домик, словно рассчитывая снова обнаружить в нём море улик. Однако на этот раз ничего не нашёл – кроме свистульки Люка, которую вручила ему леди Кэндлинг.

– А вы на сей раз что-нибудь нашли? – спросил А-ну-ка-разойдись у Фатти.

– Только запах. И ещё камень с пятном краски, – ляпнула Бетси.

Ребята дружно обернулись к ней и так свирепо уставились на неё, что бедняжка чуть не бросилась наутёк.

– Запах? – с недоумением переспросил мистер Гун. – И камень с пятном краски? Вы что, надумали опять обвести меня вокруг пальца? Больше никаких леденцов, лент, шнурков, запахов и раскрашенных камней! Хватит! Подобные улики можете приберечь для себя. И зарубите себе на носу: я уже вас предупреждал, что, если вы будете мешать следствию, вас ждут серьёзные неприятности. Понятно?

С этими словами мистер Гун развернулся и ушёл, а ребята поспешили перелезть через забор и уселись на траве, чтобы обсудить всё случившееся.

– Бетси, сколько раз тебе говорить: думай, что говоришь! – воскликнул Пип. – Ты в своём уме? Это надо же – взять и рассказать А-ну-ка-разойдись, какие мы обнаружили улики!

– Наверное... наверное, не в своём уме, – всхлипнула Бетси. – Я не хотела. Сама не пойму, как это у меня выскочило...

– Ладно, не расстраивайся, Бетси, – успокоил девочку Фатти. – Наш славный детектив всё равно не обратил на это внимания. Если это действительно важные улики, Гун нам не помеха. Не переживай!

– Да, таинственное это дело, – задумалась Дейзи. – Дело о пропавшей кошке... Интересно, куда и как она исчезла? Хотела бы я знать!

Глава девятнадцатая

Бастер – исключительно умный пёс

– Что самое поразительное во всём этом, – сказал Фатти, – так это то, что в этих двух случаях практически всё совпадает!

– Похоже, всё было специально продумано и подстроено, чтобы украсть кошку, – подхватила Дейзи.

– И опять – под подозрением только Люк, – сказал Ларри. – В три часа кошка была на месте: и Склокинг, и леди Кэндлинг видели её. Люк был возле кошачьего домика с трёх часов и до возвращения мисс Хармер, а когда мисс Хармер и Склокинг вошли в домик, то обнаружили пропажу Принцессы.

– И Люк, как и в тот раз, уверяет, что всё это время у кошачьего домика, кроме него, никто не появлялся, – задумчиво произнёс Пип. – И совершенно непонятно, как в этой ситуации можно было украсть кошку?

Сыщики замолчали. Загадка казалась неразрешимой, и всё складывалось так, что ответ мог быть только один: Люк – обманщик и вор. Однако дети упорно отказывались этому верить.

Снова и снова они обсуждали случившееся, пока наконец Бетси не позвали домой. Ребята стали прощаться: пора было по домам.

– Увидимся завтра, – мрачно сказал Фатти. – Всё равно сегодня мы уже ничего сделать не сможем. Утро вечера мудренее! Ночью я ещё раз всё обдумаю, и, может быть, завтра мы найдём выход.

– Вот если бы у нас были какие-нибудь стоящие улики да парочка подозреваемых, как в прошлый раз! – вздохнул Пип. – Боюсь, запах и пятно краски на камушке вряд ли можно счесть уликами...

– Даже старина А-ну-ка-разойдись посмеялся над ними, – сказал Фатти, вставая и направляясь к выходу. – Пока, ребята! Надо нам обязательно что-то придумать. Люку не миновать беды, если мы не сможем ему помочь.

Никто из сыщиков так и не смог толком поспать в эту ночь. Все они ворочались без сна в своих постелях, размышляя о тайне исчезнувшей кошки. Однако к утру ни у кого так и не возникло ни одной подходящей идеи, кроме Бетси, которая не решалась поделиться своими мыслями, опасаясь, что старшие ребята поднимут её на смех.

– Ну что, есть какие-нибудь идеи? – спросил Фатти, когда все встретились в саду у Пипа.

– Знаешь, – неуверенно начала Бетси, – есть у меня одна мысль про нашу улику.

– Смелей, Бетси! Что за мысль? – подбодрил её Фатти.

– Помните, в клетке всё время пахло скипидаром? – приободрившись, заговорила Бетси. – Запах был и в тот и в этот раз. Я уверена, что это неспроста. Это что-то да значит, и должно быть как-то связано с пропажей кошки. Запах – самая настоящая улика, и мы должны понять, что она означает.

– И как же ты себе это представляешь? – ехидно поинтересовался Пип.

– Можно пойти в сад леди Кэндлинг и разведать, нет ли там где-то бутылки со скипидаром, например, – робко предложила Бетси. – Наверное, это не очень нам поможет, но если запах – улика, мы хоть что-то выясним...

– Бетси права, – решительно заявил Фатти. – Она совершенно права! Оба раза мы почувствовали запах на месте преступления – и мы должны постараться выяснить, что это значит. Давайте пойдём туда и попробуем отыскать скипидар. А там, кто знает, может, отыщутся и ещё какие-то улики.

– Хорошо! Пошли прямо сейчас, – предложил Пип. – Не будем терять времени. Идём! Только осторожней: в саду может быть Склокинг. Этому джентльмену вряд ли понравится, что мы там что-то выискиваем.

Ребята перелезли через забор, а бедному Бастеру опять пришлось сидеть в заточении в сарае. Пипа отправили на разведку, и вскоре он вернулся, сообщив, что Склокинг занят чем-то прямо возле дома леди Кэндлинг.

– В общем, несколько минут у нас есть, – заключил он. – Пошли сначала к клеткам, проверим, не остался ли там запах, а потом поищем, кто и где тут хранит скипидар.

Ребята старательно обнюхали клетки и обнаружили, что запах всё ещё ощущается. В это время к кошачьему домику подошла мисс Хармер. Она была явно недовольна, обнаружив там ребят.

– Никто не должен без спроса подходить к кошкам, – сердито сказала она. – С тех пор как Принцесса снова пропала, мои нервы совершенно расшатались. Пожалуйста, не ходите сюда больше, слышите, дети?

– Мисс Хармер, а вы не пользуетесь скипидаром для чистки клеток? – вдруг выпалил Фатти.

Мисс Хармер удивлённо взглянула на него:

– Ну разумеется, нет! Я использую обычную дезинфекцию. Кошки не переносят запаха скипидара.

– А почему же тогда в клетках пахнет скипидаром? – спросил Ларри. – Понюхайте – и вы сразу почувствуете его.

Мисс Хармер потянула носом – но её обоняние было не таким тонким, как у ребят, и она не уловила никакого запаха.

– А вчера вы не почувствовали этот запах, когда вошли в кошачий домик и обнаружили, что Принцесса исчезла? – не сдавался Ларри.

– Пожалуй... – задумчиво протянула мисс Хармер. – Но точно я не могу сказать. Я была так потрясена, что смутно помню свои ощущения.

Дети снова прижались носами к клетке и стали старательно всматриваться. Но мисс Хармер настойчиво потребовала, чтобы они отошли от домика.

– Идите, идите! – подгоняла она их. – Я очень нервничаю, когда кто-то подходит к кошкам.

– Пойдёмте посмотрим в сарае, может быть, найдём там скипидар, – предложил Фатти.

Сыщики направились к двум сараям, которые стояли прямо за теплицами. В одном из них хранился садовый инвентарь, а в другом – корзины, горшки, коробки и всякая всячина.

– Вы, девочки, осмотрите этот сарай, а мы обыщем другой, – скомандовал Фатти.

Дети тщательно обыскали оба сарая, но никакого скипидара не обнаружили. Они, конечно, расстроились: ведь никто из них ещё не догадывался, что они на верном пути!

Тут Ларри заметил Люка, который с унылым видом шёл по дорожке.

– Эй, Люк, привет! У тебя такой вид, будто тебе лимон скормили за завтраком. Хватит киснуть! – ободряюще крикнул Ларри.

– Ты бы тоже скис на моём месте, – отозвался Люк. – И сдрейфил бы изрядно!

– Ладно, не дрейфь! – улыбнулся Ларри. – Видишь, выучили мы твоё словечко!

Но Люк даже не улыбнулся. Настроение у него было хуже некуда: он боялся, что в любой момент явится мистер Гун, арестует его и поведёт в тюрьму.

– А что это вы роетесь в сараях? – спросил он. – Ох и влетит вам, если вас здесь застукает Склокинг!

– Мы ищем скипидар, – ответил Фатти, выглянув из сарая.

Люк изумлённо посмотрел на него.

– Скипидар? – переспросил он. – А зачем вам скипидар? Он хранится в другом сарае. Идёмте, я покажу.

Люк повёл ребят к сараю, который обыскивали Дейзи и Бетси. Он показал на полку, где стояли разные бутылки.

– Скипидар должен быть где-то здесь, – сказал он.

Сыщики стали открывать одну бутылку за другой и обнюхивать их. Но бутылки со скипидаром тут не бывало.

– Нет здесь скипидара. Мы уже всё обыскали, – сказала Дейзи.

Люк был явно озадачен.

– Странно... Ещё вчера он был здесь. Я его тут видел. Непонятно, куда девалась эта бутылка?

Фатти ужасно взволновался: что-то ему подсказывало, что всё это неспроста.

– Тайна пропавшего скипидара... – пробормотал он.

Ребята засмеялись.

– Мы обязательно должны его найти! – настойчиво сказал Фатти.

– А зачем? – спросила Дейзи.

– Пока не знаю, но чувствую, что обязательно надо искать! – повторил он. – Может быть, бутылка пропала неспроста. Может быть, её кто-то спрятал. Мы должны найти её.

– А как ты себе это представляешь? Будем обнюхивать весь сад, как собаки? – усмехнулся Ларри.

– Вот и задание для Бастера по сыскной части! – воскликнул Фатти.

– У-у-у-у! Точно! – обрадовалась Бетси. – Бастер – удивительно умный пёс. Он в два счёта отыщет бутылку!

– Но как? – пожал плечами Ларри. – Нельзя же сказать Бастеру: «Слушай, дружище, отыщи-ка нам спрятанную бутылку со скипидаром». Он, конечно, умный пёс, но не настолько же!

– Этот вопрос мы решим, – важно ответил Фатти. – Пип, у тебя есть в сарае скипидар?

– Конечно! – кивнул Пип.

– Давай скорей принеси его, – скомандовал Фатти. – Я пойду выпущу Бастера. А вы все ждите нас возле забора – чтобы быстренько перелезть через него, если появится Склокинг.

Люк уныло побрёл работать, а сыщики дружно отправились к забору. Пип и Фатти быстро перелезли через него, и Пип побежал в дальний угол сада к сараю. Он достал оттуда маленькую банку со скипидаром, а Фатти в это время открыл другой сарай, где хранились велосипеды и где сидел Бастер. Пёс выскочил на волю и стал кружиться возле Фатти с таким восторженным лаем, словно не видел хозяина несколько лет.

– Пошли, Бастер, – сказал Фатти, взяв собаку на руки. – Есть для тебя ответственное задание!

Вскоре Пип и Фатти с Бастером были уже по ту сторону забора, где их ждали остальные.

– Где там Склокинг? – шёпотом осведомился Фатти. – Всё ещё копается возле дома?

– Да, я только что проверил, – прошептал в ответ Ларри. – На горизонте всё чисто!

– А что будет делать Бастер? – взволнованно спросила Бетси. – Он будет нашей ищейкой? Собакой-сыщиком, да?

– Надеюсь, он нас не подведёт! – С этими словами Фатти плеснул немного скипидара себе на ладонь и сунул её под нос Бастеру.

– Нюхай, дружок, нюхай! Нюхай внимательно и запоминай. Запах такой, что ни с чем не перепутаешь, да, Бастер? А теперь, давай-ка ищи этот запах. Ты ведь у нас умница, Бастер? Настоящая чистокровная ищейка!

Бастеру совсем не нравился запах скипидара. Он отворачивал мордочку от ладошки хозяина, громко чихал и тряс ушами.

– Вперёд, Бастер! Это скипидар! Ски-пи-дар! Давай! Ищи! След, Бастер, след! – скомандовал Фатти, тыкая ладошкой пёсику в нос.

Бастер пытливо взглянул на хозяина. Он прекрасно знал команду «ищи» и часто находил разные вещи для Фатти. Пёс засеменил по лужайке, высунув розовый язычок и задрав хвост трубой.

– Бедный Бастер, как бы у него вообще не отшибло нюх, – покачала головой Дейзи. – Ты чуть не удушил его этим скипидарным запахом, Фатти.

А Бастер устремился в кусты, потом выскочил из них и помчался к сараю. Пробежал взад-вперёд по дорожке, а потом направился к кошачьему домику.

– Бастер ищет кроликов, а вовсе не скипидар! – возмутился Ларри. – Смотри-ка, он нашёл кроличью нору и совсем забыл про задание!

Бастер действительно нашел дырку в земле. Он засунул туда нос, взвизгнул и принялся яростно рыть, разбрасывая землю фонтаном позади себя.

– Вылезай, глупый! – гневно крикнул Фатти. – Разве я велел тебе искать кроликов? Я же ясно сказал – «ски-пи-дар»! – И Фатти оттащил собаку от норы за хвост.

Вдруг из-под задних лап Бастера выкатился какой-то предмет. Это оказалась пробка. Фатти поднял и обнюхал её.

– Пахнет скипидаром! – взволнованно объявил он.

Ребята окружили его и стали по очереди нюхать пробку. Не было ни малейшего сомнения – от пробки пахло скипидаром!

Фатти опустился на четвереньки, засунул руку в дыру и извлёк оттуда бутылочку со старой, наполовину оторванной наклейкой, на которой, однако, отчётливо были видны первые буквы надписи – «СКИПИ». На дне её ещё оставалось немного пахучей жидкости.

– Вот то, что мы искали! – торжественно объявил Фатти, подняв вверх находку.

Бетси подбежала к дыре, бухнулась на четвереньки и с любопытством заглянула в неё.

– Ой, Фатти, а там ещё что-то есть! – воскликнула она, засовывая руку.

Теперь все столпились вокруг Бетси, с волнением ожидая, пока она достанет новую улику.

– Что это? – нетерпеливо спросил Ларри. – Ух ты! Банка с краской! У ну-ка... где-то у меня был ножик... Сейчас я поддену крышку...

В банке оказалась бежевая краска.

– Ну и ну! – покачал головой Фатти. – Ведь это та же краска, что и на камне, который мы нашли. Смотрите!

Он поднёс камушек с пятном к банке. Это был один и тот же цвет!

Ларри встал на четвереньки и тщательно обследовал дыру. Но там больше ничего не обнаружилось.

– Теперь, – подытожил Фатти, разглядывая бутылку со скипидаром и банку с краской, – осталось только узнать, кто и зачем прятал всё это в кроличьей норе?

Глава двадцатая

Поиски запаха

Сыщики были страшно взволнованы. У них на руках оказались две весомые улики. Оставалось понять, как они связаны с исчезновением кошки.

– А для чего вообще используют скипидар? – поинтересовалась Бетси.

– Чтобы отмывать кисти, стирать с вещей пятна краски, – ответил Ларри. – Ясно, что пятно на камне и скипидар как-то связаны между собой. Странно, что есть банка с краской и нет кисти. Обычно если кто-то что-то красит, то нужны кисти или валики.

– Давайте я ещё раз осмотрю ямку, – предложила Дейзи.

Но Бастер её опередил: он сунул свой блестящий чёрный нос в землю и вверх полетела новая очередь из земляных комьев. Наконец Бастер выбрался из дыры, держа в зубах маленькую тонкую кисточку – вроде той, которой рисуют дети на уроках в школе.

– Ну разве он не умница? – захлопала в ладоши Бетси.

– Проверим ещё раз! – сказал Фатти, ложась на живот и засовывая руку в дырку. Но больше там ничего не оказалось.

– Слышите? Кажется, это голос Склокинга. По-моему, он зовёт Люка, – шепнул Фатти. – Быстро все к забору! Бежим! Ларри, помоги мне разровнять землю: надо замести следы. Мы не знаем, кто всё это тут припрятал, но, кто бы это ни был, он не должен догадаться, что мы всё нашли!

Мальчишки быстро разровняли землю вокруг тайника и накидали сверху травы. Дейзи перелезла через забор и помогла перебраться Бетси. Следом примчались все остальные, включая Бастера. Они успели как раз вовремя. Буквально через минуту по ту сторону забора раздались шаги Склокинга, который шёл по дорожке, что-то бормоча себе под нос.

Ребята уселись в беседке и ещё раз внимательно рассмотрели находки.

– Одна бутылочка с остатками скипидара, одна маленькая баночка бежевой краски, одна маленькая, тоненькая и очень старая кисточка, – перечислил Фатти. – Что-то подсказывает мне, что, если бы мы только смогли догадаться, кем, как и для чего это всё использовалось, мы раскрыли бы тайну пропавшей кошки.

– Фатти, – торопливо заговорила Бетси, – может, нам стоит ещё раз наведаться в кошачий домик и обнюхать всё внутри клетки? Надо бы точно узнать, что пахнет скипидаром: кошачьи полки? Решётка? Стенки? Я, правда, сама не знаю, чем это нам поможет, но всё-таки...

– Бетси, это глупо! – ответил Пип.

– Я тоже не понимаю, что нам это даст, – согласился Ларри. – И потом, как мы залезем в клетку? Ключи ведь у мисс Хармер.

– Вообще-то, кажется, в идее Бетси что-то есть, – задумчиво сказал Фатти. – Знаешь, Ларри, пока мне тоже неясно, зачем искать место, намазанное скипидаром, но какое-то чувство мне подсказывает, что надо его искать. Бетси, сегодня твой день! Тебя посещают идеи одна лучше другой!

Бетси была счастлива получить такой комплимент. Её частенько поддразнивали и смотрели на неё сверху вниз как на самую маленькую, и теперь она страшно гордилась, что заслужила похвалу Фатти.

– Ага, но как же мы добудем ключ? – спросила Дейзи. – Мисс Хармер держит его в кармане.

Фатти глубоко задумался.

– Сегодня очень жарко, – наконец сказал он. – Наверняка мисс Хармер снимет куртку и повесит её на дерево. У кошек она уже была и сейчас, наверное, трудится в теплице. Она ведь не только ухаживает за кошками, но и работает в огороде.

– Ну-у, не знаю, – с сомнением протянул Ларри. – Теперь, после второго исчезновения Принцессы, она вряд ли оставит куртку без присмотра.

– Пошли, там разберёмся! – решительно позвал друзей Пип, вставая с лавки. Он потрогал деревянную обшивку беседки, нашёл неплотно прибитую доску и засунул в тайник все три улики. – Вот так! Тут никто их не найдёт. Идём посмотрим, чем занята мисс Хармер.

Ребята снова перелезли через забор и оказались в саду леди Кэндлинг, предварительно закрыв Бастера в сарае. Не хватало только, чтобы он носился кругами возле кошачьего домика, пока сыщики будут там всё обнюхивать и обыскивать.

Фатти вызвался пойти на разведку и вскоре действительно обнаружил мисс Хармер в одной из теплиц: она ставила подпорки под ветви персикового дерева. На ней были джинсы и холщовая рубаха. Фатти поискал глазами её куртку. Мисс Хармер, как он и предсказывал, сняла её, но повесила на гвозде внутри теплицы. Вот досада! Как достать из кармана ключ, чтобы мисс Хармер этого не заметила? Фатти вернулся и доложил обстановку.

– Надо как-то выманить её из теплицы, хоть на минуту, – сказал Пип.

Все задумались, а потом стали наперебой предлагать разные варианты – один сложнее другого. И вдруг Дейзи предложила на удивление простой способ.

– Я знаю, что делать! – воскликнула она. – Я неслышно открою двери в другом конце теплицы – у неё ведь два входа? – спрячусь рядом за каким-нибудь развесистым кустом и громко крикну: «Мисс Хармер! Мисс Хармер!» Она наверняка пойдёт к тому входу посмотреть, кто её зовёт. А в это время кто-нибудь из вас проберётся в теплицу и возьмёт ключ.

– А вдруг кто-нибудь нас застукает и будет ужасный скандал? – засомневался Ларри. – Но... в конце концов, надо рискнуть! Мы ведь сыщики, а в нашей работе без риска не обойтись! Ну, кто пойдёт брать ключ?

– Я! – заявил Пип. – Доверьтесь мне! Я очень ловкий.

– Ладно, – кивнул Фатти. – Попробуй. Значит, план такой: Дейзи прячется в кустах возле дальнего входа в теплицу, а Пип – возле ближнего, там, где работает мисс Хармер. Дейзи должна позвать мисс Хармер, и, как только та выглянет из дальней дверцы, Пип неслышно проскользнёт в беседку и вытащит ключ из куртки. Идёт?

– Хорошо придумано! – сказал Пип. – А все остальные будут ждать меня с ключом возле кошачьего домика?

– Да! Идите скорей, а то мисс Хармер закончит работу и наденет куртку, – поторопил ребят Фатти.

Дейзи и Пип отделились от остальных и потихоньку прокрались к теплице. Мисс Хармер всё ещё трудилась на том же месте. Дейзи устроилась за цветущим кустом у дальнего входа в теплицу и стала ждать, когда Пип спрячется у той двери, где висела куртка мисс Хармер. Вся операция пошла точно по плану.

– Мисс Хармер! Мисс Хармер! – прокричала Дейзи.

Мисс Хармер услышала, что её зовут. Она положила лопату и прислушалась.

Дейзи набрала в лёгкие воздуха и крикнула изо всех сил:

– МИСС ХАРМЕР!

Мисс Хармер открыла дверь теплицы и вышла наружу.

– Кто меня звал? – спросила она.

И в этот самый момент появилась мисс Тримбл. Она семенила по дорожке, поминутно поправляя очки на носу.

– Это вы меня звали, мисс Тримбл? Что вам нужно? – спросила её мисс Хармер.

Дейзи хихикнула. Далее последовал смешной разговор между двумя дамами.

– Нет, это не я, – ответила компаньонка, роняя очки. – Но я тоже слышала, как кто-то звал вас. Может, леди Кэндлинг?

– Зачем, интересно, я могла ей понадобиться? – развела руками мисс Хармер.

– Она там, за лужайкой, идёмте, я покажу вам, – услужливо предложила мисс Тримбл.

Обе пошли по дорожке к лужайке и скрылись из вида.

Пип тут же использовал свой шанс – он неслышно скользнул в теплицу с того входа, где висела куртка мисс Хармер, сунул руку в карман и быстро вытащил ключ.

Очень довольные тем, что их план удался, Пип и Дейзи помчались к кошачьему домику, где их с нетерпением ожидали остальные.

– Вот ключ! – с гордостью объявил Пип. – Давайте скорей обнюхаем клетку!

– Нет уж, в домик пойдём мы с Бетси, – удержал его Фатти. – Больше никто, а то кошки попадают в обморок. У меня нос очень чувствительный, а что касается Бетси, это ведь её идея, так что она тоже пойдёт.

Фатти и Бетси вошли в кошачий домик, аккуратно прикрыли за собой дверь и стали тщательно обнюхивать всё вокруг. От клетки пахло чистящими средствами, но кое-где всё ещё отчётливо чувствовался запах скипидара.

Дети обнюхали кошачьи полки. Кошки величественно возлежали на них, созерцая незваных гостей. Одна из кошек протянула лапку и принялась играть с волосами Фатти.

– По-моему, пахнет вот здесь, от этой полки, – сказал Фатти, после того, как тщательно обнюхал пол, потолок и прутья клетки. А ну-ка понюхай ты, Бетси!

На полке лежала большая кошка. Бетси осторожно сняла её и обнюхала полку.

– Нет, Фатти, полка ничем не пахнет.

Фатти тоже понюхал полку и недоумённо пожал плечами.

– Точно, ничем не пахнет. Но запах только что шёл отсюда.

Бетси посадила кошку на место:

– Иди, киска, садись на место.

– Странное дело! Опять запахло! – прошептал Фатти, потягивая носом. – Снова пахнет, слышишь, Бетси?

– Что за чудеса? – удивилась девочка. – Нет, это точно не полка. Слушай, наверное, пахнет от кошки! Как только я посадила её обратно на полку, снова запахло скипидаром.

Большая сиамская кошка с удивлением наблюдала, как двое странных двуногих обнюхивают её с головы до лап. Её частенько гладили, трепали по холке, чесали за ушком – но обнюхивали впервые. Судя по всему, ей это понравилось – она сладко потянулась и замурлыкала.

– Неужели это кошка пахнет скипидаром? – спросил Пип, заглянув в домик.

Фатти кивнул. Он весь раскраснелся от волнения.

– Пахнет вот тут! – объявила Бетси, показывая прямо на серединку длинного, тёмно-коричневого кошачьего хвоста.

– Точно! – подтвердил Фатти.

Он внимательно обнюхал и осмотрел хвост, которым кошка слегка помахивала из стороны в сторону.

– Фатти! Бетси! Тревога! Сюда идут! – раздался взволнованный шёпот Ларри. – Скорей, выходите!

Но, к несчастью, мистер Склокинг появился раньше, чем они успели выбраться из клетки. И грянула гроза!

Садовник не поверил своим глазам. Онемев от ярости и изумления, он уставился на дерзких детей. Фатти и Бетси стремительно выпрыгнули из клетки, захлопнули дверцу и повернули в замке ключ. Бетси дрожала как осиновый лист, да и Фатти стало не по себе. Все остальные залегли за близрастущими кустами.

– Ах вы... Вот я вас!.. Что вам тут надо?! – оглушительно заорал Склокинг. – Откуда у вас ключ? Шастаете тут, а потом у нас кошки пропадают! Хулиганы! Воришки! Всё расскажу мистеру Гуну! Он найдёт на вас управу! Будет вам урок на всю жизнь!

Глава двадцать первая

Разгадка тайны

Мистер Склокинг наконец удалился – с перекошенным от злости лицом. Бетси была в ужасе. Она ухватилась за Фатти, побледнев как полотно. Фатти тоже выглядел потрясённым.

В полном молчании они дошли до забора, перелезли через него и направились к беседке.

– Ну как же так?! Так всё хорошо шло! Пары минут нам не хватило! – сердито сказал Ларри.

Бетси залилась слезами.

– Нас посадят в тюрьму! – всхлипывала она. – Ой, мамочки! Я боюсь! Что же нам делать?

– Ты что, сдрейфила? – улыбнулся Ларри. Он хотел подбодрить Бетси, но она пропустила его шутку мимо ушей. – Не дрейфь, Бетси. Всё в порядке, – сказал Ларри, чтобы успокоить малышку, и погладил её по голове. – Надо сообщить обо всём инспектору Дженксу. Мы расскажем ему, как мы достали ключ, как вы с Фатти всё обнюхали в кошачьем домике. Не думаю, что он поверит А-ну-ка-разойдись, даже если тот напишет рапорт о том, что Склокинг обвиняет нас в воровстве. Верно, Фатти?

Фатти молчал. Ребята посмотрели на него.

– Ты тоже сдрейфил? – спросила Дейзи.

Фатти отрицательно покачал головой, продолжая о чём-то напряжённо раздумывать.

– Не о том вы беспокоитесь, – наконец сказал он. – Подумаешь, Склокинг застукал нас в клетке с кошками. Ну и что? Главное сейчас не это. Интересно, почему кошачий хвост пахнет скипидаром? И почему скипидаром пахнет каждый раз, как только исчезает Принцесса?

– Ты говорил, скипидар используют, чтобы очистить кисточки от краски или вывести пятна от краски на одежде... – сказала Бетси, вытирая слёзы. – Может быть, кошка прислонилась к чему-нибудь свежеокрашенному и с неё смывали краску скипидаром?

Фатти молча уставился на девочку. Потом вдруг он с диким воплем вскочил на ноги и изо всей силы стукнул кулаком по столу. Щёки его раскраснелись, на лбу выступили капельки пота.

– Что с тобой? – испуганно спросил Ларри. – Какая муха тебя укусила?

– Внимание, друзья! – провозгласил Фатти, усаживаясь на место. Вид у него был торжественный и взволнованный. – Малышка Бетси смотрит в самый корень! Скипидар действительно использовали, чтобы стереть краску с кошачьего хвоста. А как она там оказалась? И какого цвета была эта краска? Мы знаем какого! Мы нашли банку с этой краской и камень с пятном того же самого цвета. Это краска бежевого цвета!

Сыщики молча уставились на Фатти, который достал из тайника банку с краской, открыл крышку, обмакнул кисточку и мазнул ею по тёмно-коричневой поверхности деревянного садового стола.

– Посмотрите! – сказал он. – Узнаёте эту бежевую полоску? Точно такая должна быть на хвосте у кошки! А теперь скажите мне, что это за кошка – с бежевой полоской на хвосте?

– Принцесса! – хором ответили ребята.

Глаза у всех заблестели, лица раскраснелись. Так вот что зачем были нужны скипидар и краска!

– Вот именно! – подтвердил Фатти. – У той кошки, чей хвост пах скипидаром, на хвосте нарисовали бежевое колечко, чтобы её приняли за Принцессу, а потом краску с её хвоста стёрли скипидаром. Вот почему в клетке оба раза стоял этот запах. Похититель дважды проделал этот трюк!

– Ну и ну! – воскликнул Ларри. – Потрясающе! Кто-то придумал очень хитрый план. Подождите. Скорее всего, Принцессу выкрали ещё утром, а у другой кошки на хвосте нарисовали светлое колечко, чтобы её приняли за Принцессу – ведь все знали, что на хвосте у неё бежевая отметина.

– Вот именно! – кивнул Фатти. – А потом к клетке подходили люди – например твоя мама, Пип, вместе с леди Кэндлинг, – и все думали, глядя на крашеную кошку, что это и есть Принцесса. А потом Склокинг потихоньку стирал краску у кошки с хвоста и объявлял всем, что Принцесса пропала.

– Склокинг?! – воскликнула Бетси. Глаза её округлились. – Ты сказал – Склокинг? Но, если Склокинг смывал краску с хвоста, значит, он же хвост и красил! Значит, он и украл Принцессу!

– Ну конечно! Принцессу выкрал Склокинг! Кто же ещё? – возбуждённо говорил Фатти, расхаживая взад-вперёд по беседке. – Представляете? И каждый раз он подстраивал всё так, чтобы в краже заподозрили Люка.

– И ещё он отправлял Люка работать возле кошачьего домика, пока раскрашенная «Принцесса» сидела в клетке, а потом отмывал краску скипидаром и кричал, что ценная кошка пропала, – сердито сказал Пип. – Всё было подстроено так, что, кроме Люка, больше некого было подозревать. Ловко придумано!

– Точно! А когда Бетси проболталась про запах скипидара и пятно на камне, этот почтенный джентльмен забеспокоился и поспешил припрятать улики, – подхватил Фатти. – Может, испугался, что на банке с краской и бутылке остались отпечатки пальцев. Но старину Бастера не проведёшь! Он из-под земли вырыл эти улики.

– Давайте ещё раз – чтобы всё было ясно, – предложила Дейзи. – Значит, так. Склокинг задумал украсть Принцессу и навести подозрение на Люка. Наш злоумышленник дождался, когда у мисс Хармер будет выходной и она уедет домой – она ведь знает всех кошек, и её не проведёшь. Нарисованной отметины на хвосте тут недостаточно.

– Вот именно! – продолжил Фатти. – Значит, он ждёт, когда мисс Хармер уедет домой, крадёт Принцессу, передаёт её кому-то, потом возвращается в кошачий домик, наносит бежевой краской метку на хвост другой кошки и выдает её за Принцессу, специально показывая на неё гостям, чтобы они потом засвидетельствовали, что Принцесса была на месте. Помните, в прошлый раз леди Кэндлинг и твоя мама, Пип, в четыре часа приходили смотреть кошек, а во второй раз, в три часа, Склокинг показывал хозяйке её драгоценную Принцессу. – Фатти перевёл дух, и Ларри подхватил:

– В первый раз он всё продумал до мелочей. Он привёл с собой нашего бравого полицейского, показал ему кошек, потом ловко стёр краску с хвоста и объявил А-ну-ка-разойдись о пропаже Принцессы. Да, Склокинг всё придумал почти гениально. И какая у него выдержка! Он же сам привел бобби на место своего преступления – туда, где только что утром совершил кражу!

– А во второй раз ему удалось провести даже мисс Хармер, – хмыкнул Пип. – Помните, как он обогнал её, первым заскочив в кошачий домик, а потом якобы обнаружил, что Принцессы нет на месте. Он всех обвёл вокруг пальца – все, в том числе и Люк, были уверены, что Принцесса сидела в клетке, пока Люк трудился рядом с кошками, а на самом деле Принцессы давно уж там не было! Её выкрали ещё утром. Неудивительно, что все подозрения пали на Люка.

– Судя по всему, Принцесса в тот раз удрала от того, кому её передал Склокинг, – сказала Дейзи. – Интересно, где же она сейчас?

– Об этом Склокинг расскажет полиции, – усмехнулся Фатти. – Отлично! Я рад, что это был он, а не Люк. Нет, вы только подумайте – нарочно подкинуть в клетку свистульку Люка, чтобы ни у кого не было ни малейшего сомнения, что именно он украл кошку. Ну и подлость!

– Теперь мистера Склокинга посадят в тюрьму? – спросила Бетси.

– Конечно! – уверенно заявил Фатти.

– Вот и хорошо! – обрадовалась Бетси. – Больше он не будет придираться к Люку и жаловаться на него всем подряд.

– Надо звонить инспектору Дженксу, – предложил Пип. – Теперь, когда мы разгадали тайну исчезнувшей кошки, мы должны ему всё рассказать, не дожидаясь, пока А-ну-ка-разойдись явится нас арестовывать.

Бетси издала крик ужаса, но Фатти, смеясь, обнял её за плечи.

– Спокойно, малышка! Никто тебе ничего не сделает. Ты ни в чём не виновата. Пип правильно говорит – надо звонить инспектору.

– А как же быть с ключами от кошачьего домика? – спросил Ларри. – Мы должны вернуть их мисс Хармер.

– Да, конечно! Пошли скорей! – сказал Фатти. – В конце концов мы можем просто отдать ей ключи, сказав, что позаимствовали их у неё, и извиниться. Она, конечно, рассердится, но что же делать! Всё равно это всплывёт, и лучше самим признаться, чем ждать, пока нас примутся обыскивать.

Пять сыщиков и пёс перелезли через забор и отправилась на поиски мисс Хармер, но её нигде не было.

– Может быть, она в каком-то из сараев? – предположил Фатти.

Сыщики направились к сараю неподалёку от теплицы, который они ещё не осматривали. Фатти заглянул вовнутрь.

– Ух ты! – воскликнул он. – Так вот где Склокинг устроил свой склад! Вот его резиновые сапоги и плащ.

– И опять запах скипидара, – сказала Бетси, нюхая воздух.

– Точно! – кивнул Фатти, потянув носом. Он сунул руку в карман плаща и извлёк оттуда грязный носовой платок. На нём были инициалы Склокинга, и от него сильно пахло скипидаром.

– Ещё одна улика! – торжествующе сказал Фатти. – Этим платком Склокинг стирал краску с кошачьего хвоста! Постойте... В первый раз накануне шёл дождь, и второй раз тоже. Значит, Склокингу пришлось надеть сапоги и плащ. Давайте посмотрим!

Ребята внимательно осмотрели сапоги Склокинга и обнаружили на них капли бежевой краски. Это доказывало, что садовник был в сапогах, когда наносил метку на кошачий хвост. И конечно, именно он капнул краской на камень, который Фатти припрятал у себя в кармане.

– Надо взять эти сапоги и платок, – предложил Фатти. – Теперь у нас предостаточно улик и доказательств вины, чтобы изобличить вора. Пожалуй, нашего друга мистера Склокинга хватит удар, когда мы выложим всё это перед полицией!

Сыщики вышли из сарая и столкнулись с Люком, который по-прежнему был бледным и подавленным.

– Похоже, у вас будут неприятности, ребята! – объявил он. – Склокинг пошёл докладывать Гуну, что застукал вас в кошачьем домике и что именно вы украли кошку. Он заявил, что вы утащили Принцессу, пока я работал рядом с кошками, но ничего не сказал, чтобы прикрыть вас. Готовьтесь к худшему, ребята!

Глава двадцать вторая

Конец истории

Фатти пошёл звонить инспектору Дженксу. Ему повезло, и он застал его на рабочем месте.

– Пожалуйста, инспектор, не могли бы вы приехать к нам? Мы раскрыли тайну пропавшей кошки.

– Ах, вот как! – ответил инспектор. – А я как раз получил странное донесение от Гуна. Он сообщает, что вас обнаружили в кошачьем домике и что вы, судя по всему, замешаны в деле о краже кошки. Так что я в любом случае собирался выезжать к вам.

– Прекрасно! – обрадовался Фатти. – Вы приедете к леди Кэндлинг?

– Да, так будет лучше всего, – сказал инспектор. – Встретимся через час, хорошо?

Фатти побежал обратно к сыщикам, чтобы рассказать им о разговоре с инспектором, и застал их расстроенными и возмущёнными. Оказывается, мистер Гун уже побывал у миссис Хилтон и заявил, что её дочь поймали в чужом саду, в кошачьем домике, и что она нарушила границы частного владения. После этого полицейский направился к родителям Фатти.

– Мама ужасно рассердилась, – утирая слёзы, сказала Бетси. – Тебя не было, Фатти, и я боялась сказать что-нибудь неподходящее и не стала ничего объяснять. Мама так ругала меня!

– Ничего, Бетси, – утешил её Фатти. – Скоро приедет инспектор Дженкс, мы расскажем ему, что нам удалось узнать, и всем всё станет ясно. Через час мы встречаемся с инспектором у леди Кэндлинг. Надо захватить наши улики.

Взяв с собой бутылку со скипидаром, банку с краской, старую кисточку, испачканный краской камень, пропитанный скипидаром носовой платок и резиновые сапоги со следами краски, дети направились к дому леди Кэндлинг.

– Единственная улика, которую мы не можем взять с собой, это запах скипидара на кошачьем хвосте, – вздохнула Бетси. – А ведь она самая главная из всех улик!

– Это ты почуяла его самой первой! – сказал Фатти. – В этот раз ты была самым находчивым сыщиком!

– Смотрите! Мистер Гун вошёл в дом леди Кэндлинг, а вслед за ним и Склокинг. А вот и Люк. Привет! Куда ты идёшь?

– Мне сказали привести себя в порядок и явиться в дом к хозяйке, – мрачно ответил Люк.

– Дрейфишь? – спросил Ларри.

– Ещё как! – со вздохом ответил Люк.

– А на самом деле бояться нечего! – сказал Фатти. – Всё будет хорошо, вот увидишь. Не вешай нос!

Но Люк окончательно повесил нос и уныло побрёл мыться и переодеваться. И тут ко входу в сад леди Кэндлинг подъехал чёрный полицейский автомобиль и оттуда вышел улыбающийся инспектор Дженкс.

Он поманил ребят к себе и тихо спросил:

– Кто у нас главный подозреваемый?

– Склокинг! – решительно заявил Фатти. – Уверен, что вы так и думали, господин инспектор, но у вас не было против него улик.

– Да, я был уверен, что это не Люк, а вот Склокинг действительно подходит на роль похитителя, – кивнул инспектор. – Кроме того, мне известно то, о чём не подозреваете ни вы, ни мистер Гун: Склокинг уже один раз был замешан в краже. Тогда речь шла о породистых собаках, ну а теперь он, похоже, переключился на кошек. Ну что ж, идите в дом, а я следом.

Все участники событий собрались в просторной гостиной леди Кэндлинг.

– Садитесь, дети, – пригласила их хозяйка.

Некоторые улики Фатти оставил в коридоре, решив, что Склокингу лучше не показывать заранее резиновые сапоги, банку с краской или бутылку со скипидаром. Важно было застать сварливого садовника врасплох.

Дети расселись за столом, а Фатти скомандовал: «Бастер, к ноге!», чтобы пёс оставил в покое брюки мистера Гуна. Затем в гостиную вошёл инспектор, поздоровался с леди Кэндлинг, улыбнулся ребятам и кивнул мистеру Гуну.

– Давайте все сядем, – предложил он.

Мистер Гун надулся от важности и сурово разглядывал детей, особенно Фатти и Бетси. Ох уж эти маленькие проныры! Всюду лезут, суют носы, куда не просят! Но теперь-то они наконец получат по заслугам. Их ждут серьёзные неприятности. Склокинг уже донёс ему, что эти негодники утащили ключ от кошачьего домика, но были пойманы на месте преступления.

– Ну что же, Гун, – начал инспектор. – Я получил от вас сегодня странное донесение. Дело серьёзное, так что я решил приехать сам и выяснить всё на месте.

– Да, сэр. Дело действительно серьёзное, сэр, – начал мистер Гун, важно надув щёки. – У меня есть все основания полагать, что эти детишки, которые вечно лезут везде и всюду, коечто знают об исчезновении ценной кошки. Мне кажется, сэр, им грозят большие неприятности. Надеюсь, вы их вразумите, сэр, это безусловно пойдёт им на пользу.

– Ну что ж, готов допустить, что они действительно знают больше, чем вы думаете, Гун, – ответил инспектор Дженкс. – Давайте выслушаем их. – И он обернулся к Фатти: – Что скажете, Фредерик Алджернон Троттвиль?

Фатти понял, что настал его звёздный час. Он надулся от важности – точь-в-точь как мистер Гун! – и с расстановкой произнёс:

– Я хотел бы сделать заявление, господин инспектор. Мы – пять юных сыщиков – знаем, кто украл Принцессу!

Услышав это, Склокинг презрительно хмыкнул, и Гун последовал его примеру. Люк всё ещё трясся от страха. Очки мисс Тримбл спрыгнули с носа, что очень порадовало Бетси.

– Мы слушаем тебя, Фредерик, – сказал инспектор.

– Сэр, я готов объяснить во всех подробностях, как замышлялось и осуществлялось это преступление, – продолжал Фатти.

Все посмотрели на него с восхищением. Фатти умел подобрать верные слова.

– Мы все внимание, – кивнул инспектор, весело улыбнувшись глазами.

– Итак, инспектор, как вы знаете, Принцессу похищали дважды. В обоих случаях мисс Хармер отсутствовала, а потому забота о кошках поручалась мистеру Склокингу. Итак, главное – Принцессу похищали не после обеда, её не было в клетке с самого утра.

Все, кроме сыщиков, были удивлены, услышав это заявление. Мистер Гун открыл рот и недоумённо уставился на Фатти.

– Но как же... – начал полицейский, но инспектор остановил его.

– Не перебивайте, Гун, – строго сказал Дженкс, и А-ну-ка-разойдись больше не издал ни звука.

– Я расскажу вам, как похититель сделал это! – гордо заявил Фатти. – Он украл Принцессу утром, а на хвосте другой кошки нарисовал бежевую метку – и все, кто не очень хорошо различал кошек, конечно же приняли её за Принцессу!

Все присутствующие ахнули, а очки мисс Тримбл слетели с носа и утонули в её пышном кружевном воротничке.

– Таким образом, все, кто навещал кошек после обеда, думали, что Принцесса сидит на месте, в своей клетке, а на самом деле её уже там не было. Потом, улучив момент, вор незаметно проникал в кошачий домик, стирал краску с кошачьего хвоста тряпкой, смоченной в скипидаре, и объявлял о пропаже Принцессы. Все были уверены, что кража случилась после обеда, хотя на самом деле она произошла утром.

– Так вот почему все думали, что это я украл Принцессу! – подал голос Люк. – Ведь я был один возле кошек после обеда, и никто больше не приближался к кошачьему домику.

– Вот именно! – подтвердил Фатти. – Всё было хорошо продумано. Подозрение должно было пасть на Люка. Именно поэтому тебя каждый раз отправляли именно в это время работать возле кошачьего домика. А ещё подбросили в клетку твою свистульку.

– Кто это сделал? – Люк вскочил со стула, и лицо его запылало от гнева. – Если я доберусь до него, ему не поздоровится!

Инспектор строго посмотрел на мальчика. Тот сразу умолк и сел на своё место.

– Интересно, с чего вы всё это взяли? – спросил мистер Гун. На его лице была смесь удивления, недоверия и презрения. – Всё это – ваши нелепые выдумки. Чтобы вам поверили, вы должны предъявить доказательства!

– Доказательства? Пожалуйста! – торжествующе произнёс Фатти. Он сунул руку в карман и стал извлекать оттуда заготовленные улики. – Вот, посмотрите! Это бутылка со скипидаром. Она была спрятана в кроличьей норе вместе с банкой бежевой краски и старой кисточкой. С помощью её похититель наносил отметину на кошачий хвост. Ларри, принеси, пожалуйста, остальные улики. Они там, за дверью.

Фатти продемонстрировал всем бутылку и кисточку. Мисс Тримбл затрепетала от волнения, и очки снова спали с её носа, но руки у неё так дрожали, что она была не в силах водрузить их на положенное место. Близоруко прищурившись, она пыталась разглядеть предъявленные улики, и Фатти казался ей величайшим сыщиком в мире.

Ларри принёс резиновые сапоги и банку с краской и передал Фатти. Глаза Склокинга чуть не вылезли из орбит, когда он увидел новую порцию улик.

– Итак, – продолжал Фатти, держа в руках банку с краской, – вот краска, которую использовал похититель. А эти сапоги были на нём, когда он наносил метку на кошачий хвост. Поэтому на сапогах остались капли этой самой светло-бежевой краски. А вот носовой платок, который вор смачивал скипидаром, чтобы стереть бежевое колечко с хвоста кошки. Он очень торопился, смывая краску: ведь в первый раз следом за ним в кошачий домик направлялся мистер Гун, а во второй раз – мисс Хармер.

– Можно мне взглянуть? – попросил явно заинтересованный инспектор. Он понюхал платок, который всё ещё сильно пах скипидаром.

Фатти вынул из кармана камень, на котором осталось пятно бежевой краски, и протянул инспектору.

– Мы нашли его рядом с кошачьим домиком, сэр. Это тоже вещественное доказательство. Есть и ещё одна улика – запах скипидара в клетке у кошек. Первой его учуяла Бетси. Наша малышка – превосходный сыщик!

Бетси покраснела от удовольствия, а инспектор улыбнулся ей своей белозубой улыбкой и снова стал рассматривать платок.

– На платке есть инициалы, – объявил он. – Думаю, что по ним можно узнать имя злоумышленника.

Фатти кивнул. Люк опять вскочил с места.

– Кто же он? – задыхаясь от волнения, спросил мальчик. – Скажите же скорей!

– Да, кто же он? – не выдержала и мисс Хармер.

Инспектор строго оглядел всех собравшихся. Склокинг был бледен как полотно и тяжело дышал. Он «сдрейфил», как сказал бы Люк, и был готов провалиться сквозь землю. Трудно было узнать в нём грубого, заносчивого садовника. Постепенно взгляды всех присутствующих обратились к нему – всем стало ясно, кто настоящий вор.

– Склокинг, мы ждём ваших объяснений! – обратился к садовнику инспектор. В голосе его отчётливо звучали металлические нотки.

– Как? Неужели это Склокинг? – вскричал поражённый мистер Гун, глядя на садовника с гневом и презрением. – Вы втёрлись ко мне в доверие, водили меня смотреть на кошек, вешали на уши лапшу и делали из меня дурака!

– Между прочим, Бетси сообщила вам, что у нас есть две улики – запах в клетке и камень с пятном краски, – напомнил ему Фатти. – А вы только посмеялись над нами.

– Склокинг, куда вы дели кошку? – спросил инспектор тем же металлическим голосом. – Вы отлично понимаете, что вам предъявлены совершенно неопровержимые доказательства вашей вины. А кое-какие факты из вашего прошлого тоже свидетельствуют против вас.

Склокинг был совершенно раздавлен. Из наглого и жестокого грубияна он превратился в жалкого труса. Всем было противно смотреть на него.

– Хулиганы на самом деле всегда трусы, – шепнул Фатти Люку. – Вот теперь мы видим его истинное лицо!

Да, Склокинг предстал перед собравшимися во всей красе. Он признался во всём. Да, это он украл Принцессу, потому что думал, что выручит хорошие деньги за ценную кошку и отдаст долги. Он, конечно, расскажет, кому он её отдал, и полиция сможет вернуть кошку хозяйке. Да, он хотел навести подозрение на Люка. Да, это он наносил метку краской на хвост другой кошки, а потом стирал краску скипидаром. Да, ему пришлось дважды проделать всё это, потому что в первый раз кошка сбежала и вернулась домой. Он сожалеет и раскаивается в содеянном. Он клянётся, что подобное больше не повторится.

– Вот тут вы правы, Склокинг, – сурово произнёс инспектор Дженкс. – Подобное точно не повторится – по крайней мере в ближайшие несколько лет, поскольку вы проведёте их там, где у вас при всём желании не будет возможности заниматься такими делами. Гун, уведите его.

Гун положил свою железную пятерню на плечо Склокинга, резко поднял его на ноги и впился в него негодующим взглядом.

– А ну-ка... пошли! – свирепо рыкнул он.

Но инспектор тут же охладил его пыл.

– Кажется, вы совсем не преуспели в расследовании, Гун, – ледяным тоном сказал он. – Вы считали преступниками тех, кто хотел помочь раскрыть дело, а настоящего преступника сочли своим другом. Хотелось бы, чтобы впредь вы проявляли больше осмотрительности. Вы согласны со мной?

– Э-э-э... да, сэр! Разумеется, сэр! – насилу выдавил из себя Гун. Он совершенно растерялся и выглядел очень жалко. – Я не нарочно, сэр. Я старался изо всех сил, сэр...

– К счастью, эти дети старались больше, чем вы, и добрались до истины. Я думаю, мы должны быть благодарны им за то, что они раскрыли тайну исчезнувшей кошки. Надеюсь, вы согласны со мной, Гун?

– О да, сэр, – пробормотал Гун, покраснев от стыда. – Это очень сообразительные дети, сэр. Горжусь знакомством с ними, сэр.

– Я рад, что мы с вами поняли друг друга, Гун, – смягчился инспектор Дженкс. – Теперь, пожалуйста, уведите этого человека.

Гун ушёл вместе со Склокингом.

Юные сыщики облегчённо вздохнули.

– Наконец-то он ушёл! – воскликнула Дейзи. – Надеюсь, он больше сюда не вернётся.

– В этом вы можете не сомневаться – здесь он больше никогда не появится, – заверила детей леди Кэндлинг, которая с изумлением наблюдала за всем происходящим. – Бедный Люк! Мне больно думать, сколько тебе пришлось вынести из-за этого ужасного Склокинга.

– Спасибо вам, мадам! – сказал Люк, широко улыбаясь. Доброта леди Кэндлинг вознаградила его за все страдания. – Я так рад, что всё позади! Если вы позволите мне остаться у вас, мадам, я буду работать не покладая рук, пока вы не возьмёте нового садовника. И я никогда не забуду того, что сделали для меня эти ребята. Какие же они молодцы! Просто удивительно, как им удалось раскрыть эту тайну!

– Это Бетси вывела нас на верный путь, – сказал Фатти. – Ай да малышка! Молодчина, Бетси!

– Да нет, мы расследовали это дело все вместе, – скромно отвечала Бетси. – И Бастер тоже очень нам помог! Как хорошо, что всё выяснилось! Теперь вы вернёте Принцессу себе, леди Кэндлинг?

– Этим займусь я, – ответил инспектор, поднимаясь. – Мне нужно спешить, но на прощание я хотел бы ещё раз поблагодарить вас, ребята. Я рад, что у меня есть такие помощники – пять юных сыщиков и пёс-детектив! Надеюсь, что я и в будущем могу рассчитывать на вашу помощь.

– Конечно! – хором отвечали юные сыщики, провожая инспектора до машины. – Мы вам сразу же сообщим, если у нас появится новая загадка.

Новая загадка? За этим дело не станет. Но это будет уже совсем другая история.

Оглавление

Литературно-художественное издание
Для среднего школьного возраста

Серия «ПЯТЬ ЮНЫХ СЫЩИКОВ И ПЁС-ДЕТЕКТИВ»

БЛАЙТОН Энид
ТАЙНА ПРОПАВШЕЙ КОШКИ

Приключенческая повесть

Ответственный редактор *А. В. Купцова*
Редактор *Е. С. Вахрушева*
Художественный редактор *С. А. Карпухин*
Технический редактор *К. А. Путилова*
Корректоры *Т. И. Филиппова, Т. С. Дмитриева*
Компьютерная вёрстка *И. И. Лысова*

Подписано в печать 11.11.2022. Формат 84×108 1/32.
Бумага офсетная. Гарнитура «SchoolBook».
Печать офсетная. Усл. печ. л. 13,5.
Доп. тираж 5000 экз. D-KUS-24298-06-R. Заказ № 6302/22.
Дата изготовления 12.12.2022.
Срок службы (годности): не ограничен.
Условия хранения: в сухом помещении.

ООО «Издательская Группа «Азбука-Аттикус» –
обладатель товарного знака Machaon
115093, Москва, ул. Павловская, д. 7, эт. 2, пом. III, ком. № 1
Тел. (495) 933-76-01, факс (495) 933-76-19
E-mail: sales@atticus-group.ru

Филиал ООО «Издательская Группа «Азбука-Аттикус»
в г. Санкт-Петербурге
191123, Санкт-Петербург, Воскресенская набережная, д. 12, лит. А
Тел. (812) 327-04-55
E-mail: trade@azbooka.spb.ru

www.azbooka.ru; www.atticus-group.ru

Отпечатано в России.
Отпечатано в соответствии с предоставленными материалами
в ООО «ИПК Парето-Принт». 170546, Тверская область,
Промышленная зона Боровлево-1, комплекс № 3А
www.pareto-print.ru

Знак информационной продукции (Федеральный закон № 436-ФЗ от 29.12.2010 г.) 0+

Товар соответствует требованиям ТР ТС 007/2011 «О безопасности продукции, предназначенной для детей и подростков».